# BTEC National

# Travel & Tourism
## Book 1

Gillian Dale

www.heinemann.co.uk
✓ Free online support
✓ Useful weblinks
✓ 24 hour online ordering

01865 888058

D0257673

Heinemann
*Inspiring generations*

Heinemann Educational Publishers
Halley Court, Jordan Hill, Oxford OX2 8EJ
Part of Harcourt Education

Heinemann is the registered trademark of
Harcourt Education Limited

Text © Gillian Dale and Helen Oliver
First published 2005

10 09 08 07 06
10 9 8 7 6 5 4

British Library Cataloguing in Publication Data is available
from the British Library on request.
10-digit ISBN: 0 435446 44 4
13-digit ISBN: 978 0 435446 44 4

Edited by Jan Doorly
Designed by Lorraine Inglis
Typeset and illustrated by Tek-Art, Croydon, Surrey
Original illustrations © Harcourt Education Limited, 2005
Cover design by Wooden Ark Studio
Printed and bound in China by China Translation & Printing Services Ltd.
Cover photo: © Alamy/Pete McArthur

**Websites**

Please note that the examples of websites suggested in this book were up to date at the time of
writing. It is essential for tutors to preview each site before using it to ensure that the URL is still
accurate and the content is appropriate. We suggest that tutors bookmark useful sites and consider
enabling students to access them through the school or college intranet.

Tel: 01865 888058 www.heinemann.co.uk

# Contents

# Acknowledgements

Gillian Dale gives grateful thanks to:

Helen Oliver for Unit 5

Liz Atwal for the benefit of her expertise in human resource management

Premier Holidays, particularly Charlie Thorogood, for allowing me to observe their working practice

Rebecca Hammond for sharing her residential study project and information about her job at the Tourist Information Centre

Lisa Carmentari for telling us about her job at *Sound on Sound*

Carl Turner for sharing his degree project on Middleton Railways

Canvas Holidays and particularly Michele Bretenoux for providing information and patiently answering questions

Jan Doorly for her excellent editing

And not least David for encouragement and support

The authors and publisher would like to thank the following for permission to reproduce copyright material:

Advertising Standards Authority – page 74
Anite Travel Systems – page 256
Association of British Travel Agents (ABTA) – page 228–9
BAA Stansted – page 155–6
Blackwell Publishing/R Butler – page 134
BMRB International – page 241
Canadian Affair – page 244
Canvas Holidays – page 190–1, 195–6, 208
Center Parcs (UK) Group plc – page 6
Colombus Travel – page 109
Crystal Active, part of Crystal Holidays – page 260
Direct Mail Information Service (DMIS) – page 93
EasyJet – page 84, 114, 115
Employers' Organisation for local government – page 184

Eurostar Group Ltd – page 113
First Choice – page 78
Fitzwilliam Museum, Cambridge – page 154
Flybe – page 101
Galileo United Kingdom – page 230
Haven Group – page 254
Hilton UK & Ireland – page 84
HM Nautical Almanac Office – page 119
Holidaybreak plc – page 84
Key Note Ltd – page 241
Middleton Railway – page 273
Mike Mason/www.greekisland.co.uk – page 135
MyTravel Group plc – page 179
Newmarket Travel Service – page 153
Northenden Travel Limited – page 218
Paramount Group of Hotels – page 183–4
PersonnelToday.com/Reed Business Information – page 260
Premier Travel Ltd – page 221
responsibletravel.com – page 68
Saga Holidays – page 214
Thomas Cook – page 26, 56, 150, 180
Thomson Holidays – page 146
Tourism Australia – page 187
Travel Trade Gazette – page 36, 44, 45, 56, 71, 86, 94, 97, 143, 144, 151, 152, 154, 178, 212, 223, 225, 226, 247, 249, 251
Travel Weekly – page 82, 148–9
TravelMole Ltd – page 259
United Co-op Travel Group – page 56
Virgin Atlantic Airways Ltd – page 142
www.weatheronline.co.uk – page 108

Crown copyright material is reproduced under Class License No. C01W0000141 with the permission of the Controller of HMSO and the Queen's Printer for Scotland

The authors and publisher would like to thank the following for permission to reproduce photographs:

Alamy Images/Bananastock – page 165, 225
Alamy Images/Lyndon Beddoe – page 19
Alamy Images/Ian Dagnall – page 249
Alamy Images/Iain Davidson Photographic – page 243
Alamy Images/Robert Harding World Imagery – page 106
Alamy Images/Tim Graham – page 49
Alamy Images/Sally and Richard Greenhill – page 64
Alamy Images/Image 100 – page 179
Alamy Images/Andre Jenny – page 120
Alamy Images/Justin Kase – page 91, 112
Alamy Images/Chris McLennan – page 27
Alamy Images/Gianni Muratore – page 132
Alamy Images/Photofusion Picture Library/ David Montford – page 79
Alamy Images/John Powell Photographer – page 181
Alamy Images/Herbie Springer – page 59
Alamy Images/Travelog Picture Library – page 98
Alamy Images/Worldwide Picture Library – page 70

Alamy nrf – page 159, 270
BAA Stansted Airport – page 155
Corbis – page 13, 51, 72, 82, 117, 187, 226, 239, 265
Corbis rf – page 151, 157, 220
Corbis/Boeing Co/Reuters – page 4
Corbis/David Cumming; Eye Ubiquitous – page 122
Corbis/Kevin Fleming – page 223
Corbis/Yves Herman/Reuters – page 11
Corbis/Glen Hinkson/Reuters – page 259
Corbis/Angelo Hornak – page 37
Corbis/Dave G. Houser – page 235
Corbis/London Aerial Photo Library – page 245
Corbis/Ludovic Maisant – page 263
Corbis/Nigel Marple/Reuters – page 38
Corbis/Reuters – page 42
Corbis/Onne van der Wal – page 208
Corbis/Jim Zuckerman – page 133
Getty Images/AFP – page 121, 148
Getty Images News – page 127
Getty Images/PhotoDisc – page 3, 30, 65, 213, 260, 280
Martin Plumb – page 273
PA Photos – page 34
Ginny Stroud-Lewis – page 15, 104, 272

# Introduction

Welcome to this BTEC National Travel and Tourism course book, specifically designed to support students on the following programmes:

* BTEC National Award in Travel and Tourism
* BTEC National Certificate in Travel and Tourism
* BTEC National Diploma in Travel and Tourism.

The aim of this book is to provide a comprehensive source of information for your course. It follows the BTEC specification closely, so that you can easily see what you have covered and quickly find the information you need. Examples and case studies from travel and tourism are used to bring your course to life and make it enjoyable to study. We hope you will be encouraged to find your own examples of current practice too.

You will often be asked to carry out research for activities in the text, and this will develop your research skills and enable you to find many sources of interesting travel and tourism information, particularly on the Internet.

In some units of the book you will find information about jobs in travel and tourism and how to apply, which will be of great practical help to you.

The book is also a suitable core text for students on HND, foundation degree and first-year degree programmes. To help you plan your study, an overview of each unit and its outcomes is given at the beginning of each unit.

## Features of the book

This book has number of features to help you relate theory to practice and reinforce your learning. It also aims to help you gather evidence for assessment. You will find the following features in each unit.

### Consider this …

These are points for individual reflection or group discussion. They will widen your knowledge and help you reflect on issues that impact on travel and tourism.

### Key concepts and terms

Issues and terms that you need to be aware of are summarised under these headings. They will help you check your knowledge as you learn, and will prove to be a useful quick-reference tool.

### Theory into practice

These practical activities allow you to apply theoretical knowledge to travel and tourism tasks or research. Make sure you complete these activities as you work through each unit, to reinforce your learning.

### Case studies

Interesting examples of real situations or companies are described in case studies that link theory to practice. They will show you how the topics you are studying affect real people and businesses.

### Knowledge checks

At the end of each unit is a set of quick questions to test your knowledge of the information you have been studying. Use these to check your progress, and also as a revision tool.

### Assessment assignments

Each unit concludes with a full unit assessment, which taken as a whole fulfils all the unit requirements from Pass to Distinction. Each task is matched to the relevant criteria in the specification. If you are aiming for a Merit, make sure you complete all the Pass (P) and Merit (M) tasks. If you are aiming for a Distinction, you will also need to complete all the Distinction (D) tasks.

### Assessment activities

Assessment activities are also provided throughout each unit. These smaller assessments are linked to real situations and case studies and they can be used for practice before tackling the final assessment assignment. Alternatively, they can contribute to your unit assessment if you choose to do these instead of the final assessment at the end of each unit.

As in the assessment assignments, each task is followed by an indication of which grading criteria may be achieved by good work – P1 means the first of the Pass criteria listed in the specification, M1 the first of the Merit criteria, D1 the first of the Distinction criteria, and so on. Your tutor should check that you have completed enough activities to meet all the assessment criteria for the unit, whether from this book or from other tasks.

Tutors and students should refer to the BTEC standards for the qualification for the full BTEC Grading criteria for each unit.

## About this book

For the BTEC National Award the book covers all four core units, that is:

* The Business of Travel and Tourism
* Marketing Travel and Tourism Products and Services
* Tourist Destinations
* Customer Service in Travel and Tourism.

It also provides two specialist units to complete the qualification. These are:

* Retail Travel Operations
* Tour Operations.

For the BTEC National Certificate and Diploma programmes, the book covers all six core units, that is:

* The Travel and Tourism Industry
* The Business of Travel and Tourism

* Marketing Travel and Tourism Products and Services
* Tourist Destinations
* Customer Service in Travel and Tourism
* Working in the Travel and Tourism Industry.

It also provides four of the specialist units towards completion of these qualifications. They are:

* Retail Travel Operations
* Tour Operations
* Work-based Experience within the Travel and Tourism Industry
* Travel and Tourism Residential Study Visit.

The units for work-based experience within the travel and tourism industry and the Residential Study Visit are shorter than other units. The aim of these units is to provide guidelines to help you complete your projects which will involve practical skills and group activities.

Helen Oliver, an experienced writer and travel and tourism professional, has contributed Unit 5, Customer Service in Travel and Tourism. I have worked with Helen for many years and am very grateful to her for lending her expertise and specialist knowledge to this book.

In addition, a number of travel and tourism industry people have shared their company policies and procedures with us to allow you to develop your knowledge. Many have allowed us to use company information for case studies, and we are grateful for their help.

I do hope that you enjoy your course and find this book an excellent support for your studies. Good luck!

Gillian Dale

# The travel and tourism industry

## Introduction

The travel and tourism industry is dynamic, exciting and provides a challenging working environment. If you're reading this book, it's likely that you're considering a career in travel and tourism and that you're beginning your studies of the industry.

This unit aims to give you a sound introduction to the industry so that you learn about the nature and structure of the industry and how and why it is changing.

You will learn about the development of the industry, particularly from 1945 to the present day. You will investigate its structure and the diversity and types of organisations within it. You will study the roles of the different organisations and the products and services they provide.

You will also look at the factors which affect the travel and tourism industry in relation to how life has changed in society, how consumer expectations have changed and the way in which new products and new technology affect the industry.

### How you will be assessed

This unit is internally assessed by your tutor. A variety of exercises and activities is included in this unit to help you develop your understanding of the travel and tourism industry and prepare for the assessment. You will also have the opportunity to work on some case studies.

After completing this unit you should be able to achieve the following outcomes:

→ Investigate the development of the travel and tourism industry
→ Examine the structure of the travel and tourism industry
→ Explore the roles and responsibilities of organisations that provide travel and tourism products and services
→ Explore factors that affect the travel and tourism industry.

# Introduction to travel and tourism

You need to understand what is meant by the travel and tourism industry before you start your studies, and hopefully you will realise that it is not just about exotic holidays – although they are covered!

Tourism is the provision of services to tourists. Who are tourists? They are people who are travelling away from home to destinations for a short time. They may be travelling for the day only, or for a longer period of time, but it is always temporary. Everything that tourists do while they are away is considered part of the travel and tourism industry.

## Why do people travel?

People travel for many reasons, but they can be broadly classified as follows:

* leisure
* business
* visiting friends and relatives (VFR).

Leisure travel includes travel for holidays, cultural events, recreation, sports, religion and study.

Business travel includes all travel for business reasons, such as meetings, conferences and exhibitions. Usually business travellers have their expenses paid by their company, which can make a difference to the services they choose or have chosen on their behalf.

VFR accounts for many trips, particularly within the UK.

### Key terms

**Outbound tourists** are going out of the country.
**Inbound tourists** are coming into the country.
**Domestic tourists** are holidaying or undertaking business tourism within their own country.

Travel and tourism is very important to the UK economy. It provides many jobs – 7% of the UK workforce are in the industry – and it also provides income from tourists spending their money on goods and services. It is a fast-growing and diverse industry and its importance is recognised by the British government, which is committed to putting resources into it.

The table below shows the money earned from tourism. You will note that outbound tourism is not included – if you go on holiday to Spain most of your spending is in Spain, so it is the Spanish economy that gains. You might have purchased a flight with a UK airline, in which case your spending is included in 'fares to carriers'.

| UK TOURISM EARNINGS 2002 | |
| --- | --- |
| | £ billion |
| Day trips | 34.1 |
| UK residents overnight | 26.7 |
| Inbound | 11.7 |
| Fares to carriers | 3.1 |
| **Total** | **75.6** |

Source: 'Tomorrow's Tourism Today', Department for Culture, Media and Sport

The government can boost income from tourism in two ways; first by encouraging us to take our holidays in the UK so that the spending benefits our own economy, and second by persuading more visitors to come to the UK from abroad. In fact 86% of England's tourism income comes from domestic visitors.

# The development of the travel and tourism industry

Some important historical and more recent events have helped shape the travel and tourism industry we have today.

## Changes in travel

### Aviation

The aviation sector in travel and tourism includes airlines and airports, and the industry is heavily dependent on this sector for transporting passengers to their destinations.

*The Boeing 747 Jumbo Jet was introduced in 1969*

During the Second World War (1939–45) great advances were made in the development of aviation – in the building of planes, in navigation and communication, and in flight procedures. When peace returned to Europe it was possible to put these resources into civilian travel. There were also many RAF-trained pilots available for employment. These developments meant that aircraft became important for leisure travel.

The first British fully jet-powered passenger aircraft, the de Havilland Comet, was put in service in 1949. In 1954 two of the earlier models crashed in the Mediterranean, and service using the plane was suspended. In 1954 Boeing introduced its new passenger jet aircraft, the Boeing 707, and when it began commercial service in 1959 it dominated the market. In 1963 the Boeing 727 was introduced, one of the most successful series of passenger jetliners of the past 50 years.

In 1969 Boeing produced the 747 Jumbo Jet, a wide-bodied jet. The 747 can seat 500 passengers, though it usually holds 385. It cruises at about 600 miles per hour (965 kilometres per hour) and has a non-stop range of 7,200 miles. It usually has a forward first-class (or 'business class') section and a second level on which the cockpit and a lounge are located. This aircraft had the following impact on the package holiday market:

✱ it became possible to fly further in less time, making long-haul destinations more accessible

✱ increased capacity on the jet led to a decrease in the price per seat, bringing the price of holidays down

✱ as jumbo jets were used more, smaller aircraft were available for charter operations.

In 1976 British Airways, in collaboration with Air France, started the first supersonic airliner service, Concorde. Concorde ceased flying in 2003 but it had set the standard for luxury air travel.

## Introduction and growth of low-cost airlines

Deregulation of air travel in Europe led to the development of low-cost airlines. The European Union started the liberalisation process in 1987, when cost-related fares and certain types of discount fares were first allowed. The final stage of deregulation came in 1993.

> **Key concept**
>
> **Deregulation** – the removal of government controls from an industry to allow for a free and efficient marketplace.

What deregulation meant was that EU airlines could establish themselves in any EU member state and obtain an operating licence. All routes within the EU are available to all EU carriers. Thus an airline such as Ryanair can have a base in Frankfurt Hahn and fly to and from countries all over the EU. In 1994 EasyJet launched a low-cost airline offering two routes from Luton to Glasgow and Edinburgh. Now there are about 77 low-cost airlines flying travellers all over Europe.

In 2004 there was much expansion in routes as the EU grew to 25 states. The new member states in Eastern Europe brought opportunities for travel to and from these countries. EasyJet introduced flights to Budapest (Hungary), Ljubljana (Slovenia) and Bratislava (Slovakia). Ryanair flies to Riga in Latvia.

The impact of the low-cost airlines on the travel and tourism industry has been to encourage people to travel more and to gain new travellers – that is, people who were unused to travelling abroad but were attracted by the low prices. Many of the low-cost airlines operate from regional airports, so travel is even more convenient for people in the regions, who now have direct flights to many destinations.

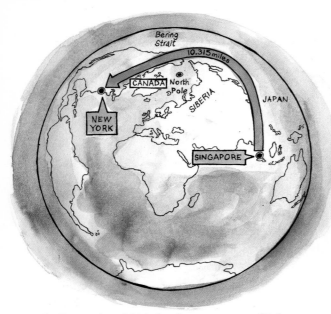

*Non-stop from Singapore to New York*

In December 2001 the first non-stop flight went around the world without refuelling. In 2004, the longest non-stop passenger flight yet was launched by Singapore Airlines. It flies from Singapore to New York, over the North Pole, in 18 hours, with no need for a refuelling stop.

The unmanned aircraft Global Hawk flew automatically from Edwards Air Force Base in the US to Australia non-stop and without refuelling in 2001. Although the technology will soon be in place for passenger aircraft to fly unmanned, it remains to be seen whether people will accept this.

## Super planes
The Airbus A380 is on its way. The aircraft can seat between 555 and 800 passengers. It is expected that there will be a range of activities on offer on board, including jacuzzis! Virgin Atlantic has ordered six of these to start delivery in 2007. However, airports which accept the aircraft have to make changes to infrastructure in order to accommodate the large plane and the large numbers of passengers boarding and disembarking. Some airports are reluctant to make such changes until major American airlines have committed themselves to these huge aircraft.

Another new aircraft is the 7E7 Dreamliner introduced by Boeing. It has lower operating costs and fuel consumption than the current Boeing 767 and a greater flight range, so it is expected to be a popular choice for airline fleets. For example, this plane can fly from the UK to Hawaii non-stop. First Choice, the tour operator, has ordered six.

## Expansion of airports
The low-cost airlines have led to more travel from regional airports, not only because these airlines choose to fly from airports with lower charges, but because charter operators have also started offering flights from regional airports such as Bristol, Bournemouth, East Midlands and Norwich. Regional departures are very popular with passengers as these airports are less crowded, therefore queues for check-in and security are shorter. Also passengers have a shorter journey to and from the airport.

It is not only regional airports that are expanding. Major airports are investing in new terminals and facilities to cater for the increased demand for air travel. In December 2003 the government announced plans for a new runway for Stansted, to be open by 2011–12.

## Channel Tunnel

A tunnel under the English Channel between France and England was just an idea for many years. But in 1986 the Anglo-French Channel Tunnel Treaty was signed and the idea could begin to become reality. The tunnel would allow the British to leave their island without flying and without risking seasickness, and encourage our continental neighbours to visit us.

In 1987 the boring for the tunnel began in the UK. Ten major British and French construction companies were involved in the building of the tunnel, collectively known as 'Transmanche'.

> **Consider this ...**
>
> The French call the English Channel 'La Manche'. Do you know, or can you find out, what this word means?

The tunnel opened in 1994. Its original budget was £4.8 billion but its final cost exceeded £10 billion.

## Super ships

A new £36-million passenger ferry has been created by a French naval architect, Gilles Vaton. It is called a *Bateau à Grande Vitesse* (BGV), which means high-speed boat. The biggest boat will carry 1,200 people and 250 cars, or 1,000 lorries as a cargo ship. Because of its high speed, the ferry would cut the journey from Portsmouth to Caen in France from six hours to under three, and the 20-hour journey from Marseilles to Algiers to nine hours. High speed is not the boat's only advantage – we already have fast catamarans operating as ferries, but the BGV can maintain its speed in all weathers, whereas the catamarans have to stay in port in rough weather.

On the French Riviera, the local council is thinking of buying a small version of the BGV, carrying 350 passengers, as a means of sea transport between Monaco and St Tropez. The aim is to reduce congestion on the Riviera's roads.

## High-speed trains

High-speed train lines such as France's extensive *Train à Grande Vitesse* (TGV) network have helped maintain the success of the railways in some countries. The TGV is operated by the French nationally owned and subsidised rail company, the SNCF. The TGV travels at speeds of over 300 kilometres per hour (186 miles per hour).

The European high-speed rail network has been extended and TGV services now run direct from Paris, the Channel Tunnel and Brussels towards Germany. The Belgian high-speed trains are known as Thalys. It is important to note that such trains require new tracks to run on, which means substantial investment.

The Eurostar service through the Channel Tunnel is operated with TGV trains, but the track on the UK side of the tunnel has only recently been renewed. New track reduces the journey time of the UK leg from London by almost half.

For the future, in order to compete with low-cost airlines, international train services in Europe will need to be overhauled. The European Commission wishes to open up competition in cross-border passenger rail links, including high-speed links like Eurostar and Thalys, to increase price competition between rival operators by 2010.

'In 2010, the high-speed trans-European network will be connected and new services will be able to develop on the basis of competition,' says EU transport commissioner Loyola de Palacio. 'Pressure from low-cost airlines is already a reality for international rail passenger services: they will have to evolve into new models, and this is without any doubt the right time to free up initiatives.'

Rail's proportion of the total EU passenger travel market has been falling for some time: it dropped from 10% in 1970 to 6% in 1998, according to European Commission data.

## Changes in products

### Holiday camps

Billy Butlin was on holiday in Skegness in the 1930s when he noticed a group of miserable holiday makers, sitting on a bench in the rain. They had nowhere to go as, in those days, when you stayed in a boarding house you were expected to leave in the morning and not come home until the evening, rain or shine. He saw the opportunity of providing for these people and decided to open a holiday camp. It opened in Skegness in 1936.

The concept was very popular and attracted about 2 million visitors a year. The appeal of Butlins was that it provided, on one site, all the facilities and entertainment a family could wish for, including childcare, swimming lessons, bingo and ballroom dancing. Between 1945 and 1960, holiday camps were at their peak, catering for about 60% of the holiday market. Warners and Pontins were other important names in the market. The holiday camp went into decline in the 1970s as demand for sunshine and package holidays abroad grew.

Butlins still exists and is owned by the Bourne Leisure Group. See the case study in Unit 4 to find out what has happened to Butlins.

---

## CASE STUDY

Center Parcs leads the short-break holiday market in the UK.

The first holiday park was opened in 1968. It was in Holland and named De Lommerbergen – Piet Derksen developed the concept. Derksen liked to escape from everyday life and get back to nature. His idea was for 'a villa in the forest'. He built 30 luxury villas and an outdoor pool in a forest in Limburg, and everything was built to harmonise with nature, a rule which still applies today.

The first park in the UK was opened in 1987 at Sherwood Forest. It offers short-break holidays, with midweek or weekend breaks all year round, and longer stays if desired. It achieves occupancy figures of over 90% at all villages and repeat bookings of more than 60% within a year. Elveden Forest opened in August 1989 and Longleat in 1994. A competitor, Oasis, was acquired in 1997.

Here is a description of one of the parks from the Center Parcs website.

### Sherwood Forest

Opened July 1987, 786 villas, 39 apartments, 400 acres, up to 4,206 guests per break. 11 themed restaurants and bars, 5 retail outlets and an extensive range of indoor and outdoor sport and leisure facilities. Most of the restaurants, bars and shops are in and around the Village Square, the open centre of the Village, where the Subtropical Swimming Paradise is also located. The newly opened Aqua Sana is an outstanding Spa facility. Indoor sports facilities are mainly located in the Jardin des Sports, quite close to the Village Square and also containing the Time Out Club for children and teenagers. There is a separate Country Club in another part of the Village, with an additional restaurant and bar and sports facilities including a golf driving range.

Source: www.centerparcs.co.uk

1 Carry out some research to find out what Center Parcs' future plans are. Try looking in the archives of the business press on the Internet.
2 What changes in society and consumer expectations have contributed to the success of Center Parcs?
3 Find out about another holiday centre (not Butlins) and compare it with Center Parcs.

---

## Package holidays

**Key concept**

A **package holiday** is one where the accommodation, transport and transfer to accommodation are put together and sold as a package.

Thomas Cook is credited with being the first person to organise a package holiday. That was a trip from Loughborough to Leicester by train – not very far at all! It was in 1841. The first package as we know it today was in 1949 and was organised by Vladimir Raitz. He took 32 passengers to Corsica on a DC3 aeroplane. He charged them £32.50. The package included accommodation in tents, return flights, transfers and full board. He established Horizon Holidays in the same year, and by the end of the 1950s the company had grown be one of the UK's major tour operators.

Other companies followed Horizon's example and package tours grew in popularity. The major growth came in the 1970s as people became more prosperous and keen to see new places. Most of the package holidays were to Spain and its islands, where hotels were built rapidly to fulfil the demand from British and German tourists.

Currency restrictions were lifted in the 1970s; before this, tourists were allowed to take only £50 in sterling out of the country. This led to an increase in the appeal of the package holiday as tourists could take more spending money with them.

## Up-to-date facilities

There are several new developments which serve to make travel easier for the tourist.

### Self-check-in at airports

Where this service is available, passengers can save time by checking in at a kiosk where they can choose their seat and print their own boarding pass. From there they can go to a 'fast bag drop' and leave their hold baggage. Passengers without baggage can go straight to the boarding gate.

### On-line check-in for airlines

Using this systems, passengers can check in without even being at the airport. From home or the office they go on-line and follow instructions to check in, choosing their seat and printing their boarding pass.

### Private jets

Those tourists who have plenty of spare cash can now hire a private jet to go on holiday. Kuoni, a tour operator, has introduced a fleet of private jets into its World Class brochure. Of course, this service is expensive – three nights in a Moroccan hotel with travel by private jet costs more than £6,000 per person.

## Changes in booking systems

Bookings in the period following the Second World War were simple to take, as airlines and tour operators had charts on the walls of their offices and took bookings by telephone or by post. These charts were fairly efficient but were of course subject to human error, and double bookings could easily arise.

As demand for travel grew, reservations departments were introduced. With the advent of computers, tour operators and airlines developed their own systems. Eventually these systems were linked to travel agencies via terminals, and travel agents could make bookings in their offices. These are known as 'Viewdata' systems. Thomson decided to accept bookings only through Viewdata, which meant that the system was essential for any travel agent. By today's standards Viewdata is unsophisticated technology, although it is still used.

Meanwhile airlines developed computer reservation systems (CRS). Airlines started to use computers in the 1950s to store the huge amount of information they needed to access. The CRS was used internally by airlines, and agents would use a publication called OAG to look up flight times and details, then telephone the airline to make a booking. Today travel agencies have direct access to the CRS systems. Global Distribution Systems (GDS) link up several CRS systems and present them to the travel agent.

## Internet booking – unpackaging

The Internet is growing rapidly as a means of booking holidays and flights. It is estimated that the British book between 5% and 10% of holidays and trips on the Internet. In America, this figure is about 30%. The growth in Internet booking can be attributed to the low-cost airlines, which educated passengers in how to book quickly and easily via the Internet and offered discounts for doing so. With increased confidence and access to

information, travellers happily book all aspects of their holiday on-line and in effect make their own packages. Travel agencies will have to redefine their role as this trend continues.

# Government intervention in tourism and legislation

The British government has always recognised the importance of tourism to the economy and has introduced new policies and laws over the years, including those described below.

## Development of Tourism Act 1969

The Act established a British Tourist Authority and Tourist Boards for England, Scotland and Wales. The British Tourist Authority and the English Tourism Council have now been merged to form VisitBritain, which is described later in this unit. The act's aim was to co-ordinate all the organisations that make up the tourism industry and provide it with a single voice.

## Transport Acts 1980 and 1985

The 1980 Transport Act ended licensing regulations affecting express coach routes and tours of over 30 miles. It led to competition between National Bus (then a public company) and private companies. The 1985 Transport Act brought about wholesale deregulation. This meant private companies could operate on any route.

## Air passenger duty

In 1996 air passenger duty was reduced on economy flights, removing a barrier to the growth of inbound tourism.

## Tourism strategy

In 1999, 'Tomorrow's Tourism', the government's tourism strategy, was published. It is still valid although it has been reviewed.

# Changes in society

## Increased car ownership

The following graph shows car ownership figures in the UK from 1970 to 2000.

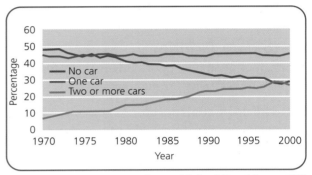

Source: National Travel Survey 2001

The fact that there are more cars on the road has had a strong impact on travel and tourism.

**Congestion**

We need more roads. In spite of successive governments trying to increase the use of public transport, few drivers are willing to abandon their cars. Public transport in the UK has a reputation for being expensive, unreliable and uncomfortable.

One scheme that has been a success is the Congestion Charge introduced to central London in 2002 by the mayor, Ken Livingstone. It currently costs £5 per day to bring a car into central London.

This encourages the use of other modes of transport and is also intended to ensure that, for those who have to use the roads, journey times are quicker and more reliable. More buses were introduced at the same time to improve public transport in the capital.

## New products to suit car use

The increase in car ownership means that more people choose to drive to their destination rather than take a train or a coach. It has also led to a demand for car use on holidays. If you have access to a car at home, why not when you are away? This demand brought about the growth of a huge car-hire industry operating internationally. Tour operators developed 'fly drive' holidays to give customers flexibility.

## Access to the countryside and attractions

Our extensive road network has been developed to accommodate cars and also freight transport. This road network means that there are very few places which are inaccessible to us by car.

Many tourists take day trips to visit attractions and the countryside. Even when people undertake pursuits such as walking or cycling, they drive to the start of their route.

### Consider this ...

What is the downside of the countryside being more accessible to us all through car ownership?

# The structure of the travel and tourism industry

Tourism is a significant contributor to the UK economy; many businesses depend on tourism, directly or indirectly. Many of the businesses in tourism are very small. Government figures show that the tourism industry consists of 127,000 businesses and that 80% of these have a turnover of less than £250,000 per year. As we saw earlier, 7% of all people in employment work in tourism, that is 2.1 million people.

The businesses which make up the travel industry are complex and diverse. In this section of the unit we will examine the various sectors which make up the industry:

> **REMEMBER!**
> Tourism is one of the largest industries in the UK, worth approximately £75.9 billion in 2002.

# Airports

The British Airports Authority (BAA) is the major organisation in airport ownership in the UK. BAA owns the airports at:

* London Heathrow
* London Stansted
* Edinburgh
* Southampton.
* London Gatwick
* Glasgow
* Aberdeen

BAA also has management contracts or stakes in ten other airports outside the UK, plus retail management contracts at two airports in the US. Nearly 200 million passengers travel through BAA airports every year.

Other major UK airports are Birmingham, Manchester and London Luton, all owned by different consortia.

Running an airport is a complex but profitable operation. The airport provides products and services to various groups of people and businesses:

* airlines are provided with the infrastructure and services to operate their flights
* customers are provided with facilities, such as restaurants and shops
* other businesses get a location in which to operate, for example, car hire, retailing or ground handling.

The airport earns revenue from all these sources but also has to work hard at keeping all its groups of customers happy.

## Assessment activity 1.1

Study an airport of your choice. This might be one that you are able to visit or one that you can examine via its website.

1 Describe the role of the airport and identify its major customer groups, e.g. airlines and freight companies. Describe the products and services on offer to each group. You could make this into a wall display with explanatory notes.

This task may provide evidence for P3 and P4.

2 Analyse the range of products and services offered by the airport and by the airlines and freight companies.

This task may provide evidence for M2.

# Airlines

British Airways is one of the world's most famous airlines and one of the largest in terms of international scheduled services. It is the largest in the UK and flies to more than 200 destinations around the world. In 2003 more than 38 million people chose to fly with the airline.

British Airways' main bases are at the London airports of Heathrow and Gatwick. The airline's products include four different types of cabin service ranging from Economy to Club World. It also fully owns subsidiaries such as British Airways CitiExpress.

## Theory into practice

Find out about the products and services available to British Airways customers. Compare economy with Club World and make a table charting your comparison. This information is available at www.ba.com.

All UK airlines are privately owned. Other major UK airlines include Britannia Airways, British Midland and Virgin Atlantic – these airlines are scheduled airlines. The UK also has many charter airlines, such as Monarch and Britannia. Hundreds of other airlines from all over the world fly in and out of UK airports, paying for the services they use.

## Key concept

**Scheduled** airlines run to a regular timetable that is changed only for the winter and summer season. The flights depart even if not all the seats have been booked.

**Charter** aircraft are usually contracted for a specific holiday season and run to a timetable set by the operator. For example, each major tour operator will need seats for its summer passengers flying to the Mediterranean. They fill every seat on the contracted aircraft and each seat forms part of the holiday package. The major tour operators own their own charter airlines and some have ventured into the low-cost market. For example, MyTravel, the tour operator, has two airlines, MyTravel and MyTravelite.

## Low-cost airlines

The principle behind the operation of a low-cost airline is to keep costs as low as possible, with few or no 'extras' offered to the customer without further charge. In this way the low-cost operators are able to offer very cheap fares. The low-cost airlines are scheduled airlines.

They practise a system known as 'yield management' which means that bookings are constantly monitored and prices are adjusted accordingly. In periods of high demand such as school holidays or weekends, prices will be higher and can even be more expensive than traditional airlines.

One of the most successful low-cost airlines is Irish-based Ryanair, which reported half-year net profits of  201 million in 2004.

Airport charges are paid per passenger and vary depending on who owns the airport and the deal negotiated by the airline. Ryanair is currently in dispute with Stansted over airport charges. Low-cost airlines often fly to regional airports because of lower charges. Ryanair recently moved its business from Birmingham to East Midlands airport, to take advantage of lower charges.

Low-cost airlines usually have a fleet of aircraft all of the same type, often Boeing 737s. This gives flexibility as the planes can be moved to any route as needed, and it also means that maintenance is simpler.

There is no business class on a low-cost flight, which means more seats can be put in the plane.

*Ryanair is one of the most successful low-cost airlines*

Ryanair's new planes do not have reclining seats or pockets for magazines, resulting in further savings.

The airlines rely heavily on newspaper advertising, which is costly, but they gain revenue by carrying advertising on their own websites. Ryanair carries advertisements on seatback covers, bringing an extra source of revenue.

The airlines charge the customer extra for food, drink, or paying by credit card, and even sell lottery tickets on board some flights. The airlines also sell hotel rooms, car hire and insurance on a commission basis.

## Regulation of air travel

**The Civil Aviation Authority** (CAA) regulates the UK aviation sector. The CAA is an independent statutory body. The responsibilities of the CAA are to:

* ensure that UK civil aviation standards are set and achieved

* regulate airlines, airports and National Air Traffic Services' economic activities and encourage a diverse and competitive industry

* manage the UK's principal travel protection scheme, the Air Travel Organisers' Licensing (ATOL) scheme, license UK airlines and manage consumer issues

* bring civil and military interests together to ensure that the airspace needs of all users are met as equitably as possible.

The CAA also advises the government on aviation issues. It receives no government funding but is funded by the charges it makes for its services.

**The Air Transport Users Council** (AUC) is the UK's consumer council for air travellers. It receives its funding from the CAA. It acts as the independent representative of air passengers and aims to complement and assist the CAA in furthering the reasonable interests of passengers.

**National Air Traffic Services** (NATS) is the organisation responsible for air traffic control. It is a public/private partnership owned by the government, a consortium of seven airlines and NATS staff. It looks after UK airspace but also the eastern part of the North Atlantic. NATS handles more than two million flights a year carrying over 180 million passengers.

The major air traffic control centres are at Swanwick, Hampshire; West Drayton, Middlesex; and Prestwick, Ayrshire. There are also air traffic control services at the country's major airports.

## Sea travel

As we live on an island, sea transport has always been an important part of our travel and tourism industry. Historically, the main mode of transport to the Continent was by sea across the English Channel. When the Channel Tunnel opened, it was expected that ferry services across the Channel would be threatened. The tunnel did take about 50% of the market, but passenger ferries have also been severely hit by low-cost airlines offering cheap fares to the Continent. It is often cheaper to fly and drive rather than take your own car.

In 1997, over 21 million passengers passed through Dover, which is the biggest port in Britain. By 2003 numbers had declined to fewer than 15 million, as the following chart shows. The first full year of Channel Tunnel operation was 1995.

| DOVER FERRY PASSENGERS ||
| --- | --- |
| 1990 | 15,532,585 |
| 1991 | 15,989,318 |
| 1992 | 17,941,400 |
| 1993 | 18,458,557 |
| 1994 | 19,123,743 |
| 1995 | 17,872,712 |
| 1996 | 18,979,719 |
| 1997 | 21,463,570 |
| 1998 | 19,441,608 |
| 1999 | 18,276,988 |
| 2000 | 16,232,191 |
| 2001 | 16,002,464 |
| 2002 | 16,442,680 |
| 2003 | 14,681,003 |

Source: Dover Harbour Board

The Channel Tunnel and low-cost flights are not the only competition faced by the ferry operators – there are also high-speed catamarans operated by SpeedFerries. SpeedFerries is offering low fares to attract customers.

Other operators in the Channel include Hoverspeed, Norfolk Line and Trans Europa, which sails from Ramsgate to Ostend. Brittany Ferries operates on longer routes to France and Spain, for example Poole to Cherbourg, Plymouth to Santander and Portsmouth to Caen, St Malo or Cherbourg.

The established ferry operator P&O revealed that its ferries lost £40 million in the financial year 2003–4, because of competition in the Channel and from low-cost airlines. The company announced 1,200 job losses in September 2004 as it cut its routes from Portsmouth to Cherbourg, Le Havre and Caen and from Rosslare to Cherbourg.

## CASE STUDY

Not all ferry travel is across the Channel. Here are some examples of other important routes:

Stranraer ➙ Belfast
Fleetwood ➙ Larne
Fishguard ➙ Rosslare
Holyhead ➙ Dublin Port
Holyhead ➙ Dun Laoghaire
Hull ➙ Zeebrugge
Hull ➙ Rotterdam
Holyhead ➙ Dublin
Pembroke ➙ Rosslare

1  Check all these ports on a map and make sure you know the location and the country of each.
2  Choose one route and find out which ferry operators serve it. Produce an information sheet detailing the services provided and extra products available on that route. A ferry brochure will help you.

### Consider this ...

Irish Ferries advertises its ferries as 'cruise ferries'. Do you think this makes them more appealing?

In the event of business failure, the Passenger Shipping Association provides financial protection to the customers of some tour operators who offer cruise and ferry-based holidays.

## The cruise market

The cruise sector has enjoyed steady growth over the past decade or more. In 2003–4, 28 new ships including the *Queen Mary 2* were launched, as companies invest in new liners. About a million British people went on a cruise in 2003. Cruise companies are doing their utmost to reach new markets such as families and younger people, rather than just the older age groups who traditionally take cruises.

Most cruises take place on the sea and most passengers from the UK take fly-cruises. This means they fly to their starting point rather than start with days at sea. The Mediterranean and the Caribbean are very popular cruise destinations. Those people who are looking for something different might take a cruise to a colder place like the Arctic to experience the beautiful scenery and the wildlife.

River cruises are also growing in popularity, and destinations include the rivers Rhine, Moselle, Danube and Nile.

Major cruise companies you may have heard of are P&O Cruises, Cunard, Royal Caribbean and Princess.

*The cruise sector has enjoyed steady growth over the last decade*

### Theory into practice

Choose a cruise from a brochure. Outline all the facilities and services included in the price of the cruise.

## Road travel

The private car dominates road travel. As we have seen, car ownership is very high in the UK, and most domestic holidays and day trips are taken by car. In addition, many people choose to hire a car when abroad, and this had led to the growth of the car-hire sector.

## Car hire

Major car-hire groups in the UK include Hertz, Avis and Europcar. All have international operations. Their products and services have become very sophisticated, making car hire very easy and convenient for customers. They offer:

* on-line or telephone pre-booking
* airport pick-up or drop-off
* a wide range of choice of vehicles
* all insurances included in fixed prices
* one-way rentals – you don't have to return the car to the same point.

One of the largest companies in car hire is Holiday Autos, which claims to be the world's largest car-rental service with access to over 750,000 cars worldwide. Holiday Autos is part of the Lastminute.com group.

## Coaches

Coach operators have adapted their products to meet consumers' changing needs and coaches today are very luxurious. Fly-coach holidays are offered so that customers do not have a lengthy initial journey but have the benefits of coach travel for touring, for example, in California.

## Rail travel

Network Rail owns and operates the national rail network in the UK. Its role is to maintain the infrastructure and renew tracks as necessary.

The train-operating companies (TOCs) lease trains from rolling-stock companies. There are 25 train-operating companies in the UK, and they compete for franchises to run each service.

The Strategic Rail Authority issues these franchises. This body also monitors the train-operating companies to make sure the interests of rail passengers are protected; they can fine the

TOCs if they fail to meet agreed standards. The TOCs are commercial companies and aim to make a profit, but they do receive government grants.

Examples of TOCs are Virgin Trains and Central Trains. The National Express Group, a British-owned transport group, owns Central Trains.

Other important aspects of the rail system are the London Underground, Docklands Light Rail and, of course, Eurostar. Eurostar is the passenger train service through the Channel Tunnel. It operates from London Waterloo and Ashford in Kent to Paris, Lille and Brussels. Eurostar is owned by London and Continental Railways, and run by a management company.

### Assessment activity 1.2

In summer 2004, an investigation was undertaken by the Rail Passenger Council, the watchdog for the rail sector. Passengers had complained that advance tickets, normally much cheaper, were not always available. For example, passengers travelling from London to Manchester should be able to buy tickets for £22. Instead they were forced to book later at higher prices – an open return from London to Manchester costs £182.

The problem occurs because Network Rail does not give the TOCs advance notice of engineering works, so timetables cannot be confirmed. Customers telephone to book advance tickets and are told they are not yet available as train times cannot be confirmed until engineering works are scheduled.

Sceptics have suggested that Network Rail is disregarding passenger interests and that the TOCs are profiting from the situation by receiving higher fares.

1 Describe the roles and responsibilities of the organisations mentioned in the case study.
This task may provide evidence for P3.

2 Describe how the problems outlined in the case study affect the travel and tourism industry.
This task may provide evidence for P5.

3 What is your opinion of this situation? How can it be resolved? Recommend a course of action, with justifications. Discuss it with your group and write up the findings.
This task may provide evidence for D2.

## Accommodation

### Types of accommodation

There are many different types of accommodation available in the travel and tourism industry.

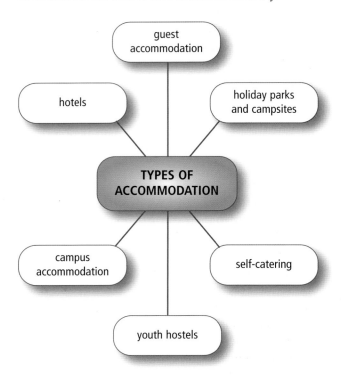

### Hotels

Hotels may be independently owned or part of large chains. The chains tend to be more impersonal, but they do provide consistency of quality throughout the world. For example, if you were to stay in a Mercure hotel in London or in Paris, the room would offer exactly the same facilities, and even the layout is often the same.

Many hotels are owned by international groups who encompass several chains within them, aiming at different types of customers. An example is InterContinental Hotels Group, a large international group that has 3,500 hotels. They are not all owned outright – some are run on a franchise arrangement. This means that the owner pays for the right to use the hotel name, but in return must follow corporate policies.

InterContinental Hotels brands are:

* Crowne Plaza

* Holiday Inn

* Express by Holiday Inn

* Holiday Inn Express
* Staybridge Suites
* Candlewood Suites.

Another major group is Accor, whose interests extend far beyond hotels. In its hotel portfolio there are some well-known brands, many of them French names because they were started in France, but they are now international.

Accor brands include:

* Novotel
* Sofitel
* Mercure
* Ibis
* Formule 1

There are many more hotel groups, and you will be familiar with names like Best Western and Moat House.

Hotels offer many products and services, catering for different customers, and the prestige and more expensive hotels like Sofitel offer greater luxury. In addition, hotels cater for both business and leisure customers so they need a range of products to suit each type. Conference customers may come for just a day but will need different services from residents.

## Guest accommodation

This includes bed and breakfast accommodation, guesthouses and farmhouses. Homeowners who wish to capitalise on having extra space available often run this type of accommodation. Many tourists consider it charming and an opportunity to experience local culture. This type of accommodation is very popular in France, where gîtes are rented out for holidays.

## Holiday parks and campsites

Holiday parks and campsites are popular with British tourists heading for France and Spain, although camping is probably less popular in the UK because of our unreliable weather. Holiday parks offer chalets and mobile homes so that tourists do not have to worry so much about the weather.

## Self-catering

Self-catering accommodation may be in holiday parks or in rented apartments or houses. Cooking facilities will be provided.

*Holiday parks offer mobile homes*

## Youth hostels

The Youth Hostel Association (YHA), which is a charity serving the needs of young people, runs youth hostels in the UK. However, you do not have to be a young person to be a member. It is very cheap to join the YHA and some of the hostels are of a very high standard, almost like hotels.

There are 226 youth hostels in both city and rural locations. The original aim of the YHA was to promote love, care and understanding of the countryside in principle and in practice.

There is also an International Youth Hostel Federation, with 5,000 hostels in 60 countries.

The YHA provides not only accommodation but a range of activity holidays.

**Campus accommodation**

Universities are keen to rent out their halls of residence outside term time. They encourage conference trade as they can also offer meeting rooms and catering facilities. This is an excellent means of using empty rooms and increasing revenue during students' holidays.

## Grading standards

VisitBritain has created quality standards for a wide range of accommodation in England. Scotland, Wales and Northern Ireland have their own schemes. Trained assessors determine these gradings.

Hotels are given a rating from one to five stars – the more stars, the higher the quality and the greater the range of facilities and level of service provided.

Guest accommodation is rated from one to five diamonds. The more diamonds, the higher the overall quality in areas such as cleanliness, service and hospitality, bedrooms, bathrooms and food quality.

Self-catering accommodation is also star-rated from one to five. The more stars awarded to an establishment, the higher the level of quality. Establishments at higher rating levels also have to meet some additional requirement for facilities.

Holiday parks and campsites are also assessed using stars. One star denotes acceptable quality. Five stars denotes exceptional quality.

The aim of the grading system is to make it easier for tourists to compare the quality of visitor accommodation offered around the country. However, as the Scottish and Welsh tourist boards use different systems and the English system uses a diamond system and a star system, it is still confusing.

When you travel abroad, you will find that there is no standard system. The star grading system is more or less accepted in Europe but cannot be wholly relied upon. Tour operators tend to use their own grading standards so that they can indicate a level of quality to their customers. An example is the 'T' system adopted by Thomson.

## Travel agents

The role of travel agents is to give advice and information, and sell and administer bookings for a number of tour operators. They also sell flights, ferry bookings, car hire, insurance and accommodation as separate products. Thus, they are distributors of products.

Many travel agents have a bureau de change. Some travel agents also do a little tour operating, for example putting together a holiday for a group.

It is estimated that there are some 7,000 travel agency shops, ranging in size from the multiples, with several hundred outlets each, to the individual shop.

Most travel agents are part of a **multiple** chain, and these dominate the business. Examples you will be familiar with are Thomas Cook, Thomson (formerly Lunn Poly) and Going Places. These particular chains are linked to tour operators and may try to prioritise their own company's products.

There has been a slight reduction in the number of branches of multiple chains in the past few years as customers choose to buy travel and tourism products through other means. The chart below shows the number of multiples owned by the UK's largest travel and tourism groups.

| MULTIPLES: NUMBER OF OUTLETS | | | |
|---|---|---|---|
| | **2004** | **2002** | **2000** |
| **Thomson** | 766 | 776 | 799 |
| **Going Places** | 668 | 696 | 800 |
| **Thomas Cook** | 618 | 668 | 697 |
| **First Choice** | 314 | 321 | 305 |

Source: TTG Multiple retailers

'Miniples' are small chains of travel agents, covering a region of the country.

**Independent** travel agents are usually run by their owner and a small team, and may have only one or two outlets. There are also independent chains – an example is Travelcare.

Travelcare is the UK's largest independent travel chain with branches nationwide and sales in excess of £430 million per year. This company is part of the Co-operative Group.

'Implants' are travel agents located within another business. They set up office within a company so that they are on hand to deal with the travel requirements of the company's personnel.

**Business** travel agents specialise in the business market.

The Association of British Travel Agents is the body representing the sector, and it also has tour operators as members. According to ABTA figures, in 2004 it had 1,043 tour operator members and 6,431 travel agency offices as members.

You will learn more about travel agents in Unit 7.

## Call centres

Almost everyone has experience of speaking to staff in call centres – they are widely used by banks and insurance companies as well as in the travel and tourism industry. It seems that customers increasingly prefer to book travel by telephone or the Internet rather than by visiting a travel agent.

The chart below compares the popularity of booking methods for ski holidays in 2001–3.

| BOOKING METHOD FOR SKI HOLIDAYS (UK) | | | |
| --- | --- | --- | --- |
| | **2003** | **2002** | **2001** |
| **Travel agent** | 44% | 49% | 55% |
| **Direct to tour operator** | 21% | 19% | 18% |
| **Own arrangement** | 21% | 22% | 24% |
| **Internet** | 14% | 10% | 3% |

Call centres are often in out-of-town locations where rents, rates and labour are cheaper. Some banks have relocated their call centres to India to take advantage of lower costs. TUI UK, a tour operator, has a call centre operating out of Newcastle under its Team Lincoln brand.

Team Lincoln sells holidays. Some call centres are operator- or airline-owned and sell on behalf of that company exclusively; others are specialist call centres and handle calls and bookings for many companies.

Call centres rely on high staff productivity to be successful. They motivate staff through incentives such as bonuses on sales targets reached. Call answering time, call durations, sales and complaints ratios are carefully monitored.

## Travel websites

Websites are the most up-to-date means of distributing travel and tourism products and services. The following chart shows the most popular websites in August 2004, by percentage of market share.

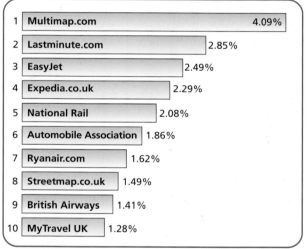

| 1 | Multimap.com | 4.09% |
| 2 | Lastminute.com | 2.85% |
| 3 | EasyJet | 2.49% |
| 4 | Expedia.co.uk | 2.29% |
| 5 | National Rail | 2.08% |
| 6 | Automobile Association | 1.86% |
| 7 | Ryanair.com | 1.62% |
| 8 | Streetmap.co.uk | 1.49% |
| 9 | British Airways | 1.41% |
| 10 | MyTravel UK | 1.28% |

Source: Hitwise Travel Report, August 2004

## Tour operators

The role of tour operators is to put together all the different components that make up a holiday and sell them as packages to the consumer. They make contracts with hoteliers, airlines and other transport companies to put the package together. All the holiday details are described in a brochure which is distributed either to travel agents or directly to customers. There are three main types of tour operators catering for the different categories of tourism:

✳ outbound
✳ inbound
✳ domestic.

## Outbound tour operators

Four major tour operators dominate the outbound market. These are often referred to as the 'big four'. They are TUI, MyTravel, First Choice and Thomas Cook. TUI UK is the UK's largest holiday company and includes the leading UK brands Thomson Holidays and Lunn Poly. It employs around 10,000 people, 7,000 of whom work overseas in around 40 holiday destinations. Its parent company, World of TUI, is the largest travel group in the world.

MyTravel is a major player in the market for air-inclusive holidays and other leisure travel services. It also has travel agents, hotels and airlines in its group.

The third large operator, First Choice, has a major travel agent in its portfolio and an airline. It offers destinations such as Majorca, Menorca, the Canaries, Spain, Turkey, Greece and the Caribbean. Winter sports destinations include France, Austria, Italy, Andorra, Bulgaria and Switzerland.

German-owned Thomas Cook also has travel agencies, airlines and hotels as well as tour operator brands, including JMC, Thomas Cook Holidays, and Club 18–30.

These companies produce an astonishing range of different holidays packaged in brochures according to type of holiday or type of customer. Here are the brochures selling holidays under the Thomson brand name:

* Summer Sun
* Platinum
* Gold
* Superfamily
* Small and Friendly
* Faraway Shores
* Florida
* Greece
* Turkey
* Lakes and Mountains
* Villas with Pools
* Al Fresco
* Price Breakers
* Cities.

There are many other tour operators in the market; some specialise in particular destinations, for example Simply Spain, or in a product, for example diving holidays.

Cosmos is the UK's largest independent tour operator and part of the Globus group of companies, a family-run organisation established in 1928 which encompasses Cosmos Tourama, Avro, Monarch Airlines and Archers Direct, along with Cosmos.

## CASE STUDY

Statistics from the Civil Aviation Authority show that the eight largest tour operators in the UK have cut capacity. TUI Group and Thomas Cook have cut capacity by 4%, MyTravel Group has cut by 9%, and First Choice Holidays Group by 17%. Cosmos has also cut by 4% in 2004, Trailfinders by 14% and Libra Holidays Group by 6%. The combined reduction in capacity, year-on-year, is 1.4 million passengers.

The big four hold 48% of capacity licensed to ATOL holders, down from 52% last year. For the year to March 2004 the leading operator was TUI, which managed to increase passengers by 13%. MyTravel suffered a decline of 13%, but still achieved second place. Next came First Choice with an increase of 21%, and then Thomas Cook.

In contrast to the drop in capacity for the big four, on-line retailers have increased capacity and grown rapidly. The Lastminute group boosted capacity by 147% and Expedia increased the number of passengers carried by 287%.

1  Some of this information was reported in an ATOL business report. Find out more about ATOL by visiting the website at www.atol.org.uk
2  Why do you think these tour operators cut capacity?
3  Why do you think Lastminute and Expedia had such big increases in passenger numbers?

Discuss your answers with your tutor.

### Key concept

**Air Travel Organisers' Licensing** (ATOL) protects air travellers and package holiday makers from losing money or being stranded abroad if air travel firms go out of business. When a tourist books a holiday the cost of this financial protection is included in the price. Any package firm that includes a flight should by law hold a licence. ATOL is managed by the Civil Aviation Authority.

### Inbound tour operators

Inbound tour operators cater for the needs of overseas visitors to the UK. An example is British Tours Ltd, which claims to be the longest-established inbound operator. It offers tours for different sizes of groups and has a wide variety of products, including a Harry Potter tour. The tours are available in many languages.

An example is a 'fun for children' tour, which includes Robin Hood and his Merry Men, Maid Marion and the bad Sheriff of Nottingham; *HMS Victory*, where Nelson lay wounded; Henry VIII's battleship the *Mary Rose*; *HMS Warrior*, England's first armoured battleship; a lively and noisy fort where children can 'fire' guns and handle swords; and Legoland, a short drive from Windsor Castle, or one of the many theme parks.

### Domestic tour operators

Domestic tour operators package holidays within the UK for UK residents. They include coach companies which place advertisements in the local newspapers. Like outbound operators, they offer beach, city, touring and special-interest holidays.

### Tour operators' associations

UKinbound is the trade body which represents tour operators and tourism suppliers to Britain. It was founded in 1977 to represent the commercial and political interests of incoming tour operators and suppliers to the British inbound tourism industry. It is a non-profit-making body governed by an elected council and funded by subscriptions from its members and from revenue-generating activities.

The Association of Independent Tour Operators (AITO) is an organisation which represents about 160 of Britain's specialist tour operators. AITO members are independent companies, most of them owner-managed, specialising in particular destinations or types of holiday.

The Federation of Tour Operators (FTO) is an organisation for outbound tour operators. It aims to ensure the long-term success of the air-inclusive holiday by influencing governments and opinion formers on the benefits to consumers of air-inclusive holidays compared to other types of holiday. Members pay an annual subscription based on the size of their organisation. All current members are also members of ABTA, and the two organisations work very closely together.

You will learn more about tour operators in Unit 11.

## Visitor attractions

The UK officially has 6,500 visitor attractions. The top 20 paid-admission attractions accounted for 45 million visits in 2003, according to the annual Survey of Visits to Visitor Attractions. These UK attractions are important to both domestic tourism market and the inbound tourism market. There are, of course, hundreds of different types of attractions, but they can be broadly divided as follows.

### Natural attractions

These include beautiful beaches, lakes and landscapes. In order to protect them, some are designated Areas of Outstanding Beauty, National Parks or Heritage Coasts.

### Man-made attractions

Man-made attractions may be historic and in the UK we have a wealth of historic houses, often cared for by the National Trust or English Heritage. We also have museums and galleries such as Tate Britain and Tate Modern, the Victoria and Albert Museum and the National Museum of Photography, Film and Television. These examples are in London, but there are museums throughout the country.

Favourite man-made attractions include theme parks, for example Alton Towers.

*Alton Towers is a well-known example of a successful theme park*

## Events

Events such as the Edinburgh Festival or the Notting Hill Carnival attract many visitors. There are many events in the business tourism sector too, such as the World Travel Market.

## Paying and non-paying

Another way of categorising attractions is to divide them into paying and non-paying. Museums, for example, are usually free, as the principle is that we should all be able to view the nation's heritage. It is usually difficult to charge visitors to natural attractions as it would mean creating barriers to access.

Non-paying attractions are still important for the economics of tourism, as they attract visitors to an area where they spend money on food, accommodation and shopping. Blackpool Pleasure Beach is the most popular free attraction with an estimated 6.5 million visits per year. However, although it is free to enter the Pleasure Beach, you have to pay to go on a ride.

| MAJOR PAID-ADMISSION ATTRACTIONS (ACTUAL OR ESTIMATED ADMISSIONS) | | | | |
|---|---|---|---|---|
| **Attraction** | **Location** | **2002** | **2001** | **% change** |
| British Airways London Eye | London | 4,090,000 | 3,850,000 | +6.2 |
| Tower of London | London | 1,940,856 | 2,019,183 | -3.9 |
| Eden Project | St Austell | 1,832,482 | 1,700,000 | +7.8 |
| Legoland | Windsor | 1,453,000 | 1,632,000 | -11.0 |
| Flamingo Land Theme Park & Zoo | Kirby Misperton | 1,393,300 | 1,322,000 | +5.4 |
| Windermere Lake Cruises | Ambleside | 1,266,027 | 1,241,918 | +1.9 |
| Drayton Manor Family Theme Park | Tamworth | 1,200,000 | 960,000 | +25.0 |
| Edinburgh Castle | Edinburgh | 1,153,317 | 1,126,680 | +2.4 |
| Chester Zoo | Chester | 1,134,949 | 1,060,433 | +7.0 |
| Canterbury Cathedral | Canterbury | 1,110,529 | 1,151,099 | -3.5 |

Source: Star UK

| MAJOR FREE-ADMISSION ATTRACTIONS (ACTUAL OR ESTIMATED ADMISSIONS) | | | | |
|---|---|---|---|---|
| **Attraction** | **Location** | **2002** | **2001** | **% change** |
| Blackpool Pleasure Beach | Blackpool | 6,200,000 | 6,500,000 | -4.6 |
| Tate Modern | London | 4,618,632 | 3,551,885 | +30.0 |
| British Museum | London | 4,607,311 | 4,800,938 | -4.0 |
| National Gallery | London | 4,130,973 | 4,918,985 | -16.0 |
| Natural History Museum | London | 2,957,501 | 1,696,176 | +74.4 |
| Victoria & Albert Museum | London | 2,661,338 | 1,446,344 | +84.0 |
| Science Museum | London | 2,628,374 | 1,352,649 | +94.3 |
| Pleasureland Theme Park | Southport | 2,000,000 | 2,000,000 | 0.0 |
| Eastbourne Pier | Eastbourne | 1,900,000 | 2,000,000 | -5.0 |
| York Minster | York | 1,570,500 | 1,600,000 | -1.9 |

Source: Star UK

To improve your knowledge of the UK visitor attractions sector, create a table similar to the one below. Use your local Tourist Information Centre and the VisitBritain website to help you complete it. Check your answers with your tutor.

| TYPE OF ATTRACTION | Two national examples | A local example |
| --- | --- | --- |
| Historic house | | |
| Garden | | |
| Museum | | |
| Art gallery | | |
| Wildlife attraction | | |
| Theme park | | |
| Historic monument | | |
| Religious building | | |

## Associations

The British Association of Leisure Parks, Piers and Attractions (BALPPA) was founded in 1936. It is non-profit-making and its role is to represent the interests of owners, managers, suppliers and developers in the UK's commercial leisure parks, piers, zoos and static attractions sector. It has about 300 members.

The International Association of Amusement Parks and Attractions (IAAPA) is a similar organisation to BALPPA but it is an international association and has members all over the world. The mission of the association is to promote safe operations, global development, professional growth and commercial success in the amusement industry.

### Consider this…

Sometimes trade associations have a **code of ethics**. These are not compulsory but members are asked to abide by them. The IAAPA includes in its code of ethics the aim 'to fill the hearts of children and all those young in spirit with joy while spending their hours of play and recreation'.

## Conference and exhibition organisers

There are hundreds of companies in the UK whose business is the organisation of exhibitions.

Some are major exhibition venues like Earls Court, Olympia, ExCel and the National Exhibition Centre (NEC) in Birmingham. Others are smaller companies that specialise in particular markets.

The venues offer wide ranges of products and services to those who wish to put on an exhibition or conference, and also to those who wish to book space at an exhibition.

An example of a venue is ExCel, based in the east of London, offering conference and exhibition space. It can offer space for a meeting for 20 people or a full exhibition which can hold 40,000 people. Customers are assigned an event manager who oversees their project and organises everything for them. A full range of services is on offer from registration and car parking to catering.

ExCel also has a subsidiary whose aim is to find new business. Although a venue might be successful and attract repeat business from year to year, it is still important to look for new markets. The company responsible for this at ExCel is the London Event Company.

People who are organising a conference expect a range of facilities to ensure their event goes smoothly. Here are some examples of the services on offer at most venues:

* dedicated entrance
* full disabled access
* on-site parking
* organiser's office
* cloakroom
* fax and photocopying facilities
* catering.

**Theory into practice**

Research an exhibition that interests you, perhaps the Good Food Show or the World Travel Market. Find out who organises it and where it is held. What services are offered by the venue to the organisers of the exhibition? What services are offered to visitors at the exhibition? Visit an exhibition if you can, otherwise use the Internet for your research.

Some small businesses may wish to organise a conference and lack either the expertise or the time to do it themselves. They can hire a conference organiser or event management company to do it for them. There are many of these types of companies and they can be found in local directories. They offer:

* venue search and liaison
* delegate invitations
* registration
* programmes
* delegate packs
* staffing
* speaker management.

Hotels offer such services, as they need to gain as much of the conference market as they can.

Some Tourist Information Centres have a conference service as it helps bring tourism to a town. They will find a venue and then usually pass on aspects of running the conference to the venue. The Tourist Information Centre will receive a commission from the venue for providing the business and may be able to sell services such as guided tours and accommodation to the conference delegates.

**Theory into practice**

Find out if there is a conference service at the Tourist Information Centre in your area. What services does it offer and how does it charge? You might find this information on its website. If you are going to visit, do so as a group or ask staff to come and talk to you at your school or college. You might combine this with the activity on page 25.

Like other sectors of travel and tourism, this one has a trade association to represent it. The Association of Exhibition Organisers (AEO) is the trade body representing companies that conceive, create, develop, manage, market, sponsor, supply or service trade exhibitions and consumer events. The AEO represents the exhibition industry both in the UK and, increasingly, around the globe.

## The public sector

The Department for Culture, Media and Sport (DCMS) is responsible for supporting the tourism industry at national level. In 1999 the government's overall strategy for the development of tourism was published in the report 'Tomorrow's Tourism'. This policy was reviewed and updated in 2004 and a new statement of the roles and responsibilities in tourism of the DCMS, VisitBritain, Regional Development Agencies, local government and the Tourism Alliance was issued, covering the following areas for action:

* marketing and e-tourism
* product quality – introducing common standards for accommodation grading schemes
* workforce skills, supporting People First, the sector skills council
* improved data and statistics.

The Tourism Review and Implementation Group (TRIG) was established in 2004. It has members from industry, the public sector and from education. Its role is to consider the wider issues affecting tourism and to monitor progress in the areas outlined above.

The Tourism Alliance was established in 2001 to represent the tourism sector. Its members are leading trade associations. It is an initiative supported by the Confederation of British Industry (CBI). The CBI provides the secretariat and research capacity for the Alliance. Its purpose is to present the industry's views and concerns more effectively to the government and to the EU.

Other government departments have responsibilities for areas of tourism. The Department for Transport looks after aviation, railways, roads, and the London Underground. The Department for Education and Skills has responsibility for sector skills councils and training organisations. The Department for the Environment, Food and Rural Affairs (DEFRA) is responsible for issues affecting the countryside, wildlife and waterways, among others.

Another government department of importance to tourism is the Foreign and Commonwealth Office (FCO). The FCO provides a consular service around the world whose function is to help British nationals in trouble, and of course to promote Britain.

The FCO website is very useful to anyone planning a trip abroad. It has a travel section which is regularly updated and warns of the risks and problems associated with travelling to over 200 countries.

### Theory into practice

Visit the FCO website at www.fco.gov.uk. Find out what the current travel advice is for Spain or for a country you are about to visit.

The structure of public sector tourism is shown in the following diagram:

The United Kingdom has four tourist boards: VisitBritain, VisitScotland, the Northern Ireland Tourist Board and the Wales Tourist Board.

VisitBritain reports to the Department for Culture, Media and Sport (DCMS). The Wales Tourist Board reports to the National Assembly for Wales and VisitScotland reports to the Scottish Executive.

### VisitBritain

The role of VisitBritain is to market Britain to the rest of the world, and England to the British. Formed by the merger of the British Tourist Authority and the English Tourism Council, its mission is to build the value of tourism by creating world-class destination brands and marketing campaigns. It also aims to build partnerships with other organisations which have a stake in British and English tourism. These organisations include the British Council, UKinbound, the British Hospitality Association and the UK Immigration Service.

Part of VisitBritain's role is to advise the government and other bodies on issues that might affect the British tourism industry. The aim is to provide advice that reflects the needs of both the tourism industry and the tourist, and to recommend courses of action to the government.

The overseas offices work closely with British diplomatic and cultural staff, the local travel trade and media, to stimulate interest in Britain.

Another example of the role of VisitBritain is its campaign to persuade high-spending tourists to come to the UK. There is no point in having a lot of inbound tourists if they don't spend their money and boost our economy.

VisitBritain has launched a magazine called *So British*, aimed chiefly at high-spending US tourists, but also at emerging markets like Russia. The magazine features luxury British brands like Harrods, Barbour and Wedgewood, and carries articles on destinations in Britain.

VisitBritain owns the VB grading scheme, which is administered by the Regional Tourist Boards.

## Regional Development Agencies

Regional Development Agencies (RDAs) have responsibility for tourism in their regions and usually work closely with Regional Tourist Boards (RTBs).

From 2003 to 2006, the RDAs will receive £3.6 million per year from the DCMS specifically for tourism. This money is to be passed on to the Regional Tourist Boards (RTBs) until the end of 2005–6. The RDAs will determine the objectives and targets the RTBs should meet in return for the funds.

## Regional Tourist Boards

The role of the Regional Tourist Board is to stimulate and manage the development of tourism to bring economic, social and environmental benefits to the people who live and work in the regions, and to provide a rewarding and enjoyable experience for visitors. The aims are:

* to attract visitors to the regions through marketing campaigns

* to help businesses give tourists a rich and rewarding experience

* to provide business support to members and to the industry as a whole.

The nine Regional Tourist Boards in England are shown below. Scotland has 14 regions.

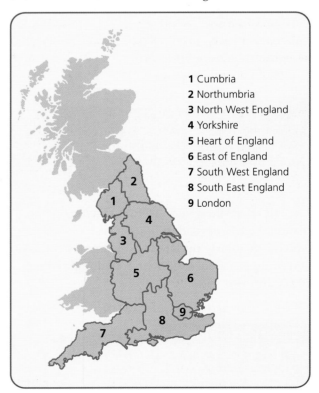

1 Cumbria
2 Northumbria
3 North West England
4 Yorkshire
5 Heart of England
6 East of England
7 South West England
8 South East England
9 London

*English Regional Tourist Boards*

The Regional Tourist Boards set out strategies for the development of tourism. They state the actions that should be taken to develop or manage tourism in the long term.

Their funding comes from membership fees (from businesses and local authorities) commercial income (such as from training courses) as well as some public funding, from DCMS, VisitBritain and the Regional Development Agencies (RDAs).

### Local authority tourism departments

Local authorities play an important role in supporting the tourism industry because of their statutory duties and because they recognise that tourism is a major contributor towards the economy. They have tourism departments and plans. Most towns also have a Tourist Information Centre (TIC). These are run independently – most are subsidised by the local council. They all rely heavily on generating income to ensure their financial viability.

The Tourist Information Centre provides a full information service for both residents and visitors. It gives information on visitor attractions and on accommodation. It usually provides a booking service for accommodation, and often incorporates a shop selling locally made crafts and gifts, as well as books of local interest. The shop is more than a service for visitors – it is an important means of generating funds.

### Theory into practice

Visit your local Tourist Information Centre. Your tutor may wish to organise a group visit. Find out about the services it offers, and try to determine how many of its services generate revenue for the TIC. Discuss your findings with the group when you return.

# Interrelationships and interdependencies in the industry

We have examined the different sectors of the travel and tourism industry, and it is obvious that the various businesses cannot work in isolation.

Each of them relies on others for its success. In this section of the unit we will examine how businesses work together, and who needs whom.

## The chain of distribution and integration

The chain of distribution is the means of getting the product to the consumer. It applies in any industry, and traditionally takes this form:

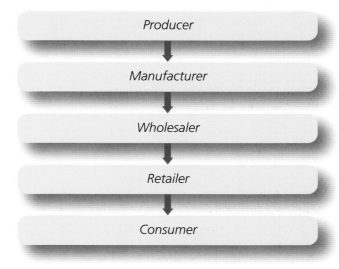

In the travel and tourism industry there is also a traditional chain of distribution:

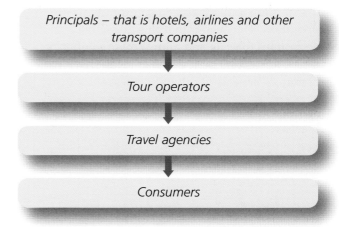

In this traditional chain of distribution, businesses fit neatly into a category such as 'travel agency' and perform the role of that business. However, the industry is much more complex than that and in many cases the traditional chain has been shortened.

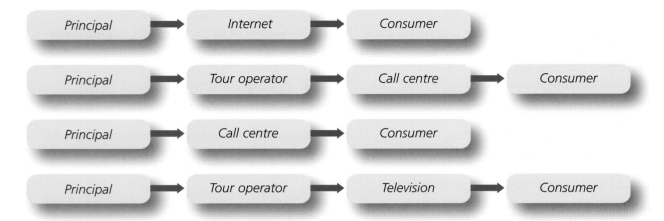

The diagram above gives some examples.

In addition, companies do not stick rigidly to one line of business. They tend to buy or merge with other businesses, always striving for greater commercial success and market dominance. When companies do this it is known as vertical or horizontal integration.

Vertical integration occurs when two companies at different levels in the chain of distribution merge or are bought. This may be backwards integration – for example a tour operator buys a hotel – or forwards integration, for example a tour operator may buy a travel agency.

Tour operators have bought or created airlines, hotels and travel agencies. This means they own all the different components in the chain of distribution and are able to control the whole operation. They claim that this gives them economies of scale and allows them to offer better prices to customers. It can also mean that smaller operators are forced out of business.

### Key concept

**Economies of scale** occur when a company is able to spread its costs over mass-produced goods or services. Savings can be achieved through discounts for bulk purchasing, rationalisation of administration systems and management, and lower production costs.

If a tour operator buys another tour operator at the same level in the chain of distribution, this is known as horizontal integration. A recent example was the acquisition of Travelselect by Lastminute.com. The company bought Travelselect for £9 million, raising the money in new shares. Lastminute bought Travelselect to provide access to a further 39 airlines and on-line access to Eurostar, giving it a wider range of products to sell.

All of the major tour operators in the UK are vertically and horizontally integrated, owning their own travel agencies, airlines and hotels besides different tour-operating businesses. In fact, their operations are not limited to the UK; all are global operations.

The Thomas Cook Group has companies in all parts of the chain of distribution: airlines, hotels, tour operators, travel and incoming agencies. Its global and UK operations are described on its website.

> The group encompasses 33 tour operators, about 3,600 travel agencies, a portfolio of 76,000 controlled hotel beds, a fleet of 77 aircraft and a workforce numbering some 24,600. The company is represented in the sales markets of Germany, Great Britain, Ireland, France, Belgium, Luxembourg, the Netherlands, Austria, Hungary, Poland, Slovakia, Slovenia, Egypt, India and Canada.
>
> The UK's third-largest vertically integrated leisure business comprises the tour operator brands Thomas Cook, Thomas Cook Signature, JMC, Neilson, Style, Club 18–30, Cultura, Time Off, Sunset, Sunworld Ireland and roomsandhotels.com Under the tour operator brand Thomas Cook, the company offers package holidays.
>
> With more than 1,500 outlets, Thomas Cook UK is the market leader in the British travel agency business. It also owns Thomas Cook Airlines UK, Britain's second-biggest charter carrier with 24 aircraft.
>
> Source: www.thomascook.info/tck/de/en/nws

At an Institute of Travel and Tourism conference in 2004, the chief executive of Thomas Cook UK explained why Thomas Cook had become a vertically integrated company: 'We were a successful retailer, but felt vulnerable without our own product. We also wanted to control the quality of the holidays we were selling – that was important for the brand.'

There are those, however, who think that vertical integration is no longer suitable for today's market, because it means that capital is tied up in assets and is subject to risk. Also, if customers do not want to buy from the High Street agencies, many of the chain stores will close as tour operators invest in other types of distribution.

## Support networks

We have seen in this unit that the travel and tourism industry is made up of diverse businesses of all different sizes and locations. It is essential that there are means for these organisations to work together.

In each sector of the industry, we have seen that there are regulatory and trade bodies whose role it is to advise members and represent them, particularly to the government. In addition we have seen that the role of the public sector is one of supporting and guiding different businesses so that everyone, including tourists, employees and management, can benefit from tourism while minimising problems.

# Factors which affect the travel and tourism industry today

## Destinations

Tourists are constantly looking for new and more exciting destinations. There are very few new destinations to visit these days as improved transport has already made almost everywhere accessible. ABTA carries out its own research through its members and predicts that the following destinations will rise in popularity, but for different reasons.

### New Zealand

According to ABTA these two islands regularly top travel surveys and more and more British people are choosing to visit them. New Zealand offers beautiful scenery with rainforests, glaciers, fjords and geothermal pools. It has a lot to offer for adventure tourists, as white-water rafting, jetboating and bungee jumping are all available. The *Lord of the Rings* films have also been an influence in attracting visitors to New Zealand.

*New Zealand's beautiful scenery, shown in the* Lord of the Rings, *attracts visitors*

## Croatia

Croatia could be described as a revamped destination as it was a popular resort for UK travellers before the Balkan wars in the 1990s. At that time Croatia was part of Yugoslavia. Now that the area is peaceful again more and more tourists are going, not only for its beauty but because it is very cheap. The popular areas are the beautiful resorts of Dubrovnik, Split and Rovign on the Dalmatian coast. There are also hundreds of idyllic islands dotted along this coast and it is ideal for sailing.

## Bulgaria

According to ABTA statistics, bookings for Bulgaria reached 110,000 in 2003 and the UK is Bulgaria's third-largest market after Germany and Greece. Bulgaria has a lot to offer; it has beaches along the Black Sea coast, lively cities and skiing in the winter. It is improving all the time with investment in infrastructure and new hotels.

## Tasmania

Another destination growing in popularity according to ABTA is Tasmania. It lies off the coast of southeast Australia. Tasmania has one of the most beautiful beaches in the world, Wineglass Bay. It also has a World Heritage site, Cradle Mountain Lake St Clair.

---

### Assessment activity 1.4

ABTA reports that Eastern European destinations are seeing a surge in demand. Write a short informal report for a travel agent. Make sure you give examples of specific destinations.

1 Describe the factors that have led to this increase in demand.

   This task may provide evidence for P5.

2 Analyse the effect of these factors on the travel and tourism industry.

   This task may provide evidence for M3.

3 Evaluate the effect of the factors that have led to this increase in demand and recommend how travel agents should respond.

   This task may provide evidence for D2.

---

# Changes in society

## Pattern of taking holidays

In 2004 the education minister Charles Clarke gave the go-ahead for plans to change the school year to a six-term year. The school year will be divided into terms of more equal length than the old three-term system. This will impact on holiday seasons for tour operators and should lead to more even prices throughout the summer. It is hoped there will be less of a peak of demand in the summer as parents have more choice about when to take a holiday. There has been a recognised problem of children being taken out of school to go on family holidays at cheaper periods, and the new school year may solve this to some extent.

Another change in holiday patterns is that people are taking more short breaks. There has been an immense growth in this market, both within Britain and with people travelling abroad. Cities are very popular destinations, especially London, New York and Amsterdam.

## Increased income and expectations

We are wealthier as a nation and have higher expectations than in the past. Most people have been abroad and expect to take at least one holiday a year, in contrast to previous generations. People's income can be described as follows:

* gross income – pay before deductions like tax, National Insurance, etc.

* net income – pay in hand after deductions – also known as disposable income

* spending money – the amount left over after essential outgoings such as rent or mortgage payments. This is also known as discretionary income.

---

### Key concept

**Disposable income** – what's left after tax, National Insurance and pension contributions are deducted from pay.

**Discretionary income** – what's left after essentials like rent or mortgage, food and the cost of travel to work.

---

Discretionary income is important in our industry because without it you can't go on holiday or travel. Fortunately, most people have a greater discretionary income these days, and travel is relatively cheap.

Official figures show disposable income rather than discretionary income, as it is easier to measure.

## Improved education

The government aims to improve the level of education achieved by people from all sectors of society. It aims to get more students into university and more of the population achieving at least a Level 2 qualification.

The more educated we are, the more we are aware of the world and its possibilities. We are curious about different cultures and languages and keen to experience them. As we live in a multicultural society we are more familiar with different religions, foods and cultures and less anxious about the unfamiliarity involved in travelling to new places.

## More leisure time

The increase in leisure time can be attributed to several factors:

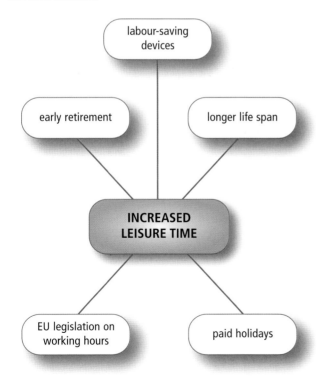

Most households have a range of labour-saving appliances, including dishwasher, washing machine and microwave. This means the household chores are not the drudgery they once were and we are free to use our time to do other things.

People are also living longer. One of the most important markets in travel and tourism is the 'grey' market. This refers to older people who have plenty of time and available funds and want to travel. Older people these days are usually in good health due to the success of the National Health Service and the availability of good food. Contributing to private pension schemes over their working years has led to a good income in retirement for many people. If the mortgage has been paid off and the children have left home, older people can party! Saga is the most famous tour operator catering for older people, but all tour operators are aware of and marketing to this group.

It has become common for people to retire earlier, even in their fifties, and take advantage of good pension arrangements. This trend will reverse in the future as many pension schemes have experienced difficulties, and the government is also encouraging people to work longer. As the older section of the population increases, the younger working people cannot generate enough in taxes to support a large section of the population not working. This is a concern for the British government, which is constantly reviewing pension schemes to find ways around the problem.

It is a legal requirement for employers to give their staff paid holidays, and now most UK employees receive at least four weeks' holiday a year. This had led to people being able to take more holidays than the traditional summer break, and many people also take a winter holiday and/or several short breaks. Those who benefit from flexitime working can arrange their hours so that they are able to take weekend breaks.

How we spend our leisure time varies greatly according to taste, age, income and expectations. There is, however, an increase in demand for travel and attractions to visit.

## Activities on offer

About 50,000 couples get married abroad each year, according to ABTA. Although exotic holidays are expensive, they are much cheaper than a traditional wedding at home. Some couples persuade a few friends to holiday with them to attend the wedding. The top destinations for weddings abroad are the Caribbean, Sri Lanka, Mauritius and Florida.

Most people still choose a beach holiday but other types of holiday are increasing in popularity. Activity holidays, which include cycling, skiing and water sports, now make up 8% of package holidays. One of the reasons people are slightly less keen on beach holidays is awareness about the dangers of spending too long in the sun. If tourists are not going to sunbathe, they need something else to do.

Some companies have found their niche in catering for particular types of activity holidays. One example is Cycling for Softies. It provides bikes and all the equipment you might need at the starting point of your holiday. The cycling is fairly gentle and each night is spent in a different hotel along the route where the holidaymakers can relax and enjoy dinner.

Another area of growth is the 'spa' holiday. Activities such as yoga are included and guests have massage and other treatments. You will find many hotels now described as 'spa hotels'.

*Cycling holidays are an example of the activities available*

## Political factors

The travel and tourism industry is frequently affected by political factors such as terrorism, changes in government policy or health and safety concerns.

### Terrorism

The devastating terrorist attacks of 11 September 2001 in the United States also had an impact on the UK and the worldwide tourism industry, as people were afraid to fly, particularly American tourists. The result was a decline in visitors to Britain and a decline in worldwide travel for leisure and for business.

In October 2002 a terrorist bomb in Bali resulted in over 200 deaths. The tourism industry in Bali was ruined, and only began to pick up again two years later.

There have been similar bombings in Istanbul, in Kenya and in Madrid over the past few years. Each of these events results in a loss of tourism for the area involved until such time as travellers begin to forget about the incidents and feel safer.

### Changes in policy

The US government has made changes to immigration requirements in order to improve security. Eventually, all entrants to the US will be fingerprinted. Visitors from some 27 countries, including the UK, are to be fingerprinted and photographed on arrival as part of the fight against terrorism. The US authorities had hoped to admit only visitors who carried a passport with biometric data, but most countries are not ready for this development.

Sometimes regulations do not allow residents of one country to enter another. For example, due to trade embargos imposed on Cuba, US residents cannot travel to Cuba except in exceptional circumstances.

## Health and safety

Foot and mouth disease had a devastating effect on travel and tourism in the UK in 2001. Animal, rural and farm-based attractions were badly affected by the crisis caused by the disease. Overall, 26% of attractions were forced to close for part of their normal opening season in 2001.

Countryside locations and footpaths were closed by the government at the height of the epidemic and this led to a 25% drop in visits to farm attractions.

Some zoos also had to close. One attraction, the Ashton Court Estate, a country park in Bristol, had a 31% fall in visits.

Fortunately, figures from the following year saw a large increase in visits to farms, gardens and countryside attractions, as tourism recovered from the foot and mouth outbreak: farm visits were up 50%.

In the winter of 2002–3 an outbreak of the respiratory disease SARS affected tourism, particularly in the Far East. People were discouraged from travelling to and from countries which were affected, such as Hong Kong and Canada.

Natural disasters, too, bring about a decline in tourism. Examples include hurricanes affecting the tropics and earthquakes in areas such as Turkey.

### ✱ REMEMBER!

Natural disasters are considered an 'Act of God' and not covered by insurance. Thus, if your flight is delayed for technical reasons you will be compensated, but if the plane is struck by lightning, you will not.

### Assessment activity 1.5

Look in the quality newspapers and find examples of events that have affected the travel and tourism industry in the past week.

1 Describe these events and how they have affected the industry.
   This task may provide evidence for P5.

2 Analyse the way in which such factors impact on the industry.
   This task may provide evidence for M3.

3 Say what you think the industry could do in response to such events. Recommend courses of action and give your justifications.
   This task may provide evidence for D2.

### Knowledge check

1 How did the development of low-cost airlines impact on travel and tourism?

2 What is meant by deregulation?

3 What are the elements of a package holiday?

4 What legislation covers tourism in the UK?

5 What are the problems affecting the UK railways?

6 Describe the different methods of distributing travel and tourism products to consumers.

7 Why is Croatia increasing in popularity as a holiday destination?

8 What is the difference between scheduled and charter airlines?

9 What are the drawbacks of accommodation grading schemes?

10 How do call centres motivate their staff?

11 Who are the 'big four' tour operators?

12 What is horizontal integration?

13 What is vertical integration?

14 Which government department is responsible for tourism?

15 What is the role of a Tourist Information Centre?

16 What is the role of the AUC?

# UNIT 1 ASSESSMENT ASSIGNMENT

Your college has a thriving travel and tourism department and wishes to ensure its continued success. In order to do this it wants to carry on recruiting students who are enthusiastic about the industry and interested in pursuing a career in one of its diverse sectors. Each year the college holds two open days and these are well attended and efficiently organised, but the students who come have already decided they are interested in travel and tourism and are easy to recruit.

Your tutor thinks it would be a good idea to 'spread the word' about travel and tourism, and proposes a road show for local secondary schools. The purpose is to spend half a day in each school mounting an exhibition/information session/interactive activities for Year 10 pupils. This will differ from the usual careers evening sessions in that it will be organised by students and it will be about the travel and tourism industry, not just the courses. It is hoped that the pupils will be so enthused by what you tell them that they will come flocking to college to study travel and tourism.

For the following tasks you might produce a display with illustrations and explanatory notes, and an information sheet to be distributed to pupils.

1  The pupils need to know about the development of the travel and tourism industry. Describe key developments that have had an influence in bringing about the industry we have today.

   This task may provide evidence for P1.

2  Explain how these developments have shaped the structure of the industry today.

   This task may provide evidence for M1.

3  Evaluate the effectiveness of the current structure of the travel and tourism industry in meeting customer needs and responding to external factors.

   This task may provide evidence for D1.

4  To give pupils an overview of the industry, describe the structure of the industry. To do this effectively you should include the following:
   • an explanation of different sectors and how they work together
   • an example of one organisation in each sector and its role
   • examples of the products and services provided by these organisations.

   This task may provide evidence for P2, P3 and P4.

5  Analyse the range of products and services provided by different organisations in travel and tourism.

   This task may provide evidence for M2.

6  It is important that pupils understand the dynamic nature of the industry and how it responds to current events and changes in society.
   • Provide a general description of the factors that affect the travel and tourism industry today.

     This task may provide evidence for P5.
   • Give a detailed analysis of two factors that affect the industry today.

     This task may provide evidence for M3.
   • Recommend how the industry could respond to these factors. For example, you might discuss how rising fuel prices affect airlines, the prices of seats and consequently holidays. You should recommend courses of action for airlines or tour operators to deal with this problem and justify your recommendations.

     This task provides evidence for D2.

**UNIT 2**

# The business of travel and tourism

## Introduction

In the last unit you were introduced to the different sectors in the travel and tourism industry and you looked at some examples of organisations within the sectors. This unit investigates the types of organisations in terms of their operation and their ownership and also looks at the organisations that lend support to travel and tourism companies.

You will examine the financial and administrative systems that exist in travel and tourism, including systems relating to banking, payments, purchasing, sales and processing data. These systems vary according to the size and nature of the business and we will study those differences and look at various examples.

You will explore management and communication systems used in the travel and tourism industry, considering levels of staffing, use of technology and staff responsibilities. The structures of very large companies will be compared with small and medium-sized operations.

### How you will be assessed

This unit is assessed by an integrated vocational assignment (IVA) set by Edexcel. The assignment covers units 2 and 3. Your centre will assess the IVA using Edexcel's assessment criteria. A variety of exercises and activities is included in this unit to help you develop your understanding of the business of travel and tourism and prepare for the IVA. You will also have the opportunity to work on some case studies.

After completing this unit you should be able to achieve the following outcomes:

→ Investigate different types of travel and tourism organisations, their ownership and the organisations that provide support

→ Examine financial and administrative systems within the travel and tourism industry

→ Explore management structures and communication systems in the travel and tourism industry.

# Types of organisations

This unit provides you with an introduction to the business world that will be invaluable to your understanding of how travel and tourism businesses operate, and how any business operates. Although you are studying travel and tourism now, you may find yourself in another industry one day – for example, there is much overlap between the IT industry and others, including travel and tourism. Everyone needs to learn about technology these days, and what you learn here will stand you in good stead and help you understand business affairs.

You may decide in the future to start your own business. Does that seem very ambitious? As you proceed through this unit you will find out about some very enterprising people who started up businesses; some are small operations and others have grown into multinational companies. You, too, might one day start your own travel and tourism business and this unit will give you the basic information you need. On the other hand, if you decide to work for a major company, you will have an understanding of how it operates and the support systems it needs.

A good example of a successful set-up can be found in the story of Lastminute.com. Have you heard of it? If not, look at its website before you read on.

## CASE STUDY

The idea for a website selling holidays at the last minute at cheap prices came from Brent Hoberman. Martha Lane Fox was a colleague of his and became involved in the idea; the two of them worked together on the company's business plan for eight months. Lane Fox and Hoberman bought the lastminute.com domain name for £5,000 in 1998. They needed to raise capital to start their business and this proved to be difficult as, at that time, people didn't fully understand the Internet and its potential. Hoberman and Lane Fox had to reassure investors that the Internet would take off.

It did, and the company now offers customers everything to do with going away, going out and staying in including package holidays, short breaks, hotels, flights, train tickets, theatre tickets, restaurants and sports events. It also offers home food delivery, DVD rentals and personalised TV listings. Everything is at the last minute, which is defined as within three months.

Martha Lane Fox attracted a lot of publicity and was interviewed in papers and magazines,

*Martha Lane Fox and Brent Hoberman of Lastminute.com*

gaining interest in the new venture. In March 2000, at the height of the dot.com boom, Lastminute.com was floated on the stock market. The company's share price rose to a high of 487.5p. Lastminute shares rose 28% on the first day of trading, representing a valuation of £732 million and earning the company £113.5 million. Martha Lane Fox personally had a fortune of £40 million. However, in 2001 the dot.com bubble burst, and the Lastminute share price fell to an all-time low of 18.75p. Lane Fox's fortune was now only £9 million.

At this point many dot.com businesses went bust, but Lastminute.com staged a strong recovery. In 2003 Lastminute.com announced its first full-year profit, £200,000 against losses of £16.2 million a year earlier. Martha Lane Fox decided to resign from her post as managing director. She was only 30 years old, and her 3.6% stake in the company, which she still has, was then worth about £26 million.

Since those exciting early days, Lastminute.com has become the most recognised e-commerce brand in London and the second most recognised in the UK. The company has acquired many other businesses including a flight consolidator called TravelSelect.com which provides access to more airlines, a tour operator called the Destination Group, and a company called TravelPrice.com, a competitor trading in France, Spain and Italy. The next acquisition was eXhilaration, a lifestyle company offering adventures such as bungee jumping or Ferrari driving.

Lastminute.com also trades in Sweden, the Netherlands, Belgium, Italy and France and has joint ventures in Japan, Australia, South Africa and Spain.

1 Lastminute.com is an intermediary (middleman). What do you think might happen to it as more and more suppliers such as airlines sell their product directly on the Internet?
2 Why do you think Lastminute.com has a policy of acquiring different companies?

# Ownership and support

## Types of organisation

Organisations can take many different forms. We will look at the different types in this section, remembering that they are not mutually exclusive.

### Independent

If you start up in business by yourself you are likely to form an independent organisation. This means you are not linked to any other group and you can make all your own business decisions. However, you may decide to join a trade association like ABTA so that you can benefit from the support and advice that it offers.

An independent business often has only one or a few outlets, and may specialise in a certain area of travel and tourism.

### Miniples and multiples

Retail travel agents tend to be grouped as miniples or multiples. Miniples are small chains, often within a regional area, whereas multiples have many branches across the nation. Some examples of these are given in Unit 1 and discussed in detail in Unit 7.

### Franchise

A franchise is a type of organisation which allows an individual to start up his or her own business but to minimise the risks by being part of an existing organisation. An organisation, the franchisor, sets up a contract with the person wanting to enter the business, the franchisee, including the following:

* permission to trade under the corporate name
* assistance and advice in running the business
* provision of stock and trading materials
* help in finding premises.

In return the franchisee must pay a premium, and a percentage of the revenue earned by the new business.

### CASE STUDY

Global is an example of a travel and tourism franchise. It offers franchisees the chance to start their own travel business from home or an office. The Global website shows what is on offer:

* a complete induction to the Global Travel Group, including an introduction to the travel industry for those who require it
* an introduction to Global technology, sales, marketing and customer service
* follow-up training and regular workshop seminars covering a wide range of topics including business management, industry developments and NVQs in most travel-related subjects.

1 What are the benefits of taking on a franchise?
2 What are the drawbacks of taking on a franchise?
You can find out more about franchising from the British Franchise Association.

## International

A company is an international organisation as soon as it operates in more than one country. This is very common today and all of our 'big four' tour operators are international companies. Lastminute.com developed into an international company.

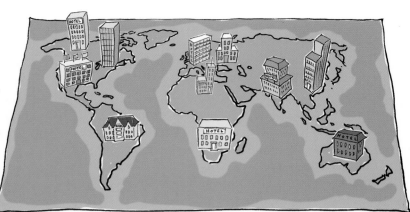

When companies operate throughout the world in almost every country, then they are not merely international but global. McDonald's is the best-known example. In travel and tourism, there are many global hotel groups such as Accor and Marriott.

> ✳ **REMEMBER!**
>
> The big four tour operators in the UK are First Choice, MyTravel, Thomas Cook and TUI UK.

## Categories of organisation

Organisations are categorised as public, private or voluntary. You need to know what these terms mean and be able to determine for yourself which category a company falls into.

### Public sector

Public sector organisations receive their funds from local or central government and usually aim to provide a service. Examples include the national and Regional Tourist Boards and some visitor attractions. (Many examples are given in Unit 1.) Funds for public sector tourism organisations come from central government through the Department for Culture, Media and Sport (DCMS) or from local councils. These organisations are judged on issues such as numbers of visitors achieved and quality, rather than on financial success.

In some countries the state owns and runs companies, re-investing the profits into other state ventures. Many transport facilities are state-owned, although not in the UK where privatisation has taken place. Privatisation means the state selling assets previously in the public sector to the private sector, to raise money. The Aer Lingus case study gives an example.

---

### CASE STUDY

**Rivals eye Aer Lingus sell-off**

**by TTG reporters**

**A NUMBER of players have emerged as contenders to take over Aer Lingus if the Irish government decides to privatise the state-owned airline.**

Aer Lingus chief executive Willie Walsh has announced his interest in a possible management buy-out. And Ryanair chairman David Bonderman is rumoured to be considering a bid, as are Aer Lingus pilots.

But reports that British Airways is interested have been firmly denied by the UK flag-carrier.

The Irish government has made it clear that it will not be rushed into a sale of the company, which is valued by experts at around €500 million. Dublin has stressed it will not strike a deal just 'to suit financiers', and a decision on Aer Lingus's future is not expected until at least the autumn.

Irish transport minister Seamus Brennan said the airline was a vital national strategic asset, and added that if the government were to sell the company, Walsh and his team would have to 'join the queue' with other potential investors.

According to industry sources, Walsh has already been offered the top job at Swissair and roles at other major airlines, but has so far stuck with the Irish carrier.

*Travel Trade Gazette*, 30 July 2004

1 **Why do you think the Irish government is considering privatising the airline?**
2 **What is a management buy-out?**
3 **What are the advantages and disadvantages of privatisation and a management buy-out?**

The **DCMS** is the government department responsible for tourism. It also looks after the arts, sport and recreation, the lottery, museums, film, broadcasting, press freedom and regulation, the built heritage and the royal estate.

## Theory into practice

Find out which travel and tourism organisations in your area are in the public sector. Compare your findings with your group.

## Private sector

Most organisations in the travel and tourism industry are privately owned. These organisations may be huge companies like British Airways, or small businesses. They usually aim to make a profit and are commercial companies. When they fail to make a profit over a period of time they are likely to cease trading.

All theme parks, restaurants, tour operators and travel agents in the UK are privately owned. There are different types of private ownership, ranging from sole trader to public limited companies. These will be discussed later.

## Voluntary sector

Voluntary organisations often have charitable status. Many are run by volunteers, although some have paid employees. They may be pressure groups, such as Greenpeace and Tourism Concern. Others, for example the National Trust, aim to preserve and protect historic buildings and landscapes.

Voluntary organisations do not aim to make a profit, but this does not mean they are not commercial. Any revenue they gain will be re-invested to further the aims of the company.

## CASE STUDY

National Trust and English Heritage share many similarities in their roles and responsibilities. However, in terms of ownership and funding they are very different.

English Heritage is the government's statutory adviser on the historic environment. It is officially known as the Historic Buildings and Monuments Commission for England. Its

*Lanhydrock House, Cornwall*

powers and responsibilities are set out in the National Heritage Act (1983, amended 2002) and today it reports to Parliament through the Secretary of State for Culture, Media and Sport.

The organisation is sponsored by the Department for Culture, Media and Sport. It also works closely with the Office of the Deputy Prime Minister, which is responsible for planning, housing, transport and the constitutional framework within which most decisions affecting the historic environment are made; and the Department for Environment, Food and Rural Affairs on rural issues.

English Heritage is funded in part by the government and in part from revenue earned from historic properties and other services.

The National Trust is a registered charity and is independent of government. It relies on the generosity of its supporters, through membership subscriptions, gifts, legacies and the contribution of many thousands of volunteers. All its revenue is re-invested in the care and maintenance of the land and buildings under its protection. However, four out of every five of its historic houses run at a loss and the National Trust is always in need of financial support.

1  **Draw up a table comparing the National Trust and English Heritage. Include the following:**
   - **type of organisation**
   - **sources of funding and other support**
   - **advantages and disadvantages of the two types of ownership.**

2  **Accompany the table with explanatory notes on how the type of ownership affects the support available for the operation of the organisations.**

**Consider this ...**

In 2002–3, English Heritage received public funding of £115.2 million, and income from other sources was £38.4 million. What do you think the other sources are?

# Business policies

## Takeovers

Sometimes a business has a policy of acquisition, of buying out other companies. Look back to the case study on Lastminute.com on page 34 to see which companies it bought out. Companies take over other businesses to grow and to reduce the competition.

Takeovers happen constantly in travel and tourism. Recent examples include the purchase of the Southlands Hotel in Scarborough by the coach company Shearings. Shearings already owns 37 hotels in the UK. This is an example of vertical integration.

Takeovers can be friendly or hostile – a hostile bid means that a company management does not want the company to be taken over, but the decision must be made by the shareholders.

## Mergers

A merger differs from a takeover in that two companies agree to become one. They can, however, result from takeovers. An example is the merger of the two city-break companies Bridge and Cresta, which merged in 2004. Both companies had previously been taken over by the MyTravel Group. Cresta and Bridge were rivals and this had not changed since they became part of MyTravel. The two companies were located in separate parts of the country with their own management. The merger will avoid duplication as the companies will share one management team in one location, and costs will be reduced. There is no reason to get rid of the brand names, as both can be retained.

**Theory into practice**

Find out what the current situation is with Cresta and Bridge. Research on the Internet and find out if both brands still exist and whether they are in competition. Check also on the parent company. Discuss your findings with your group.

## Public–private partnerships

This type of partnership is a collaboration between a public body, such as a local authority or central government, and a private company.

The Labour government in the UK wants to expand the range of public–private partnerships because it believes it is the best way to secure the improvements in public services that Labour promises. The government believes private companies are often more efficient and better run than bureaucratic public bodies. Some consider that management skills and financial expertise from the private sector can create better value for money for taxpayers. These partnerships are in services like health, but there are often public–private partnerships in tourism as governments cannot afford to resource new developments by themselves.

Before the Olympics in Athens in 2004, Greece launched an investment drive to attract 500 million of private investment into tourism. Hellenic Tourist Properties (ETA), a state-run organisation, was seeking to develop its 300 sites throughout Greece, through long-term leases and joint operation with private investors. It wanted to finance new hotels, campsites and golf courses. The aim was to make Greece a more attractive tourist destination, especially because of the Olympics.

*Greece launched a drive to attract more investment in tourism before the 2004 Olympics*

# Types of ownership

## Sole trader

A small independent firm usually operates as a sole trader. This means that the owner is personally responsible for all amounts owed to creditors and the government. It also means that should the sole trader not be able to make suitable arrangements to settle any debts, personal possessions will be taken by creditors. Although this is a simple business set-up, sole traders are very vulnerable because if their venture fails they can lose everything including their home.

## Partnership

This is when two or more people combine to form a company; the maximum number of partners allowed by law is 20. Each partner receives a percentage of the return of the business, depending upon how much they invested. Each partner is responsible for all the debts incurred by the business, no matter which partner incurred them.

## Private limited company

There are different types of private companies – the differences lie in the amount of liability the owners have if the company goes bankrupt. Private limited companies issue shares that can be bought and sold only with the permission of the board of directors. Each shareholder's liability to pay the company's debts is limited to the amount that they have not yet paid for company shares that they own.

It is also possible to set up a private company limited by guarantee. In this case, the owners agree on liability limits when they set up the company. This structure is often used to limit the personal liability of directors.

There are also private unlimited companies, where there is no limit to liability.

Most small businesses are private rather than public limited companies.

## Public limited companies and flotation

The shares of a public limited company (plc) can be traded on the Stock Exchange.

A company can become a plc only if it has share capital of £50,000, at least two shareholders, two directors and a qualified company secretary.

A business is said to be floated when it enters the stock market for the first time. It first has to meet the criteria described above. The advantages of floating a company are:

* you get back the money you invested in the company and hopefully a lot more – remember Martha Lane Fox!

* you issue shares and therefore raise new capital to develop your business

* you can motivate your employees by issuing shares to them

* it is good for your reputation – it shows you are an established company

* it is easier to acquire other businesses – you can use shares in your existing company to trade, as well as cash.

Of course, there are also disadvantages:

* share prices can go down as well as up and the value of your business fluctuates with them

* you will need a lot of professional advice to carry out the flotation, and this is expensive

* there is always a risk of a takeover

* shareholders will have a say in the running of the company

* public accounts have to be issued.

# Support organisations

## Sources of funding

If you are setting up in business you will need enough set-up capital to run the business until it begins to make a profit. Companies of all sizes also have to raise funds from time to time to finance growth, new ventures or takeovers. Various sources of funding are available according to the nature of the business and its ownership.

### Family and friends

Many small businesses are financed by families and can grow to be huge family enterprises. Friends may wish to invest in a business and reap profits without hands-on commitment.

### Banks

Banks are an obvious source of funds and they can offer loans. A loan is an amount of money borrowed for a set period and with an agreed repayment schedule. The repayment amount will depend on the loan size and the interest rate. The bank will lend only if the money is guaranteed, which may mean using a house as security or a family member as guarantor. Banks will also probably ask to see a business plan.

Overdraft facilities are also available from banks. These are more flexible than a loan as you have an agreed overdraft amount and can borrow what you need up to that limit. It is very quick to arrange an overdraft and you don't need to provide so much security, but if you do exceed the agreed limit you will have to pay penalties and this can be expensive.

### Grants

There are many sources of grants and in travel and tourism the Regional Tourist Board is able to advise on possible sources. Grants are usually from government or EU funds; they are one-off payments and do not have to be repaid, nor does interest have to be paid. There are strict criteria for eligibility when applying for grants, and a grant will not usually be given for the full cost of a project or venture.

## CASE STUDY

An example of a current scheme is the Tourism Capital Grants Scheme in the East of England region. To be eligible for a grant, the proposed development must:

- involve capital spending and a tangible new asset (maintenance and repairs not included)
- provide facilities for tourists, as opposed to the local community
- have planning permission
- have a total eligible capital cost of over £6,000
- conform to VisitBritain minimum quality standards on completion of the project
- be a member of, or join, a marketing organisation
- be committed to training
- provide paid employment.

1 **Discuss with your colleagues the kind of projects you think would be eligible for this grant scheme.**
2 **Why is it necessary to join a marketing organisation?**
3 **Why is training mentioned?**

The National Lottery is a source of grants. The DCMS has responsibility within government for National Lottery policy but does not award the grants. There are 16 distributing bodies responsible for awarding lottery grants; the Heritage Lottery Fund and the Arts Council are probably the bodies most relevant to travel and tourism. Camelot runs the lottery games and is responsible for the provision of lottery terminals and promoting the National Lottery. Camelot takes no part in awarding lottery grants.

Commercial companies whose aim is to make a profit are rarely eligible for grants as they come from public funds.

### Theory into practice

Go to the National Lottery website and find out which organisations related to travel and tourism have been awarded lottery grants. Remember they are likely to be in the heritage sector. Discuss with your group what the funds were spent on.

### Business angels

Business angels are wealthy individuals interested in investing their own funds in growing companies. They do not usually invest in very large corporations, but in start-ups. Most investments are less than £75,000.

They are often people who have experience of running a business and therefore are a source of advice. There is a National Business Angels Network whose role is to bring potential angels and businesses together.

### Venture capital

Venture capital is also known as private equity finance. Venture capitalists are often major companies which will invest large sums of money in return for shares in a business. They are looking for a high earning potential and a return on investment within a specified time. In other words, they expect the company to grow and be sold on very quickly at a large profit.

Venture capitalists are experienced at business and bring expertise and advice. They will require financial projections and will exert a great deal of control over the business.

The British Venture Capital Association helps larger businesses locate venture capital companies.

## *Support services*

A large business will use a full range of support services, including the following.

* **Stockbrokers** offer general financial advice on corporate finance-related transactions. They can advise on mergers and acquisitions, disposals, equity issues and flotation.

* **Solicitors** advise on legal matters and ensure the company operates according to current legislation. Some large companies employ their own solicitors.

* **Banks** are not only a source of funds but handle all financial transactions and can give advice on financial matters.

* **Auditors** check the final accounts and accounting systems of companies.

* **Registrars** deal with all matters relating to registration and certification of shares and making dividend payments.

* **Business Link** is managed by the Department for Trade and Industry, a government department. It provides invaluable advice for those setting up their own businesses. It is also possible to attend subsidised training courses run by Business Link on many aspects of business.

* **Trade associations** are very important for business support, particularly for small and medium-sized businesses which are less likely to employ experts in the different areas of business. The associations represent the interests of their members and press for changes needed in trading conditions or legislation by consulting with relevant bodies and lobbying government. In addition the associations provide advice and information to their members and try to keep them up to date with events which may affect their business. Examples of trade associations include the Association of British Travel Agents (ABTA) and Air Travel Organisers' Licensing (ATOL). The relevant trade associations for each sector can be found in Unit 1.

* **Enterprise bodies** are usually set up by government but are not government departments. They operate independently from ministers, although ministers remain accountable to Parliament for their performance.

Scottish Enterprise and Highlands and Islands Enterprise are examples of enterprise bodies set up to deliver economic development policies through a network of 22 local enterprise companies. They are funded by the Scottish Executive and aim to help new businesses get under way and support and develop existing businesses. These do not have to be travel and tourism businesses.

## CASE STUDY

*In August 2002, EasyJet bought Go*

EasyJet has its main base at Luton airport, and its offices are named 'Easyland'. EasyJet is a low-cost airline and offers over 170 routes from 50 European airports.

The airline was started in 1995 by Stelios Haji-Ioannou. He started with two routes from Luton to Glasgow and Edinburgh. His father owned a shipping line and he received money from his father to start up the airline. Although it is now a listed company on the Stock Exchange, the family remains the major shareholder.

In August 2002, EasyJet bought another low-cost airline, Go, at a cost of £375 million, boosting the growth of EasyJet.

During the financial year to 30 September 2003, the company reported pre-tax profits of £52 million on a turnover of £932 million and carried 20.3 million passengers. Haji-Ioannou has started up several other Easy brands and has sold £19 million of his shares to do so. He calls this 'selling his past to finance his future'.

Two of his start-up businesses, EasyInternetcafé and EasyCar, have together mounted up losses of over £100 million, although EasyCar is forecast to break even in 2005.

Haji-Ioannou could have raised finance from banks, business angels or venture capitalists but these sources would have meant letting go of control of his businesses. He prefers to keep control and if EasyCar is floated soon, as expected, he will find his investment is rewarded.

1 **Describe the EasyJet organisation, including its ownership, and the organisations that could provide funding and other types of support and advice. Include the following: banks, business angels, family, venture capitalists, trade associations and regulatory bodies such as the CAA.**

2 **Explain the advantages and disadvantages of different types of ownership for EasyJet and how the ownership affects the type of support available for its operation.**

# Financial and administrative systems

When businesses are set up, systems have to be put in place to manage their finances and administration. To begin with these systems could be fairly simple, but large organisations have much more complex systems and employ internal and external expertise to manage them. In this section we will look at the range of systems available to travel and tourism businesses.

## Financial systems

### Types of bank accounts

You are probably familiar with personal bank accounts, as if you have a job you need an account in order to get paid. **Business accounts** operate on the same basis but there are different kinds of accounts according to need.

Anyone starting up a business should open up a separate business account in order to keep careful accounts of transactions separate from personal finances. They would also be offered the services of a business adviser. This person will not necessarily have expertise in travel and tourism but will be able to advise in general terms. Service charges are made for business accounts.

**Current accounts** are used for day-to-day transactions. The rate of interest is very low or not payable at all, but funds are immediately available.

**Deposit accounts** earn interest on funds but with high-interest accounts, the money is not immediately accessible. In business these are often termed 'reserve funds' as they are kept for emergencies or for new ventures.

### Theory into practice

Visit one of the major banks in your town. Find out about the different types of business accounts and services available. You shouldn't need to ask for information – leaflets and brochures will be readily available. Decide which account and services would be suitable for someone setting up a small travel agency. Make notes on the services chosen and give reasons for your choice. Check your work with your tutor.

Travel and tourism businesses such as tour operators and airlines have to be able to trade in other currencies. In order to simplify trading they open **foreign currency accounts**. These allow them to manage their international cash flow and pay suppliers in their own currencies.

For example, tour operators have euro accounts and can pay hoteliers, etc., from them. Having a foreign currency account also helps reduce the risk of adverse exchange rates – this is discussed in more detail on pages 45–6. Banks offer all kinds of currency accounts, for example:

* euro accounts
* dollar accounts
* multi-currency cheque accounts.

Currency accounts can be held in the UK or overseas. Where businesses have offices overseas it is advantageous to have an **overseas bank account** funded by local resources.

Like foreign currency accounts, these accounts assist in the management of international cash flow and help reduce the risks associated with trading in foreign currencies. These accounts need not be with a different, foreign bank. The major banks are international, for example HSBC has offices in 79 countries.

### Receiving and making payments

Of course, payments are an essential part of any business. The business needs to collect payments efficiently from its customers. Suppliers, salaries and pensions have to be paid, and taxes, National Insurance and VAT have to be paid to the government. Offering a choice of payment methods to customers is important as it gives choice and helps the business receive payment on time. There are four main methods of payment – cash, cheque, cards or electronic means. The nature of the business determines which of these are suitable.

**Cash**

It is very unlikely that a business will pay suppliers in cash for security reasons. However, it is not unlikely that customers will make payments to a retail operation in cash. In fact large amounts of cash are still used in payment for holidays. If a business holds a lot of cash then security is an issue and a safe will be essential. Travel agents make use of night safes at the bank to deposit cash at the end of the day. Larger shops do not risk taking cash to the bank but have it collected by a security firm. This is called a bulk cash deposit service.

> ### Consider this ...
> Have you ever had responsibility for a large amount of cash? It can be alarming. A local arts venue was hosting a rock concert by a well-known band. The band insisted on being paid in cash at the end of the gig, so the manager had to collect the cash from the bank and keep it on her person until the end of the concert. She was very relieved to hand it over.

## Cheques

These are a traditional way of making and receiving payments. Cheques can be sent by post or paid directly into suppliers' bank accounts. For payments received, these might be in sterling or in another currency. Cheques received in payment are paid into the bank like cash.

A cheque guarantee card is needed with a cheque – most cheque guarantee cards have a £100 limit. If payment over the limit is accepted, the cheque could be returned unpaid because the guarantee does not apply. With travel and tourism services there is often time for a cheque to clear before the products or services are taken – for example, a holiday is paid for several weeks before departure and any cheque payment has time to clear.

## Electronic funds transfers

These are widely used both within the UK and internationally. They can be used to make same-day transfers, at a fee.

## BACS direct credit – electronic funds transfer

Direct credit is a simple, reliable and secure way of making electronic payments to individuals or other businesses, rather than using cash or cheques. Direct credit is provided by BACS Ltd on behalf of the UK payments industry. It is particularly suitable for customers making large volumes of payments.

## SWIFT

SWIFT stands for the Society for Worldwide Interbank Financial Telecommunications. It provides a secure payments system for financial institutions in more than 190 countries. It is the fastest way of making international payments.

## International banker's drafts

This is a type of cheque issued directly from the bank on behalf of a client. The draft is guaranteed as the bank has already ascertained that there are sufficient funds to cover it. A banker's draft in sterling can be paid into the bank in the normal way. A banker's draft in another currency will be subject to the current exchange rate and will take longer to clear, unless the company has an account in that currency.

## Standing orders

This is an easy way of setting up regular payments, for example to suppliers. A mandate is completed requesting the bank to pay the amount due on a particular date. It is a safe and efficient way of making and receiving payments and is carried out electronically.

## Direct debits

A direct debit allows payments to be taken directly from an account. It differs from a standing order in that the amounts can vary.

## Card processing

Accepting credit and debit cards widens the scope for being paid. Card payments can be made face to face, by telephone, post or over the Internet. UK businesses now use chip and PIN technology on credit card payments, which means that instead of signing a receipt, cardholders type in a Personal Identity Number (PIN) to confirm a transaction. The following extract from the *Travel Trade Gazette* explains how it works.

## *Security*

Basic security means taking care of cash and cheques by keeping them in a safe and not allowing unauthorised access. However, we have seen that electronic methods are now more common, especially for large international businesses. The use of the Internet and other technology has provided many significant benefits protect on-line transactions with customers.

It is also important to keep data secure on computers, which can be done by the use of a firewall. This is a security system installed on a computer network to restrict traffic. It can block unauthorised access to private networks such as an intranet.

When trade is carried out on-line, it is sometimes necessary to ensure that the people being dealt with are who they claim to be. Digital certificates, pieces of technology on the identified individual's system, perform this task. They are sometimes known as electronic signatures. They are issued by an organisation to identify an individual or a company.

## Currency conversions

As travel and tourism organisations operate internationally and sometimes globally, foreign currency risk has an impact on their trading. When making and receiving payments to and from other countries, a conversion takes place from one currency to another. As the exchange rate changes from day to day according to the economic conditions of the time, the currency conversion can work for or against a company.

to business because it permits the fast transmission of information, but there are security risks. Many customers may be concerned about making payments over the Internet with their credit or debit cards, fearing that the card information can be accessed by fraudsters.

Secure sockets layer (SSL) is the standard security technology for creating an encrypted link between a web server and a browser. This link ensures that all data passed between the web server and browser remains private and integral. It is used by millions of websites to

Foreign currency risk has to be carefully managed by businesses, but the more different countries and currencies that are being dealt with the more complex and risky the situation becomes. Companies have to identify the amount of risk and understand the potential losses they face.

There are various ways of managing currency conversion.

### Spot dealing

This is when currency is converted as it is needed at the current market rate. This leaves the company vulnerable to variations in the exchange rate. If the company has foreign currency accounts, it is protected to an extent against risk, but financial managers still have to decide when to convert currencies.

### Forward contracts

This is a means of reducing the risk, as it allows budgeting at a guaranteed rate of exchange. An agreement is made with the bank to buy or sell currency on a certain date at a fixed rate of exchange. Forward contracts are also used to hedge fuel prices. Of course they are a gamble, as exchange rates can vary either way.

## CASE STUDY

### Fuel price rises cause concern for airlines
#### August 2004

Fuel price rises have caused anxiety amongst airline shareholders worried about dividends and loss of profits. Jet fuel is the second-biggest cost for airlines after staff costs, accounting for up to 20% of operating expenses.

The Iraq war is blamed for the rise in oil prices and according to estimates from the International Air Travel Association, the airline industry will break even this year only if the average price of oil is $33 a barrel. At an average price of $40 a barrel, the industry will lose $6.9 billion.

BA has carried out some hedging but has still added fuel surcharges to fares. Other airlines are reviewing their fuel-hedging policies as the rise in oil prices forces carriers to choose either to lock in now before oil climbs higher, or wait and hope prices fall.

Lufthansa is one of the most comfortably hedged major airlines. It hedged about 89% of its fuel requirements this year and 35% of fuel needs for 2005.

1  What is meant by fuel-hedging policies?
2  Find out whether BA still has fuel surcharges.

## Financial records

Every organisation, from the sole trader to the largest company, has to produce financial records. A sole trader must, at least, record incoming cash and outgoings and produce a tax return. A plc is required to publish a full set of formal accounts.

All financial transactions within a business have to be recorded. The organisation's management need up-to-date financial information to help them run the business efficiently. In very small organisations paper systems may be sufficient, but most companies rely on information technology to produce financial information.

* **Petty cash** is needed for small day-to-day purchases and expenses. An amount of cash is kept for these purposes and any amounts spent are recorded in the petty cash book, with receipts.

* **The sales ledger** records the sales the company has made, the amount of money received for goods or services, and the money still outstanding from debtors. Copies of invoices are kept alongside the sales ledger. These have to be kept for six years.

* **The purchase ledger** records outgoing payments to suppliers or money still owed to suppliers, against their invoices. It allows the business to see how much money is owed at any one time.

* **Cash books** record all the money that comes into and goes out of a business. The cash book should record all transactions, however made, and be divided into two separate sections, receipts and payments.

* **Profit and loss accounts** show the income received and the expenses and overheads paid over a period of time, leaving a profit or loss figure for the period. Not all income is from sales – it may be from rentals or the sale of assets, for example.

* **The balance sheet** gives a view of the state of the company's finances at a given point in time. It shows all the assets of an organisation including any property and equipment, which are known as fixed assets. Any money in the bank is a financial asset. The assets are set against liabilities and must balance each other. Liabilities are the owner's capital or the shareholders' capital in the business. Other liabilities are any debts the company owes.

*An example of a cash book page*

All of these accounts can be kept on a computer rather than in books. All large companies use **computerised accounting**. Those who can afford it have tailor-made packages and their own accounting departments, employing expertise in both accountancy and IT systems.

Smaller companies are more likely to buy accounting software. Bought-in systems are cheaper than tailor-made ones but will have some features that are not needed and perhaps some that do not entirely fit the needs of the business. Sage is a popular accounting package.

Computerised systems should provide all the necessary information for annual returns, tax returns and value added tax (VAT) returns. Any reports needed should be easily accessible as long as the data has been input correctly.

## External accounts

Financial information about an organisation is of interest to many people. Shareholders and potential shareholders are interested in dividends to be paid and the value of their shares. Employees want to know if the company, and therefore their job, is secure. Any creditors, including banks, are interested in the ability of the organisation to pay its debts. The government will expect to receive taxes from a profitable company.

Sole traders do not have to make their **annual accounts** public, although they are likely to keep them for their own use. Private and public limited companies, however, must comply with the Companies Act and complete an annual return. They must also supply a signed set of accounts to Companies House every year.

From January 2005, Europe's listed companies have to conform to International Financial Reporting Standards. The aim of these standards is to create one single set of accounting standards that can be applied anywhere in the world. This will make it easier for investors to compare the performance of companies across international boundaries. But the new rules will cause a lot of work for companies, and particularly their accountants, as they prepare accounts that meet the standards.

**Key concept**

An **annual return** is a record of key company information which must be provided annually. Annual returns are filed at Companies House in London and are made publicly available.

Most large organisations incorporate their annual accounts into an **annual report**. This gives information about the current activities in the business as well as the figures in the accounts. All shareholders receive a copy of the annual report.

An **audit** is a check on the accounts and accounting system of an organisation. All companies in the UK have to have their final accounts audited by a professional accountant from outside the company.

**Key concept**

An **audit** checks that the accounts show a true and fair view of the affairs of the company.

## Tax returns

Every sole trader must complete a self-assessment tax return. Tax has to be paid on profits from the business. Expenses can be deducted from income to calculate how much profit is left (if any). If all the internal accounting systems have been properly managed, it is relatively easy to complete the tax return.

Corporation tax has to be paid by companies on their profits. The company must file tax returns with the Inland Revenue.

**Theory into practice**

Study the annual report of a company that interests you. You can ask for a free copy of any annual report from the Financial Times Annual Reports service or you can find an annual report on a company's website. Perhaps you would like to study the annual report from Lastminute.com – it is on the website.

Look at the profit and loss account and the balance sheet. Can you make any judgements about the financial status of the company? Who are the major shareholders? Make some notes and compare your findings with other companies researched by your group.

## Value added tax (VAT)

VAT is a tax on sales of goods and services. The current rate of VAT in the UK is 17.5%. Some goods, for example foods, are exempt.

All VAT-registered businesses have to complete a VAT return form for each tax period, usually every three months. A business must be registered for VAT once its turnover reaches £58,000, and must charge VAT on its goods and services, and keep records of VAT paid on purchases. The following information is included in the VAT return:

✱ VAT charged to customers

✱ VAT paid by the business to suppliers.

The difference between the amount of VAT received and the amount paid out must be calculated. If a business pays out more than it receives, it can claim this back, but if it receives more than it pays, this amount must be paid to HM Customs and Excise, a government department.

## Administrative systems

Administrative systems are the procedures used by an organisation to ensure that routine and non-routine tasks are effectively carried out to required standards. The larger the organisation, the more complex and numerous its administrative systems are likely to be. Some organisations try very hard to reduce bureaucracy and maintain an informal working environment. EasyJet is an example of one where paperwork is kept to a minimum.

Some administrative systems are general and apply to any business with appropriate variations, for example different kinds of booking systems. Others are specific to a particular business, for example procedures for currency exchange in a bureau de change.

We will look at systems for a ski chalet. The ski chalet is part of a vast multinational operation, but the procedures to be followed are provided in a manual designed purely for ski chalet staff. The list of paperwork is shown opposite.

We will look at some examples of procedures. Of course, staff in a ski chalet do not have access to a computer so all their procedures are carried out manually.

*Ski chalet staff must deal with the necessary paperwork*

**Pre-season paperwork**
1  Chalet inventory
2  Staff apartment inventory
3  Chalet meter readings
4  Staff apartment meter readings
5  Menu planner
6  Any additional forms handed out

**Weekly to chalet controller**
1  Chalet cash book
2  Receipts – numbered
3  Menu planner
4  Invoices – signed
5  Credit notes and statements
6  Weekly incident/accident report forms
7  Weekly chalet report

**Monthly to chalet controller**
1  Goods received sheets
2  Statement of chalet costs
3  Bednights chart
4  Telephone log sheets
5  All weekly paperwork items

## Purchases

Purchase orders are made to buy goods or services from suppliers. In a ski chalet the staff do

**CHALET PURCHASE ORDER BOOK**

Supplier ............................................. Client code: ............. Order days ........ Delivery days ........

| Minimum order quantity | Product | Date of order | | | | | | | | |
|---|---|---|---|---|---|---|---|---|---|---|
| | | | | | | | | | | |
| | | | | | | | | | | |
| | | | | | | | | | | |

not need to ask for quotes from suppliers. The company has already decided on food suppliers and the staff are issued with their contact details in order to make purchases from them. The example above is a purchase order to be completed manually.

Once the order is received by a supplier it will either confirm the order by telephone or send the goods with a delivery note. The delivery note has the same details as the order.

Once the goods are delivered or the service is received, the supplier will send an invoice to a specified office. This will be in the resort, not head office. The invoice is a request for payment and includes all the details of what was delivered, costs including discounts, VAT if appropriate, and any delivery charges. When this is received the company matches up all the documents related to

that order and pays the invoice according to the terms agreed.

## Sales

In the ski chalet, staff are told how many guests and who they are by head office, so sales records are kept there. However, they do have to record 'bednights' as a check on the accommodation being used and to allow budgeting for expenses. The example shows the type of form to be completed.

Sales records are an important source of management information. In a travel agency a daily sales report can be automatically produced by the computer system. Each time an agent makes a sale he or she inputs the data and it is recorded. The manager is then able to assess whether targets are being met and is able to take action in problem areas. The daily reports are

**CHALET BEDNIGHTS CHART**

Resort .......................................................................

Chalet .......................................................................

Costing period from ................... to ..................... Total no. of days ...................

| Group name | Arrival date | Departure date | No. in group | No. of nights included | Total bednights clients | Total bednights staff | Extra meals |
|---|---|---|---|---|---|---|---|
| | | | | | | | |
| | | | | | | | |
| | | | | | | | |

amalgamated into weekly reports, and so on.

In a hotel, bookings are recorded. Again they may be manual or computerised. Large organisations always have computer reservation systems. The clerk is able to see which rooms are available on the screen and, having confirmed the customer's requirements, enters the booking into the computer. The system will generate the customer's invoice at the end of the stay, including any extras.

## Customer database

Customer records are of vital importance to a company. Travel agents and tour operators in particular are fortunate in that they are able to collect substantial amounts of information about their customers, because they usually give many personal details when booking holidays. This information can be used for research purposes or to send out promotions and direct mail.

The regulations of the Data Protection Act must be followed in the keeping of any customer information.

Manual records can be kept easily and many travel agents still use manual files. A computer database is more efficient as it allows searches to be made on specific fields so it would be possible, for example, to send a leaflet about a luxury cruise to all customers who spent more than £1,000 per person on their last holiday.

There is no need for the ski chalet staff in our example to keep customer records, as they are held on a database at head office.

## On-line bookings

When you are making a booking on-line the procedure is clear for you to see as customers are expected to manage the process themselves. All the seller has to do is ensure that explicit instructions are given to the user.

## Meetings and company records

A limited company is required to hold an annual general meeting (AGM). Members of the company and accountants have to have 21 days' notice of the meeting.

For other meetings only 14 days' notice is required, and unlimited companies have to give only 7 days' notice.

Sometimes, extraordinary meetings are called to discuss special issues. Companies House must be sent a copy of decisions taken at these meetings within 15 days. Minutes must be kept of general meetings and of those held by directors.
A company secretary will be responsible for making sure all these conditions are adhered to. Companies must keep official records of

✱ the shareholders and the shares they own

✱ directors and company secretaries

✱ directors' other commercial interests

✱ loans.

**Theory into practice**

You are the assistant to the operations manager at a small theme park in your local area. It attracts only people in the immediate region and closes in the winter.

1 All the systems need a complete overhaul. Your role is to suggest suitable examples of the following systems for the theme park:
   • receiving payments
   • keeping sales records.
   For each system you suggest, you must explain its operation.

2 For each system you suggest, explain how the system meets the needs of the organisation.

# Management structures and communication systems

## Management structures

Every business, from the sole trader to the largest company, is organised in a particular way. The structure should be such that it fits the current aims and practices of the business and when it no longer fits, restructuring should take place.

Businesses can be organised by:

* function
* geographical area
* product
* matrix.

### *Functional organisation*

If a business is organised by function, it will be divided into departments fulfilling different functions. Examples include human resources and marketing departments.

This is a simple method of organisation as it is clear to everyone what the different departments do. Within each department there is a manager or director, with line management reporting to them. The advantages are:

* there are clear lines of management
* it is clear what the responsibilities of each department are.

The disadvantages are:

* there may be lack of communication between departments, with each unaware of what others are doing and how they impact on each other
* as this is a traditional model, people may be reluctant to change the structure.

Look at the TUI UK organisation structure below to see an example of functional management.

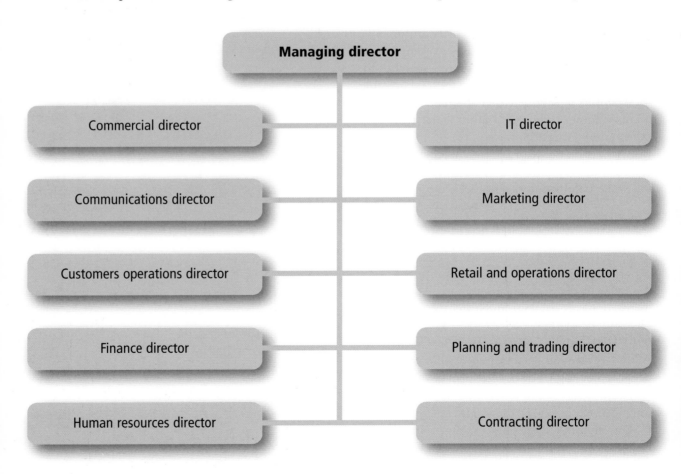

| Managing director |
| --- |

| Commercial director | IT director |
| Communications director | Marketing director |
| Customers operations director | Retail and operations director |
| Finance director | Planning and trading director |
| Human resources director | Contracting director |

## Geographical organisation

A business can be organised according to geographical area. This is sensible for multinational organisations, where each country or region can be managed as a unit of business. The advantages are:

* the impact of language and cultural differences within the company is reduced

* local needs can be catered for

* positive competition can be encouraged between regions.

The disadvantages are:

* there may be duplication of resources and staff

* there is a potential for conflict between local and central managers.

## Product organisation

In travel and tourism a product management structure is very common with large businesses that have a number of brands. With this structure each department has responsibility for a brand and all the management functions that go along with operating that brand. The advantages of this type of structure are:

* each brand caters for a particular market segment which is well known by the managers

* there can be positive competition between brands.

The disadvantages are:

* there may be unhealthy rivalry between brands

* there will be duplication of resources and staff

* there may be a lack of central control.

## Matrix organisation

Matrix management is becoming increasingly popular. It combines aspects of product management with functional management, and is sometimes used where a new project is planned. Under the matrix system, individuals are given responsibilities within a project area reporting to a project manager, but will also retain their usual responsibilities reporting to their departmental manager. The advantages are:

* it gives staff the chance to use their skills across the business

* it is very flexible.

The disadvantages are:

* staff may have divided loyalties as they report to more than one manager

* it may not be clear where responsibilities lie.

## Organisation charts

An organisation chart shows the structure of the company and how the work is divided into different areas. It also shows the lines of responsibility between staff, so that it is apparent who is responsible to whom. An employee studying a chart will find the possible promotion routes.

The chart may show a hierarchical structure or line relationship. This is a very traditional structure and shows a chain of command with each person responsible to the person above them. It is sometimes referred to as a pyramid structure.

Senior managers

Middle managers

Supervisors

Agents

Trainees

Many organisations today would be depicted in a chart as a flatter structure. There are fewer layers of management, and each manager has a broader span of control. Restructuring of organisations often involves getting rid of middle managers and flattening the structure.

## CASE STUDY

Paramount Holidays has restructured its sales team, combining the Paramount Holidays team with the Adventure Travel division.

In keeping with the company's mission of delivering excellent customer service and to enable the company to fully focus on the many differing distribution channels, the company has made some changes in responsibilities for the current teams. This will enable them to have a greater focus on account management, customer service and stronger communication with travel agents.

As part of the restructuring, Jamal Desai, sales director, will take responsibility for the sales function of the Adventure Travel division in addition to Paramount Holidays. Reporting to Jamal will be two head of sales roles, south and north.

Susan Levinsky will have responsibility for sales in the south, based in Ashford. Her remit also includes responsibility for the relationship with Paramount Retail. Supporting Susan are Helena MacIntyre, regional sales manager, south west; Georgina Stevens, recently promoted to regional sales manager, Midlands; and as a result of Clive Bevan's move to Paramount Ski Lakes and Mountains, a vacancy exists for regional sales manager, south east.

The company is also currently recruiting for a head of sales, north. In the interim, Frederick Chambers and Monty Davies, regional sales managers for the north and Scotland respectively, will report directly to Jamal.

Other retail agents represent an important part of the business. The majority of Vertigo Travel agents have recently agreed to sell Paramount car hire as their preferred car-hire supplier. In order to give more focus to these key accounts, Parminder Shah, in addition to her responsibilities for Paramount Holidays, will be national account manager with responsibility at a commercial level for charter flights and Paramount car hire with Vertigo Travel.

1 **What kind of management structure is apparent from the information given?**

2 **Draw up an organisation chart for the sales department adding other functions and roles as you think appropriate.**

3 **Explain how the management structure fits the needs of the sales department at Paramount Holidays.**

## Factors affecting organisational structure

There are several factors which affect the type of organisational structure chosen. These are as follows.

### Size

A company with few staff requires only a simple organisatonal structure. Lines of communication can be informal and not many managers are needed. As the company grows, more formal structures are needed and there is an increase in paperwork and bureaucracy.

### Location

International organisations require offices and facilities in more than one country. This may lead to decentralisation of functions and dispersed staff and managers.

> **Key concept**
>
> In a **centralised structure**, senior managers in a central location or head office make most decisions.
>
> In a **decentralised structure**, staff work in teams in different locations and are led by local managers.

### Nature of business

If a travel and tourism organisation offers a specialised, fairly straightforward product, for example walking holidays in Madeira, the organisational structure is likely to be fairly simple, with a personal approach.

### Management style

Management is about motivating people to act in certain ways so that the team can achieve its common goal. Different managers prefer different organisational structures to enable them to practise their management style. A good manager must inform, motivate and develop the team.

An **autocratic** manager makes all the decisions and announces them to the team. This person is the boss and so has full control. The main advantage of this kind of leadership is that decisions are made quickly, as no consultation is involved. Its other advantages include:

* where there is a need for urgent action the autocrat will take control

* some team members gain security from being told what to do.

The disadvantages are:

* team members may become frustrated at their lack of control

* there may not be room for the team to express creativity

* there may be over-dependence on the leader.

Autocratic management belongs in a traditional hierarchical structure.

With **consultative** management, the leader still makes the decisions but discusses them with the team. The advantages include:

* the team is informed of what is going on

* open discussion is encouraged

* the manager spends time with the team.

The disadvantages include:

* the team may feel involved but frustrated by having no real power.

With **democratic** management, the decision-making is shared among the team. The advantages include:

* ideas are encouraged from everyone

* there is greater involvement and commitment from team members

* the team is likely to be supportive of the leader

* the team is fully informed.

The disadvantages include:

* some team members may not be able to cope with being involved in decision-making

* the democratic process can take too long

* the leader may not agree with the decisions of the team

* powerful team members may take over.

With **laissez-faire** management the team is left to sort itself out and get on with its work. The manager does not get involved and therefore is not leading the team.

The advantages include:

* highly motivated and skilled people are able to get on with their tasks

* the team is empowered.

The disadvantages include:

* new team members will be uninformed

* the team may be left with little or no direction.

# Communication systems

**Consider this ...**

If you were working in a ski resort as a chalet manager, how would you communicate with your company?

## *Internal communications*

### Verbal

Verbal communication can be as informal and as simple as members of staff discussing a problem with each other, or a manager giving information or instructions. Staff enjoy socialising at break times and will discuss their work. This is the most common way of communicating within an organisation.

Verbal communication can take place more formally at meetings. Meetings may be scheduled or ad hoc, that is, held as they become necessary. In one low-cost airline the management team meets for the first hour of each day to discuss developments and determine strategy.

Meetings are more formal than conversations. In a business meeting there is usually an agenda, or list of items to be discussed, and minutes are taken to record what has been agreed. In a more informal meeting there may not be an agenda and minutes, but there is the risk that decisions will not be actioned in these circumstances.

The telephone is also a means of verbal communication within an organisation. It is easy for staff members to call each other and internal networks can be set up even where staff are in different locations.

In international operations it is cheaper to set up a telephone conference than for personnel to travel for a meeting. However, as you cannot see body language during a telephone conference some nuances of conversation may be missed. To solve this problem, video-conferencing became very popular in the 1990s, but it is less so now.

It works via interactive two-way video.

The services offered for conferencing are very sophisticated. BT offers a service where up to 50 people worldwide can join in a conference, although it is doubtful whether much would be achieved with so many people!

Interviews are another type of verbal communication. They can be used in different ways:

* to discuss a problem with a line manager
* to participate in an appraisal interview
* for disciplinary reasons.

### Written

Written communications within an organisation include **minutes of meetings**. These record decisions made and who is to action them, and they are distributed to all relevant staff.

**Notice boards** are also used to give staff news items about company developments or forthcoming events. The notice board is a one-way communication system and therefore can be a cause of conflict if it is used to inform staff of unpopular decisions, as staff cannot easily communicate their concerns.

**Memos** have become far less common as a means of written communication with the advent of e-mail, but they are still used in some organisations. A memo is a brief informal document which is used to pass on information within a company.

**Letters** are rarely used as a form of internal communication except in formal situations involving warnings, redundancy or dismissal.

Large companies often have an **in-house magazine or newsletter**. This helps staff in different locations to be aware of company developments, and can also serve as a morale booster as it reports on successes within teams.

Here are some examples of how the Co-op Travel Group and Thomas Cook keep in touch within their organisations.

UNITED CO-OP hosts a staff forum called Reform Councils. It is open to more than 900 members of staff within the retail division, plus the Apollo and Barrow Travel call centres.

Forty-nine trained staff are responsible for gathering information and feedback for the regular council meetings, which occur about four times a year. Topics can range from pay and conditions to uniforms and sales development.

'Training takes time and commitment but it is well worthwhile – everyone knows what is expected of them. The feedback has been excellent,' says Jane Webb, group human resources manager.

The council representatives are of all ages and experience, and include branch managers, travel advisers, foreign exchange staff and apprentices. Some are also members of the shop workers' union, and there are even shop stewards and full-time union officials on the councils.

'The union people can really help us because they have ideas from other companies,' says Webb.

'We have a good relationship and have the same objectives. It also benefits them as they understand the company's issues and financial performance, so are more realistic.'

THOMAS COOK has an intranet 'Get in Touch' facility, to which all staff have access. There is also a dedicated e-mail address for staff to send feedback direct to UK chief executive Manny Fontenla-Novoa. A spokeswoman added: 'We issue an annual staff questionnaire to gain a temperature check on morale and motivation within the company.'

Cook also runs panel sessions – made up of a cross-section of the business – which are held regularly to provide feedback on new ideas and marketing initiatives. Other internal forms of communication include a quarterly magazine and monthly videos for stores.

*Travel Trade Gazette*, 30 July 2004

### Electronic

Electronic communications for internal use include e-mail, which is a popular way for staff to communicate with one another, and intranets.

An intranet is a website that has restricted access, usually for employees only. It may hold information that a company wishes to share internally but not externally. There are several benefits of using such a system, and some risks. The benefits are:

* internal users are able to communicate quickly over the intranet

* there can be better communication of objectives and guidelines to company employees

* teams can communicate well across all departments and locations

* team members may feel empowered as they are able to share knowledge and have access to information

* there are reduced costs for printing and distribution of information

* people have quicker access to information.

The risks include:

* where many people have access to a system, there is potential for security lapses to allow unauthorised access

* there is a possibility that employees perceive too much information is available and suffer from information overload

* employees may be unable to decide which information is relevant to them

* users may attempt to set up their own web pages and abuse the system.

## External communications

### Verbal

Verbal communication takes place in person with customers when they come into business premises, and in meetings with suppliers.

The telephone is a vital means of remaining in contact with both customers and suppliers. A company of any considerable size will have a switchboard with a trained operator. The operator's role is to answer the telephone quickly with the appropriate greeting and then to pass on calls to the correct departments. Call centres have established their businesses by using the telephone and their staff are highly trained.

> ### Consider this ...
> Many call centres are opening in Scotland, as research has shown that customers like the gentle lilt of a Scottish voice. Companies are also taking advantage of lower overheads.

Voice message services are provided by all telephone companies. They are used both for internal and external communications and mean that however busy staff are, they do not have to miss calls. Of course, voicemail means there is no excuse for not calling back!

### Written

Written communications take several forms. **Fax** is still used a great deal for communicating from business to business, but it is rivalled by e-mail. It is useful for sending diagrams or pictures which are not easily attached to e-mail.

Formal business **letters** have retained their importance as a communication tool, particularly when dealing with complaints. It is not necessary for large travel and tourism organisations to compose a fresh letter each time they wish to communicate with a customer. Standard letters are prepared and generated by a computer, with personal details added at the touch of a mouse.

**Company magazines** are a popular communication tool for airlines, which provide them for customers on flights. They are used to sell in-flight products and to give destination information. They can also be used to promote a positive corporate image.

> ### Theory into practice
> Next time you or a family member takes a flight, keep the in-flight magazine. Go through it and find examples of how it is used to communicate in a positive way with customers. You could make a display out of your research findings.

**Annual reports** were discussed earlier as a means of reporting financial results. They are also a way of telling shareholders and other interested parties what the company is aiming to do in the future, and what has happened in the past year.

## Electronic

There are many advantages to **e-mail** communication with customers and suppliers, particularly when they are in international locations

An **extranet** is an extension of an intranet, for the purpose of providing information about the company to selected other companies or individuals. Examples include customer support information or information about new products.

The **Internet** is having a major impact on the industry, as a source of information for choosing and planning holidays and other forms of travel, and for making bookings. Companies are able to use the Internet to communicate their products and services to customers and to gain feedback, as it is interactive.

**Theory into practice**

In your role as assistant to the operations manager at a small theme park (see page 51) you have been asked to draw up a report on suitable communication systems to be used both externally and internally. Produce the report, describing the different types of system and explaining why they are appropriate.

**Knowledge check**

1　Describe how a franchise operates.

2　What are the differences between public, private and voluntary organisations?

3　Explain how English Heritage benefits from being in the public sector.

4　What is the difference between a takeover and a merger?

5　What does 'flotation' mean?

6　Give three examples of sources of funds for setting up a business.

7　How do trade associations support businesses?

8　Explain why a tour operator might hold a foreign currency account.

9　Explain three different ways of making payments to a supplier.

10　Why do airlines fix the price of fuel in advance?

11　Explain the purposes of an annual report for a plc.

12　Describe the advantages and disadvantages of a matrix organisation structure.

13　Explain the terms 'intranet' and 'extranet'.

Slovenia Tours is a tour operation business providing holidays in Slovenia to inbound tourists. Since Slovenia's entry into the EU it realises that there is potential to increase its business and to attract tourists from throughout Europe to Slovenia. It has decided that the UK is an important market and is considering setting up an office base in the UK.

*One of Slovenia's attractions is the castle in its capital, Ljubljana*

The problem is that Slovenia Tours has no idea how businesses operate in the UK and it needs help and advice in order to start.

You work for a Regional Tourist Board as a marketing assistant. Your tourist board has been given funding by the Regional Development Agency for projects which might attract new businesses to the region. Your manager has agreed to provide help and advice to Slovenia Tours, and you have been assigned to help prepare a series of notes and presentations for this purpose. Your aim is to give an explanation of the operation and ownership of travel and tourism businesses in the UK.

Slovenia Tours needs to understand the different types of travel and tourism organisations in the UK and their ownership.

1   Describe three different types of travel and tourism organisations and their ownership.

2   Describe the organisations that provide support to them and their role.

3   Explain the advantages and disadvantages of different types of ownership for one of your chosen organisations and explain how the ownership affects the type of support available to it.

Slovenia Tours will need to set up administrative, financial and communication systems in its British office. It will eventually have offices in major cities throughout Europe and they must be able to communicate easily with the head office in Slovenia. Remember that they will be selling holidays to Slovenia to British customers.

4   Describe the role and purposes of financial systems in the travel and tourism industry including banking, making and receiving payments, and security.

5   Describe the role and purpose of administrative systems in the travel and tourism industry including purchasing, sales and processing data.

6   Describe different types of communication systems used in the travel and tourism industry.

7   Select appropriate administrative, financial and communication systems for Slovenia Tours and explain how they will be used. Use flow charts, etc. if appropriate.

8  Justify how the selected systems meet the needs of Slovenia Tours.

9  Devise a suitable management structure for the UK office of Slovenia Tours and produce an organisation chart for the office.

10 Explain how the management structure is appropriate to the needs of Slovenia Tours.

# UNIT 3

# Marketing travel and tourism products and services

## Introduction

This unit introduces you to marketing in the context of the travel and tourism industry. You will look at definitions of marketing, its functions and how market segmentation is used in travel and tourism. You will also learn about the distinctive nature of the industry and the issues raised in applying the general principles of marketing.

You will consider different methods of market research, and how they are used in travel and tourism. The concept of the marketing mix will be introduced, and you will consider how it applies to travel and tourism organisations in practice.

### *How you will be assessed*

This unit is assessed by an integrated vocational assignment (IVA) set by Edexcel. The assignment covers units 2 and 3. Your centre will assess the IVA using Edexcel's assessment criteria. A variety of exercises and activities is included in this chapter to help you understand the principles of marketing in travel and tourism and prepare for the IVA. You will also have the opportunity to work on some case studies to further your understanding.

After completing this unit you should be able to achieve the following outcomes:

→ Explore marketing in the context of the travel and tourism industry
→ Examine different methods of market research and how they are used by the travel and tourism industry
→ Consider how the marketing mix could be applied to a travel and tourism organisation
→ Apply practical marketing skills for the travel and tourism industry.

# Introduction to marketing principles

Before you try to understand the processes of marketing and how they occur in practice, you need to understand what is meant by the concept of marketing. If you ask people what they understand by marketing, they often mention advertising or selling; these things are not marketing, but they are a part of it. Marketing embraces all business decisions that are made in order to get a product or service to the right customer or consumer.

A company which has adopted the core philosophies of marketing puts the customer at the heart of its business. Every product made has a customer who needs or wants that product, even if they don't quite know it yet. For every service that is offered, the company has established that there are customers who would like to use that service. Of course, this doesn't always work out in practice. If it did, no companies would fail. But companies that are successful in the long term are those which are carefully providing for the needs of their customers.

An organisation that aims to practise successful marketing tries to have excellent customer knowledge and to anticipate customers' needs. Most travel and tourism companies understand that putting the customer first is crucial to success in business.

## Definitions

### Marketing

This is how the Chartered Institute of Marketing (CIM) defines marketing:

> *The management process responsible for identifying, anticipating and satisfying customer requirements profitably.*

There is an argument that 'profitably' is not an essential word in the definition – not all organisations aim to make a profit. Charities give all the money they make to the cause they work for. They have to market themselves to raise that money. Public organisations such as tourist boards provide services to consumers, but don't usually make a profit. They still use marketing principles to ensure that the services they provide are right for their customers.

Here is another definition, provided by a famous marketing expert called Philip Kotler.

> *The marketing concept holds that the key to achieving organisational goals lies in determining the needs and wants of target markets and delivering the desired satisfaction more efficiently and effectively than the competition.*

Again the importance of the customer is emphasised, but now there is also mention of the competition. Travel and tourism is a very competitive industry. Consider how many holiday companies there are to choose from when you book a holiday. So to be successful, a company has to not only provide what the customer wants but do it better than competitors.

Another marketing expert, Peter Drucker, suggests the following definition:

> *The aim of marketing is to make selling superfluous. The aim is to know and to understand the customer so well that the product or service fits him/her and sells itself!*

It is difficult to think of travel and tourism companies that have reached the stage where customers flock to them because the product or service is exactly right. But this is certainly something to aim for.

### Theory into practice

Ask ten people what they understand by marketing. Write down what they say and bring your notes for discussion with your colleagues. How many people are close to the definitions given?

### Customer service

As part of your course you are also studying customer service. You may be wondering how customer service and marketing differ from each other. Good customer service is part of the marketing process; it is concerned with how the product or service is presented to the customer, how the company is presented to the customer and how the customer is dealt with. Good customer service involves developing personal service skills. The function of marketing, however, is to encompass the whole process of deciding which products and services the customer will want and how they will be delivered to the customer.

## Functions of marketing

The functions of marketing are to:

* find out about customer needs
* produce products and services that meet those needs
* know the market – including competitors
* make sure the whole organisation is marketing-orientated
* find and communicate with customers
* manage any threats that affect the marketing process.

In the UK, marketing has been a high-profile aspect of business since the 1970s, and today it would be difficult to find travel and tourism companies that do not acknowledge its importance. Most will have a marketing department or marketing manager.

It is important to recognise that the marketing department cannot operate in isolation. Its work will impact on all other sections of the business, so marketers must hold a position within an organisation which allows them influence on other departments. What would be the point of the marketing department of a tour operator carrying out research and finding out that no one parties in Faliraki any more if the contracting department did not act on the information?

A newer business philosophy which you may come across in your studies is Total Quality Management (TQM). This concept arose from the Japanese management approach known as *Kaizen*, and involves all members of an organisation constantly trying to improve quality in the processes they use, the products and services they produce, and the culture in which they work. It can be summed up as a management approach to long-term success through customer satisfaction.

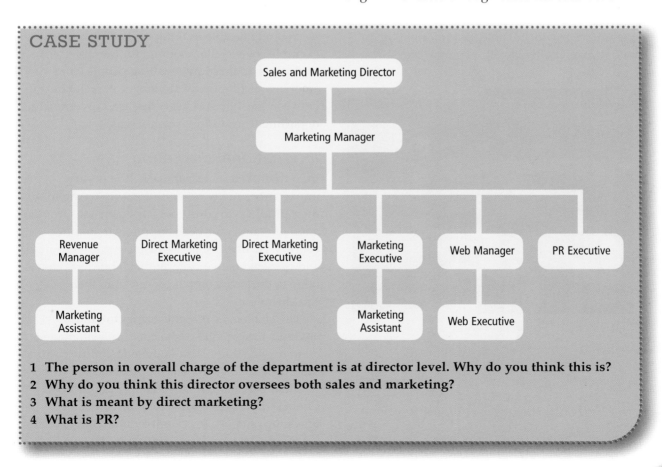

## CASE STUDY

1  **The person in overall charge of the department is at director level. Why do you think this is?**
2  **Why do you think this director oversees both sales and marketing?**
3  **What is meant by direct marketing?**
4  **What is PR?**

# Types of marketing

Marketing can be described as a set of tools which allow a company to achieve its aims. So far, we have talked about marketing to customers or consumers.

## Consumer marketing

Many of the travel and tourism companies with which you come into contact are practising consumer marketing. Examples include travel agents, airlines and Tourist Information Centres.

## Business to business marketing (B2B)

Marketing to other businesses doesn't mean that customers are forgotten. Instead it recognises that there are different kinds of customers, including other businesses who in turn serve the final consumer, or even further businesses.

For example, an airport must market its services to airlines. They are customers of the airport, just as passengers are the customers of airlines. Travel agents are customers of tour operators. When a travel agent sells a holiday, it is on behalf of a tour operator. Agents expect the tour operator to provide reliable, fast information on holiday availability, as well as glossy brochures.

**Theory into practice**

1 Think about an airline being the customer of an airport. List other organisations that have the airline as their customer.

2 Think about the airport. Does it have any other customers? Who are they? Are they companies or individuals? Discuss your thoughts with others in your group.

## Service marketing

In travel and tourism, marketing is often used to sell a service rather than a product. This may be B2B or consumer marketing. The marketing of services can provide a particular challenge because of the nature of the product. Read more about this in the section on the marketing mix, page 66.

## Social marketing

The issue of profitability in the definition of marketing was discussed at the beginning of this unit. Sometimes a function of marketing is to promote a cause which brings a social benefit rather than profit, for example 'responsible tourism'. The idea of responsible tourism is that tourists are more aware of their environment when on holiday and take measures to protect it. The idea encourages businesses to make sure they don't detract from a community, but enhance it. The International Centre for Responsible Tourism is a not-for-profit organisation that promotes responsible tourism both with businesses and with consumers.

You will be able to think of many other examples of social marketing, for example campaigns to discourage young people from smoking, or to raise awareness of the relationship between lifestyle and heart disease. Government departments fund these campaigns.

## International marketing

In tourism, international marketing is very important as many organisations are trying to sell their products to consumers or businesses from another country, or need suppliers in another country. Airlines must do business with airports and passengers over international borders. Hotels hope to attract incoming tourists into their establishments.

The challenges that this brings are fairly obvious. Knowledge of the country's language is often needed, but also a knowledge of the cultural differences and customary approaches to business.

There are many financial implications, too. Changes in foreign exchange rates affect the financing of deals, for example in paying hoteliers for rooms. Making payments across borders is

*When doing business, cultural and language differences can be a challenge*

expensive, even within the EU. Travel and tourism operations are usually well prepared for these problems.

## Marketing orientation

### Product orientation

Companies which follow a product-oriented approach to business concentrate on making good-quality products which in their experience have sold well. They strive to improve production techniques and systems, but take little notice of market changes and trends. They hope that the product is so good that customers will come to them and demand it.

Sometimes, when a company has invested in production equipment, for example to build holiday caravans, it will want to keep on producing them so that the production line does not become obsolete. This type of company may run into trouble as consumer needs change, and the product may become unpopular.

### Sales orientation

In a sales-orientated company, the goods or services are produced and then a huge effort is put into selling and promoting them. Profits are made through sales volume, but this strategy can bring only short-term success because if the consumer has a bad experience of the product or it is of poor quality, there will be no repeat business. An example of this in travel and tourism is where holidays are sold which involve poor

accommodation in run-down resorts. They may at first attract custom through heavy promotion based on low prices, but the holiday makers will not enjoy the holiday and will not use the company again.

### Marketing orientation

A marketing-orientated company identifies its customers' needs, produces products and services to fit those needs, delivers the product to the customer in the right place and at a price which suits them, and gains profits through customer satisfaction. This is what successful companies are doing all the time.

## Customer needs and wants

There is no need to distinguish between needs and wants in marketing. As far as the marketing process is concerned, they are the same thing. The important factor is to find out what they are. We think we *need* a lot of products and services when in fact we just *want* them! How many times have you heard people say 'I need a holiday'? Do they need it or want it? It doesn't matter, as long as they are going to buy one.

However, it is important to realise that customers' wants and needs vary, and products, services and marketing techniques must also vary to meet those needs. The travel and tourism industry is very competitive. If the company does not cater for the needs of a customer, the customer will be able to choose from many others that do.

### Consider this ...

Think of all the products or services you bought in the past two days. Did you need them, or want them?

## Market segmentation

To find out about customer needs, you have to find out as much as you can about your customer. If all your customers have the same needs you can satisfy them with only one product or service and one set of marketing activities. This is known as undifferentiated marketing or a total market approach. It is very unusual, and you are unlikely to find examples of it in the travel and tourism industry.

It is more likely that the organisation has identified different groups of customers, and that within each group customers have similar needs and characteristics. The market is all the people who buy or might buy the product. Dividing the market into groups of people with similar needs and characteristics is called market segmentation.

Having identified these market segments, a company has to decide whether to cater for all the segments, with different products and marketing strategies for each one, or to cater for some of the segments with different products and strategies, or to cater for just one specific market segment. The latter is known as 'niche marketing' and is highly specialised. An example is diving holidays, which require specialist knowledge of locations and equipment. There could, of course, be differentiation within the diving market.

The segments that the company chooses to target with its marketing are known as target markets. Later in this unit we will discuss the methods of segmenting the market.

## The marketing mix

The marketing mix describes the key elements that an organisation uses to achieve its objectives and meet the needs of its customers. These elements are commonly known as the four Ps:

The four Ps give us the core of a company's marketing strategy. The use of the four Ps will be discussed later in this unit.

Marketing is a continuous process. A company which is just starting out or is reassessing its position in the market will first have to stop and take stock of all its activities and what is happening in the market. It will then review this position throughout the life of the company, following five stages.

## Identifying and researching the market

First, it is usual to search for a 'gap in the market', that is a customer need that is not being catered for, or not catered for well enough. Market research sometimes uncovers such gaps, but the opportunity may just be spotted by someone. Market research is then needed to find out whether customers are receptive to the idea.

## Product development

The next step is to develop the product or service, including its name or 'brand'. This brings us to the first of the four Ps, product. The product must have some quality that sets it apart from the competition – this is known as the Unique Selling Proposition (USP).

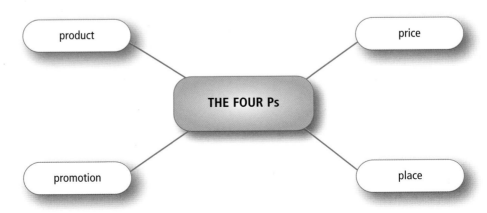

## Price

The product or service must have a price, and the price-setting stage is the second of the four Ps. The price may or may not be fixed.

## Place

Distribution channels must be determined. These are the means of getting the product or service to the customer. Place refers to place of purchase, and not where the customer is going – this can cause confusion in travel and tourism. The traditional chain of distribution in travel and tourism, as you saw in Unit 1, looks like this:

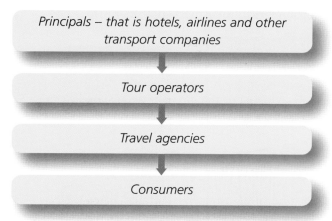

Principals – that is hotels, airlines and other transport companies

↓

Tour operators

↓

Travel agencies

↓

Consumers

## Promotion

The product or service has to be promoted so that the consumer is aware of it. This is the 'face' of marketing, the activities we all see as they are carried out in the public domain. They may take place through different advertising media, promotions or public relations activities. This specialised branch of marketing is known as 'marketing communications'.

If marketing has been effective, then sales will take place. After-sales service is also important, remembering that the marketing focus is on customer satisfaction, so it should be considered to be part of the product mix.

Some organisations are proactive and telephone their customers after they have bought a product to ensure they are satisfied with it. Many travel agents do this when customers return from holiday. Travel and tourism organisations do not always have face-to-face contact with customers but they can invite feedback by e-mail or make their complaints policy very clear and easy to use.

Research must take place at all stages of the marketing process to ensure that customer needs are being met. Constant monitoring of marketing activities is also important.

## Constraints and issues in marketing travel and tourism

### Moral issues

Moral issues for travel and tourism include matters relating to social responsibility and ethics. For example, the tourism industry depends heavily on the natural environment and therefore has a moral obligation to protect that environment. Green tourism, otherwise known as sustainable tourism or responsible tourism, is of increasing importance because of the enormous growth in travel. However, some of the biggest tour operators have been accused of paying lip service to responsible tourism and not having real policies to safeguard the environment. An organisation called Responsible Travel has organised a petition to lobby three tour operators on their environmental policies, and invites members of the public to send in stories about environmental degradation.

Of course, there are significant marketing advantages to going green. A recent MORI poll showed that 61% of consumers believe that environmental issues are important when choosing a holiday. As this is a topical subject, green marketing campaigns also attract positive publicity from the media.

## Health and safety

Travel and tourism organisations are subject to health and safety legislation. However, these laws differ internationally. Tour operators in particular have an obligation to ensure the health and safety of their customers on holiday and should have extensive procedures in place for this.

## Accessibility for people with disabilities

In some countries, such as the UK, access for people with disabilities is taken very seriously and legislation is in place to ensure accessibility. For example, all new buildings must be accessible to people in wheelchairs.

Tour operators may find that other countries do not have such policies and that access is restricted, particularly at historic sites. Again, tour operators need to make checks and advise customers in their marketing literature.

**Consider this …**

Not all buildings are easily accessible to people with disabilities. Think about the provisions made in a cinema or theatre near where you live.

## Adverse publicity

There is a saying that 'all publicity is good publicity'. Think about your own opinion of that. Adverse, or unfavourable, publicity can come from many sources. There is an example in the case study above of tourists being asked for negative feedback. Television programmes such as *Holidays from Hell* play on negative experiences, and the holiday companies or airlines involved cannot stop such publicity.

Tourists often write to newspapers with complaints, which are then published. Organisations have no control over this kind of negative publicity.

Here is an example of a newspaper reader's complaint:

> Is it just me or is anyone else fed up with being asked for detailed personal information under the pretence of doing market research? Three times on my recent holiday to Tenerife I was asked to complete a ridiculously long questionnaire. They say they want holiday makers' feedback so that they can improve customer service, etc., so why do they want to know about my income, what car I drive and where I've got my mortgage? Presumably if I gave all this information I would then be inundated with mailshots trying to sell me all sorts of rubbish. I am sick of it!

## External constraints

Travel and tourism companies need to be aware of the external factors that affect the operation of their business. An analysis of these factors is described as a PEST analysis, because the factors involved are categorised as:

* political

* economic

* social

* technological.

A PEST analysis should take place at regular intervals as part of a review of marketing activities. Management should be constantly aware of topical issues which may impact on business, even when a formal analysis is not taking place.

Companies also need to undertake a thorough analysis of internal factors affecting operations. This is known as a SWOT analysis, looking at the company's:

* strengths

* weaknesses

* opportunities

* threats.

You need to know how to carry out these types of analyses and use the information gathered.

### Key concept

**PEST** – a PEST analysis helps an organisation to take stock of the external factors affecting its business, identifying political, economic, social and technological factors. The PEST analysis helps with the SWOT analysis as it can point to opportunities and threats.

The following are some of the external (PEST) factors which currently affect travel and tourism companies.

### Political factors

These often relate to changes in legislation introduced by government. A recent example of legislation affecting our industry is the Denied Boarding, Cancellation and Delay EU Regulation, which was accepted in 2004, becoming operational in 2005. This regulation gives passengers much greater compensation when flights are delayed or cancelled. Airlines are mostly unhappy about these new regulations and think that they will have to pay out a lot in compensation. Airlines' associations are presenting a legal challenge to the regulations, claiming that they will lead to higher fares and less choice for consumers.

### Theory into practice

Find out what EU regulations promise to consumers in cases of flight delay or cancellation. What do you think of this? Carry out a debate. Half the group should represent airlines and the other half consumer groups.

When regulations are proposed, various groups campaign to or 'lobby' Parliament to get their views heard and try to make sure that legislation represents their interests. The airline associations lobby on behalf of airlines and the Association of British Travel Agents (ABTA) lobbies for travel agents. ABTA and similar organisations help their members to keep up to date with industry changes, as it is sometimes difficult to monitor new developments.

Tour operators have to be aware of the political situation in the destinations they offer. Some places can become very dangerous because of a political situation. This changes rapidly, but tourists will avoid places where there have recently been serious incidences of unrest or terrorism. For example, the Bali bombing deterred tourists for some time, and currently it is not advisable to visit many parts of the Middle East because of terrorist activity.

Many such occurrences cause great problems to tour operators as they are unexpected and cannot be planned for. Tour operators may have to repatriate holiday makers when an incident occurs, and switch destinations for those who have booked to go there. The Foreign Office website gives the current situation on safety in countries all over the world.

### Economic factors

Changes in taxes affect tourism as they raise costs. Passengers on airlines have become used to paying air passenger duty, as they are also used to paying road tax. When taxes are raised or newly introduced they become contentious. In the US a room tax is added to your hotel bill. In the Balearics an environmental tax for tourists was introduced in 2001 and caused great controversy.

## CASE STUDY

Spain, 12 April 2001

Hoteliers and tourist boards in the Balearics were up in arms yesterday when a controversial new tourist tax was approved in Parliament. The cost to tourists is only a euro a day, but that could amount to £35 extra on a holiday for a family of four over two weeks.

The aim of the tax is to raise about £40 million annually to help the islands fight environmental problems. The tax is imposed on the tourists as they contribute to the environmental problems.

Hotel owners think that holiday makers will go elsewhere because of the tax. Even the Majorcan Tourist Board is against the tax. The president of the tourist board commented, 'We said right at the start and we repeat, we don't like the tourist tax'. He said also that the entire tourist industry was against the tax.

1 What do you think about the tax? Is it a good thing or not?
2 Find out about some other tourist taxes by carrying out research on the Internet.
3 The tax was abolished in October 2003. Why do you think this was?

Another important economic factor is interest rates. If rates rise it can affect a business's ability to repay loans.

The exchange rate can also dramatically affect a company's costs. For example, a tour operator with contracted accommodation in Spain will pay in euros. A weak pound will buy fewer euros and will bring increased costs to the tour operator. Eleven European countries have adopted the euro, and although the UK has retained sterling and is not a member of the euro zone, travel and tourism businesses in the UK are still affected by the euro. Customers who come from the Continent may expect to use euros in the UK and in fact some hotels and shops will accept them, giving change in sterling.

Rises in fuel prices also affect the economic health of airlines and tour operators, as the following case study shows. Read it carefully and answer the questions.

## Social factors

Travel and tourism businesses operate in a rapidly changing market. It is important that marketers take notice of social changes affecting their customers.

People in the UK today generally live longer and are healthier. They have more money to spend than previous generations, and time to spend it. Older people make up a vital market for travel and tourism operators, who have lost no

## CASE STUDY

### EasyJet fears oil hike

EASYJET has warned its full-year profits will be hit to the tune of £4 million if oil prices continue to ride high.

The no-frills airline said profits could slip to about £52 million if oil prices stay at more than $40 a barrel. The airline has hedged 55% of its fuel to the end of September.

However, it ruled out adding a surcharge to its tickets as airlines such as British Airways, Virgin Atlantic and Singapore Airlines have done.

EasyJet piled further pressure on its share price – which plummeted by 21% on Monday to 158 pence – when it warned of a tougher trading environment later this year.

Chief executive Ray Webster said: 'We indicated in our interim announcement that we were seeing unprofitable and unrealistic pricing by airlines across all sectors of the European industry.

'We expect this to continue during the rest of the year. While demand for low-cost travel remains strong, the forward pricing environment is exceptionally competitive.'

His words echo those of Ryanair chief executive Michael O'Leary, who warned of a fares 'bloodbath' this winter.

Revenue climbed by almost a quarter year-on-year to hit £1.015 billion in the 12 months to May.

This outstripped Ryanair's annual revenue which also climbed, by 28%, to about £671 million.

But the Irish airline's profit is more than double EasyJet's at about £128 million.

Passenger figures rose by 23% to 22 million in the year to May. But load factors dipped by two percentage points to 81%.

*Travel Trade Gazette*, 11 June 2004

1 **Investigate and explain these terms:**
   - **no-frills**
   - **hedging**
   - **surcharge**
   - **forward pricing environment**
   - **revenue**
   - **profit**
   - **load factor.**
2 **Explain how a rise in fuel prices affects an airline's profits.**
3 **What measures could an airline take to avoid the risk to profits?**

*Older people make up a vital market for travel and tourism operators*

time in creating holidays specifically for them in off-peak periods. This market is known as the 'grey' market.

Tastes change from season to season. Tourists want to visit new destinations, and as travel costs are comparatively cheaper than a few years ago, much of the world is easily accessible. Short breaks are wanted, not just a traditional summer holiday. More people want to stay in mobile homes rather than tents, and so tour operators provide them. Sunbathing is not so popular now, as the public is increasingly aware of the risks of skin cancer.

Tour operators therefore provide different types of holidays. There are city breaks, adventure holidays and spa holidays, all providing the tourist with a variety of things to do while they are away. 'Cultural tourism' is the term coined for holidays which include excursions to sites of interest, museums and galleries.

The media has a great influence on our culture. Films make us aware of places and inspire us to visit. Tourism to New Zealand has increased since the release of the *Lord of the Rings* trilogy of films which was made there. Tourism New Zealand research shows that 10% of foreigners visiting are at least partly motivated by the chance to tour sites shown in the films.

In New York you can relive a favourite television programme and sign up for a guided *Sex in the City* tour.

## Technological factors

Technology is probably the area of greatest change, as there are rapid developments in many areas. The building of the Channel Tunnel opened up our small island to our neighbours and allowed us more options for outbound travel. Aircraft are being developed that will hold many hundreds of passengers, and airport runways are being expanded to accommodate them. Self-check-in is becoming more common at airports, including checking in your own baggage. It is possible to hire a car without any personal contact, collecting keys and making payment via a vending machine.

The Internet has revolutionised the way we book our holidays and travel. On-line booking systems are common for all modes of transport and for many holidays. Hotel bookings can also be made on-line, showing you a view of your room and the facilities.

Travel agents are under great threat from the Internet. Their commissions have been slashed as operators cut costs and encourage Internet bookings. If tourists can do their research on the web, 'see' their destinations and book easily, why use a travel agent? Those agencies that survive will be the ones that adapt their role so that they offer a specialist service and excellent advice, rather than just a booking service. In fact, those that survive will be those that practise the best marketing.

### Theory into practice

You have read many examples of PEST factors that may influence marketing in travel and tourism. Remember that these influences can occur on a local, national or international level.

1 Work with a partner and choose a tourist facility in your area. This could be a tourist attraction, a tourist office or a hotel. Describe the facility and its location. What is its target market?

2 Identify all the political, economic, social and technological factors that will impact on its future planning. You may need to do some research to find out what is going on in your local area, for example new housing developments that will bring new customers. Look at what is happening nationally as well. Present your findings to your group and discuss the variations that occur. Are any of the factors you have identified opportunities or threats?

3 Explain how these factors will affect the application of marketing principles by your chosen tourist facility.

## Regulations and consumer issues

Travel and tourism companies are subject to many regulations and pieces of legislation. In this section we will look at those issues which specifically affect marketing activities.

The **Consumer Protection Act 1987** makes it an offence to give customers a misleading price indication about goods and services. It lays down rules about the use of terms such as 'reduced' and 'bargain'. Price indications given verbally are also covered. In travel and tourism, this legislation has most relevance to brochures and advertising.

The **Trade Descriptions Act 1968** is one of the most important pieces of consumer legislation, and section 14 is its most relevant part for travel and tourism. This section deals with the supply of goods and services. It states that it is an offence to make a statement that is known to be false or to recklessly make a statement which is false. This applies to the provision of services, facilities and accommodation and the location of amenities for any accommodation. An offence can be committed even when there is no intention to deceive the customer.

The **Unfair Terms in Consumer Contracts Regulations 1999** apply to all contracts. When you book a holiday, a hotel room or a flight you enter into a contract with the seller. The seller will publish terms and conditions associated with that contract – you can read these in any holiday brochure.

These regulations protect consumers against unfair terms in contracts. Sometimes attempts are made to introduce terms and conditions that may reduce the consumer's statutory rights or may impose unfair burdens on the consumer over and above the obligations of the ordinary rules of law.

The **Data Protection Act 1998** provides rights for those who have information held about them in 'relevant filing systems'. This may be on computer or in paper files. The act also requires those who record and use personal information to follow sound practice.

An individual can have access to information held about him or her and, if necessary, have it corrected or deleted. People must have the opportunity to consent to the collection and processing of their data. Personal data must be kept secure, up to date and not for longer than necessary.

The Data Protection Registrar, an independent officer who reports directly to Parliament, administers this act. If you want to have access to information about yourself, you must make a written request to the holder of the information. Travel and tourism companies hold a lot of customer information, which must be revealed if a customer asks for it.

The **British Code of Advertising** has the following main general principles.

✳ All advertisements should be legal, decent, honest and truthful.

✳ All advertisements should be prepared with a sense of responsibility to consumers and society.

✳ All advertisements should respect the principles of fair competition generally accepted in business.

✳ No advertisements should bring advertising into disrepute.

✳ Marketing communications must conform with the code. Primary responsibility for observing the code falls on marketers. Others involved in preparing and publishing marketing communications such as agencies, publishers and other service suppliers also accept an obligation to abide by the code.

* Any unreasonable delay in responding to the Advertising Standards Authority's enquiries may be considered a breach of the code.

The **Advertising Standards Authority** (ASA) is an independent body set up by the advertising industry to police the rules for advertising, sales promotion and direct marketing. The system is one of self-regulation aiming to protect consumers and maintain the integrity of marketing communications. The ASA continually checks a sample of advertisements, but also relies on the public to complain about advertisements which do not comply with the code. The ASA can ask for an offending advertisement to be withdrawn or changed. Of course, some complaints are judged to be unfounded, as shown in the example below.

The following is an adjudication made by the ASA after a complaint.

---

### Wales Cottage Holidays

Date:      14 June 2000
Media:    National press
Sector:   Holidays and travel
Industry complaint from: Pembrokeshire

**Complaint:** Coastal Cottages of Pembrokeshire objected to a national press advertisement for holiday cottages. It stated 'WALES Cottage HOLIDAYS 555 throughout Wales including "Best in the UK"'. The complainants objected to the claim 'Best in the UK' because they believed it wrongly implied the advertisers had been voted best in the UK.

#### Adjudication:

Complaint not upheld

The advertisers said the claim was based on a national newspaper supplement article 'Britain's top 25 holiday cottages', in which two of their holiday cottages featured. They said respondents to the advertisement were sent a brochure and an insert that explained that. Although it considered that the advertisement should have qualified the claim, the Authority concluded that the advertisers had justified their use of the claim. The Authority considered that the claim did not imply that the advertisers had been voted best in the UK. The Authority considered that the claim was acceptable.

Source: www.asa.org.uk

---

# Marketing research

Marketing research is imperative in the marketing process, especially in travel and tourism where not enough is known about why consumers behave as they do. Marketing research enables an organisation to find out about the market, the competition and what consumers want.

Many different methods are used to carry out research, depending on the purpose of the specific research project. Research may be carried out on behalf of a company by a specialist research agency, or it may be done by the company itself, in-house.

## Areas of research

Research may be related to any area of the marketing mix or to the market overall. The most complex area of marketing research relates to consumer behaviour. We will examine these areas of research in more detail before studying the methods of marketing research.

### Market research

Market research is a category of marketing research that involves finding out about the market for a product or service. Remember that the market for a product is all the users or potential users for that product. Therefore, in market research, we would like to find out who these people are, how many of them there are, what they are like, where they are, and so on.

We also want to know who else provides products or services in this market and how many sales (or how much market share) they have. Market share can also be measured in financial terms. If a competitor is performing better than we are, we need to find out why. We should find out what the sales are worth for the whole market and whether the sales trend is up or down.

### Product research

For a physical product such as a new type of aircraft, a long period of research and development is needed, including testing the product to make sure it works and is safe. At the same time, the developer must find out about the market for the product. Who wants this aircraft? What features do they want incorporated?

Tour operators research destinations to add to their product portfolio. Again, they need to find out whether there is a need for the product – are many people likely to go to this destination? These questions take the marketer from product research into market research.

## Price research

The price charged for a product must represent good value to the consumer. This does not mean the product has to be cheap. The most expensive cocktail in the world is over £200 and available in a bar in Paris. It is made with a very rare brandy and some people are prepared to buy it. Research that concerns price might involve finding out what competitors charge for similar products, or asking consumers what they would be prepared to pay.

## Promotion research

This might include looking for new methods of promoting the product or the company, assessing competitors' promotional activity, or trying to evaluate the success of a promotional campaign. It is difficult to determine whether promotions work. Even if there is an increase in sales, we can never be absolutely sure whether it is due to the promotion or to some other factor, like the weather.

## Place research

This area of research means finding out whether the distribution methods being used are the most suitable to reach the consumer, and finding new ways of reaching the customer.

## Consumer research

Consumer behaviour research is very difficult to conduct, as consumers themselves often cannot explain why they act as they do. Although challenging, this area of research is possibly the most useful as it can lead to an understanding of consumer needs, and their attitudes to a product, and help a company to determine which products or services will fulfil consumer needs.

# Market segmentation – classifying consumers

In order to market their product effectively, travel and tourism companies must segment the market, as we saw on page 65. The market is divided into groups of people with similar characteristics, each group making up one segment. The segments at which the company directs its marketing activity are the target markets.

Market segmentation can be done in various ways. Most companies choose to use not just one but a combination of methods.

## Demographic segmentation

Demographics is the study of the make-up of the population. Demographic trends illustrate how the population is changing. Factors that affect the make-up of the population are the birth rate and life expectancy.

Currently we have an ageing population as people live longer and the proportion of people in older age groups increases. This is, of course, of interest to marketers, who have termed older people the 'grey market'. The birth rate is low at the moment but in the post-Second World War years many babies were born as families were reunited and looked to the future. These babies are now in their fifties, and due to the sheer numbers of them, they have been an influential and important market all their lives. They are known in marketing as the 'baby boomers'.

When demographic segmentation is used, consumers are grouped according to:

* age
* sex
* ethnic grouping
* family life cycle.

The family life cycle is a useful, if old-fashioned, method of segmentation. The stages of the life cycle are as follows:

* young singles
* young marrieds
* full nest 1 (youngest child under 6)
* full nest 2 (youngest child 6 or over)
* full nest 3 (older, but still dependent children)
* empty nest 1 (children gone)
* empty nest 2 (children gone, parents retired)
* solitary survivor.

These life stages do not relate to age, but to family development. The idea is that needs and wants change according to where we are in this cycle.

Families with young children expect hotels to provide appropriate services for them and look for family holidays, whereas an empty-nest couple is looking for different services and may have a greater disposable income.

## Socio-economic segmentation

In this method of segmentation the population is divided according to socio-economic grouping. These groupings are based on occupation, not income. The classifications are used extensively by advertising media to describe their readership.

| SOCIAL GRADE | SOCIAL STATUS | OCCUPATION |
|---|---|---|
| A | Upper middle class | Higher managerial, administrative or professional |
| B | Middle class | Intermediate managerial, administrative or professional |
| C1 | Lower middle class | Supervisory or clerical, and junior managerial, administrative or professional |
| C2 | Skilled working class | Skilled manual workers |
| D | Working class | Semi-skilled and unskilled manual workers |
| E | Those at lowest level of subsistence | State pensioners, casual or lowest-grade workers |

## Geographic segmentation

The marketing data company CACI has produced the classification called ACORN (A Classification of Residential Neighbourhoods) based on postcodes. Every street in the UK is included and categorised into 54 typical neighbourhood categories. Streets which have broadly similar residents are categorised together. The classification is arrived at using information drawn from the census and from market research data.

**Theory into practice**

Go to the website www.upmystreet.co.uk. Enter your postcode and then click on ACORN profile. Find out what your profile is. You can get a detailed profile if you wish.

Travel and tourism companies can easily find out the geographic location of their customers as they usually have access to addresses on their database. The geographic area from which the customers are drawn is known as the 'catchment area'. The catchment area is very important for tourist attractions as they need to draw customers from as wide an area as possible. Organisations such as VisitBritain need to know from which countries incoming tourists originate in order to target their marketing activities.

## Psychographic segmentation

With this type of segmentation, consumers are categorised according to personality types, lifestyle and motivation. When it is done well, it is very effective in determining targets, but it is difficult to do accurately. It is very relevant to travel and tourism. For example, environmentally aware people will be interested in sustainable tourism products.

---

## CASE STUDY

Researchers sometimes come up with their own psychographic categories. In 2001 the English Tourism Council did some research about reviving the UK's coastal resorts. It came up with the following groups:

- Conformists – this is the largest group – they desire sameness and familiarity. They like a comfortable environment, chatty atmospheres and scenic fresh air. They want to be surrounded by people like them.
- Sentimentals – this group does not respond to any trends. Any change or drop in standards can alienate them.
- Seekers – these people are image-driven and like to see themselves as trendy. They like to be in the right place with the right people. They like to have fun but often have responsibilities and are constrained by budget.

- Radicals – free spirits and frequent travellers. They work hard and play hard and like to discover a destination before other people. They want distinctive restaurants, pubs, bars, clubs and nightlife.
- Independents – seek out different cultural experiences away from the crowd. Upmarket restaurants, sports, heritage, accommodation and beaches are important to them.
- Pragmatists – highly cultured and artisan people. They enjoy peace and quiet and go to places where they can enjoy the outdoors and fresh air. They are the least willing to spend money and 20% of them never take a holiday.

1 **How do you think this study will help VisitBritain promote coastal Britain?**
2 **Decide what media you might use to reach each of these groups. (Read through the section on promotion to help you do this.)**

---

**Consider this ...**

In 2003, the English Tourism Council became part of the new organisation VisitBritain. Which of the English Tourism Council's groups do you think you belong to?

Draw up profiles of the type of people you would expect to be attracted by the different First Choice brands. Make them as detailed as you can using the information in this section.

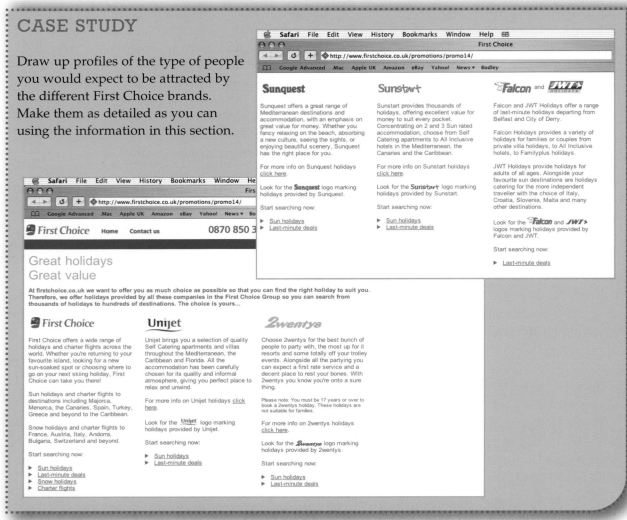

Source: www.firstchoice.co.uk

# Research methodology

## Types of data

Data is often divided into the categories quantitative and qualitative.

**Quantitative** data consists of facts and figures, for example the number of people admitted to a museum in one day. **Qualitative** data is more difficult to collect and to analyse as it is about why people behave as they do and what they think. Sometimes consumers themselves have trouble knowing why they choose to buy certain things.

Data can also be **primary** or **secondary**.

### Primary data

This is data that has been collected for the first time – it didn't already exist somewhere. It is sometimes called field research. Researchers do this type of research only when they are sure that the information they require has not been collected elsewhere.

Methods of collecting primary data include:

* surveys
* questionnaires
* observation
* focus groups.

**Surveys** are interviews carried out with consumers. They may be completed by mail, telephone, personal interview or through an Internet site. They are usually based on a **questionnaire** rather than free discussion.

The table opposite shows the advantages and disadvantages of the different survey methods.

| SURVEY METHOD | ADVANTAGE | DISADVANTAGES |
| --- | --- | --- |
| Personal interview | Interviewer can explain questions to respondent | May introduce bias |
| | Response rate is good | Very expensive to administer because of interviewer's time |
| | Can use 'prompts' to aid recall | Difficult to recruit trained interviewers |
| Telephone interview | Easy to carry out | People find telephone calls intrusive |
| | Many calls can be carried out in a short time | No visual prompts |
| | Response rate is fairly good | |
| | Personal contact with respondent | |
| Mail questionnaire | Cheap to administer | Very low response rate |
| | Few staff needed | Needs an appropriate list of addresses |
| | | No explanation of questions to respondents |
| Internet questionnaire | Easy to administer | Limited to respondents who access that website, therefore biased |
| | Instant response | No explanation of questions to respondents |

*Surveys can be carried out by interviewing passers-by in the street*

It has become common practice for tour operators to give their customers questionnaires to complete at the end of their holiday. The response rates are usually good for these types of surveys, particularly if the holiday makers are travelling by plane. They are a captive audience and air crew can easily collect the completed questionnaires.

The results of these surveys help with planning for the next season and show up faults which the company can then investigate.

### Key terms

**Respondent** – the person who is answering the questions.

**Closed question** – one with a limited range of answers, sometimes just yes or no or a number.

**Open question** – one where any answer can be given.

**Filter question** – one that allows the respondent to omit certain questions which may not be applicable. For example, 'If you answer no to question 5, go to question 11'.

**Classification data** – the age, sex and occupation of the respondent. This is used to group respondents into categories.

**Quota** – the number of people in different age or socio-economic groups to be questioned.

**Happiness Holidays Questionnaire**
**Help us and you could win a FREE holiday worth up to £1,000!**

At Happiness Holidays, we are committed to making sure that you have the best holiday possible. To help us achieve this, we would like to ask for your help. By providing your views and comments in this questionnaire, you can tell us what you think about your holiday and where you feel there is room for improvement. As a way of saying thank you, you will be entered into our FREE PRIZE DRAW to a win a holiday – so don't forget to include your contact details.

**SECTION 1 Your holiday booking**

1  Please state your holiday start date: Day ☐☐ Month ☐☐ Year ☐☐

2  At which resort are you staying?

..........................................................................................

3  When did you book your holiday? Month ☐☐ Year ☐☐

4  Is this your first holiday with Happiness Holidays? Yes ☐ No ☐
   If no, when was the last occasion? Year ☐☐ Which resort? ........................
   How many Happiness Holidays have you taken in the past five years? ☐

5  How did you hear about Happiness Holidays?
   Television ad ☐          National newspaper ad ☐          Magazine ad ☐
   Internet banner ad ☐          Friend's recommendation ☐
   Newspaper/magazine article ☐          Internet search engine ☐          Travel agent ☐

6  How did you book your holiday?
   Direct ☐          Through travel agent ☐

7  Did you use a brochure or the Happiness website to obtain holiday information?
   Brochure ☐          Website ☐          Both ☐

**SECTION 2  Your holiday satisfaction**

8  How do you rate your holiday overall?

   Better than expected ☐          As good as expected ☐          Worse than expected ☐

   If worse, please state why: ...............................................................
   ..........................................................................................

9  Was there anything you particularly liked about your Happiness Holiday? If so, what?
   ..........................................................................................
   ..........................................................................................

10 How do you rate the value for money of your holiday?
   Excellent ☐          Very good ☐          Satisfactory ☐          Less than satisfactory ☐

11 How likely are you to book another holiday or short break with us?
   Already booked ☐          Very likely ☐          Quite likely ☐          Not likely ☐

**SECTION 3 About you**

**12** Please state the age and gender of the person who made the booking  Male ☐  Female ☐

18–24 ☐    25–34 ☐    35–44 ☐    45–54 ☐    55–64 ☐    65+ ☐

**13** Please describe the occupation of the principal wage earner in your household

Unskilled worker ☐    Skilled worker ☐    Lower management ☐

Middle management ☐    Senior management ☐    Director ☐    Self-employed ☐

Part-time worker ☐    Homemaker ☐    Retired ☐    Student ☐    Unemployed ☐

**14** While daily newspapers do you regularly read?

The Sun ☐    The Star ☐    Daily Mirror ☐    Daily Mail ☐    Daily Express ☐

The Times ☐    Daily Telegraph ☐    The Guardian ☐    The Independent ☐

The Financial Times ☐

**15** Would you be interested in receiving future holiday news and special offers from
Happiness Holidays?   Yes ☐    No ☐

**1  Which questions are examples of open questions?**

**2  Why is a free holiday on offer?**

**3  Why does Happiness Holidays ask which newspapers are read by the respondent?**

**4  Which classification data is asked for?**

**5  Where could this questionnaire be distributed?**

**6  What is your opinion of the questionnaire?**

---

When designing a questionnaire, remember the following points.

✱ Before you write any questions, make a list of what you want to find out.

✱ Go through the list and discard anything that is not absolutely essential.

✱ Go through the list again and try to order the information you require in a logical way.

✱ Write the questionnaire asking general questions first and them more specific questions. Never ask more than one thing in a question.

✱ Avoid bias in a question.

✱ Try to use closed questions – the answers are easier to analyse.

✱ Use a limited number of open questions if you want to find out the respondent's opinion.

✱ Use a filter question if the respondent does not need to answer every question.

✱ Always put classification data at the end. It is not a good idea to start off by asking respondents how old they are and what they

do for a living. The exception to this rule is when you need to establish whether the respondent fits a quota.

**Theory into practice**

1  Using the guidelines given above, design a short questionnaire to be given to your colleagues or friends and family. It could be about where they are going for holidays, or plans for future travel. Make sure it has no more than ten questions and limit the open questions to one. Don't forget to ask for classification data.

2  Ask at least ten people to answer your questions and then try to analyse the data according to age/gender groups.

3  Explain what kind of travel and tourism organisation would find your questionnaire useful, and how they would produce it.

4  Explain how your questionnaire meets the needs of the travel and tourism organisation you have chosen.

**Observation** is a very simple and yet effective research method. There are several ways of doing this; in its simplest form, observers can watch consumers, for example at airports, and report on how they behave. Cameras can be used instead of live observers, and the tapes can be analysed at a later date. The observer will use a checklist or take notes to aid later recall.

**Mystery shoppers** can be used in any sector; staff pose as customers and report on the performance of travel agencies, for example. Journalists in travel and tourism often use this technique, as shown in the extract below from *Travel Weekly*.

*Mystery Shopper* wanted to go sailing in either Greece or Turkey for two weeks but as a novice she was hoping to find an operation that would provide instruction as well as all equipment and facilities and somewhere to stay while she learnt the ropes.

She also wanted the chance to be able to sail solo, once she was good enough. She'd heard there were operators who ran sailing clubs in the Mediterranean but she couldn't remember their names.

A couple of travel agents visited couldn't remember their names either and only a couple were able to come up with the right brochures. Unfortunately, only one of the agents seemed to be clued up about sailing holidays – and she was one of those unable to produce a single brochure.

*Travel Weekly*, 12 July 2004

Undercover journalists often use the **participant observation** method of research. It involves full participation, so if you were researching a travel agency, you would get a job and become a travel agent in order to observe the others.

Observation is not cheap as you need observers or cameras, and it is time consuming. The observer can also bias the results unless he or she is completely unobtrusive. The results are also subject to analysis by an observer – who may not be completely objective.

**Focus groups** are another type of primary research. With this method a group of people is invited to participate in a group discussion in someone's home, a hotel or an office. They may be offered an incentive to attend, such as a flight voucher. The objective of the discussion is to find out people's attitudes to a product or service. A group leader, often a psychologist, leads the discussion.

### Secondary data

Secondary research is sometimes called desk research as it can be done at a desk, computer or in a library. It collects data that already exists and is available to researchers. This data sometimes has to be paid for and it may be internal or external to the organisation. Secondary research is done first – it may lead to primary research if you do not find everything you need to know.

Sources of secondary data that are internal to an organisation include:

* sales records
* customer database
* costs
* profits
* load factors (airlines)
* productivity.

External sources of secondary data include:

* World Tourism Organisation (WTO) – statistics on worldwide tourism
* tourist board websites
* VisitBritain and Star UK websites
* UK International Passenger survey – statistics on inbound and outbound tourism

* *Social Trends* and *Cultural Trends* (Her Majesty's Stationery Office publications)

* Keynotes and Mintel reports – regular reports on everything you can think of; available only to subscribers, but libraries often subscribe

* National Readership Survey figures for newspapers

* Department for Culture, Media and Sport statistics

* travel trade reports

* newspaper surveys and reports.

### Theory into practice

Visit www.vts.rdn.ac.uk and find the travel and tourism tutorial. Take a tour and find out where you can gather travel and tourism information on the web. Remember this is secondary data.

## Marketing research plan

There must be a reason for the research – a set of objectives. What do we want to know? It could be that an organisation wants to know:

* who is buying the products

* why sales are going up

* why sales are going down

* what people think of the organisation's image

* what new destinations should be introduced.

The range of possibilities for research is endless, but a single piece of research should not try to cover too much ground.

## Planning the research strategy

Once we know what we are trying to find out, we can consider the methodology necessary to find the information. Do we need to do secondary or primary research, or both?

* Who do we want to ask?

* How will we sample?

* How will we reach them/what method of data collection should we use?

* Where will we do the research?

* Who will do the research?

* When will we do the research?

## Sampling

It's not usually possible to ask everyone who might be relevant to take part in research. If, for example, every single holiday maker completes a questionnaire, this is called a census. A census covers the whole population where the population is all the possible respondents for that survey.

It is more usual to interview a sample of customers, as it is very expensive to carry out a census. The sample should be representative of the whole body of customers, otherwise the results will be biased.

With **random probability sampling**, every member of the population has an equal chance of being selected. The company could use its own database as the source of respondents, and a percentage of these could be selected at random. When a national survey is undertaken, the electoral register can be used as the source of respondents.

**Quota sampling** is a method where not everyone has an equal chance of being selected. The choice of respondents is up to the interviewer, but he or she has a quota to fulfil based on factors such as age, gender and socio-economic group.

With **stratified sampling** the population is divided into groups or strata, according to common characteristics. Then, a random sample is taken from each group.

## Collection of data

At this stage the research is carried out and the data is captured. This may be on paper or electronically. Personal interviewers are usually issued with lap-top computers to make the whole process much easier.

## Analysis of data

It is possible to analyse data by hand, but time-consuming and laborious. Computer analysis is the most common technique, and ensures cross-tabulation of data. It is more difficult to analyse qualitative data electronically, because of the diversity of responses.

## Evaluation of data

Once the data has been produced and analysed it must be interpreted and conclusions must be drawn from it. Recommendations will be made so that the findings can be acted on. The data, the conclusions and the recommendations should be presented in a report.

# Marketing mix

Before any travel and tourism organisation can determine its marketing mix it needs to plan. Plans may be short term, perhaps for a year, or longer term, up to five years and beyond. The organisation must have an idea or **vision** of where it wants to be in its market in the future. It may even plan to enter a different market.

## Marketing planning

A marketing audit is first carried out, including the PEST analysis and the SWOT analysis (see page 69).

The organisation should then be in a position to set its objectives. Objectives are goals, and set out what the company is trying to achieve. They focus on where the company is heading and clarify what the business aims to do. For example, a hotel is not just in the business of providing a bed for a night, but offers a host of other services that affect the consumer's choice.

### Mission statements

Goals can be summarised in a mission statement. This is a short statement, consisting of a few lines, which states what the company aims to do. Mission statements are usually published in company literature, on websites and in the reception areas of company offices. The mission statement is useful to customers as it tells them what to expect in terms of product or service. It is also useful to employees as it focuses them on what the company wants to achieve.

It would be surprising to find a mission statement that says the company wants to make a lot of money, even if we think companies do. It is likely that the emphasis will be on service.

Here are some examples of mission statements from travel and tourism organisations. First, Holidaybreak plc:

> Holidaybreak is the UK's leading operator of specialist holiday businesses. Group companies retain a distinctive identity whilst sharing expertise and exploiting opportunities in our common interest.
>
> Our aim is to achieve continuing profitable growth by developing our existing business market leading brands in the UK and European holiday markets and through acquisition in the travel sector.

This statement manages to tell us a lot about the company in those few lines. It tells us who Holidaybreak is, and that there are different companies under the Holidaybreak umbrella. We know it is already profitable as it talks about 'continuing profitable growth' and we know that the company wants to acquire more travel businesses.

The Hilton mission statement is much shorter and simpler, but still conveys useful information about the company culture.

> To always exceed customer expectations by delivering quality service through exceptional teamwork.

And here is the EasyJet mission statement:

> To provide our customers with safe, good value, point to point air services. To effect and to offer a consistent and reliable product and fares appealing to leisure and business markets on a range of European routes. To achieve this we will develop our people and establish lasting relationships with our suppliers.

Some organisations write a 'vision statement' as well. This summarises the goals that the company hopes to achieve in the long term, recognising that these goals are not likely to be achieved in the short term but do show the direction the company is working in.

### Theory into practice

Find three examples of vision or mission statements for travel and tourism organisations. For each example try to find at least three facts about that company from the statement. List the facts and discuss them with your group.

## Objectives

Objectives should reflect the mission statement but will be very specific. The objectives may be strategic (general) or operational (broken down to specific targets).

Examples of strategic objectives include the following:

The SMART approach is often used to help set objectives. This means that objectives should be:

* Specific – it is evident what has to be achieved

* Measurable – there will be evidence as to whether the target has been achieved

* Achievable – it is possible that this can be done

* Realistic/Relevant – moving the company towards longer-term goals

* Timed – there must be a time limit on when this is to be achieved.

Operational objectives are more specific and allow the organisation to achieve its strategic aims or objectives.

First Choice is likely to make more acquisitions in the activity and specialist sectors. 'There is not a shortage of businesses around. They will be small, bolt-on acquisitions,' said Long.

*Travel Trade Gazette*, 11 June 2004

1 Identify three of First Choice's marketing objectives from the article.
2 Decide whether the objectives are strategic or operational.
3 Go through the objectives and match them with the terms of SMART objective-setting. Say whether and how the objectives are SMART.

## The marketing mix

You have already been introduced to the four Ps – product, price, promotion and place – that make up the marketing mix. These elements are used in combinations that form the operational objectives for an organisation. The four Ps are the tools that allow the organisation to meet its strategic objectives.

We will study each of the four Ps in turn, but always remember that they are interdependent.

### *Product*

According to *Principles of Marketing* by Kotler and Armstrong:

> 'A product is anything that can be offered to a market for attention, acquisition, use or consumption that might satisfy a want or a need. It includes physical objects, services, persons, places, organisations and ideas.'

This definition shows that a service is also considered to be a product, and in travel and tourism, businesses are predominantly concerned with the marketing of services.

The marketing for services may be different from that for a physical product as it is highly dependent on the people delivering the service. A fifth P, people, is often added to the marketing mix for services.

### Nature of the product

When you buy a product, it is usually **tangible** – you can touch it. If you receive poor service when buying a bed you can forget about it when you enjoy wonderful nights of good sleep on the bed itself. Buying a travel and tourism service is rarely like that, because travel and tourism products are rarely tangible.

Another challenge for marketers is that the service is **inseparable** from the person providing it. In a restaurant, the food may be of a consistent quality because of the use of high-quality produce and standard recipes. However, the diner's experience will still be ruined if the waiter is having a bad day. Hence the reason for the importance of the fifth P, people.

Travel and tourism products and services are often **perishable** (like food going off in a supermarket). Once a flight has left the airport it is too late to sell any more seats. They have perished. Airlines have to make sure their flights are as full as possible to make a profit.

### Theory into practice

1 Look at a holiday brochure. Choose a holiday and write down everything that is included in the price. You can include items for which you must pay a supplement if you wish.

2 Try to decide which aspects are tangible products and which are services. Make a table of your findings and compare it with a colleague's. For example, a free T-shirt is tangible. The services of the rep are intangible.

Another way of looking at products is to examine their features and benefits. The product features represent the core value of the product. For example, the features or core of a package holiday are the accommodation and transport. There will be a whole range of added features, depending on the holiday chosen. These might include food, sports facilities and entertainment.

The features convert into benefits for the consumer, such as relaxation, the opportunity to go sightseeing or to learn a new skill such as windsurfing.

Companies are always looking for new features to add to their products and services. They want to give further benefits to the customer and maintain competitive advantage. Theme parks introduce new rides each season to attract customers. Cinemas sell a wider range of foods and drinks and offer plusher seats and more leg room.

Marketers hope to find a unique selling proposition (USP), something that makes their product different and ensures it stands out from the opposition.

## Branding

The brand is the name and image that goes with the product, and it aims to suggest something about the product itself. Some brand names such as Thomson or Thomas Cook are well-established and have built up a good reputation. Under these 'family' brand names the company owns other familiar brands. For example, Lunn Poly and Portland are part of the Thomson group. Thomson itself is part of the TUI group. TUI is not as well known as Thomson in the UK, so when TUI acquired Thomson it wisely decided to retain the original brand names.

### Consider this ...

How many holiday brands can you think of? Do the brand names suggest anything about the company? What kind of image does each brand try to project?

Branding can cost a lot of money as companies spend on research trying to find exactly the right name, logo and image. It is particularly important when the brand has to work in several countries and languages. Finding a name often starts with a brainstorm activity where people are asked for their ideas, a short list is made and more research carried out with consumers before a name is selected.

Branding is used as part of **differentiation**. This is where an organisation tries to ensure that its product or service is different from that of the competition. It is promoted in terms of its differences, usually claiming to be of better quality.

If a brand is successful, it can build up **brand loyalty** among consumers, where they begin to prefer it over its competitors.

## Niche products

Much of the UK holiday market has been characterised by mass-market tour operators throughout the 1990s and at the beginning of the 21st century. There has, however, always been room for niche operators, which are usually smaller and highly specialised. They may specialise in a particular type of product, for example diving holidays, or a particular area, say Madeira, or they may market to a particular group of people – perhaps the over-50s like the organisation Saga. This is called niche marketing.

## Product life cycle

This concept is used to show how a product moves through different stages in its life, until it becomes obsolete. It is useful in marketing as the stage of the life cycle has an impact on how the product should be marketed.

It is also important that a company has products in each stage of the life cycle. If all the products were in the decline stage, the company would soon be heading for bankruptcy.

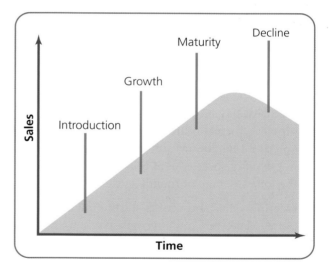

* **Introduction:** The launch of a new product is a very exciting, but tense, period. A lot of the marketing budget is assigned to advertising letting customers know it exists. Developing the product will have cost both time and money, so little or no profit is expected in the introduction stage. If the product is accepted by the market then some contribution to costs will be made. The people most likely to buy the new product or try out a new service are

known as 'innovators'. They are the kind of people who like to be the first to try something new. The price charged at this stage is often high – this appeals to innovators, who do not mind paying for exclusivity – and it helps to repay costs. Some products never go beyond this stage. Recently, an airline failed before it had flown a single plane, because its finance deal broke down.

✳ **Growth:** This is the most profitable stage in the product's life cycle and companies are eager to gain these profits while they can. Word-of-mouth promotion is important at this stage, as consumers hear about the new product and want to try it. Competitors will rapidly enter the market, bringing out their own versions of the new idea. Because of this increased competition, it is important for companies to try to build up some brand loyalty. The promotional budget is usually devoted to stressing the product's benefits over competitive products (differentiation).

✳ **Maturity:** Competition is at its most intense at this stage. Weaker competition will be squeezed out of the market by aggressive marketing strategies. Marketing efforts focus on being competitive, often by promoting low prices. The low-cost airlines are currently in maturity, having had years of unprecedented growth. In spite of this, newcomers are still entering the market, although new entrants are not usually successful at this stage. Maturity is the longest stage of the life cycle.

✳ **Decline:** Sales and profits start to fall at this point. Marketers must recognise when products are likely to move into this stage, as they must decide whether it is worth staying in the market. An organisation should be diversifying into other markets or products at the beginning of the decline stage (at the latest) to ensure survival. But there are examples of companies who have managed stay profitable because they are the only player in a market that everyone else has abandoned – in effect they become niche marketers.

Successful companies have products at each stage of the life cycle. It is difficult to predict how long each stage will last, as many external factors affect the product's life. In travel and tourism, the product life cycle can be applied to products, services and destinations.

> ## Theory into practice
>
> For this exercise you will need to draw a template of the product life cycle. If you do this on an overhead transparency you will be able to overlay your work onto it and show your findings to the group.
>
> Study this list of destinations below and decide where you think they are in terms of the product life cycle. Put them onto your template.
>
> - Costa Brava
> - Costa de la Luz
> - Bali
> - Kenya
> - Prague
> - Paris
> - Bulgaria
> - Barbados
> - Haiti.
>
> Repeat the exercise, this time with these travel products and services:
>
> - free meals on flights
> - leisure centres in hotels
> - Internet booking for holidays
> - Channel ferries
> - spa holidays
> - self-check-in
> - A380 aircraft
> - super ships.
>
> Be prepared to justify your decisions and discuss with your group.

## Price

The second element of the marketing mix is price. Travel and tourism organisations must use pricing as a means of achieving their objectives. If the company doesn't get the price right it will not make a profit.

The simplest approach to pricing is the 'cost plus' method. For this the organisation calculates the cost of producing the product and then adds a percentage to give the return it wants as profit. Although it is simple, it is not the most effective approach to pricing. If sales targets are not met, there won't be a profit. Also, this approach ignores the basic premise of marketing, about identifying customer needs. Every approach to pricing should start with the principle of asking 'What is our customer prepared to pay? Are all the customers going to pay the same price?'

There are many different pricing strategies. A company will determine the strategy to be adopted by considering the stage the product has reached in its life cycle, competitors' activity and the prices of other products offered by the company.

## Market skimming

This pricing strategy normally applies to a new product, particularly anything that involves new technology. When the product is launched costs are high and the company needs to recover the costs as quickly as possible. The new product appeals to innovators who can afford to pay a premium price for it. This introductory high price gives the product an air of exclusivity, which may appeal to certain consumers, but may be lowered as the product enters the growth stage of the life cycle, in order to attract new customers.

## Market penetration

This is another common strategy for the introduction of new products. In this case, a very low price is set. The idea is that the low price attracts customers and builds market share quickly. The most common use for this type of pricing is with fast-moving consumer goods such as household products and groceries. It is a useful short-term strategy, but problems may arise in trying to hold onto customers when the price rises to a more realistic level.

## Competitive pricing

This is used in highly competitive markets where companies keenly watch the prices of their competitors and react quickly to any lowering of prices by reducing their own. This happens constantly in airline and tour operation businesses. It also relies on a lack of brand loyalty among customers, as they must be prepared to switch brands to get the best price. It can be a dangerous strategy if prices drop so low that weak companies fail and others lose money.

## Odd pricing

This simple approach to pricing can be used in conjunction with any of the others. It assumes that customers will feel that the price is cheaper because it is an odd number rather than the next-highest round number, say £499 rather than £500 – the idea is that psychologically this seems significantly less than £500. Although it is common practice no one knows whether it works. What do you think?

## Promotional pricing

With this approach the price is linked to a special promotion for a limited period of time. Sometimes the customer has to collect tokens to be eligible for the special price. This draws attention to the product and gains publicity, so it especially useful for new products. Tourist attractions often use this method of pricing.

## Differential pricing

With this method, different prices are charged for different groups of people. For example, in museums and cinemas, senior citizens and students can expect to pay reduced prices. On trains, the purchase of a Railcard (family or young person's) gives the holder access to discounted fares.

Hotels have set rates but they are usually flexible. If you are looking for a hotel room and you book on the day, always ask for their 'best rate'. You are sure to get a discounted price because remember, the hotel room is perishable. If no one takes it, it hasn't made any money.

## Seasonal pricing

This is particularly important in the tourism industry. The whole season is divided into three – peak, shoulder and off-peak. Peak season always coincides with school holidays and is when prices are at their highest. This causes problems for parents, who have to pay the highest prices. Some parents take their children out of school to avoid peak-season holidays, but now that they can be fined £100 for doing so, this is likely to be a less popular option.

It is not just tour operators who charge higher prices at times of high demand. Airlines charge more on Friday afternoons and at the end of weekends, and rail fares cost more during rush hours.

## CASE STUDY

There have been complaints about 'unfair and unjustified' travel and holiday prices during school holidays. Executives from Britain's biggest tour operators have been asked to explain why prices go up so much at the end of term.

Groups such as Working Families have pushed for an enquiry. A representative said, 'I do think parents are between a rock and a hard place. On the one hand, most do not like taking their children out of school in term time but, unfortunately, once it gets to holiday time, prices do shoot up.'

This enquiry is well timed. Parents now face fines of £100 for taking their children out of school during term time. But July and August are the most expensive times to go away, with prices rising by almost £1,000 on a fortnight's holiday in Spain for a family of four.

A spokesman for the Association of British Travel Agents said, 'If you look at the big travel companies' financial results, you will see that they make a loss or only a tiny profit out of season. If they did not charge the higher prices during the peak they would soon be out of business.'

1  **What do you think about the high prices? Are they justified?**
2  **Look at some brochures and compare prices from season to season. Work out the percentage increases.**
3  **What extra costs do you think tour operators have in the peak season?**
4  **Make notes on your answers and discuss them with your group.**

## Place

This is the element of the marketing mix that considers how to get the product or service to the customer in the right place. The means of getting the product to the customer is known as the **channel** or **chain of distribution**. In the travel and tourism industry, the channel is complicated by the fact that there is often no tangible product to pass from one to another through the channel.

### Types of distribution channel

The traditional channel of distribution in travel and tourism is set out below.

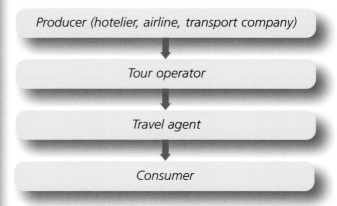

Producer (hotelier, airline, transport company)
↓
Tour operator
↓
Travel agent
↓
Consumer

As we saw in Unit 1, there are many variations on this traditional channel, including use of the Internet, telephone call centres, and so on.

The Internet has considerably reduced distribution costs for airlines. Some low-cost airlines take more than 80% of bookings via the Internet. This is good news for the airlines and for consumers, but it is not so good for travel agents. Travel agents work on a commission basis. They take a small commission from the principal for every product sold. However, airlines have drastically cut travel agents' commissions and in some cases do not use agents at all. If this trend follows with tour operators, then travel agents will be in a very vulnerable position.

TUI announced in 2004 that it was closing some of its less profitable Lunn Poly (now Thomson) stores as more business went on-line. Internet sales for TUI were at 4% of business but expected to rise to 24% by the year 2010.

Another development in distribution from TUI is the launch of television distribution with a

TV Channel. You may have seen this channel. It is a sales channel and sells holidays, not only from Lunn Poly but from other suppliers too. Other tour operators also have sales channels. In fact, annual holiday sales through television channels have reached 400,000.

However, travel agents still offer a valuable service, particularly for tour operators, some of whom have acquired chains of travel agents (vertical integration) in order to better control their representation to the public. Going Places is owned by MyTravel and Thomson (TUI) owns its own travel agencies. Thomas Cook has both a tour operation and a travel agency operation.

There are advantages to the tour operator of selling through travel agents:

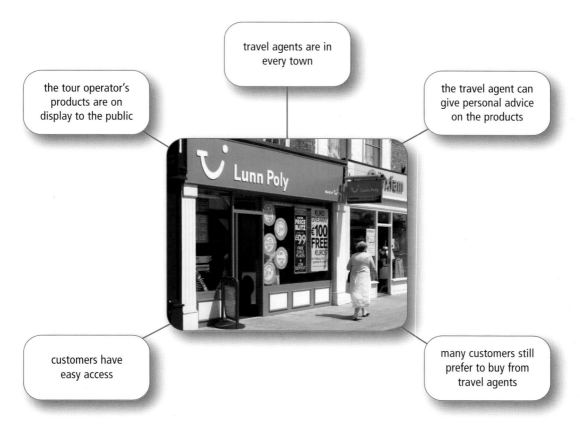

the tour operator's products are on display to the public

travel agents are in every town

the travel agent can give personal advice on the products

customers have easy access

many customers still prefer to buy from travel agents

Disadvantages to tour operators of selling through travel agents include:

* commission must be paid
* the agent decides how to rack the brochures and may not give prominence to a tour operator's product
* tour operators have little control over the quality or method of selling
* travel agents take add-on sales, for example car hire and insurance.

Advantages of direct selling include:

* control over how the product is sold
* no commission to be paid to a third party
* no problem with brochure racking.

Disadvantages of direct selling include:

* no High Street presence
* high cost of advertising to reach potential customers
* call-centre operation is needed, even if only to back up the Internet.

### Global Distribution Systems

Several companies provide electronic distribution services through computerised reservation systems and Internet-based systems. You may have heard of Galileo, Amadeus, Sabre or Worldspan, all of whom offer Global Distribution Systems.

The major low-cost airlines do not use Global Distribution Systems because of the commission payable, although this situation may change as these companies negotiate to attract low-cost airline business.

### Tourist attractions

Tourist attractions have different considerations in terms of the 'place' mix. Customers have to travel to them in order to enjoy what they have to offer. This means the location of the attraction is important, as it must be accessible to customers. Purpose-built attractions such as Disneyland Paris are located near to major road networks. Hotels and ample parking are provided in the vicinity to ease access for visitors and to encourage them to stay longer.

Channels of distribution are still essential to allow visitors to buy tickets. Travel agents sell tickets to attractions, as do tourist offices. The Internet is a source of direct booking and tickets can also be booked by telephone for most attractions. Tourist attractions are very aware of the educational market, and sell group tickets directly to schools and colleges at a discount, combining price and place.

## Promotion

In order to achieve their marketing objectives, travel and tourism companies must make both consumers and trade customers aware of their products and services. The tools they use to do this are collectively known as promotion and form part of the marketing mix.

*Marketing: Concepts and Strategies* by Dibb, Simkin, Pride and Ferrell offers us this definition of promotion:

> ‘The role of promotion in a company is to communicate with individuals, groups or organisations with the aim of directly or indirectly facilitating exchanges by informing and persuading one or more of the audiences to accept the firm's products.’

We see that the role is communication, and this branch of marketing is often described as 'marketing communications'. The individuals, groups or organisations at whom the promotion is targeted are known as the 'target audience'.

### Purpose of promotion

The definition given above suggests that the purpose of promotion is to inform or persuade. This is often the intention of a promotional campaign, but remember that promotion is being used with the other elements of the mix to help the organisation achieve its marketing objectives.

The purpose may be to:

* inform the public about a new product or service
* inform the public about a change to the product or company
* increase sales
* increase market share
* give reassurance to existing customers
* respond to competitors' promotions
* remind consumers that the company is there
* reinforce the corporate image.

These objectives will be achieved only if the company chooses the right promotional mix – the right medium must be chosen to reach the consumer, and the timing must be right.

### Timing

The right time for promotion is when the purchaser is at the stage of deciding what to buy. For example, hotels will advertise their services when a special event in their vicinity, such as a sporting event, is coming up. Theatres send out programme guides at the beginning of each season so that people can book ahead and plan their theatre trips. Holiday companies traditionally start their major campaigns just after Christmas. Once the festivities are over, people start to think about their holidays.

Timing is not just about the right time of year; marketers must also consider what day and what time to place advertisements. These decisions will be constrained by their budget.

### Budget

Promotional budgets can run into millions. It is easy to see why when you consider that a 30-second spot on national television can cost as much as £25,000. Companies can spend only what they can afford, and it is possible to have a good campaign on a very tight budget by using regional media or by devoting the budget to cheaper public relations activities.

A company will use past experience to set budgets for new campaigns and may set a budget as a percentage of estimated sales to be derived from the campaign.

### Target audience

The entire budget is wasted if the promotional campaign does not reach its intended audience. If advertising needs to be aimed at a mass audience, then television is often the best medium. In the average home in Britain the television is on for more than five hours a day. Of course, that doesn't mean the viewer is watching your advertisement or even that there is a viewer!

Usually the advertiser wishes to reach a particular group of people and will choose a medium where the profile of the audience matches the profile of the intended customer. All the media publish profiles of their audience, that is their gender, age group and socio-economic group. These profiles help advertisers to select appropriate media. There are several companies that carry out audience research to produce these profiles. One example is the National Readership Survey, which tells us who reads which newspaper. Another example is the Broadcasters' Audience Research Board (BARB), which collects information every week about the number of people watching television.

## Promotional methods

### Advertising

The Advertising Association describes advertising as 'messages paid for by those who send them, intended to inform or influence people who receive them'.

Advertising is paid for and is placed in the media. The media is the collective term for television, newspapers, radio, magazines, directories, outdoor sites and advertising on transport. It also includes the Internet, although this still tends to be described as 'new media'. New media also includes new forms of advertising such as text messaging.

| SHARE OF TOTAL ADVERTISING EXPENDITURE 2003–1994 | | | | | | | | | | |
|---|---|---|---|---|---|---|---|---|---|---|
| | 2003 | 2002 | 2001 | 2000 | 1999 | 1998 | 1997 | 1996 | 1995 | 1994 |
| **Press** | 48.6% | 49.6% | 51.4% | 50.6% | 51.1% | 52.2% | 52.2% | 53.1% | 54.2% | 54.8% |
| **TV** | 25.3% | 25.8% | 25.1% | 27.3% | 28.0% | 28.0% | 27.7% | 28.0% | 28.4% | 28.5% |
| **Direct mail** | 14.3% | 14.2% | 13.5% | 12.0% | 12.2% | 11.6% | 12.3% | 11.6% | 10.3% | 10.4% |
| **Internet** | 2.2% | 1.2% | 1.0% | 0.9% | 0.3% | 0.1% | 0.06% | – | – | – |
| **Outdoor & transport** | 5.2% | 4.8% | 4.8% | 4.8% | 4.2% | 4.3% | 4.1% | 3.9% | 3.7% | 3.5% |
| **Radio** | 3.4% | 3.3% | 3.2% | 3.5% | 3.4% | 3.2% | 3.0% | 2.9% | 2.7% | 2.4% |
| **Cinema** | 1.0% | 1.1% | 1.0% | 0.8% | 0.8% | 0.7% | 0.7% | 0.6% | 0.6% | 0.5% |

Source: WARC/Royal Mail/DMIS

## Television

There are two organisations responsible for television broadcasting in the UK. One is the British Broadcasting Corporation (BBC), which does not carry advertising and is funded by payment of a licence fee. The second is Ofcom. Ofcom is the regulator for all UK communications industries, not just television. It also covers radio, telecommunications and wireless communications.

Ofcom's mission statement is:

> Ofcom exists to further the interests of citizen-consumers through a regulatory regime which, where appropriate, encourages competition.

Ofcom publishes codes about what is and is not allowed in television advertising. Here are a few examples:

* Only 7 minutes per hour of advertising is allowed (on some channels, 12 minutes are allowed).

* It must be evident what is a programme and what is an advertisement, so there must be obvious breaks in between.

* Some programmes must not be interrupted by advertising, for example religious programmes or royal ceremonies.

The codes are very detailed. You can find out more about them and the role of Ofcom by visiting the Ofcom website at www.ofcom.org.uk.

Advertisers wishing to use television have dozens of commercial channels to choose from with the advent of cable and satellite services. Advertising is sold in 'spots'. One spot is usually 30 seconds long. There is no fixed rate for a spot, as the price varies according to time of day – peak time is 5.30–10.30 pm when most people are watching. Premium rates will be charged if a particularly popular programme such as an important football match is being shown.

Advertisers buy a package of spots. If you watch television for any length of time you will note that the same advertisements are repeated often. This is to ensure that the message reaches as many people as possible. The number of people viewing an advertisement is called the 'reach'. The final episode of *Friends* was broadcast in May 2004

in the US. It attracted over 50 million viewers and advertisers paid over £1 million for 30-second spots. All the spots were sold by January 2004. In this country, 4.1 million viewers watched the final episode of *Sex and the City* on Channel 4.

There are many advantages to television advertising:

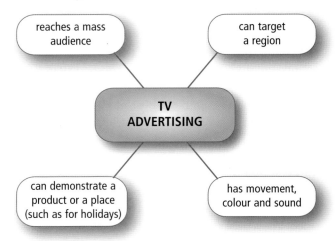

It is, however, very expensive. Not only are spots expensive but there are also the production costs of the advertisement to cover.

> ### Thomson's £3m TV ad campaign
>
> A £3 MILLION television advertising campaign to promote Thomson will start on Sunday – the operator's first since January 2001.
>
> Although the TUI group has advertised its Lunn Poly retail chain on TV, promotion of the Thomson brand has been restricted for the last few years to branding of Tottenham Hotspur Football Club and a Welsh ice-hockey team.
>
> The new 'time is too precious' campaign will take the form of two 40-second commercials on terrestrial and satellite TV.
>
> Marketing director Hugh Edwards said TUI would soon be able to reveal its new television programme sponsorship deal.
>
> *Travel Trade Gazette*, 14 May 2004

Another form of advertising on television is sponsorship. Sponsors pay to be associated with a programme and their logo and product shots appear at the beginning, end and at either side of each commercial break.

## Radio

As with television, it is the commercial sector of radio that carries advertising. BBC radio stations are funded by the same licence fee as television. There are many local commercial stations and you should note the ones in your locality. There are also some national commercial stations, for example Virgin Radio.

You can find out about radio stations by visiting the Radio Advertising Bureau (RAB) website at www.rab.co.uk. This is an independent body that gives information on advertising issues to industry members, but also to the public.

Spots are sold on radio in the same way as on television, with peak times attracting greater revenue. In 2003–4 commercial radio advertising revenue was £611.6 million in the UK, according to the RAB.

Radio advertising is becoming more popular. One of the reasons is the advent of digital radio, which allows greater targeting. Advertisers who wish to reach 15–24-year-olds often use radio as they represent a large part of radio audiences, with RAB reporting a 20% growth in listening hours for this group since 1999.

The advantages of radio advertising are:

Audience research for radio – including the BBC – is carried out by Radio Joint Audience Research (Rajar). Ofcom is the regulatory body.

## Press media

The term 'press' refers to newspapers, magazines and directories.

National Readership Survey Ltd is a non-profit-making body that provides estimates of the number and type of people who read Britain's newspapers and magazines. The survey covers about 250 publications. The reader profiles are broken down by age, sex, region, and other demographic and lifestyle characteristics. Publishers of press media use these profiles to sell advertising space, and advertisers use them to target the correct audience through appropriate media.

For **national newspapers**, the UK has 12 daily newspapers and 11 Sunday newspapers. The *Sun* has the biggest circulation of all the national dailies and the *News of the World* is the most popular Sunday newspaper. Between them they attracted an advertising spend of £1,930 million in 2002.

Advertising is sold by the page, half-page or column. Prices vary according to the position of the advert. The front and back pages are most expensive, as they are most prominent. The newspapers with

the highest circulation command the highest rates; therefore the *Sun* is the most expensive.

The advantages of national newspaper advertising are:

most people in the UK read a newspaper

can tie in with topical events

very precise profiling is possible

NATIONAL NEWSPAPER ADVERTISING

can include colour

flexible: only a short time between placing the advert and publication

### Theory into practice

Find out the latest circulation figures for Britain's newspapers. You can do this by looking at a newspaper's website, looking at the National Readership Survey website or by studying a publication called BRAD in your library. Draw up a bar chart comparing the figures.

There are also hundreds of **regional newspapers**, some of which are free. Some are very highly regarded, such as the *London Evening Standard* and the *Yorkshire Post*. Circulations vary and some are very small, but for a company that wants to advertise its services in a particular locality, they are useful and inexpensive. Regional newspapers attracted a spend of £2,870 million in 2002, even greater than the national newspapers. Much of this goes on classified advertising, which is more likely to be read in a regional paper than in a national.

**Magazines** come in different categories:

* consumer magazines
* business and professional journals.

There are over 3,000 titles of consumer magazines in the UK, so the advertiser can be very precise about target audience.

One of the biggest sellers is the *Radio Times*, which has a circulation of over 1 million. Some hobby magazines sell only a few thousand copies.

There are several travel magazines aimed at consumers, and many aimed at buyers or owners of property abroad. These can be useful media for transport companies. Women's magazines are also an important category of consumer magazines.

Business and professional publications are aimed at people within particular industries. There are two important ones for travel and tourism, with which you should be familiar. These are *Travel Weekly* and *Travel and Tourism Gazette*.

The advantages of magazine advertising are that it offers:

precise targeting

MAGAZINE ADVERTISING

'inserts' and regional targeting

colourful, glossy adverts

A disadvantage of magazine advertising is that the copy must be ready to go to press quite a while before publication, so it is not so flexible as newspaper advertising. It is not suitable for the last-minute discounted offers which are popular in the tourism market.

An **advertorial** is a promotion that is written in the style of a feature. It looks like the editorial pages but is promoting a company or a product. Readers will probably assume that it is a feature unless they look closely at the small print, which will state 'advertising feature'.

## CASE STUDY

weddings&honeymoons

### Passion renewed

**Kathryn Liston speaks to a former travel agent who recently renewed her vows in the Caribbean**

fORMER TRAVEL AGENT JULIE Roberts wanted to do something different after deciding to renew her vows with husband Alan for her silver wedding anniversary.

Julie, who used to work at Hayes Travel in Prestatyn, north Wales hit upon the idea of having the ceremony abroad.

"I scoured the brochures to see what was on offer worldwide," explains Julie. "I looked at the Maldives, Mauritius and other romantic destinations before opting for Jamaica."

She chose the Breezes Runaway Bay resort, near Ocho Rios, from the Thomson Holidays weddings programme. This offered all-inclusive arrangements, no children, a wedding package and plenty to do – while Julie was content to read a book on the beach, Alan was looking for more active pursuits.

Julie opted to upgrade to the Premium flight service which includes more legroom and free drinks. Even though the couple did not get to sit together on the flight on the way out or back , the rest of the arrangements went smoothly.

"The whole process could not have been easier," she says. "I told the travel agent what we wanted, and the date of our anniversary and they faxed the hotel which said we could have the ceremony on the date we wanted.

"When we checked in I told reception about our plans and they said someone would be in touch the day before, which they did. The wedding co-ordinator rang our room and invited us to choose the flowers and the photographic package we wanted. They did the rest."

Julie said she feared it might be a bit tacky but it was not what she expected. "The reverend who conducted the ceremony was a lovely guy, who made it all very special. It was much more personal than I thought it would be."

Photographs were followed by a horse-drawn carriage and then dinner at the resort restaurant.

So did the occasion live up to expectations? "Oh yes," she says. "The main advantage of having a wedding abroad is that there is much less work involved than having it at home. I know that from first-hand experience having arranged two daughters' weddings. It was all so simple to do. I couldn't fault it. We were really pleased with Breezes. The staff were so friendly, and it was a very genuine friendliness."

She believes that overseas weddings are a good option for those getting married for the second time or those who want to renew their vows, but for a first marriage, you could end up missing friends and family - unless you bring them out with you of course.

■ **See page 30 for your chance to win a Thomson wedding**

*Travel Trade Gazette* Weddings Supplement, August 2004

1  **What is the purpose of this feature?**
2  **Julie used to be a travel agent. Is this important in the feature? If so, why?**
3  **What features of the product are promoted?**
4  **In your opinion, does it work?**
**Discuss your answers with a colleague.**

## Cinema

As with any media, marketers look at the audience profile before deciding on a campaign. For cinema, Cinema and Video Audience Research (CAVIAR) provides this information. Advertisers aiming to reach 15–24-year-olds may well choose cinema advertising as cinema-going is the number one leisure activity for this group.

Overall, 86% of the population say they go to the cinema. However, the current annual average is only three visits per person. There is also a seasonal pattern to cinema-going. In 2003 the busiest months were August, October and December, school holiday periods. (Not surprisingly, the biggest box office takings were from *Finding Nemo*.)

Total advertising spend on cinema in 2002 was £180 million, much less than any other form of media.

The advantages of cinema advertising are:

the audience is seated and highly receptive

can be targeted regionally

**CINEMA ADVERTISING**

good for reaching 15–24-year-olds

still advertisements are cheap to produce for small local businesses

However, the production costs of full advertisements are high and the advertisement will not have the same reach as television.

### Theory into practice

Next time you go to the cinema, take a notebook with you. List all the advertisements you see including the still advertisements at the beginning. Try to decide who the target audience is. Is it always 15–24-year-olds? Are the advertisements linked to the film in any way? Are any travel and tourism organisations showing advertisements?

Discuss your findings with your group.

*Billboards are strategically placed*

## Outdoor and transport

Outdoor media usually means billboards.

These are placed all over the country in strategic sites, usually on roadsides. Companies which specialise in outdoor advertising sell the space to advertisers. Advertisements can also be placed on taxis, buses, in the London Underground, at railway stations and at bus stops. Large colourful posters are excellent for the travel and tourism industry, reminding commuters that they can get away to sunnier places.

## Internet

As soon as you connect to the Internet you will find advertising messages. These can be linked to searches, so that if you search for low airfares, for example, you will find pop-ups for travel sites such as E-bookers will appear. The Internet advertising spend is growing year on year as it becomes more widely used.

Advertisers choose sites which they think their potential customers will visit. They can buy banner advertisements or pop-up advertisements on the host site. These not only advertise but link to the advertiser's own website. It is even cheaper to buy a text-only link.

## Brochures and leaflets

These are essential promotional tools for tour operators. They are costly to produce, but provide a showcase for the company's products and services.

Getting the brochure out on time is important, because if it is not available when the booking of main holidays begins, sales will be lost. This means that the information in the brochure has to be collated and prices fixed a long time before the season in question. This can cause major headaches for tour operators and lead to extensive discounting during the season.

Other organisations in the travel and tourism industry produce leaflets but these are usually smaller and less costly, so it is easier to change them more regularly.

## Public relations

Public relations is a major part of the promotional mix and very important to those travel and tourism companies that have small marketing budgets. This is because public relations activities are much cheaper than other forms of promotion. Public relations may be carried out in-house or contracted out to a specialist PR agency.

The responsibilities of the public relations department may include the following:

* generating press releases
* media liaison
* organising events
* organising exhibitions
* publication of newsletters
* organising receptions.

### Press releases

Press releases are used to place favourable reports about a company in the media or to inform them about a new product. They are extremely cheap to produce and can result in a lot of free publicity.

A good press release should have the following features:

* it should be targeted at the right audience, via appropriate media
* it should be presented in such a way that it can be inserted into a news page or feature with little alteration – this saves work for the receiving editor
* there should be an attention-grabbing headline
* the press release should be dated and show the corporate logo and address
* if an event is being publicised, the venue, date and time must be given
* a photo can be included
* contact details for further information must be given.

---

## CASE STUDY

Study the press release below.

**BRENTWOOD COLLEGE OF TRAVEL AND TOURISM STUDIES**
Trenton Park  Brentwood  BD5 6AG

### Press Release
21st May 2005

Second-year travel and tourism students at Brentwood College are racing to Paris!

As part of their course they are required to arrange a residential study. The students decided to make their trip as challenging as possible and to race each other! Their trip takes place in the first week in October and lasts for four days.

The 14 students will be travelling by various routes including Eurostar, air from Gatwick, and car and ferry. They will carry out an evaluation of each route in terms of speed, cost, convenience and service.

Their tutor Billie Myson says: 'This will be the hardest assignment the students have ever attempted. They have arranged every detail of the trip by themselves. I am very proud of them and look forward to the trip and to hearing their final reports.'

Photo of group attached

For further information please contact Billie Myson on 0146 777565 or Joanna Smith on 07789 567432.

1 **Compare the press release with the criteria shown above. Does it match them all?**
2 **The press release concerns students on a travel and tourism course.**
   • **What is the purpose of the press release?**
   • **What media are likely to be approached?**
   • **Why would these media be chosen?**

# Sales promotion

Sales promotion includes all those activities which aim to bring about an early or extra purchase of a product, and they are found extensively in the travel and tourism industry. A sales promotion is very useful for boosting sales in the short term but will run for only a few weeks, otherwise the impact is lost.

Examples of sales promotions are money-off coupons, competitions, buy-one-get-one-free offers and loyalty schemes. Most hotel chains offer incentives such as free nights to regular guests through loyalty schemes. Airlines also operate loyalty schemes, the most famous of which is the AirMiles scheme. This has even been extended to some shops.

Trade promotions are very common in travel and tourism, where call centres and travel agents receive financial or other incentives for sales.

# Direct marketing

Direct marketing, as its name suggests, deals directly with the consumer, and can take several forms.

## Direct mail

Direct mail is a form of direct marketing where advertising is sent in the post to the customer, personally addressed. It is sometimes referred to as junk mail – but by consumers, not advertisers! This is because we receive a lot – 5,438 million items were sent in 2003 – and throw a lot of it away. The response rate is about 11%, but it is still a popular promotional tool in travel and tourism.

## Direct response

Direct response is a form of direct marketing that does not depend on the mail, so it can be used in all the same media as advertising. The difference is that a response is solicited. The reader might be invited to send for a brochure or send an e-mail asking for information. The value of direct-response marketing is that it is easier to monitor than advertising. You are able to measure the response rate, and with every response you gather more customer information.

## Telemarketing

Telemarketing is similar to direct mail except that the telephone is used. Cold calling, that is making unsolicited calls, is very unpopular with consumers and is not often used in travel and tourism. However, telemarketing is important in selling holidays and travel to callers who are responding to advertising or other forms of promotion, and there are many call centres in travel and tourism businesses.

# How do promotional methods work?

According to AIDA theory, the aim of promotional activities is to take the consumer through four key stages that lead to the adoption of a product, service or idea.

AIDA stands for:

* Attention – the promotion attracts the attention of the customer.

* Interest – having spotted the promotion, the customer is sufficiently interested to want to know more.

* Desire – the customer decides that he or she wants it! The information about the product has stimulated the customer's desire for it.

* Action – the final stage, the customer knows what action to take to complete the purchase.

## Knowledge check

1  Give a definition of marketing.

2  Explain the following terms as they are used in travel and tourism marketing – 'inseparable', 'tangible' and 'perishable'.

3  What does B2B marketing mean?

4  Explain the term 'gap in the market'.

5  What are the four elements of the marketing mix?

6  Why is the Trade Descriptions Act important in marketing travel and tourism?

7  What is a PEST analysis?

8  What is a SWOT analysis?

9  What is the function of the ASA?

10 Explain the different methods of segmenting the market.

11 What is the difference between qualitative and quantitative data?

12 Explain the advantages and disadvantages of different survey methods.

13 What is the difference between primary and secondary research?

14 Describe some different methods of sampling.

15 What is a mission statement?

16 What is niche marketing?

17 Describe the stages of the product life cycle.

18 Explain two pricing strategies.

19 What are the different types of press media?

20 What are the differences between public relations and advertising?

## UNIT 3 PREPARATION FOR ASSESSMENT

### Flybe

Flybe is an Exeter-based low-cost airline and is currently the third largest low-cost airline in Europe. It has a unique low-fare airline business model designed to be very different from Ryanair and other low-cost airlines.

Flybe was launched on 18 July 2002, but it grew out of an airline that started life in 1979 as Jersey European. Exeter became the company's headquarters in 1985 and was also a base for technical services. Jersey European gained its first London route in 1991 from Guernsey to London Gatwick and shortly afterwards the Jersey–London route came into operation.

Also in the 1990s, routes were introduced from Belfast City to London, and Belfast City to Birmingham. Business class service was launched, making Jersey European the first domestic airline to offer two classes of service. Jersey European won the 'Best UK Regional Airline' award in 1993 and in 1994.

Jet maintenance was brought to Exeter in 1994, which expanded the scope for third-party services. In 1995, the fleet consisted of seven jets. Three new business lounges were opened at Belfast City, Jersey and Guernsey and the Ticket to Freedom frequent-flyer loyalty scheme was launched.

In 1996 the first franchise routes in conjunction with Air France began offering flights from London Heathrow to Toulouse and Lyon. This partnership continued to expand in 1997 to include Birmingham International to Paris Charles de Gaulle and Glasgow.

In 1999 expansion continued with the acquisition of 11 Bombardier Dash 8s and four Canadair Regional Jets. A major new base at London City was introduced, with services to Dublin and Edinburgh. The brand was changed to British European and then to Flybe.

In 2001, after the terrorist attacks in September of that year, the airline found itself with problems and losses. The situation was critical and a transformation plan was required, with the following objectives:

1 Traditional distribution channels are expensive. Flybe aimed to get 80% of sales through the Internet. Travel agent commission was reduced from 7% to 1% and the lowest fares were available only on the Internet.

2 It was decided to re-align pricing, product and terms and conditions to reduce costs and increase ancillary revenues. This means charging for catering and excess baggage. Prices were to be transparent, with no hidden extras and no refunds offered. The target was to achieve £25 million per annum of ancillary revenue.

3   The route network was to be rationalised to create profitable routes and defendable bases. The strategy to achieve this was to continue the 'Backbone Britain' policy, to pick up routes in continental Europe and to open new bases in Birmingham, Bristol and Exeter. It was also decided to develop volume routes in Germany, Italy, France and the Nordic countries. The market split was 65% leisure and 35% business.

4   The aim was to consistently reduce costs but exceed customer expectations. A customer satisfaction survey was undertaken, with good results.

5   People matter – staff and customers were to be involved in the transformation. A policy of 'open channel' communications was adopted, alongside a no-blame culture, allowing staff to report incidents without fear of reprisal or blame.

Flybe also has an aviation services division employing 350 people in engineering at Exeter. Support was given from the Regional Development Agency.

Flybe runs aggressive newspaper advertising campaigns and also undertakes local sponsorship of football teams.

Flybe claims to be a 'national regional' airline meeting UK regional domestic needs. 75% of routes support the 'Backbone of Britain' strategy. 10% of routes are to France, capitalising on the second-home market and repeat business. 10% of routes go to the Spanish beaches. 5% of routes are Air France franchises, but this contract is coming to an end.

Flybe offers 1.8 million seats per annum out of Birmingham, 1.65 million seats per annum out of Southampton, and 716,000 seats per annum out of Exeter and Bristol.

Flybe differentiates prices for business travel. It offers:

- cancellation allowed from three hours before a trip without charge
- an executive lounge
- complimentary drinks
- a frequent flyer programme.

1   Carry out research into the aviation sector and describe the constraints and issues affecting the sector. You can do this by carrying out a SWOT and PEST analysis for Flybe. Describe how Flybe could develop the marketing mix.

2   Explain how constraints and issues affect the application of the principles of marketing at Flybe.

3   Evaluate how the marketing activities at Flybe meet the needs of the organisation and the customers.

4   Describe the methods of market research that would be appropriate for Flybe, and how they would be used.

5   Produce a market research plan justifying your selection of research methodology.

6   Produce two different types of promotional material suitable for Flybe.

7   Explain how your materials meet the needs of the company and explain the stages of producing the materials.

8   Produce a questionnaire or an observation checklist that could be used by Flybe in the course of the market research.

9   Explain how the research documentation meets Flybe's needs and explain the stages of producing the research documentation.

# UNIT 4

# Tourist destinations

# Introduction

This unit will provide you with the opportunity to explore all aspects of tourist destinations. It will build on the knowledge you already have about destinations, and you will extend your knowledge of key geographical features.

Major transport routes and gateways between tourism generating and receiving areas will be examined, and you will consider the effects of the transport links on tourism in destinations. You will also examine the effect of different time zones on travel and tourism.

You will study the factors that contribute towards the appeal of a destination, including access, culture, motivation, geographical features and attractions.

You will learn how to carry out effective research using the Internet and a series of reference materials such as atlases, brochures and travel guides. You will use your research skills to investigate some worldwide destinations and assess the tourism potential of locations that are not yet established for tourists. You will identify gaps in provision and recommend how destinations could attract more tourists.

## How you will be assessed

This unit is internally assessed by your tutor. A variety of exercises and activities is included in this unit to help you understand all aspects of tourist destinations and prepare for the assessment. You will also have the opportunity to work on some case studies to further your understanding.

After completing this unit you should be able to achieve the following outcomes:

→ Use sources of reference and research skills to provide a range of information
→ Examine major transport routes that link tourist generating and receiving areas
→ Explore the factors that contribute towards a destination's appeal
→ Investigate the tourism potential of different locations.

# Sources of reference and research skills

## Reference materials

You will need to become proficient in using a range of reference material to investigate destinations.

### Atlases

A good atlas is essential to anyone working in travel and tourism. Any library will have a selection of good atlases. The *World Travel Atlas* (Columbus Press) has been designed for the travel trade and for students. It is also available on-line and is a good source of facts and figures which are updated every year.

### Country guides, area guides, resort and city guides

These types of guides are extensively available in bookshops and libraries. They are constantly updated, so do check the dates of library editions as many libraries cannot afford to update their whole collection of travel guides regularly.

Some of these guides are very well produced and include maps, hotel and restaurant recommendations, and plenty of information on what to see and do. They are ideal for tourists but not so useful for students, who may need to research facts and figures on tourism and trends.

The *World Travel Guide* is probably the best-known directory for the travel trade. It contains factual information on every country including transport, accommodation, visa requirements, health and a social profile.

### Manuals

OAG produces a comprehensive series of guides for air and rail. The travel trade commonly uses these. Some of them are quite complex to follow, and demand a knowledge of time zones and airline codes.

### Timetables

Timetables are published by all transport carriers and are readily available in published form and on the Internet. Airports amalgamate the timetables of their carriers and post them on their websites.

*Brochures are visually appealing and easy to understand*

### Brochures

These give a lot of destination information. They are visually appealing and easy to understand. But remember that their purpose is to sell, and therefore they are likely to give a biased view, always positive. They will not provide you with statistical information about tourism.

### The Internet

The Internet is a wonderful source of information. However, there are so many sites that you will have to learn how to search properly to find what you want, and to make sure the information is reliable.

You should first make sure you are familiar with search websites such as Yahoo and Google. You have the option of searching UK or worldwide, and it is often easier to limit yourself to UK searches to begin with. If you enter 'Travel and tourism' you will find thousands of sites listed and many will have little relevance to you. But it is worth spending some time surfing these sites and bookmarking those which are useful in your favourites list. (If you do not have your own computer, make a note of the addresses.)

Some websites are themselves directories and link to other useful tourism information sites.

Examples are www.altis.ac.uk and www.tourismeducation.org.

If you are searching for information on destinations the following websites will help you:

* www.geographia.com – destination information
* www.worldatlas.com – useful for maps and country information, and it has some map tests.

Many travel guides are available on line. Examples include www.fodors.com and www.lonelyplanet.com.

The World Tourism Organisation (WTO) is a useful source of statistics on visitor numbers to destinations. You might find the printed version in your library, but it is also available on-line at www.world-tourism.org. You will find some excellent information freely available on this site but detailed reports are available only to subscribers.

## Gazetteers

Gazetteers are the same as travel guides, presenting information on destinations. OAG produces a series of gazetteers and these are available on the Internet. Visit www.virgin.net/travel/resortfinder.

## Hotel guides

All major chains produce their own guides listing their hotel locations, facilities and services. Remember that these are sales tools like brochures and will present only positive information.

There are travel trade hotel guides which travel agents refer to. These give independent reviews of hotels and are useful for checking hotels before you visit them.

## Language books

Like travel guides, language books aimed at travellers are extensively available. They are conveniently divided into sections with useful phrases, for example a hotel section with phrases useful for booking a room.

## CD Rom

Much atlas and resort information is available on CD Rom from various companies. Some companies, such as the AirMiles travel company, use CD Rom to issue a regular company magazine.

## Travel trade journals

Your library should have copies of travel trade journals, which give up-to-date features on the industry and on specific destinations. If you wish you can subscribe to these publications with a student subscription. The national and regional press also carry regular travel pages, which are full of informative features and advertising.

### Theory into practice

Go to the website www.world-tourism.org.

1 Find the mission statement on the site. Summarise it in your own words.

2 Look at the section on how the WTO works. Find out what the regional commissions are. Write an explanation and name them.

3 Go to the statistics section. Find WTO's 'Tourism 2020 Vision'. Where are the top three receiving regions expected to be?

4 What will world international arrivals be?

5 Download the report 'Tourism Highlights'.

6 Find out the latest figure for world international tourism arrivals.

7 What was the 1990 figure?

8 What is the percentage change?

9 Find the same figures for receipts.

10 What is the difference between receipts and arrivals (latest figures)?

11 What does this mean?

12 Why are receipts shown in US dollars?

13 Find the top five world tourism destinations (arrivals and receipts). Are they the same? Explain any differences.

Ask your tutor to check your work.

### Key terms

**Tourism receiver** – a country that tourists choose to visit. France is a major receiver.

**Tourism generator** – a country where tourists originate. The UK is a major tourism generator.

**Tourist arrivals** – numbers of tourists visiting a country expressed in numbers of visits.

**Tourist receipts** – the amount of money spent in a country by tourists.

# Research skills

During your studies you are expected to carry out research, both individually and in groups. Learning how to do research properly is very important to you, because not only does it help you find the information you need to complete your assessments and succeed in your studies, but it gives you skills you can apply in whatever career you choose in the future.

Good research skills are particularly important if you work in travel and tourism as you must have up-to-date, relevant and accurate information to pass on to customers and colleagues. Unit 3, Marketing Travel and Tourism Products and Services, explains how professional marketing research is carried out, and you will find it useful to refer to that unit. However, this unit is concerned with research skills and the specific types of research that will help you succeed in your studies and in your future career in travel and tourism.

Researching involves the following:

* being clear about what you need to find out

* knowing where to search for information

* assessing the validity of a source and cross-referencing information

* collecting and presenting relevant information

* drawing conclusions about your findings

* acknowledging your sources.

## What you need to find out

It is vital to be clear about your objectives, so it is worth spending some time on this preparation stage. Research is time-consuming and it is easy to get side-tracked, so make sure you know exactly what you are looking for.

If you are researching for an assessment you will have been given a brief. Your tutor will also give you a verbal interpretation of the brief. Listen carefully and make notes – you will not remember all the information later. You may be given tips about where to find relevant information; ask questions and clarify anything you are unsure about. Make a list of the different things you need to find out, and write down key words to help your search.

*Madeira is an example of a destination you might research*

Imagine that your task is to research the island of Madeira and the factors which make it appealing as a tourist destination. You might start by compiling the following list.

> **What do I need to find out?**
> * location of the island
> * transport links from the UK
> * who goes there
> * what the climate is like
> * which companies offer packages there
> * what kinds of hotels there are
> * what there is to do.

Before you start any research, you should consider your list carefully. You will be faced with vast amounts of information, particularly on the Internet, so you need to make sure you are looking only for essential information. The brief here is very simple: 'the island of Madeira and the factors which make it appealing as a tourist destination'.

Which two items in the list above should be discarded? You have not been asked who goes there or which companies offer packages. Discard these for the moment. If you think that these will provide useful extra information to help you answer the original brief and improve your grade, come back to them later if you have time.

You were not asked to find the location of Madeira either, but this is essential to include for your own knowledge and to set your work in context.

You may be carrying out research in a work situation, probably in response to an enquiry from a customer or a colleague. Make notes on what you need to find out or complete an enquiry form if they are supplied.

When searching on the Internet remember to use a search engine such as Google. You can search for images, news stories, search Google's directory or search the web. The directory differs from the web in that it is edited and sorted into categories.

Be as specific as you can with your key words to narrow your search. If you want to search for an exact phrase, put it in inverted commas. You might notice some of your results are termed 'sponsored results'. This means those companies have paid to be listed and may come up first.

Remember that search engines provide help if you get stuck. Look for the help link on the main page.

## Where to search for information

You have been given a list of useful sources of information in this unit. However, this is just a starting point and you should keep your own list of useful sources of information. Internet sites can be bookmarked as 'favourites' if you have your own computer. A notebook is useful for other sources.

Use your list of things you need to find out, and against each one suggest a source of that particular piece of information. You may need to add some key words to your list. You may also need to find more than one source of information for each item in order to check its validity.

Look at the Madeira example again.

| What do I need to find out? | Possible source |
| --- | --- |
| Location of the island | Atlas |
| Transport links from the UK | Airport/airline websites, package holiday brochures |
| What the climate is like | Brochures, websites |
| What kinds of hotels there are | Brochures, resort guides |
| What there is to do | Brochures, resort guides, tourist organisation websites |

Key words might help you with the 'What there is to do' question. Try sports, beaches, walking, nightlife, and restaurants.

You will note that one source can give you a lot of the information you need, but you should always use more than one source to show that you have carried out your research properly and assessed the validity of your information.

On the other hand, you don't need to refer to every source of information on a topic. For example, information on climate is available from several sources. Choose one valid source, check briefly that other sources confirm your findings, and then discard them.

## The validity of a source

You need to make sure that your source of information is accurate, up to date and unbiased. It is important to do this with every source but it is more difficult to assess Internet websites as anyone can set up a website, and they do not always give accurate or objective information.

Ask the following questions to decide whether your source is valid.

### Who wrote it?

Is the person or organisation well qualified to write it? For example, you can be fairly sure that a published text book is written by a highly qualified person. A letter in a newspaper complaining about a hotel may not be valid – it represents only one person's experience. Newspaper articles tend to be more trustworthy, but again they can reflect the paper's politics and opinions, so be careful.

### What is the purpose of the information source?

If you are using a holiday brochure, remember its purpose is to sell so it may be biased in favour of a hotel or destination. It certainly won't tell you if there was an outbreak of food poisoning last season. A publication like *World Travel Guide* is more reliable than brochures as it gives factual information for the travel trade and is not trying to sell particular destinations.

### Is the information up to date?

When was it written? If it is a web page, when was it last updated? If information isn't up to date, don't use it. Of course, if you are researching a topic that does not change, such as the history of the development of tourism in the UK, then an older text book will still be useful.

## Does the author give sources of facts and figures?

You need to check this as you too need to quote sources. You may be able to go back to the quoted source and check for accuracy.

## Does the author seem to be biased in the presentation of information?

You will recognise bias when you have experience of using different sources. Initially it is difficult to recognise, but you can practise by reading several newspaper accounts of the same event.

### Theory into practice

Consider the following extracts and sources of information on Madeira and comment on their validity. Compare your findings with the rest of your group.

1 A holiday brochure selling packages to Madeira.

2 This extract from a holiday guide on Madeira:

> **Customs and entry formalities:** Most visitors, including citizens of all EC countries, the USA, Canada, Eire, Australia and New Zealand, need only a valid passport – no visa – to enter Madeira.
>
> **Currency restrictions:** Tourists may bring an unlimited amount of Portuguese or foreign currency into Madeira. No more than 100,000 escudos or the equivalent of 500,000 in foreign currency may be exported per person per trip.

3 A current weather chart from www.weatheronline.co.uk, such as the following:

| CURRENT WEATHER CHART: AZORES, MADEIRA | | |
|---|---|---|
| | **Maximum temperature** | **Weather Mon. afternoon (local time)** |
| Lajes/Terceira | 27°C | Various clouds |
| Horta/Faial | 26°C | Various clouds, slight shower |
| Angra do Heroismo | 26°C | Various clouds |
| Flores | 25°C | Various clouds, heavy shower |
| Porto Santo | 25°C | Cloudy |
| Horta | 25°C | Various clouds |
| Funchal/Madeira | 24°C | Various clouds, vigorous wind: 5Bft. |
| | **Temperature noon** | **Weather Mon. afternoon (local time)** |
| Santa Maria | 25°C | Various clouds, slight shower |

4 This hotel review of a Funchal hotel from an Internet hotel booking site – posted September 2002:

> This is the most fantastic hotel ever. Been there two years in a row and plan to go back this year. The service is second to none as is the location, access and facilities. You will be treated as individuals and made to feel welcome by all staff. By far the best hotel ever.

5 The following extract on Madeira from *World Travel Guide*:

# Madeira

☐ international airport

40km
20mls

Porto Santo
Porto Santo
Baixo

**MADEIRA**

Ponta do Pargo
Porto do Moniz
Santana
Pico Ruivo 1862m
Baia de Zarco
**Madeira**
Cabo Girão
Santa Cruz
**FUNCHAL**
Chão
Deserta Grande

ATLANTIC OCEAN

Ilhas Selvagens
Bugio

DAB-MI40

**Location:** Atlantic Ocean, 535 nautical miles southwest of Lisbon.

**Direcção Regional de Turismo** (Regional Tourist Office)
Avenida Arriaga, 18, 9004-519 Funchal, Madeira
Tel: (291) 229 057. Fax: (291) 232 151.
E-mail: info@madeiratourism.org
Web site: http://www.madeiratourism.org

## General

**AREA:** 794 sq km (314 sq miles).
**POPULATION:** 253,800 (1992).
**POPULATION DENSITY:** 319.6 per sq km.
**CAPITAL:** Funchal. **Population:** 126,889 (1991).
**GEOGRAPHY:** The group comprises the main island of Madeira, the smaller island of Porto Santo and the three uninhabited islets of Ilheu Chao, Deserta Grande and Ilheu de Bugio. The islands are hilly and of volcanic origin and the coast of Madeira is steep and rocky with deep eroded lava gorges running down to the sea. These are particularly impressive on the north coast of Madeira island. The largest of a group of five islands formed by volcanic eruption, Madeira is in fact the summit of a mountain range rising 6.5km (4 miles) from the sea bed. Its volcanic origin can be clearly seen in its mountainous interior and in the lava streams which break up the line of cliffs on its coast. At Cabo Girão, west of the capital of Funchal, is the second-highest cliff in the world. Inland, Pico Ruivo is the island's highest point (1862m/6109ft) with the slightly lower Pico de Arieiro (1810m/5940ft) nearby. Both are destinations for sightseeing tours, commanding fine views of the surrounding mountains. Madeira's volcanic origin means that it has no sandy beaches, although there is a small beach, Prainha, near the whaling village of Canical on the extreme east of the island. Madeira itself is 58km (36 miles) long and 23km (14 miles) wide. Porto Santo is much smaller, only 14km (9 miles) long and 5km (3 miles) wide, with a long, golden sandy beach, complementing Madeira.
**TIME:** GMT + 1 (GMT + 2 from last Sunday in March to Saturday before last Sunday in October).
**ELECTRICITY:** 220 volts AC, 50Hz. Round 2-pin plugs are in use.
**COMMUNICATIONS:** Services are similar to those offered on the mainland.
**BBC World Service and Voice of America frequencies:** From time to time these change.

| BBC: | | | | |
|---|---|---|---|---|
| MHz | 12.10 | 9.410 | 6.195 | 3.955 |
| Voice of America: | | | | |
| MHz | 15.26 | 9.760 | 1.197 | 0.792 |

Extract taken from *World Travel Guide* published by Columbus Travel Guides

## Collecting and presenting information

If your research is for an assessment you may have been told how to present your information – for example, it may be in the form of a report or a display. This will help you but you still need a plan. Your plan gives you a structure to work to, enabling you to make sure you have covered everything and that it is presented in a logical order.

When you are collecting information, organise it as you collect it. If you are making notes from the Internet or a book, group all the notes relating to a particular topic together. If you are photocopying or printing, highlight the relevant points immediately, and organise topics together.

If you are finding out information for customers, the same rules apply. Make sure you have all the relevant information to hand and present it in a logical order.

If you are writing an assessment, everything you write must be in your own words. It is unacceptable to copy from another source unless it is a direct quote, which must be acknowledged with details of the source and the date. If you do copy directly from a source without acknowledgement, this is called plagiarism and is very serious.

You can attach information from brochures and the Internet in appendices. This means they should be labelled Appendix 1, 2, etc. and attached to the back of your work. They must be referred to in the body of your work. For example, in your report you might state that 'Funchal has several 4-star hotels. These are listed in Appendix 1.'

You should also provide an introduction and contents page for your assessment.

If you are presenting information to colleagues or customers, you may need visuals to help you. You could use a map to show location or a suitable brochure.

## Drawing conclusions about your findings

In an assessment, you should always have a conclusion. This is a brief summary of what you have found out. If you are giving an oral presentation, you should remind your audience of the main points of what you have just told them. This applies to giving information to customers too – summarise the information to help them retain the key points.

## Acknowledging your sources

A bibliography should be included with an assessment. This is a list of every source you have used, with titles, authors, publishers and dates. Journals and websites should also be listed.

Direct quotes should be acknowledged within the text. Photos, maps or graphs should be clearly labelled with the source and date.

When dealing with customers it will be enough to mention the source of information and give them further sources to look at if they require more information.

## Locating continents and major tourist destinations

Part of your research skills will involve finding out the location of major tourist destinations,

particularly those which are most popular and those which you choose to study in depth. The following activity is designed to revise or kickstart your geographical knowledge.

### Theory into practice

For this exercise you will need a world map. You can download a map from www.geoexplorer.co.uk or you can use an outline map from your world atlas.

1 In the activity on page 105 you looked at the World Tourism website and found out which countries had the most tourism arrivals. Locate these countries on the world map. Find out the name of the capital city for each country and locate these also.

2 Locate and name the following on the map:
- the equator
- the northern hemisphere
- the southern hemisphere
- Europe, Africa, America, Australasia and Asia
- the Atlantic, Pacific and Indian oceans
- the Alps, Andes and Himalayas.

Use an atlas to help you complete your map and ask your tutor to check your work.

### ✱ REMEMBER!

When carrying out **research** you need to:
- plan well – don't just browse unless you have hours to spare
- check the validity of your sources
- never plagiarise
- present your work in a logical way with headings
- use appendices and always refer to them in the main body of your report
- add a bibliography.

# Transport routes

Without effective transport routes, tourists cannot reach their destination. Indeed, the transport available is usually a factor in choosing a destination. In this section we will examine the transport routes that link major tourism generating and receiving areas.

## Road

Domestic travellers within the UK are more likely to travel by road than by any other means. Car ownership is at its highest ever – 44% of households own one car, 23% own two cars and 5% have three or more cars, according to the 2001 census. Results from the United Kingdom Tourism Survey show that, for the past four years, 73% of domestic tourism trips were made by car.

As our roads are also for transporting goods, this means they are under a lot of pressure. The UK has a good network of motorways but they are frequently congested, particularly the M1, M6 and M25.

In general, use of our roads is free, apart from road tax and petrol, of course. Petrol is very expensive in the UK, so it is an important cost consideration. There are a few toll roads, for example the Dartford crossings via the M25, and the M6 north of Birmingham now has an optional toll section so that motorists can avoid congestion. Motorways on the Continent are not free – tolls are charged and add a substantial cost to a car journey.

## Major routes by road

Even when tourists are to travel to their destination by air they may use the road network to reach the airport. Possible hold-ups from traffic congestion have to be taken into consideration when planning the journey to the airport.

It is straightforward for tourists travelling between the UK and the rest of Europe to make their journey by road. The Channel ports, both sea and rail, give immediate access to motorway networks in France and the UK. From northern France there are excellent motorways connecting with the rest of Europe. These motorways are less congested than those in the UK, so make for more pleasant driving. Major roads have been reclassified throughout Europe with 'E' numbers to clarify route planning for motorists.

Traditionally, campers heading for France and Spain travel by road, and the ferry costs are included in their camping package. Camping operators provide information about driving abroad and route maps. However, with many

| TRANSPORT USED BY UK RESIDENTS IN THE UK | Percentage of trips | | | |
|---|---|---|---|---|
| | 2003 | 2002 | 2001 | 2000 |
| Car | 73 | 73 | 73 | 73 |
| Train | 12 | 12 | 12 | 13 |
| Regular bus/coach | 4 | 4 | 4 | 5 |
| Organised coach | 2 | 2 | 2 | 2 |
| Motorised caravan/camper van | 1 | 1 | 1 | 1 |
| Motor cycle | less than 1 | less than 1 | less than 1 | less than 1 |
| Bicycle | less than 1 | less than 1 | less than 1 | less than 1 |
| Plane | 5 | 4 | 4 | 4 |
| Boat/ship | less than 1 | 1 | 1 | 1 |
| Other | 2 | 2 | 3 | 2 |

Source: United Kingdom Tourism Survey

*The possibility of traffic hold-ups must always be taken into account when planning*

low-cost flights available, campers are more often choosing to fly to their destinations.

Tourists with limited budgets may choose to travel by coach. There are some excellent services both in the UK and beyond. The main disadvantage is the length of journeys, particularly in continental Europe where the speed of coaches is restricted below the normal speed limit. Eurolines is a well-known international scheduled service coach operator. A typical service is the trip from Birmingham to Paris at a cost of £49. However, the journey takes 11 hours.

Fly-drive holidays are very popular in the US. Petrol is cheap and if tourists have the use of a car they have the opportunity to visit more than one destination. For example, car hire in Florida would allow a family to visit Disneyworld and the Everglades. However, tourists may not choose to drive very long distances in the US as they are unfamiliar with the road system, and the speed limit is restrictive.

## Rail

The rail network in the UK is complex and beleaguered by problems. Some serious crashes like the one at Potters Bar in May 2002 undermined public confidence, and the services have a reputation for being expensive and not punctual.

There are different train-operating companies for different regions, and another company is responsible for all the tracks and systems.

Network Rail is the not-for-profit company which owns and operates the rail network. There are 25 train-operating companies which hold franchises to run each service. Examples include Virgin Rail and Stagecoach.

London has a comprehensive underground rail system, and Glasgow and Newcastle have metro systems. The London Docklands Light Railway has been very successful in improving transport links and reducing road congestion.

The Channel Tunnel opened in 1994 and provides a vital rail link with France and Belgium. Work continues on the second section of the UK high-speed rail line and is due for completion in 2007.

The major Eurostar terminals are located in London Waterloo, Paris Gare du Nord and Brussels. Eurostar also has stations in Ashford and Lille. The map on page 113 shows Eurostar's connections.

Eurostar also offers passengers connecting tickets to many cities and destinations in Europe. This service makes travel by rail much easier for UK-originating passengers, as they can book the whole trip through Eurostar and get all the travel information they need without contacting the rail networks in the countries they wish to travel to.

Some of the destinations served by Eurostar and connecting Continental rail services are shown on page 113.

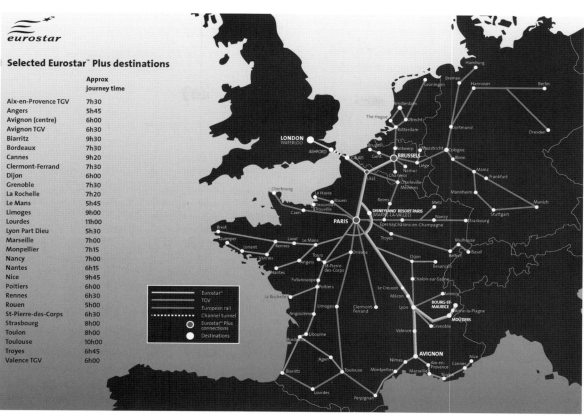

# eurostar

## Selected Eurostar™ Plus destinations

| | Approx journey time |
|---|---|
| Aix-en-Provence TGV | 7h30 |
| Angers | 5h45 |
| Avignon (centre) | 6h00 |
| Avignon TGV | 6h30 |
| Biarritz | 9h30 |
| Bordeaux | 7h30 |
| Cannes | 9h20 |
| Clermont-Ferrand | 7h30 |
| Dijon | 6h00 |
| Grenoble | 7h30 |
| La Rochelle | 7h20 |
| Le Mans | 5h45 |
| Limoges | 9h00 |
| Lourdes | 11h00 |
| Lyon Part Dieu | 5h30 |
| Marseille | 7h00 |
| Monpellier | 7h15 |
| Nancy | 7h00 |
| Nantes | 6h15 |
| Nice | 9h45 |
| Poitiers | 6h00 |
| Rennes | 6h30 |
| Rouen | 5h00 |
| St-Pierre-des-Corps | 6h30 |
| Strasbourg | 8h00 |
| Toulon | 8h00 |
| Toulouse | 10h00 |
| Troyes | 6h45 |
| Valence TGV | 6h00 |

Map legend:
Eurostar™ / TGV / European rail / Channel tunnel / Eurostar™ Plus connections / Destinations

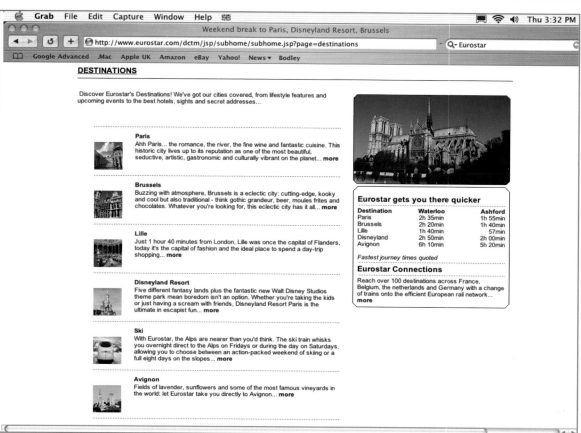

Weekend break to Paris, Disneyland Resort, Brussels

http://www.eurostar.com/dctm/jsp/subhome/subhome.jsp?page=destinations

Q- Eurostar

Google Advanced  .Mac  Apple UK  Amazon  eBay  Yahoo!  News ▾  Bodley

## DESTINATIONS

Discover Eurostar's Destinations! We've got our cities covered, from lifestyle features and upcoming events to the best hotels, sights and secret addresses...

**Paris**
Ahh Paris... the romance, the river, the fine wine and fantastic cuisine. This historic city lives up to its reputation as one of the most beautiful, seductive, artistic, gastronomic and culturally vibrant on the planet... **more**

**Brussels**
Buzzing with atmosphere, Brussels is a eclectic city: cutting-edge, kooky and cool but also traditional - think gothic grandeur, beer, moules frites and chocolates. Whatever you're looking for, this eclectic city has it all... **more**

**Lille**
Just 1 hour 40 minutes from London, Lille was once the capital of Flanders, today it's the capital of fashion and the ideal place to spend a day-trip shopping... **more**

**Disneyland Resort**
Five different fantasy lands plus the fantastic new Walt Disney Studios theme park mean boredom isn't an option. Whether you're taking the kids or just having a scream with friends, Disneyland Resort Paris is the ultimate in escapist fun... **more**

**Ski**
With Eurostar, the Alps are nearer than you'd think. The ski train whisks you overnight direct to the Alps on Fridays or during the day on Saturdays, allowing you to choose between an action-packed weekend of skiing or a full eight days on the slopes... **more**

**Avignon**
Fields of lavender, sunflowers and some of the most famous vineyards in the world: let Eurostar take you directly to Avignon... **more**

### Eurostar gets you there quicker

| Destination | Waterloo | Ashford |
|---|---|---|
| Paris | 2h 35min | 1h 55min |
| Brussels | 2h 20min | 1h 40min |
| Lille | 1h 40min | 57min |
| Disneyland | 2h 50min | 2h 00min |
| Avignon | 6h 10min | 5h 20min |

*Fastest journey times quoted*

### Eurostar Connections

Reach over 100 destinations across France, Belgium, the netherlands and Germany with a change of trains onto the efficient European rail network...
**more**

## Air

Air travel is the main form of long-distance travel and the most rapidly expanding transport sector. To cope with increased demand for air travel, many gateway airports have had to expand capacity. For London, Heathrow is building a fifth terminal, and Stansted has plans for a second runway. There are over 50 regional airports in the UK, but distances are not so great as to make air travel a preferred option within the UK. However, services from cities in Scotland and Ireland to London do very well. Air travel is the most favoured form of travel for inbound tourists to the UK.

| TRANSPORT USED TO TRAVEL TO THE UK BY OVERSEAS VISITORS Percentage of visits | | | |
|---|---|---|---|
| | 2002 | 2001 | 2000 |
| Air | 71 | 70 | 71 |
| Sea | 18 | 18 | 17 |
| Tunnel | 11 | 12 | 12 |

Source: International Passenger Survey

There are two main categories of air travel: scheduled and charter. Tourists travelling on a package holiday are likely to be travelling on a charter plane, often owned by the tour operator they are travelling with. For example, Thomson is a tour operator and has a sister airline company called Britannia. Charter airlines will sell seat-only deals to fill up their flights and achieve better load factors.

Scheduled flights are sold on a seat-only basis and run to a timetable, revised for winter and summer schedules. Charters operate according to holiday demand and do not operate every day to the same destination.

Low-cost airlines have developed over the past few years. They offer very few services such as catering or allocated seats, but do offer low fares. The low fares are not available at peak times or to late bookers.

### CASE STUDY

The following extract from the EasyJet information pack on its website gives an explanation of how a low-cost airline achieves its low fares:

#### how we do it

easyJet offers a simple, no frills service at rock bottom fares. Fares can be offered at such good value due to the following main reasons:

easyJet **IS A TICKETLESS AIRLINE**... All you need to fly is your passport and your booking reference. This is less hassle for the customer, who doesn't have to worry about collecting tickets before travelling, and is cost-effective for easyJet.

**EFFICIENT USE OF AIRPORTS**... easyJet flies to main destination airports throughout Europe, but gains efficiencies through rapid turnaround times, and progressive landing charges agreements with the airports. By reducing turnarounds to 30 minutes and below, easyJet can achieve extra rotations on the high-frequency routes, thereby maximising utilisation rates of its aircraft.

**THERE'S NO SUCH THING AS A FREE LUNCH**... so easyJet doesn't offer one. Plastic trays of airline food only mean more expensive flights. easyJet passengers are given the choice as to whether they wish to buy themselves drinks or snacks from the in-flight easyKiosk. Our customer feedback illustrates that passengers do not want a meal on board a short-haul flight. They prefer to pay less for the flight and have a choice to purchase snacks on board if desired.

1 **Visit the Ryanair website and see if its explanation of low costs is the same.**
2 **Compare with EasyJet and make notes.**
3 **Discuss your findings with your group.**

The airline industry is very competitive and many low-cost operators have entered the market throughout Europe. Some of the new airlines are operating from eastern Europe as the recent entry into the European Union of several eastern European countries has encouraged travel to and from this area. Passengers are not always aware whether they are travelling on a scheduled service, low-cost scheduled service or charter flight, as the distinctions between the different airlines become less obvious.

## Routes by air

Airline routes are very complex as each airline has its own routes, but enters into different types of partnership with other airlines to extend its networks. British Airways (BA) is one of the world's major airlines so it serves as a good example. BA flies to many destinations worldwide.

British Airways is a hub-and-spoke network; that is, it uses major airport gateways as hubs and flies passengers from regional airports (the spokes) to join other direct flights at the hub. The flights from the hub may be to major airports or to regional airports.

In contrast, EasyJet is a point-to-point airline. All flights are in pairs – for example, Stansted to Nice and Nice back to Stansted. EasyJet is a very successful airline working with a much simpler route network than British Airways – all its flights are within Europe.

The maps below show the airports that EasyJet uses.

### Key terms

A **scheduled airline** operates flights to a timetable. Low-cost airlines are usually scheduled services.

**Charter flights** operate to holiday destinations and are chartered for periods of holiday demand.

**Hub-and-spoke** airlines offer connecting services between regions and major airports.

**Point-to-point** services operate between paired cities or towns.

## Airport gateways

Airports are gateways to travel destinations. London is served by four major airports: Heathrow, Gatwick, Stansted and Luton. There is also a small airport in the Docklands area of London, London City Airport. This airport is used mainly by business travellers.

Gateway airports are always the busiest. Sometimes the gateway is to another flight. Transfer passengers are those who fly to a hub airport and transfer to another flight. Examples of major hubs are Heathrow and Paris Charles de Gaulle. The worldwide airline Air France is based at Charles de Gaulle. Passengers fly to this Parisian airport from other cities to join other flights.

## CASE STUDY

These were the top ten UK airports (by passenger numbers) in 2002:

| 1 | Heathrow | 63 million |
|---|---|---|
| 2 | Gatwick | 29.5 million |
| 3 | Manchester | 18.6 million |
| 4 | Stansted | 16 million |
| 5 | Birmingham | 7.9 million |
| 6 | Glasgow | 7.8 million |
| 7 | Edinburgh | 6.9 million |
| 8 | Luton | 6.4 million |
| 9 | Belfast Int. | 3.6 million |
| 10 | Bristol | 3.4 million |

Source: www.world-airport-codes.com

Locate each of the airports on a map of the UK. You can download a map from www.geoexplorer.com or you can use the map in your atlas.

You will note that Heathrow is by far the busiest airport. Visit Heathrow's website and find out the following.
- Who owns Heathrow airport?
- What other airports does this company own?
- Find five examples of domestic (inside the UK) cities linked by air to Heathrow. For each example state the airline operating the flight.
- Find five examples of European holiday destinations served by flights from Heathrow. Again state the airlines operating the flights.
- Find five examples of worldwide city destinations served by Heathrow. Again state the airlines operating the flights.

## CASE STUDY

These were the top ten world airports (by passenger numbers) in 2003.

| 1 | Hartsfield-Jackson Atlanta International | 79,086,792 |
|---|---|---|
| 2 | O'Hare International | 69,354,154 |
| 3 | London Heathrow | 63,468,620 |
| 4 | Tokyo International | 63,172,925 |
| 5 | Los Angeles International | 54,969,053 |
| 6 | Dallas–Fort Worth International | 53,243,061 |
| 7 | Frankfurt International | 48,351,664 |
| 8 | Charles de Gaulle International | 48,122,038 |
| 9 | Schipol | 39,959,161 |
| 10 | Denver International | 37,462,428 |

Source: Airports Council International

Find out in which country each of these airports is located. Locate and name them on a world map. You can download a map from www.geoexplorer.com or you can use a map from your atlas.

Find out the airport codes for each airport listed. Use the website www.world-airport-codes.com or a manual.

Choose one of the airports other than Heathrow and answer the following:
- Who owns the airport?
- What other airports does this company own?
- Find five examples of domestic (in the same country) cities linked by air to your chosen airport. For each example state the airline operating the flight.
- Find five examples of European holiday destinations served by flights from your chosen airport. Again state the airlines operating the flights.
- Find five examples of worldwide city destinations served by your chosen airport. Again state the airlines operating the flights.

# Water

Ferry services across the English Channel are surviving despite the building of the Channel Tunnel. P&O operates a service from Dover to Calais, as does Sea France. Hoverspeed operates the fastest sea crossing by sea cat from Dover to Calais and Newhaven to Dieppe.

Great Britain is linked by ferry to its neighbours in Ireland and also to Holland and Scandinavia. Because of competition from air travel and the Channel Tunnel, operators such as P&O are offering many new products and services to encourage people to travel by sea. P&O offers shopping cruises, entertainment cruises and city cruises, including two-night cruises from Hull to Holland or Belgium.

*Cruising offers the chance to see many different destinations and take part in varied activities*

## Cruising

Cruising is growing in popularity and its appeal is spreading to different markets, not just the traditional 'grey' market – older people with time and money at their disposal. Two new cruise companies, Island Cruises and Ocean Village, aim their product at first-time cruisers including the family market. The atmosphere on these ships is much less formal than on traditional ships.

In the UK in 2003, cruise passenger bookings reached 963,500, a rise of 17.4% on the previous year. Cruises range from a few nights to a tour lasting several months. The appeal of cruising lies in the chance to see many different destinations without having to change hotel room or keep repacking suitcases. Everything is included in the initial price, apart from drinks and tips, so it is easy to budget. Many varied activities are provided on board to keep passengers entertained.

## Ports

Like airports, ports are gateways. They are embarkation points for ferry services and also for cruise passengers. UK-originating cruise passengers may fly to a port to start their cruise or may leave by sea from the UK, usually Southampton. The advantage of a fly-cruise is that the passengers avoid long days at sea before they reach intended destinations.

Miami is one of the busiest cruise ports in the world, and is able to handle very large ships. A range of services is offered at a cruise terminal, including the following:

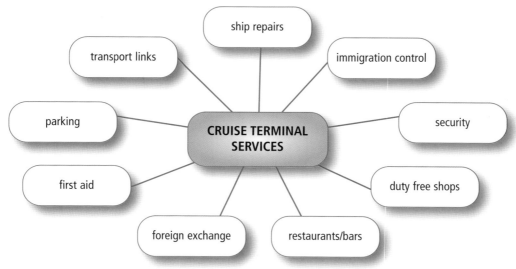

The Kidman family is going to the Vendée in France for a camping holiday. They live in London. They went last year and drove to their campsite, having crossed the Channel using the Shuttle. They are also considering flying or rail this year and want to know which route is the best option for them. The family consists of parents, a ten-year-old and an eight-year-old. Cost is a consideration, but convenience is also important.

1 Draw up a table showing the different routes. (You may first need to locate the Vendée region.)

This task may provide evidence for P2.

2 Describe the advantages and disadvantages of the different routes and draw some conclusions about how the features of the routes add to the appeal of the Vendée as a destination.

This task may provide evidence for M1.

## Time zones

Greenwich Mean Time (GMT) is the standard time for the world. Each time zone to the east of Greenwich time zone is ahead of GMT, that is +1 hour, +2 hours, etc. Each time zone to the west is behind GMT, that is –1 hour, –2 hours, etc. Going eastwards you add hours to GMT, and going westwards you subtract hours from GMT. GMT is also known as Zulu.

### Daylight-saving time

Daylight-saving or summer time has been adopted in most regions of the world. In the UK it is known as British Summer Time. At 1 am GMT on the last Sunday in March, the clocks go forward by one hour, and on the last Sunday in October they revert to GMT. Other countries may introduce daylight-saving time on different dates.

The purpose of the change is so that the hours when people are working or studying better match the period of available daylight. When travelling, people must ensure that time changes are included in time calculations.

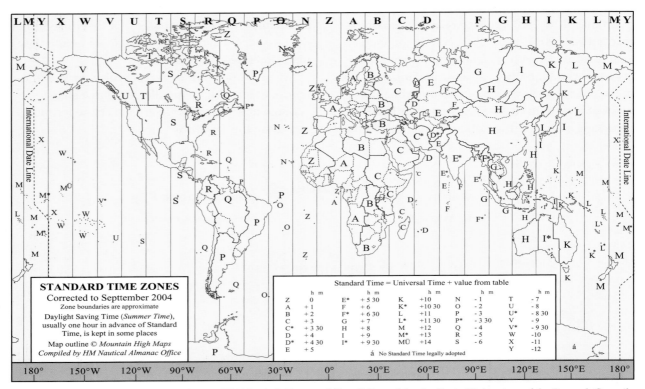

Source: HM Nautical Almanac Office, © Council for the Central Laboratory of the Research Councils

1 A friend on holiday in Portugal telephones you at 2 pm on 1 September. What time is it in Portugal?

2 You come back from holiday in France on 3 September and your flight leaves Montpellier at 17.35 and arrives in the UK at 18.35 (local times). How long was the flight?

3 You are going to New York for Christmas shopping at the beginning of December. Your flight leaves the UK at 9.30 am and the flight takes seven hours. What time is it in New York on arrival?

## International Date Line

The International Date Line is the imaginary line on the Earth that separates two consecutive calendar days. Travelling east across the line takes the traveller back one day; travelling west takes the traveller forward one day. It is most apparent for cruise passengers.

On a map it is shown as 180° away from the meridian that goes through Greenwich, on the line of longitude.

### CASE STUDY

New Zealand has one time zone, which is 12 hours ahead of GMT. Daylight-saving time (DST) is in effect from mid-October until mid-March. The clocks advance by one hour for DST. Travellers who arrive from the northern hemisphere cross the international dateline and lose a full day, and on returning from New Zealand regain a full day.

Crossing time zones can cause 'jet lag' – usually going east is worse for this than going west. The reason for it is that inbuilt bodily rhythms have been disturbed and it can take a few days for the body to readjust to the new time zone. The 12-hour difference in New Zealand could mean it takes several days to return to normal. Travellers may find that they are falling asleep during the day and staying awake at night.

Find out what can be done to alleviate jet lag. Produce a short information sheet that could be given to air passengers before their flight.

### Consider this ...

If you leave Sydney at 1 am in the summer, how can it be light all the way by air to London?

# Factors contributing to the appeal of a destination

This section is not designed to be a guide to different destinations. Rather, its purpose is to develop your understanding of why different destinations appeal to different types of tourists, and to help you develop your own research skills through the use of case studies. We will look at examples of destinations in the UK, Europe and worldwide and examine the different types of destinations.

### Consider this ...

What were the things about your destination that appealed to you on your last holiday?

We will look at factors which contribute to the appeal of a destination, including:

* access
* culture
* motivation for travel
* geographical features
* natural attractions
* purpose-built attractions.

## Access

Most tourists do not want to travel too far from their country of origin for trips, for reasons of time, cost and convenience. Tourists choosing to travel long distances, for example to Australia from the UK, make that trip infrequently and tend to go for a longer period of time. The Caribbean is more popular with US tourists than those from the UK as the flight times, and therefore costs, are lower.

UK tourists most commonly take city breaks in Europe as they can easily access the destination for a weekend and still put in a full week's work. Short breaks to New York are also popular, but UK tourists tend to stay for four or five days.

Travellers will also take into consideration how much further they have to travel to the destination having arrived at the gateway airport or port. Until a few years ago tourists visiting Tobago had to change to a local flight in Port of Spain, Trinidad, as the runway could not accommodate large jets. Since the runway was extended to cater for jumbos, the provision of direct flights has brought about an increase in tourism.

Skiers have to carefully consider access to the resort when deciding how to travel. Even if they fly to a gateway airport such as Geneva or Lyon, they will still be faced with a lengthy drive or rail journey into the mountains.

*Bratislava is one eastern European capital that will expect increased tourism*

### Theory into practice

Imagine you are taking a week's skiing trip to Courcheval in France. Find out the possible routes from your home. Include all modes of transport. Draw up a table showing the pros and cons of each route – remember to consider transport directly to the destination. Which route has the best access from your home and to Courcheval? Say which route you would choose and why. Ask your tutor to check your work.

Different types of tourists require different things from their transport route. Those with plenty of time and no small children may make the journey an integral part of the trip, enjoying driving and stopovers en route. Others want to arrive at their end destination as quickly as possible.

Access is not just about transport links. Politics and economics also affect access. Only 15 years ago, eastern Europeans were not free to travel to their relatives and friends in the west, and vice versa. Even when they received their political freedom with the fall of the Berlin Wall and the dissolution of the Soviet Union, the people of those developing nations could scarcely afford to travel. However, western Europeans could benefit from visiting new destinations they could easily afford. Prague is a good example, now in the top ten of city breaks from the UK.

A dramatic event of 2004 will have an effect on travel within Europe, both from east to west and west to east – another ten countries were accepted

into the European Union. These countries are currently described as 'accession' countries and bring the total numbers of EU countries to 25.

Most of these countries have not experienced much tourism so far, so their potential for development is great. There are already examples of airlines operating between the UK and new member states. Remember that these countries are not so far part of the Eurozone (those countries whose currency is the euro) but retain their own currencies.

### ✱ REMEMBER!

The countries joining the EU in 2004 were:

- Cyprus
- Czech Republic
- Estonia
- Hungary
- Latvia
- Lithuania
- Malta
- Poland
- Slovakia
- Slovenia.

### Theory into practice

Locate and name these new entrants to the EU on a map. Find out the names of the other 15 member states of the EU. Locate and name them also on the map.

Choose one of the countries that entered the EU in 2004 that is not yet very popular with tourists. Find out what is currently provided for tourists in that country or in one destination within it. Look at transport both to the destination and within it.

1 Describe the accommodation, facilities, attractions and information and identify gaps in provision for tourists.

This task may provide evidence for P4.

2 Decide whether you think the destination has potential for tourism, and explain why.

This task may provide evidence for M3.

3 Who is likely to visit? What developments would you recommend to attract tourists and why?

This task may provide evidence for D2.

# Culture

**Consider this ...**

Think of somewhere you have been where you felt you were in a different culture. In what ways did it feel different?

Some tourists love to experience a different culture and lifestyle when on holiday. Some do not! Some hope to find bars and restaurants serving the same food as they get at home and access to their usual daily newspaper. Certain resorts in Spain, for example Torremolinos and Benidorm, cater so well for British, German and Dutch tourists that the Spanish culture is hidden. In contrast, Barcelona is typically Spanish with authentic restaurants and Spanish culture thoroughly evident.

Cultural and sporting events attract tourists, for example the Olympics in Athens or the Euro 2004 football championships in Portugal. Sometimes tourists need to be educated in what to expect from the host country and its culture, so that their behaviour and dress are respectful and do not offend.

*Sports events such as Euro 2004 in Portugal attract visitors whose behaviour comes under scrutiny*

Lille is an example of a city destination which is fast rising in popularity. It is situated in northern France near the Belgium border. Two major factors, access and culture, explain its appeal.

For UK tourists, access to Lille is excellent by Eurostar. There are nine trains a day from London Waterloo and the journey time is 1 hour 40 minutes. This is less time than some people spend commuting! There are also three buses a day from London Victoria, operated by Eurolines. Although not so rapid as the train, this is an inexpensive way to travel.

Lille airport is 10 kilometres from the town but there are no direct flights to London. To fly to Lille it would be necessary to fly to another hub in France and out again. There are, however, air links to other European cities such as Barcelona, and to many French airports.

Lille was named European Capital of Culture for 2004. A different city is nominated every year

– Cork is the European Capital of Culture for 2005. The European Commission provides funding to:

- promote diverse cultural activities to a range of people
- increase social cohesion
- create a sustainable cultural heritage.

Lille had over 2,000 different exhibitions and performances during 2004 attracting many new tourists. Once in the city, tourists found many other features of Lille to enjoy. There is a medieval town centre, Vieux Lille, with cobbled streets and individual shops. The architecture is interesting, with Gothic churches, and there are good restaurants and bars.

1 Find out which city is currently European Capital of Culture. Describe the following factors and how they contribute to the city's appeal:
- location of the city
- access for UK tourists
- special activities planned for the year
- other tourist attractions in the city.

This task may provide evidence for P3.

2 Choose two different types of visitor, for example a family or a group of 18-year-olds. Say how this city appeals to the customers. Compare your findings with another destination in the UK or outside Europe.

This task may provide evidence for M2.

## CASE STUDY

The Notting Hill Carnival takes place in Ladbroke Grove in London every August Bank Holiday weekend. The festivities last for three days. The first carnival was in 1966, and was started by West Indian immigrants in the area. These were mainly Trinidadians who wanted to replicate the flavour of their wonderful carnivals at home. The first carnival was fairly small, but now it is a massive spectacular attracting up to 2 million people.

The carnival reflects the multicultural nature of our society, with groups representing many different backgrounds, including the

Philippines, Central and South America and Bangladesh. People celebrate their own musical and artistic traditions.

For two days of the carnival there are three live stages featuring local bands, as well as artists from around the world. Visitors can buy exotic foods from all over the world at street stalls or buy traditional arts and crafts.

Perhaps the most exciting part of the carnival is the three-mile-long procession which takes place. People parade in magnificent costumes, alongside soca and steel bands.

If you can visit Notting Hill Carnival, go and see what it's like. Otherwise find out about a similar (possibly much smaller-scale) event in your area that represents the local culture. Describe the event in detail. Find out if the event attracts tourists and if that is its purpose. Compile some facts and figures on the event and share your findings with your group.

## Motivation for travel

Why do people travel? Why do people go on holiday? A great deal of research has been done into motivation for travel, but consumer behaviour is a difficult area to research as sometimes we ourselves don't know exactly why we do something. There are probably as many reasons for going away as there are tourists who go. Tourists on holiday together at the same resort do not necessarily have the same motivation for being there.

### Consider this ...

Think about your last trip away. What motivated you to travel? Was it to visit friends or relatives? In that case your motivation might have been a desire to reinforce friendship or family bonds. Perhaps you were motivated by a sense of duty to visit an elderly family member.

A trip or holiday may have more than one motivating force behind it. Football fans who visited Portugal for Euro 2004 might have been motivated by a desire to see their team win and also a wish to relax in the sun.

Types of motivation for travel and tourism include the following.

### Physical reasons

Tourists may be motivated by the need for rest and relaxation, having worked hard all year. This motive could manifest itself in the choice of a simple beach holiday for relaxation in the sun. It might be reflected in the choice of a spa holiday where rest and well-being are emphasised.

### Social reasons

Some tourists take a holiday in order to meet new people. This is especially true of singles holidays or 18–30-type holidays. Some people combine their love of activity holidays with meeting a new group of people, perhaps by joining a walking or cycling tour.

### Love/romance

The most obvious examples of holidays in the 'romance' category are the markets that have grown up for wedding packages or honeymoons.

### Desire for adventure

Some tourists want to spend their time away enjoying new experiences and may opt for adventure holidays ranging from safaris to white-water rafting.

### Education

Many tourists visit the UK in order to participate in English-language courses, and many language schools have opened up to cater for them – language courses can be found in all major cities.

Many UK students undertake educational trips abroad as part of their courses, including for the purposes of language learning.

### Culture

Those who visit a destination to study the architecture, the arts and music are motivated by a desire to experience culture. In its wider sense many tourists want to experience the language, lifestyle, food and drink offered by another culture. We often describe those who like to travel further and further afield in search of new experiences as having 'wanderlust'.

## Escape

Often tourists want to escape from their busy lives at home or work, and that in itself is motivation to travel. It is also common for tourists to want to escape the British climate, hence the sale of summer sun and winter sun holidays.

## Pull factors

Those motivators which arise from our own needs and desires or our own experiences at home can be described as 'push' factors in tourist motivation. We can also be motivated by external factors, which are known as 'pull' factors.

Examples include advertising of particular destinations, seeing holiday or other television programmes about resorts, or even copying our favourite celebrities. The *Times* newspaper runs a column entitled 'How to holiday like a celebrity'. The British Tourist Board, VisitBritain, has campaigns aimed at overseas tourists to try to encourage them to come to the UK. Celebrity concerts attract tourists – a Robbie Williams concert in Dublin in 2002 led to an increase in sales of trips to Dublin of 20% year on year, according to short-break specialist Cresta.

A favourable exchange rate also increases our motivation to travel. In the early years of the 21st century the US dollar was very weak against sterling. This led to increased tourism to the US from the UK – in the first four months of 2004, UK arrivals to the US jumped by 16% to 1,331,000, compared with the same period last year. There are some factors which decrease our motivation to travel to a destination. High levels of crime dissuade tourists. Reports of terrorism may put an end to tourism in an area for a lengthy period of time, as occurred in Bali after an appalling bomb attack on a nightclub in 2002. Pollution or natural disasters such as floods or earthquakes also decrease motivation to travel to a destination.

### Theory into practice

Make a small survey of some friends or colleagues. Ask them to think about a recent trip away. It doesn't have to be a holiday – it might be a day out or a visit to friends. Ask them why they chose that particular trip. What motivated them?

Try to categorise the motivating factors as shown above. Ask too about the external motivators. Did someone else's experience or an advertisement motivate them? Remember that there may be more than one motivator.

Put your results in a table – it might look like this:

| TRAVELLER | PUSH MOTIVATION | PULL MOTIVATION |
| --- | --- | --- |
| Susie – hen night in London | Social – to support her friend | All her girlfriends were encouraging her to go |
|  |  |  |
|  |  |  |
|  |  |  |
|  |  |  |
|  |  |  |

Guess the motivation of the people described in the left column, and match it with a suitable holiday on the right.

| PEOPLE | HOLIDAY |
| --- | --- |
| Joe and Parminder are about to celebrate their first anniversary – Joe is going to surprise Parminder with a weekend away | Two weeks in Cyprus in Ayia Napa with lots of clubs and bars |
| Sarah, a tourism lecturer, is arranging a trip for 20 tourism students | A few days in a 4-star hotel with all facilities on the seafront in Bournemouth |
| Paul is very overweight and concerned about it – he is worried about his health | Five days on the Costa del Sol, including talks from a holiday representative and visits to three hotels |
| A group of six lads have been friends since school and spend every weekend out on the town – they want to go away for two weeks together | A week at a detox and yoga centre |
| Kelly is exhausted – she has spent the past six months looking after her new baby. Her mum is going to babysit for five days so Kelly can go away with her husband for a rest | A round-the-world ticket and a backpack |
| Veronica is taking a year out travelling after working in the city for five years – she has little money after having spent all her high earnings on a new flat | Flight only to Delhi |
| Moassem and Raj are planning a trip to India to visit their elderly relatives whom they haven't seen for four years | Weekend in Venice including a trip on a gondola |
| Graham and Martin have a weekend free from their busy air-crew jobs – they can take free flights and they want to take in some galleries and have a couple of special quiet dinners | A couple of days in Florence staying in the city centre |

Did you guess the motivating factors? They are listed below. Match them to the appropriate people.

- education
- relaxation
- romance
- health
- social
- wanderlust
- culture
- duty.

## CASE STUDY

Different motivation does not necessarily mean a different destination. Some destinations have so much to offer that they are suitable for all types of people. One of the top city break destinations, Paris, is a good example.

You may wish to choose Paris to research for your assessment, and this case study will help you start. You will need plenty of information about Paris. Consider using the following:

- atlas/road map
- brochures
- travel guides
- Internet sites
- French tourist office or website.

Remember that you must use more than one source of information and you must cross-reference for validity, as discussed earlier.

First, ensure you can locate Paris. Find it on a map, and research access from the UK. Start from your home town and find at least two different routes to get there.

Choose two of the travellers mentioned in the 'Theory into Practice' activity above and research what they could do in Paris and where they could stay. Write up your findings in a brief article suitable for a travel feature. Everything you choose must fit their motivation. For example, if you choose romance, you will need to find:

- a charming hotel with character – and perhaps a four-poster in the room
- somewhere to buy flowers
- somewhere to buy chocolates
- a romantic restaurant
- a romantic walk along the river
- a boat ride on the river in a *bateau mouche*.

# Geographical features

The geographical features of a region can add to its appeal, particularly where the geography lends itself to particular activities such as walking, mountaineering or fishing. Particular features of the topography may appeal to different types of visitors.

The appeal of the seaside is obvious to us all, but the sea can also provide a variety of activities of interest to tourists such as water-skiing, surfing, deep-sea fishing or whale watching.

Mountainous regions are popular for walking in the summer but have an even greater attraction in the winter for skiers.

On volcanic islands like Tenerife and St Lucia, tourists can climb to the centre of volcanoes and bathe in sulphur pools. The ruins of Pompeii are also a great tourist attraction.

Rainforests are not just for intrepid explorers. On some Caribbean islands such as Grenada, tourists can climb up waterfalls and ramble through the rainforest, all under the care of a local guide.

Even desert safaris can be made available to people on package holidays in Tunisia or Morocco.

Tourists need to be aware when arranging trips about climate zones and seasonal variations. This sounds obvious, but many tourists arrive in Thailand, for example, and find it is the monsoon season and they didn't check first. The problem of encountering poor weather, unexpected by the tourist, has increased as people have ventured further afield.

Unexpected climatic conditions can be a disaster for tourism and for the destination, as the article below about Prague in August 2002 illustrates.

**Worst floods in 200 years**

Czech residents were forced out of their homes as central Europe faced the worst floods known for over 200 years. The River Vltava burst its banks, causing death and destruction. Fourteen people died in the Czech Republic alone. Buildings crumbled and great piles of mud were left by the flood waters.

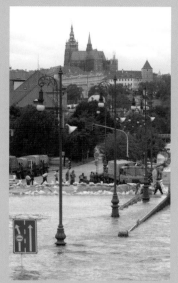

The floods were caused by a period of heavy sustained rainfall over about a week. The water rose up through the sewers, and the basement of the National Theatre was flooded.

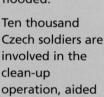

Ten thousand Czech soldiers are involved in the clean-up operation, aided by civilians. The EU has pledged $50 million in aid to help the Czech Republic, which hopes to join the EU in 2004.

In neighbouring Slovakia, a state of emergency has been declared as the Danube threatens to flood the capital, Bratislava.

1  **Find out about the long-term effects of the floods on tourism in Prague.**
2  **Has the city recovered?**
3  **What was the economic effect of the floods?**
4  **How will the entry of the Czech Republic into the EU affect tourism?**
5  **Can you find statistics on tourism in the Czech Republic? Try Internet searches, newspaper archives and World Tourism Organisation statistics.**

Make notes on your findings. If you choose to study Prague for your assessment, you will have made a useful start.

# Natural attractions

Natural attractions appeal to tourists who want to gaze at the world's wonders such as Niagara Falls or the beautiful lakes in the UK's Lake District. Lakes, rivers and mountains can provide the setting for a wide variety of leisure and sporting activities. Every tourist area will have some kind of natural attraction in or near to the destination that can be promoted to tourists. It may be beaches, lakes, mountains or rolling countryside.

### Theory into practice

Find a natural attraction close to where you live. It may be something that already attracts tourists. If this is so, find out how many tourists visit, when and what the appeal is. If the attraction does not yet appeal to tourists, consider the potential and suggest what developments could be made to encourage tourists to visit. Prepare some notes for a presentation on your findings to the rest of your group.

## Built attractions

Buildings that attract tourists may be historic, like the colleges in Oxford and Cambridge, or built to attract tourists, for example theme parks. Attractions can be built to enhance the existing tourism potential of a destination. Consider coastal resorts, where water parks and fairgrounds have been introduced to appeal to tourists.

# Destinations

In this part of the unit you will find out about the different types of destinations and look at some examples and their appeal.

## Towns and cities

City breaks are one of the fastest-growing sectors in UK domestic and outbound tourism.

Perhaps surprisingly, more UK domestic holidays are taken in cities and towns than in seaside resorts, as the chart on page 128 shows. In 2002, 29% of domestic holidays were to cities or large towns, whereas 27% of trips were to seaside resorts.

| TYPES OF LOCATION STAYED AT FOR DOMESTIC HOLIDAY TRIPS Percentage of trips | | | |
|---|---|---|---|
| | 2002 | 2001 | 2000 |
| Large city/large town | 29 | 28 | 27 |
| Seaside | 27 | 28 | 28 |
| Countryside/village | 25 | 26 | 26 |
| Small town | 19 | 17 | 17 |
| Not specified | 1 | 1 | 1 |

Source: United Kingdom Tourism Survey

Paris was the top-selling city destination in 2003 for most city-break tour operators. London, not unexpectedly, is the top UK city destination, for both domestic travellers and overseas visitors.

VisitBritain has run three domestic campaigns to persuade UK residents to take breaks in Britain, seemingly with some success as Blackpool was seventh in the league according to research carried out by Cheapflights. Other city destinations consistently in the top ten are Dublin, Rome, Amsterdam, Barcelona and New York.

### Consider this ...

Why are city breaks so popular? Why would they appeal to you?

### Theory into practice

The table below shows the top towns visited by overseas residents in 2002. Locate and name these destinations on a map of the UK. Copy the table and for each town or city name the nearest airport and motorway or major road. Locate these on your map. You can download a map from www.geoexplorer.com or you can use a map from your atlas.

| TOP TOWNS VISITED BY OVERSEAS RESIDENTS 2002 | | | |
|---|---|---|---|
| City/town | Airport | Motorway | Visits (in thousands) |
| London | | | 11,600 |
| Edinburgh | | | 850 |
| Birmingham | | | 670 |
| Manchester | | | 590 |
| Glasgow | | | 400 |
| Oxford | | | 390 |
| Bristol | | | 310 |
| Cambridge | | | 280 |
| Cardiff | | | 280 |
| Newcastle upon Tyne | | | 240 |
| Brighton | | | 230 |
| York | | | 230 |
| Bath | | | 200 |

Source: International Passenger Survey

European destinations have become more accessible because of low-cost airlines and Eurostar. New York is attractive because the dollar is weak against the pound.

Traditional summer holidays are no longer the norm, with many people choosing to take frequent short breaks. People have higher disposable incomes than ever before and can afford to travel. Globalisation of society and mass communication leads to a desire to see other places and learn about other cultures.

By looking at some examples of cities we can analyse the appeal in more detail.

## CASE STUDY

York is a popular city destination for both domestic and overseas tourists. According to information from York Tourism, it attracted 4 million tourists in 2002 with a spend of £293 million.

Most visitors arrive in York by car as it is easily accessible by road. It does, however, also have good rail links. There are regional airports within reach but international visitors are likely to travel via London or Manchester.

The city has many historic and cultural attractions, the most famous being York Minster, the Jorvik Centre and the Castle Museum. These are purpose-built attractions.

Motivation for travel to the city varies according to the type of tourist. Many visit to see a historic city but there are those who come for the good shopping or to be entertained at the horse races.

Geographically, York benefits from its proximity to the beautiful Yorkshire countryside, the moors and the dales, and many tourists combine a visit to the countryside with their city visit.

Local attractions include:
- Jorvik Centre – a ride back to life more than 1,000 years ago, with many items on display that were discovered in an archaeological dig on the site
- Gothic York Minster
- medieval city walls
- Barley Hall – a timber-framed house dating form the Wars of the Roses
- nearby stately homes – Bishopthorpe Palace and Sutton Park
- shopping in the streets of Stonegate and Petergate.

Repeat business is important to York, otherwise overall visitor numbers would fall. A series of one-off or annual events is arranged in order to attract visitors. Look at the York Tourism website (www.york-tourism.co.uk/visitors) for the latest examples.

Information about tourism in York provided by York Tourism for 2002:
- 4 million visitors a year
- £293 million spent in York each year
- 9,570 jobs in York created by tourism
- 65% travel to York by car, 23% by train, and 2% by regular bus.

The following information is for the period from April 2003 to March 2004:
- 11,000 year-round and seasonal bedspaces
- 48.8% bed occupancy, 62.1% room occupancy
- the largest number of visitors is in the 35–64 age groups and in the ABC1 socio-economic groups
- the great majority are independent travellers (90%)
- over 1.5 million of the 4 million visitors to York have been, or will go, to other parts of Yorkshire during their current visit to York
- 77% of visitors in 2003–4 have been to York before – a strong showing for repeat business and up from 58% in 1996–7
- 19.5% of visitors are from overseas (30% of these from North America, 41% Europe). In 1995–6, 34% were from overseas.

1  **What is another term for the amount of money spent by tourists?**
2  **Why is there a difference between bed occupancy and room occupancy?**
3  **How could York attract more young people?**
4  **Why was there a strong decline in the number of overseas visitors between 1996 and 2002?**
5  **Do some research and identify five attractions in York or the surrounding area that might appeal to a visiting couple in their fifties from the US.**

You might decide to use York for your assessment, in which case you will find this activity has provided a start to your in-depth research.

# Coastal/seaside areas

The traditional idea of a holiday is two weeks by the seaside. For UK tourists this changed in the 1970s, from two weeks by the sea in Britain to two weeks by the sea in Spain or another Mediterranean resort. France was always a popular overseas destination as our nearest neighbour, but there were 12.5 million trips to Spain by UK-originating tourists in 2002, 0.4 million more than to France. France and Spain between them accounted for 41% of all trips abroad from the UK. Not all these trips are for seaside holidays. Spain's cities are becoming very popular, especially Barcelona, and Paris is the top city destination.

Coastal resorts provide something for all the family – the sea, a beach and some form of entertainment. Tourists from northern European countries such as the UK and Germany tend to travel south to the Mediterranean for a better climate. There is no need to go long-haul for the sun in summer.

Spain's resorts attract many package holiday makers, but change is occurring. A market report from Cheapflights in 2004 showed that Alicante and Malaga were third and fourth in the top-ten flight destinations but these were flight-only sales, not packages. This meant that either passengers were staying with friends and relatives or had booked their own accommodation. Likewise, at the February half-term in 2004, families were heading for Spanish beaches with Tenerife, Málaga, Lanzarote and Alicante in the top places. This was according to research from Travelsupermarket. The fifth place went to Geneva, showing the popularity of ski holidays.

The Spanish costas are very popular with the British, Germans and Dutch. Some tour operators such as First Choice think that the Costa Brava has had its day and have dropped it from their programme.

The Costa del Sol is a popular choice for second homes, and a great deal of development is taking place. Another area of extensive development is the relatively unknown Costa de la Luz, towards Portugal.

The Spanish islands are very popular destinations. There are two groups of islands: the Balearics, located to the east of the mainland in the Mediterranean, and the Canaries, located off the coast of Africa in the Atlantic.

The Balearics consist of Majorca, Minorca, Ibiza and Formentera. Formentera is the least developed of the four and is reached by a 45-minute ferry ride from Ibiza. All are suitable for family holidays, but Majorca (Magaluf) and Ibiza (San Antonio and beyond) have also built up reputations as clubbing destinations for young people.

The Canaries are a group of islands with tourism concentrated on the four largest. These are Tenerife, Gran Canaria, Lanzarote and Fuerteventura. The islands are dry with sparse vegetation, and are mainly volcanic. Fuerteventura has wide, sandy beaches but those on Tenerife are unappealing, consisting of black volcanic sand.

## The appeal of Spain

There are both scheduled and chartered flights to Spain from all major airports in the UK and from the rest of western Europe. From the UK there are also ferry services to Bilbao and Santander. The ferry services are useful if travellers are happy to have a fairly long sea journey and then drive to their final destination.

Many UK visitors drive through France to Spain. There are good ferry links from Barcelona to the Balearics. Tourists or immigrants from Africa to Spain and France enter via the southern ports such as Algeciras. Most visitors to the Canaries arrive by air, because of their location.

On the Spanish mainland transport is easy, with good rail and bus links and easily accessible car hire. Spain is also cheap compared with many destinations, which aids its accessibility.

The culture varies according to the area or resort in Spain and there are vast differences. In the cities the visitor is most likely to experience authentic Spanish culture with opportunities to see opera, dancing and arts events and try Spanish dishes and tapas. Around Holy Week there are many religious festivals in all areas.

On the Costa del Sol, in most of the Balearics and the Canaries the lifestyle and even use of English are similar to that at home. In some purpose-built resorts in the Canaries there are no local people to be found. Even the Spaniards here have arrived from other regions of Spain to find work in tourism.

The sun rather than wanderlust is the main motivation for travel to Spain, with decades of development having taken place to cater for western European sun-worshippers. Those looking for unspoilt Spain will head away from the costas and islands to the interior or northern coastal areas. Those motivated by the love of culture will travel to the cities of Barcelona to view the architecture of Gaudí or to Seville to experience the Easter festivities and religious parades.

Spain has beautiful coastlines (stretching 4,964 kilometres), and mountainous areas where skiing is popular in the Pyrenees and the Sierra Nevada. The climate is mild, with up to ten hours of sun in the summer and the highest temperatures in the south. The Canaries enjoy a temperate climate all year round and therefore attract those looking for winter sun.

Each area of Spain has its particular attractions. The cities have museums. Granada is famous for its beautiful setting and historical palace and buildings. There are plenty of attractions offering entertainment for families, such as waterparks and the famous theme park Portaventura, situated on the east coast near to Barcelona.

## Theory into practice

Mark the following costas on a map of Spain. Identify the gateway airports serving these areas. Find out which are the major resorts in the areas and locate and name them on the map. You can download a map from www.geoexplorer.com or you can use a map from your atlas.

- Costa Calida
- Costa de la Luz
- Costa Blanca
- Costa de Almería
- Costa Brava.
- Costa del Sol
- Costa Verde
- Costa Cantábrica
- Costa Dorada

## Theory into practice

Answer the following quiz questions on Spain.

1  In which city is the Prado museum?
2  Which city is famous for Gaudí's architecture?
3  Name the Balearic Islands.
4  Name the Canary Islands.
5  In which city is the Alhambra palace?
6  Which city hosted the 1992 Olympic Games?
7  Which football team signed David Beckham in 2003?
8  Which country, also famous for tourism, borders Spain to the west?
9  Gibraltar is a territory of which country?
10  What is the native language of Barcelona?

## ✳ REMEMBER!

Spain vies with France as the number one destination for UK tourists.

It has something to offer for everyone – beautiful beaches and cultural cities; it is well served by air links; it is inexpensive; and it is welcoming to tourists.

## Purpose-built resorts

A purpose-built resort is an area that has been developed solely for tourism. It has accommodation, transport links and tourist facilities and entertainment. Examples range from holiday centres like Center Parcs and Disneyland in Paris and the US, to a town carved out of the rock in Puerto Rico, Gran Canaria. In the UK one of our oldest and most famous purpose-built resorts is Butlins.

*Butlins is one of the most famous purpose-built resorts*

There are three Butlins resorts in the UK, all situated in seaside locations. They are at Bognor Regis, Minehead and Skegness. Each resort offers different kinds of accommodation, eating places, shops, swimming pools and plenty of entertainment. The main target is families on a limited budget, although Butlins has worked hard at extending the season by offering specialist short breaks and catering for the conference market.

Traditionally, Butlins was known as a holiday 'camp' rather than holiday centre, and it had an image of being cheap and cheerful. Billy Butlin opened the first camp in 1936. It remained a family operation until 1972 when it was bought by Rank.

Butlins now belongs to Bourne Leisure, one of Britain's largest holiday companies. It was acquired from Rank as part of a package of several holiday companies.

Rank spent £139 million refurbishing the three resorts over two years from 1998. One thousand new chalets were built, and a huge pavilion was added to each site with indoor shops and entertainment. But in spite of this investment Butlins did not attract enough customers and losses were made.

Bourne Leisure considered selling the operation but decided to try to turn around the business. The main problem was the family target. Now, families are the target only in peak season and the rest of the time Butlins offers 'entertainment breaks' aimed at adults.

Bourne has also invested £30 million in upgrading accommodation, landscaping, and updating the Redcoats' uniforms. In 2004 a spa centre opened at the Skegness resort. So far the results have been good, with turnover and spend per head increasing. Bourne has further plans – it intends to give each resort its own theme and to attract more conference business, as a Butlins resort can accommodate at least 5,000 people.

Find out more about the conference market at Butlins. Butlins brochures will be useful, and you could search for the Butlins and Bourne Leisure sites on the Internet.

1 Choose one of the three resorts and describe the appeal to customers. Remember to include transport links and all the other factors discussed in this unit.

 This task may provide evidence for P3.

2 Describe the appeal to a conference customer. Your customer is likely to be a large company or public sector operation which needs a large venue for a conference. Compare your findings with the appeal of another conference venue in Europe or worldwide.

 This task may provide evidence for M2.

## Natural and rural areas

Sometimes a natural or rural area is a destination in its own right. Ski resorts are obvious examples. There are many in Europe, including St Anton and Seefeld in Austria, and Interlaken and Wenden in Switzerland.

The areas around Italy's lakes are popular destinations, especially lakes Garda, Como, Maggiore and Orta.

In the UK we have 11 national parks which were designated under the National Parks and Access to the Countryside Act of 1949. These parks are attractive to tourists because of the natural habitat, and they are protected from development.

### Theory into practice

Find out the names of all the national parks in the UK and make sure you know their locations.

## CASE STUDY

The Everglades include an area of national park covering over a million acres in south Florida but this is only one-fifth of the Everglades area. Tourists visiting the resorts of Florida such as Orlando and the west coast beaches may also opt to visit this beautiful natural habitat.

The area is designated a World Heritage Site and a Wetland of International Importance. The Everglades comprise one of the largest freshwater marshes in North America and offer sawgrass marshes, wet prairies and mangrove swamps between the open seas of the coast and the uplands and freshwater wetlands. There are walking trails in the park and some that are suitable for bicycles. Tourists can also take boat trips through the swamps and look out for alligators. Most tourists visit the Everglades for a day trip from one of the neighbouring resorts, as the conditions are unpleasant for a long stay because of plenty of biting insects such as mosquitoes.

1 **Find out which resorts in Florida are near to the Everglades.**
2 **Suggest a day's activities for a group of friends visiting the Everglades. They will arrive by car. Use the Internet or brochures to gather your information and put it together in an information sheet.**

## Historical and cultural areas

Earlier in this unit we saw how culture is a factor that adds to the appeal of a destination, particularly some of Europe's cities. We saw too how a destination could be nominated European Capital of Culture and use this to promote itself to tourists.

Sometimes the history and culture of a region are so interesting that the whole tourist industry is based on that culture. Peru's wonderful Inca history has led to tourists following the 'Inca trail'. The following case study is an example of such tourism.

## CASE STUDY

Hiram Bingham, an American explorer, first discovered Machu Picchu in 1911. It is an Inca city located 120 kilometres north west of Cusco in Peru, and before discovery it was hidden by dense jungle on the mountains where it is located, 2,400 metres above sea level.

The city's stone constructions are spread over a narrow and uneven mountain top, bordering a sheer 400-metre drop over the Urubamba River canyon. Because of the fascinating architecture the site has been designated a Unesco World Heritage site and has become one of South America's major travel destinations.

Many adventure holiday companies offer tours there, and local operators sell day tours from Cusco. The only means of transport is a train from Cusco to Aguas Calientes, the nearest town to Machu Picchu. Then there is a 20-minute bus journey up the mountain to the ruins.

The popularity of the site has led to problems – it is in danger of being destroyed because of the large number of visitors. In the late 1990s visitors were restricted to 500 per day to protect the site. Unesco is considering a further restriction to 100 visitors per day.

1 **Find out more about Machu Picchu by researching on the Internet and in other resources. Report your findings.**
2 **Present the arguments for and against restricting visitor numbers. You could use your ideas for a debate in your group.**

## Business destinations

In 2003 research was commissioned by VisitScotland to find out more about trends in the business tourism market, particularly in conferences and meetings.

Association meetings are more frequent than corporate meetings, and therefore make up an important market for business tourism destinations. The US holds most international association meetings but France, Spain and Germany are also important. Barcelona, Paris, London, Brussels and Vienna are among the top city destinations. The UK is third for international association meetings but first in Europe for international corporate meetings.

Meetings are usually held in conference centres or hotels. May, June, September and October were found to be the most popular months for conferences.

### Theory into practice

Choose one of the business city destinations mentioned above. Produce a fact sheet suitable for distribution to a business person attending a conference. Include information on time (GMT or other), currency and exchange rate, language, business hours, transport, facilities for business, business hints, and attractions for spending free time.

# Tourism potential

Having looked at the appeal of destinations for tourists and at tourist motivation, it should be obvious that destinations have to change over time to accommodate the changing motivation and needs of tourists. Developments in transport and access open up new areas of the world and allow them to be developed for tourism. Governments and representatives from interested private sector companies have to work together to plan and develop areas so that tourism is sustainable and evolves without detriment to the interests of local people.

Study of the destination life cycle developed by R. Butler in 1980 helps us to understand how tourist areas develop and evolve. It cannot be strictly applied to all destinations, but is a useful planning guide and shows how destinations can be viewed as resources which have a finite life. Some communities become dependent on tourism and if a destination goes into decline their livelihood is at risk, as are the resources and infrastructure invested in tourism.

The diagram below depicts the destination life cycle. You will note the resemblance to the product life cycle (see page 87).

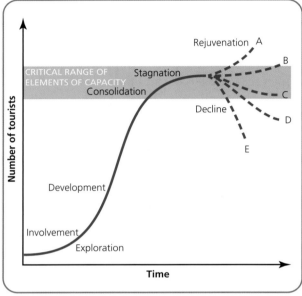

Source: Butler, 1980

## Stage 1 Exploration

At this stage there are few tourists. Awareness of the destination is very limited. In fact the few tourists are more likely to be termed 'travellers', as they are the type of people who are looking for adventure and new experiences. They will have found their own independent transport to the destination as the area will have poor access. There are few facilities and basic infrastructure. Nothing has been put in place for tourism and as there are so few tourists their impact is negligible. The local culture remains intact and the natural attractions undisturbed, adding to the attraction for the independent traveller.

## Stage 2 Involvement

The destination begins to develop, travel companies start to organise transport links and there is an increase in tourist numbers. Local people may start to take advantage of the new opportunities opening up to them and build facilities such as restaurants and offer accommodation in their homes. The public sector starts to investigate how tourism can be developed and to invest in facilities and infrastructure. There may be some advertising of the destination.

## Stage 3 Development

The early 'explorers' will no longer visit this destination. Instead the tourists are more institutionalised and likely to arrive on organised tours. There is a rapid growth in the number of tourists. The local people start to lose control of development as private companies move in and take control. There will be marked changes in infrastructure and in the appearance of the destination. There may be massive building projects for accommodation and also of attractions. The public sector's role is very important at this stage if the resident population's interests are to be protected and if tourism is to be sustainable. A tourist season will have emerged and there is heavy advertising to market the destination.

## Stage 4 Consolidation

Tourist numbers are still growing but not so rapidly. The host population has reached the state of resentment to tourists rather than expressing an interest in the visitors. There is extensive marketing to try to extend the season and attract yet more visitors.

## Stage 5 Stagnation

This is the stage of mass tourism. Peak numbers have been reached and the types of tourists are those who are looking for much the same experience as at home, possibly with a better climate. The natural environment may have been spoilt or hidden by the man-made attractions and infrastructure in place. The problems and negative impacts of tourism are most evident. The destination is over-commercialised and overcrowded.

## Stage 6 Decline

Some of the tourist facilities are closed or fall into disrepair as tourist numbers decline and the tourists go elsewhere. The destination may lose tourism altogether.

## Stage 7 Rejuvenation

If action is taken, destination managers can avoid the decline and the resort can be rejuvenated. This involves sometimes drastic action and redevelopment and the injection of capital.

A destination with tourism potential will be located at the start of the destination life cycle in 'exploration' or 'involvement'.

### CASE STUDY

**Faliraki**

Once a tiny fishing village you would be hard put to find a fisherman here now. Dubbed 'lively' in the brochures it is, in fact, little more than a noisy teenage play pen. Jet skiing, go-karting, even bungy jumping are on offer to the daily influx of frolicky young visitors whose idea of fun appears to be getting drunk on fizzy beer and making as much noise as they possibly can. And noise there is, brain-addling at night as the bars and clubs wind up to full power. The din is in evidence several kilometres away. Drinks cost up to six times supermarket prices and street touts for the clubs and bars can be persistent and aggressive. Beaches are a grey, gritty sand and packed with holidaymakers from dawn to well after dusk. Food here is as plastic as you would expect and the only good meal to be had is snapped up by millions of mosquitoes homing in from the nearby lowland to gorge on the bare teenage flesh. Perversely, recent hotel complexes have adopted a Cycladic village theme for those wishing to enjoy the 'Greek experience'. If you have a two-watt bulb for a brain and an ever-open wallet you will feel very much at home with the majority of visitors in this Greek version of the Spanish costas.

Source: www.greekisland.co.uk

1 **At what stage of the destination life cycle is Faliraki?**

2 **In your opinion does it have any future tourism potential? Consider what measures can be taken to attract tourists to Faliraki. Make some notes and discuss your ideas with your group.**

1 Give examples of sources of information on resorts.

2 Explain the terms 'tourism receiver' and 'tourism generator'.

3 What is the purpose of a search engine?

4 How do low-cost airlines keep costs down?

5 How does access affect the appeal of a destination?

6 Describe three different motivators for travel.

7 Why do tourists choose city breaks?

8 Why is Spain so attractive to the British?

9 Describe the stages of the destination life cycle.

10 Give examples of culture contributing to the appeal of a destination.

# UNIT 4 ASSESSMENT ASSIGNMENT

You work as an assistant for a tourism development consultant, Paul Richards. Paul is very experienced in assessing the tourism potential of destinations and putting together development plans, liaising with public and private interested parties. He is currently preparing background material that can be used in future presentations to show the scope of his business to potential clients. He needs to prepare presentation notes, information sheets or exhibition material which cover the following:

- why transport links are important in attracting tourists to a destination
- the factors that contribute to the appeal of destinations.

This information will demonstrate to potential clients the breadth of work that the company covers. Paul has asked you to carry out the research to provide the information for this presentation.

Identify three tourism-receiving areas, one in the UK, one in Europe and one worldwide. For each identify one of its tourism-generating areas. For example, you could choose:

| | |
|---|---|
| Receiving destination UK – York | Generating area – United States |
| Receiving destination Europe – Majorca | Generating area – Holland |
| Receiving destination worldwide – Orlando | Generating area – UK |

For the following tasks, effective use of an appropriate range of resources and research skills will provide evidence for P1. Carrying out sustained and independent research using accurate, reliable and sufficient data, and cross-checking for reliability, will provide evidence for D1.

1 Describe the transport routes that link each receiving destination with its tourist-generating area. For example, describe the transport routes that link the UK with Orlando. Make sure you include all modes of transport as applicable, that is, including road, sea and air links. Include gateways and transfers from gateways to final destinations. You might present this information in the form of an information sheet with maps, or as a poster with illustrations and explanations of the routes.

This task may provide evidence for P2.

2 For each of your chosen receiving destinations explain how the transport routes add to the appeal of that destination for different types of visitor. You should consider factors such as convenience, comfort, cost and length of journey. You might present this information as another poster or additional information sheet.

This task may provide evidence for M1

3 For each of your chosen destinations describe the factors that contribute to the appeal of the destination. Include all the factors discussed in this unit:

- access
- culture
- motivation of tourists
- geographical features
- natural and built attractions.

You might produce this information in the form of a fact file or brochure with illustrations.

This task may provide evidence for P3.

4   Identify three different types of visitors and compare and contrast the appeal of each of your chosen receiving destinations for the different visitor types. You might present this information in the form of a table like the one below. This could be added to a fact file or included in a poster. You should draw some conclusions from your comparison.

This task may provide evidence for M2.

| DESTINATION | HONEYMOON COUPLE | FAMILY WITH YOUNG CHILDREN | GROUP OF SINGLE FRIENDS |
|---|---|---|---|
| London | | | |
| Majorca | | | |
| Orlando | | | |

Paul also requires you to carry out research into destinations which have potential for tourism. He will use this information to make a proactive approach to local government in those areas, hoping to gain some new business.

5   Choose two destinations which have not yet been developed for tourism. The destinations should be in different locations. Remember the destination life cycle when making your choice – the destinations should be at the early stages of the cycle or at the stage where rejuvenation is possible. Locate and name your destinations on separate maps. Describe the current provision for tourism in these destinations.

This task may provide evidence for P4.

6   Explain why you think each area has potential for tourism.

This task may provide evidence for M3.

7   Explain how the location, infrastructure, transport links, accommodation and facilities could be developed to attract tourists. Justify your suggestions. This information could be presented in the form of a report for Paul or it could be presented in the form of information sheets. Provide a bibliography and ensure you use a range of cross-referenced and up-to-date, accurate resources.

This task may provide evidence for D2.

# UNIT 5

## SECTION 1: MANDATORY UNITS

# Customer service in travel and tourism

# Introduction

Customer Service in Travel and Tourism is a core unit for the qualification and an important skill for everyone working in the industry. It is essential to travel and tourism organisations that their staff provide excellent customer service. Many organisations provide similar products and services, and it may be that the level of customer service provided will determine with whom potential customers decide to book. This unit will develop your understanding of why customer service is so important to travel and tourism organisations, and give you the opportunity to develop skills so that you can deliver excellent customer service.

### How you will be assessed

This unit is internally assessed by your tutor. Throughout the unit activities and tasks will help you to develop your knowledge and understanding. Case studies are included to add industry relevance and demonstrate how aspects of customer service are carried out in particular travel and tourism organisations.

After completing this unit you should be able to achieve the following outcomes:

→ Explore how customer service is provided and the benefits it brings to the travel and tourism industry
→ Examine the issues and implications of delivering quality customer service
→ Use customer service skills to deal with customer situations
→ Demonstrate selling skills within travel and tourism contexts.

# Customer service and benefits

## Principles

The objective of travel and tourism organisations is not to meet customer expectations, but to *exceed* them. After all, many of the flights, holidays and hotels we book are very similar and are often within the same price range. So which company customers choose to book can be determined by the level of service provided – how friendly the travel consultant was, how quickly a phone call was returned, the personality of the receptionist or the cleanliness of the aircraft. As a travel and tourism employee you will need to be aware of the principles of customer service to ensure that customers book with you rather than your competitors.

### First impressions count!

> **Consider this ...**
>
> Have you ever walked into a shop and walked out again within a very short space of time? What was it that made you leave? What aspects created the impression that it was not worth waiting?

It takes customers just ten seconds to form their first impression. These first impressions could be formed by seeing:

* a queue of customers – or being served immediately
* staff talking to each other and ignoring their customers – or being greeted with a smile
* scruffy staff who are chewing gum – or well-dressed staff with a professional appearance
* staff slouching over desks – or positive behaviour and body language
* eating in the office – or clear, tidy desks.

Once a negative first impression is formed, it is very difficult to change.

> **✱ REMEMBER!**
>
> Research shows that it costs five times as much to attract a new customer as to retain an existing one. Organisations need to ensure that they retain their customers.

**Personal presentation** is an important element of a first impression. Your personal presentation reveals how you feel about yourself, your customers and your level of professionalism. Travel and tourism is such a 'people' business that you should be aware of the importance of personal presentation and the impact it will have on customers and their confidence in your ability to provide a good service. Customers will judge you (and the organisation you work for) on:

* your appearance – what you are wearing, whether it is neat and tidy or in need of ironing
* how you care for yourself – is your hair neat, jewellery discreet and nails clean?
* your body language – how you express yourself (see page 141)
* how you greet your customer – are you enthusiastic and smiling?
* how organised you are – is your desk neat and the filing system organised, enabling you to find information quickly and easily?

In order to encourage good personal presentation, some organisations provide staff with a uniform. This is usual for staff in roles dealing directly with customers such as in a travel agency, working in an overseas resort, a local guide or in a Tourist Information Centre.

There are many benefits of staff being in uniform:

* customers immediately know who the staff are – this is particularly important in some roles, e.g. as an overseas resort representative or a ride attendant at a theme park

* a corporate image is developed

* staff feel they are part of the company – and the team

* the organisation has direct control over what staff wear.

Guidelines regarding the wearing of the uniform, caring for it and other aspects of personal presentation are usually provided. For example, Virgin Atlantic requires its female cabin crew to manicure and varnish their nails.

**Consider this ...**

Uniforms are not usually provided for staff who do not deal with customers. Examples include tour operators' head office staff, airline administration staff and back-office staff at tourist attractions. However, many do provide a dress code. Why do they consider this necessary? What impact does this have?

## CASE STUDY

Travel and tourism employers take a dim view of staff wanting to express their individuality too strongly, preferring to present a more conventional face to their customers. Forget tattoos! And body piercing is strictly limited to the ear lobes. As each summer arrives, so do workplace issues over skimpy attire, and the tattoos and piercing that may be exposed as a result.

However, it is clear that a balance has to be struck between the employers' business interests and the reasonable freedom of the employee. Many travel and tourism organisations now provide guidelines regarding dress codes. Examples are shown below.

| Thomas Cook | Customer-facing staff are not allowed to wear facial studs or body piercing. Women are allowed to wear earrings, but men are not. Tattoos must be covered. |
|---|---|
| First Choice | Uniforms are made to measure – thus ruling out problems of rising hemlines! |
| Thomson | Staff are not allowed to alter their uniforms. |
| Virgin Holidays | Nose studs are allowed only for religious reasons. Business dress must be worn by all customer-facing staff. For hairstyles, no Mohican cuts or weird and wacky colours are allowed. |
| MM Group (a call centre representing EasyJet and the UK Passport Agency) | Formal dress is required at all times. |

1  Do you think guidelines should be issued to all employees? Within the same organisation, should customer-facing and back-office staff receive the same guidelines?

2  Why do you think the MM Group (a call centre) insists on business dress?

**Body language** is another important element that can form a first impression. It is estimated that we convey more messages by the way we stand, use eye contact, hold our heads, gesticulate and use facial expressions than we do with our words.

## Theory into practice

Work with a partner. Take it in turns to choose one of the feelings listed below and to act it out. Use facial expressions, gesticulate, etc. but don't speak! How successful is your partner at interpreting your body language?

- angry
- upset
- exhausted
- cheerful/happy
- confused
- bored
- excited

Similarly our **tone of voice** can indicate how we are really feeling. We can use the same words in two different situations but our tone of voice may make the words carry an opposite meaning. It's not what we say but how we say it that makes the difference.

Your body language and tone of voice will determine whether the word 'hello' is meant as a cheery sign that you recognise someone, a threat, a put down or an ecstatic greeting! A good actor will be able to convey at least a dozen different meanings with the word 'no'.

## Consider this ...

An important aspect of providing good customer service is recognising customers' feelings. Watching body language and listening to the tone of voice are the best ways of working out what your customer is really feeling.

## Theory into practice

Work with a partner. Imagine you have just been asked to a party. Say 'Thanks, I would love to come' (or a similar positive phrase indicating you wish to go). Say the phrase in as many different tones as you can. You partner must interpret what you are really meaning – some of these may indicate that you do not want to go at all! You must use the same words each time and change only your tone of voice to indicate a different meaning.

## Key concept

Research shows that the tone of voice we use and our body language convey much more than the words we use.

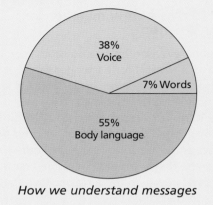

*How we understand messages*

## Theory into practice

How are these people feeling?

## CASE STUDY

Read the following extract from the Virgin Atlantic Cabin Crew Manual.

### Your role as a crew member for Virgin Atlantic

The primary reason for having cabin crew on board an aircraft is for passenger safety. It is, however, no good being a role model in safety aspects, if levels of customer service are inadequate. The ongoing success of Virgin Atlantic depends on the service we offer and the care and concern we extend to our customers. They will judge us in the first ten seconds of boarding the aircraft. Have they been acknowledged? Have they received a genuine smile? Are the crew giving out positive body language? Has sufficient eye contact been used? Has a friendly and approachable stance been intimated? Is the appearance and grooming of the crew perfect? All these things from you, in addition to the appearance of the aircraft and cabin!

It is imperative that a good impression is created from the outset. You will not get a second chance to make a first impression. You are 'the company' from the customers' viewpoint.

After the first impression has been created, it is important that consistency is maintained throughout the flight.

Our objective must be that our customer service always exceeds passenger expectations and that there is no doubt that they will travel with Virgin Atlantic Airways on their next trip.

1  What does Virgin mean by a 'genuine' smile?
2  Why is eye contact so important?
3  What does a 'friendly and approachable stance' mean?
4  How can you be 'the company' for the customers?
5  Give three examples of how cabin crew can give consistent service.

## Communication

Whatever form of communication you have with customers (whether on the telephone, face to face or in writing), the aim is to exceed customers' expectations and send them away satisfied.

Later in the unit communication skills will be examined in more detail. Whatever the situation, the following sequence is likely to happen in a face-to-face meeting with a customer:

**Greet the customer**

> Remember, first impressions count! Smile as you greet the customer. Be warm, friendly and positive.

**Listen carefully – each customer is an individual**

> All customers are individuals with differing feelings and different needs. Some will have very different opinions from you!

**Establish the customer's needs**

> The customer will tell you some of his or her needs but you may need to ask further questions.

**Whatever service is required, you need to be able to work quickly and accurately to provide it**

> Your product knowledge will determine how quickly and efficiently you can work. Do you know where Bournemouth, Benidorm and Barcelona are – or do you have to look them up? Is your drawer organised, is your diary up to date and can you find your way around the computer reservation systems easily?

**Meet the customer's needs (and exceed customer expectations!)**

> Your aim is to provide the customer with what he or she wants and in doing so to exceed expectations. You will need good customer service skills to do this. Selling skills may also be required.

**Produce a satisfied customer**

> The ultimate objective is a satisfied customer who has had an enjoyable experience being served by you.

Customers buy products or services because they believe they **need** them, e.g. a drink, car or holiday. **Expectations** refer to what the customer expects from the product or service. A drink may satisfy a need (thirst) but not meet expectations if it does not taste as good as the customer thought it would. So if a customer enters a travel agency needing a summer holiday for a family of four, he or she may also have certain expectations about the costs, ideal locations and activities available. You could meet these needs (by selling a holiday for the family) but to exceed expectations you will need also to provide details of excursion possibilities, airport transfers, free child places and car hire.

Read the extract from the *Travel Trade Gazette*, 'Nuptials in the nude'. Would you be equal to dealing with such requests? Remember, each customer must be treated as an individual and whatever the request, surprise should not be shown! The customer must never be humiliated.

## Nuptials in the nude? You've got to be joking

YOU'VE CHOSEN the perfect holiday to the Maldives to get romantic with your partner. Your bag is packed but there's one problem … you are undecided about which of your lovers to take with you.

The solution? Ask the travel agent if they can put 'to be confirmed' on your booking to give you time to choose the perfect travelling companion.

The situation may be a real dilemma for the cheating lothario, but is nonetheless highly entertaining for the agent taking the booking.

This is just one of the more bizarre requests received by travel agents, which have been published in a list following a survey by Virgin Flightstore. Travel agents were asked to divulge the funniest requests they have had from customers.

One client requested a wife-swap holiday, while another couple asked for a nudist wedding abroad.

Meanwhile, a transvestite customer asked what would be suitable attire for him to wear while away – dressed as both a woman and a man.

And let's not forget the first-time flyer who asked for a window seat – so she could open it for air.

*Travel Trade Gazette*, 2 July 2004

## CASE STUDY

'Mystery shopping' is used by many companies to assess the performance of their staff. Organisations employ people to visit shops or make sales enquires, pretending to want to purchase products and services. They assess the performance of staff and submit reports.

The mystery shopper below wanted to purchase a holiday. She asked for a two-week holiday in August for three single mums with children. She visited four agents and submitted the following report:

### Agent 1

*Brochures offered: None*

This agency was so busy that I had to call back. When I returned a consultant approached me and I explained that I wanted to book something for the school holidays, and that we were looking for a good deal, probably self-catering. The clerk then questioned if a villa would be suitable.

I was told that for the time of year we wanted to travel the price would be between £1,800 and £3,200. Villas were mentioned again and I got the impression that the agent was only interested in selling villa holidays.

I wasn't offered any brochures during my visit and I felt uncomfortable, as though my enquiry wasn't that important. I wasn't even asked if I would like to sit down.

I asked for a business card but was disappointed to find that it didn't have the agent's name on it.

*Score out of 100: 24 points*

### Agent 2

*Brochures offered: Aspro Holidays; Airtours*

I was offered a seat immediately. An agent searched through different options and asked whether I wanted half-board or self-catering, for how long we wanted to travel and from which airport.

All this information was fed into the computer and various options appeared on the screen.

The clerk highlighted relevant deals and was very efficient, but after a while I began to get confused. There were two offers that caught my eye but she could not find one of them in a brochure.

By now – one hour later – I was totally confused and felt loaded with too much information. I then had to prompt the agent to give me details for the two holidays she had first mentioned.

*Score out of 100: 63 points*

## Agent 3

*Brochures offered: JMC; Thomson Summer Sun*

I was approached promptly by a junior member of staff. I said I was looking for a holiday during the school summer breaks and was referred to another agent who asked me to take a seat.

I told her my full requirements, and she found a couple of options for Menorca and Portugal. She mentioned that they were late deals.

Although she was professional and efficient, I felt there were other options she could have told me about.

Although the options offered fitted my criteria, I felt there was too much use of the computer and not enough individual tailoring applied during the enquiry.

I felt her product knowledge was excellent but she just didn't 'sell' the holiday to me. The price was probably right for my budget but I did not feel inspired by the agent's sales technique.

A bit more of a personal touch would have been welcome.

*Score out of 100: 70 points*

## Agent 4

*Brochures offered: Skytours; Thomson Summer Sun*

I was met by a friendly consultant who offered me a seat and made me feel relaxed. All members of staff were smiling and busy doing various tasks.

My agent seemed genuinely interested in me as a customer and made every effort to ask key questions before searching the computer. After a lengthy discussion I was shown a variety of options on the computer and we picked out particular deals while making use of the brochures.

The clerk was very helpful and an excellent listener – she pointed out hotels which were particularly suitable for children.

She didn't just provide me with the facts, she also took the trouble to tailor-make a holiday to suit my individual requirements.

An excellent service.

*Score out of 100: 87 points*

## All in all – summary

The winning agent not only offered several child-friendly holiday options, but also made the mystery shopper feel perfectly at ease. This ability should not be underestimated.

The runner-up was helpful but could have offered more information on specific destinations. She did not create a sense of urgency to book.

The second runner-up scored quite well, but needed to give more details about the two preferred options. Instead, the mystery shopper was bombarded with a wealth of information about less suitable holidays.

The fourth-placed agent scored poorly. The shopper felt pushed towards a villa holiday only, regardless of the request. There was no interest shown in the request. No brochures were used.

*Travel Trade Gazette*, 23 July 2004

1  **Make a list of all the factors the mystery shopper used to form her judgements about the agencies visited.**
2  **Use the list to create a set of guidelines for dealing with customers in a travel agency.**

Product knowledge is an important aspect of customer service. However, a travel consultant in a travel agency cannot be familiar with all destinations worldwide. How can he or she ensure that an excellent service is still provided?

## ✱ REMEMBER!

Everyone working in travel needs to know the phonetic alphabet and the 24-hour clock. They will help you provide an error-free service. Make sure you learn them!

## Speed and accuracy of service

In order to be able to provide a fast and efficient service, several skills are needed. First, you must be organised. You will not be able to know everything – but you must know where to find out about it! So if a customer wants to book a long-haul holiday bird-watching in Madagascar, you should know which resources to use to establish which tour operators sell such specialist holidays.

Second, you need product knowledge, that is ideally you will know where Madagascar is. However, again if you don't it is important that you can quickly look it up on the Internet, bespoke software or in the *World Travel Guide* and establish that it is an island in the Indian Ocean, off the coast of Mozambique.

Product knowledge also includes information about your organisation – what it sells, who to refer complaints to, opening times, and how to use the computer and telephone systems effectively. All of these will help you to provide a speedy and accurate service.

The phonetic alphabet is used for clarity in various forms of communication. For example, pilots use it on radios and a tour operator may use it on the telephone.

The 24-hour clock is used by the travel industry worldwide to avoid mistakes and confusion between am and pm when reading timetables.

The day starts at one minute past midnight (0001) and the following 12 hours follow the normal system; 1 pm becomes 1300 hours, 2 pm is 1400 hours and so on until we reach midnight. In the travel industry, midnight is not represented as 2400 hours but as 2359 hours in order to make it clear which day is being referred to. The next day is 0001 hours.

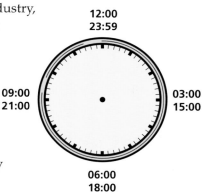

| PHONETIC ALPHABET | | | | | | | | |
|---|---|---|---|---|---|---|---|---|
| A | Alpha | | B | Bravo | | C | Charlie | |
| D | Delta | | E | Echo | | F | Foxtrot | |
| G | Golf | | H | Hotel | | I | India | |
| J | Juliet | | K | Kilo | | L | Lima | |
| M | Mike | | N | November | | O | Oscar | |
| P | Papa | | Q | Quebec | | R | Romeo | |
| S | Sierra | | T | Tango | | U | Uniform | |
| V | Victor | | W | Whiskey | | X | X-ray | |
| Y | Yankee | | Z | Zulu | | | | |

## Working as a team

Teamwork can be wonderful – and it can also be very difficult. You will be able to recall projects where friction has arisen with colleagues because someone has not done their fair share of the work.

All work in the travel industry involves teamwork at some stage. If a team works well, it is more likely to provide an excellent service. Imagine arriving in your holiday resort and finding that someone in the resort team had not told the transfer rep that the flight was going to be early!

A good team will:

* want to achieve the same goals
* have a leader
* involve everyone in the team
* be confident and have self-esteem
* communicate well with each other
* make clear decisions
* pay attention to detail

* respect and trust each other
* have clear roles and responsibilities
* support each other
* have a 'can do' approach.

You will look at teamwork in more detail in Unit 6. The case study below shows an extract from Thomson Holidays' Children's Representatives Programme.

## Customer charters

A customer charter is a document written by an organisation to tell customers about the minimum levels of service they can expect from the organisation. It acts as a guarantee of service to the customer but can also be used as a guide to staff. It may include, for example, how quickly a complaint will be dealt with, when tickets will be received and how customer will be compensated in the event of cancellation or delay. Sometimes this information is included in the booking conditions.

## CASE STUDY

### Resort teams

Teams in resort are large and you will be working with many people, not just Thomson staff but hoteliers and officials to name but two. There should always be an attitude of open co-operation within teams, an ideal of working towards the same goal. Although this is sometimes difficult it is essential to focus on what is really important – the customers and their holiday. It is easy to get carried away with personal thoughts and feelings when working in a team but everyone should have their focus on the customer; they pay the wages at the end of the day.

The start of the season is the ideal opportunity to set up your working standards with everyone you are likely to work with. There will probably be one or two people who would not be the colleagues you would choose; your challenge will be to work well with these people despite your personal feelings. If you do that, then the customers will benefit and so will you. There is much more achievement in working well for a full season with someone you don't really like, than there is in

moaning and feeling sorry for yourself all summer. Who knows, with your efforts, you may even end up good friends (it often happens!).

Many problems occur in teams because members don't know or understand each other well enough, so make sure you try hard. Talk to your colleagues and really listen to them. Other issues come up because of misunderstandings, which usually occur because of a lack of agreement about standards you will work to, who will do what, etc. It is important that you get the team together and discuss the problems.

It is sometimes difficult to talk to a colleague about something you are unhappy with – but you are much more likely to get it sorted if you do talk!

Source: Children's Representatives Programme,
Thomson Holidays

1 Why do problems occur in teams?
2 How can they be prevented?
3 What are the potential benefits of working in a team?

# Benefits of providing excellent customer service

It is recognised that the provision of excellent customer service is essential to a travel and tourism organisation, with benefits for both the staff and the customers.

## Customer benefits

If the principles of good customer service are followed, satisfied customers will feel they have been greeted warmly, dealt with by friendly and efficient staff, and received the goods or services they want. They will go away having had their needs met and an enjoyable experience.

Over the long term, customer loyalty will develop – so that a customer would not dream of going elsewhere. They will tell their friends about your products and services too.

> Positive first impression
> Professional presentation/appearance of all staff
> Customer greeted warmly
> Positive body language
> Accurate information provided quickly
> Clear and accurate communication
> Colleagues working well as a team

> Customers' needs are met
> The experience is enjoyable
> The experience is stress-free
> Customers like the organisation and want to return (customer loyalty)

> Satisfied customers

## Staff benefits

Providing excellent service, and as a result dealing with satisfied customers, is very rewarding for employees. It is satisfying to be thanked for kindness, efficiency, solving a problem or providing advice. Positive feedback from customers provides job satisfaction and a feeling of well-being. This can contribute towards a good working environment in which everyone is working as a team and supporting each other. For some individuals this may lead to promotion – perhaps with a pay increase. The overall result of excellent service and satisfied customers is a staff team that is productive and positive.

Further benefits to staff may include job security – after all, with a good sales record, customers who keep returning and positive feedback, your position in the organisation will be secure. This may enhance your prospects for training and promotion – and may give you a sense of personal satisfaction as well as financial security.

## Benefits to the organisation

All businesses are dependent upon their customers. Whether public, private or voluntary, all organisations aim to provide a high level of customer satisfaction, so that the customers return (bringing repeat business) and ensure the continuation of the organisation. Increased sales may result from repeat business or the fact that the satisfied customers tell other people – who then wish to purchase the same product or service. All this results in increased profits for the organisation.

The public image of a company is the view held of that company by the general public. This is difficult to determine but is often related to what you read in the press about the company. It will be influenced by the service people receive from sales consultants, experience of the product or service and after-sales service.

For example, imagine you book a flight on the Internet. You may already have an image of the airline from previous experiences or word of mouth. However, this image will also be influenced by the design of the website, its ease of use, and the destinations available. Once on the flight, your image will be further amended by the appearance and customer service levels of the cabin crew, the pilot and whether or not you and your luggage arrive at the same destination on time! The image you had of the airline before the flight could be very different from the one you have when you arrive at your destination.

Competitive advantage may also result from excellent customer service. Customers will choose to travel with those companies that offer a reliable and consistent service.

Excellent service

↓

Satisfied customers

↓

Good public image and public relations
Positive relationships with the press
Customers return (repeat business)
Good working environment for staff
A positive, happy workforce

↓

Increased sales/profits

## CASE STUDY

### Cunard pushes reality of QM2

Report by **Sarah Thomas**

**CUNARD boss Peter Shanks has hit out at media coverage of the four-hour delay on the homecoming voyage of Queen Mary 2 to Southampton.**

The company faced a barrage of negative press last week following a technical fault. Cunard is determined to bring agents on board to show them the reality of the ship.

European senior vice-president Peter Shanks said: 'QM2 is a very high-profile ship, which has its upsides, but it also means there are stories which are wide of the mark. We have plans for key journalists and agents to come on board to see how the ship is performing.'

This latest incident occurred when bow thruster doors failed to close in Lisbon and had to be shut manually. The 1,310-cabin liner was due to set sail for Southampton at the conclusion of a 16-day voyage from Fort Lauderdale. Shanks said the 'negative slant' of the press had been out of proportion.

He said flights and accommodation details for late-returning passengers due to travel elsewhere were dealt with by Cunard, while outgoing passengers were offered lunch and complimentary drinks. The ship set sail again at 9.15 pm instead of its scheduled time of 6 pm on Easter Monday.

'We did our absolute best to look after customers', he said.

The national press was due to join the ship last week, while plans to host a number of trade partners during the summer are also under way.

Shanks said these plans had always been in place regardless of press coverage.

He added bookings were currently holding up 'extremely well' and there was 'no correlation' between booking performance and negative coverage.

*Travel Weekly, 19 April 2004*

1  **Why had the *Queen Mary* 2 received bad publicity? Why is Cunard critical of the press?**
2  **Name two things Cunard did to minimise problems for passengers caused by the delay.**
3  **How is Cunard planning to improve press relations?**

**Theory into practice**

Use the Internet to investigate the aims and objectives of three travel and tourism organisations. You may also wish to look at their mission statements. What other objectives do organisations have? How important do you think customer service is to each organisation?

Front-line staff, that is those dealing directly with customers, may be the only people from the organisation that customers meet. For example, the only people from an airline that customers meet are the cabin crew and check-in staff, while the resort representatives will be the only people the customer meet from a tour operator. These staff have a key role in determining customer satisfaction levels. It is therefore essential that travel organisations train front-line staff well – the costs of poor service far outweigh the costs of training.

**Theory into practice**

1  We know that it costs five times as much to attract a new customer as to retain an existing one. List the costs involved in attracting new customers and those involved in retaining existing ones.

2  It is estimated that dissatisfied customers tell between six and eight other people, while satisfied customers tell one. What implications does this have for organisations?

## Customer types

You have already seen that the objective of customer service is to meet customer needs and exceed expectations. In order to do this it is first necessary to *understand* customers' needs – but this is easier said that done. After all, there are many different types of customers all of whom have different needs.

To be able to provide excellent customer service, organisations must understand their customers, recognise their differing needs and provide products and services that meet their requirements. For example, a tour operator will provide a different holiday and range of excursions for a single person, a group of young people wanting to go clubbing, and a couple wanting to escape the British winter. Similarly, on a day trip to a theme park a young couple will have different needs from a family with two children.

### Internal and external customers

Before looking at different customer types it is important to differentiate between internal and external customers. Colleagues are known as

**internal customers**, while people outside the organisation are known as **external customers**.

It is perhaps more obvious why caring for external customers is so important. After all, an organisation is dependent upon them to buy products and services. Without external customers, organisations don't exist – they need sales to make profits and pay wages.

But internal customer service is also important to an organisation. How you deal with colleagues, how you behave in the office and your level of efficiency will all affect your working relationships. This can impact upon how well a team works together, relationships with managers and overall productivity. All of these can also have an effect on job satisfaction and staff morale – which in turn can influence the customer service provided.

Internal customers include the following.

✳ Colleagues who work together – this may be on a daily basis, such as in a travel agency, or on an ad hoc basis, such as cabin crew.

✳ People in different departments who support the customer-facing staff – accounts departments are a good example of support staff whose levels of service can have a high impact. How quickly they send out refunds or are able to answer invoice queries will have a direct influence on the level of customer service that front-office staff can provide.

✳ Managers and supervisors – how quickly, efficiently and accurately you deliver information to your boss will also determine his or her level of efficiency. Leaving tasks to the last minute, delivering sloppy work or not meeting deadlines will affect how well your boss can work – and his or her attitude towards you.

✳ Suppliers – people or organisations that contribute towards the product or service you provide have an important effect on overall service. Examples include food companies that provide airlines with in-flight meals; cleaning organisations that clean the offices each morning; a coach company that provides airport transfers for the tour operator; a company that prints leaflets for the Tourist Information Centre.

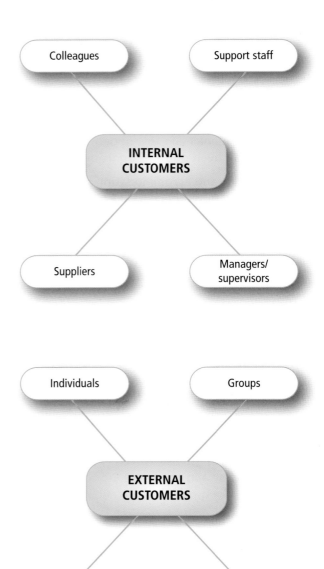

We will now examine some of the different types of external customers and how their needs may differ.

## Individuals

People travel alone for many different reasons. They may be travelling on business, wanting to participate in a specialist activity, or hoping to meet a partner. Some may choose to travel alone, while others may do so reluctantly. Some single travellers are young (18–30) while many are over 50 and some over 70. All such individuals will have differing needs. These must be provided for by airlines, tour operators, airports, hotels and their staff.

## CASE STUDY

### Friendship adds Prague breaks

SINGLES specialist Friendship Travel has added city breaks to Prague and Istanbul, as well as holidays in the Caribbean, to its brochure for this winter and next summer.

The operator, which claims to be the only singles company to sell through the trade, has reported an increase in demand for city breaks.

Two-night breaks in Prague start at £298 for departures on November 26. The price includes flights, transfers and half-board accommodation at the four-star Hotel Movenpick.

Seven-night Caribbean holidays start at £849, including flights from Gatwick, transfers and all-inclusive accommodation in the Dominican Republic.

Managing director Colum McLornan said: 'All-inclusive options in the Caribbean are an ideal choice for the single holidaymaker.

'Guests can relax and take in the free on-site activities during the day, then enjoy the companionship of other members of the group in the evening.'

Friendship Travel caters for the over-25s and pays 10% commission to agents.

*Travel Trade Gazette*, 6 August 2004

1  **Friendship Travel is a specialist tour operator catering for single customers. List all the products and services it could provide to meet the needs of these customers (e.g. room share, dinners at set times so that everyone eats together).**
2  **Check its website for more information and to see if you have missed anything.**

# CASE STUDY

## ARE YOU SLEEPING COMFORTABLY?

### British Airways Club World

LOUNGE: BA's Terraces lounges are oases of calm: tinkling water, piped birdsong and soft colours. A Molton Brown spa offers massages, and the business centre has high-speed Internet access. 10/10

SEAT: Can you get a good night's sleep? The answer is yes, but there's still that odd seat divider to sort out and downstairs on a full plane can resemble a dormitory. But lots of space, good-sized TV screen and footstool make this still one of the comfiest beds in the air. 9/10

SERVICE: When the service is good, it's impeccable; but when it's not so good it can make a six-hour flight seem much longer. 9/10

EXTRAS: The Molton Brown products in the amenity kit and the open snack bar are nice touches, but BA has a long way to go if it wants to match Virgin's in-flight masseuse. 6/10

FOOD: BA's cuisine is hard to beat, as is its well-thought-out wine list. Starters range from chilli prawns to light salads, and main courses include salmon, green chicken tikka and roast beef. 10/10

ENTERTAINMENT: Good-sized screens and large selection of channels, but it's antiquated compared with Virgin's on-demand entertainment system. 8/10

OVERALL IMPRESSION: Style and luxury means Club World will always be popular with the business traveller, especially with new touches such as the sleeper service (with bigger pillows and thicker blankets). But for some travellers it's not private enough and BA needs to address this issue before rivals steal its crown.

TOTAL: 52/60

### Virgin Atlantic Upper Class Suite

LOUNGE: Funky and hip, the Virgin Clubhouse at Heathrow has a bar, games zone, business area, spa and upstairs quiet zone. Lots to do and an excellent selection of food. 10/10

SEAT: Just four abreast, so no clambering over people even by the window. And due to the design, each seat is self-contained with a stool for your feet, shoe storage or a guest for dinner. The seat flips over to form a fully flat bed. A big table for eating or working, and lots of space above and below for storage. 10/10

SERVICE: Virgin is known for its service and delivers in spades. Nothing seems too much trouble for the crew, who go out of their way to ensure you are comfortable. 10/10

EXTRAS: On-board massage is unique to Virgin and a great extra; the amenity kit includes the excellent red-eye reduction eye mask. The bar is another great idea and is now at the back of the cabin to avoid disturbing other passengers. 10/10

FOOD: The food in the lounge – sushi and dim sum – is delicious, and a perfect light meal pre-flight. On board, the selection is not as extensive as you might expect. 8/10

ENTERTAINMENT: Virgin's on-demand system allows you to watch what you want when you want. Large selection of new and old movies, TV programmes, music and games. 10/10

OVERALL IMPRESSION: The Upper Class Suite ticks all the boxes for the executive: privacy, comfort and lots of space. Virgin has set the business travel bar extremely high and it's difficult to see how it will be topped.

TOTAL: 58/60

*Travel Trade Gazette* Business, August 2004

1  List all the products and services that BA and Virgin Atlantic provide for their business customers.
2  Is there anything else they could do to ensure the comfort of these passengers?
3  Why is so much provided for business customers?

## Groups

Groups include school groups, special interest groups, and friendship groups.

Some groups may all know each other and have similar needs (such as a group of young men wishing to go on a day trip white-water rafting). They may be happy to be treated as a single entity for the purpose of their day trip. However, a coach party of Americans who have booked a Blue Badge Guide for their tour of Cambridge may all have differing needs. Some will want to visit King's College, others may wish to go shopping and others may want to enjoy an afternoon's punting on the river.

For those dealing with groups, it is important to remember that the group is actually made up of many individuals – and to consider their individual needs. This can be very demanding.

## Customers with special/specific needs

Some customers may have specific needs, which may require additional and sensitive customer service. This may be because they:

* do not speak English

* come from a different culture (e.g. ethnic minorities)

* have special dietary needs

* are minors travelling alone

* are travelling with young children

* have mobility problems (e.g. wheelchair users)

* have a hearing impairment

* have a visual impairment

* have speech difficulties.

## CASE STUDY

Newmarket Travel Service looks after the travel arrangements of Group Organisers. Our clients include a large number of sports and social clubs from across the spectrum of commerce and industry, a wide and diverse selection of special interest groups and a large number of groups from Probus, U3A, National Trust Associations and Active Retired Association groups.

For over twenty years we have delivered a friendly and efficient service to our clients, as well as high quality, value for money travel arrangements to the tens of thousands of passengers who have travelled with us.

Our Group Travel Advisors can help you with your travel arrangements to a range of destinations which currently includes the UK, Europe, North America and even further afield. We arrange a vast array of short breaks by coach and air and a significant number of coach-inclusive touring programmes.

If your group is looking for something a little different, our 'Tailor Made' service can be used. Our experience, resources and purchasing power can be harnessed to produce a competitive quotation for a wide range of travel arrangements for groups.

Thousands of smaller groups – friends from the office, club, family circle – have, since 1994, taken advantage of our 'Minimum Ten' programme of breaks and tours. We pick you up from your chosen pick-up point (if it's a coach-inclusive break) and guarantee the price, just as long as your group consists of at least ten passengers. All the tours are supported by posters and detailed itineraries, helping you 'sell' the trip to your friends and fellow group members.

Our knowledgeable and friendly team is waiting to help you. We look forward to the pleasure of your group's company … and Happy Travelling!

Source: www.newmarkettravel.co.uk

1  Who does Newmarket Travel Service cater for? (Give five examples.)
2  What specialist services does Newmarket Travel Service offer for the groups?

It is clear that all customers with specific needs must be treated individually. Many people are unsure how to deal with specific needs and this can result in customers feeling insulted or patronised.

The extract below gives an example of how organisations can meet such needs effectively. It is from the 'Exhibitions/Events/Courses' leaflet of the Fitzwilliam Museum in Cambridge.

### Access

The Courtyard Entrance provides street-level entry to the Museum with easy access to the main temporary exhibitions gallery and to galleries and services on all floors. This entrance should be used by **groups, schools, wheelchair users** and those who find stairs difficult.

### Visitors with disabilities

Museum wheelchairs are available at the Courtyard Entrance on request. Fully accessible WCs and lift access to all floors. Induction loop available for gallery talks and events. A large-print Information and Events leaflet is available. Special sessions and events for visitors with sensory or mobility impairment or other particular need; contact Education Department on 01223 332904.

### Consider this ...

The Disability Discrimination Act 1995 introduced new laws aimed at ending the discrimination some customers faced. The law requires service providers to make 'reasonable adjustments' to ensure their premises are accessible to those with a sensory, physical or mental disability which seriously affects their day-to-day activities. Around 8.6 million people, or 1 in 7 of the UK population, fall into this category.

The Disability Discrimination Act covers building design and construction, building approaches and exits, as well as public places such as footpaths and parks. Printed material, such as brochures or menus, may also need to be available in braille or audio formats, and websites should be suitable for disabled users.

### Theory into practice

Investigate a large hotel, an airport, an airline or a mass-market tour operator. What particular products or services does this organisation provide to meet the needs of different customers? You may wish to consider the needs of single women travellers, business customers, children travelling alone (airlines only), people of different ethnic origins, group bookings, people of different religions, disabled travellers.

## CASE STUDY

### Thomas Cook

THOMAS COOK aims to recruit more mature staff in a bid to match staff with its customer profile.

The company says shop staff do not reflect the ageing of the UK population – 67% of sales consultants are aged 16–34 while just 3% are aged 55 or over.

But consumers aged over 55 represent a quarter of all sales made through Thomas Cook stores.

Cook's head of human resources development, Colin Dalby, admitted the 'low pay environment' made recruiting older people more difficult.

A more diverse age range is just one element of Thomas Cook's aim for its retail sales workforce.

It is also chasing a rise in male recruits – at present 89 out of every 100 sales staff are women; a wider ethnic mix; and staff who are able to work more flexible hours.

'At the moment, our peak store trading hours are between 11.00 and 15.00 – but this is when staff are out for lunch. This is a real problem for shops,' said Dalby.

To combat this problem, Thomas Cook aims to recruit more flexible staff, such as 'key time workers' over the lunch period, staff on nil-hour contracts who can be called up at short notice, long-term temps and graduates.

*Travel Trade Gazette*, 25 June 2004

1 **Why is Thomas Cook recruiting more mature staff?**
2 **What does 'customer profile' mean?**
3 **List the other changes that Thomas Cook intends to make to its staffing profile.**
4 **Do you think these will help provide excellent service?**

*Customer Services team at BAA Stansted*

Hi, I am Paula Heffron, Head of Customer Services at BAA Stansted. I am delighted that you are studying customer service. It is an issue we take very seriously within BAA and at Stansted Airport and we are very proud of the service we offer.

You will appreciate that handling over 20 million passengers a year, up to 75,000 in one day, can be a challenging operation with the variety of scenarios it presents. Add to this that the general public are, rightly, more and more demanding of excellent service (even if they are travelling on one of the low-cost airlines), which brings in itself a host of customer service challenges. Life is never dull for my customer service duty team and our front-line staff.

It takes a small army of front-of-house staff and behind-the-scenes staff to ensure an airport operates efficiently and effectively, and that all our customers receive the best possible service. All of our passenger-facing staff receive customer training on induction and in their refresher training, and all are trained in dealing with special needs passengers, how to handle and defuse difficult situations, and many speak foreign languages. All of the team are first-aid trained and many staff are defibrillator-trained to assist with life-threatening collapses.

We take part in the government's Defibrillators in Public Places campaign and currently have

23 defibs at Stansted, with staff from many organisations trained to use them. They have saved several lives to date at the airport, and the team have received lovely letters of thanks from families.

We are also fortunate to have an on-site paramedic supplied by the Essex Ambulance Trust and co-funded by Stansted Airport for 18 hours a day. This is to ensure a rapid response to passengers who require first aid or emergency treatment, and they attend many calls daily, from simple first aid requests to life-threatening conditions. Our airport information desk is open 20 hours per day to provide face-to-face information and services to passengers and all our information staff are multilingual and very knowledgeable about anything and everything passengers want to know!

We have a team of passenger service assistants who ensure that 3,500 free trolleys are available to passengers on arrival and departure, and who also provide free assistance to special needs passengers and anyone requiring assistance, e.g. parents with children, the elderly, etc. We have help points located in the short-stay car parks and on the terminal forecourt from where assistance can be summoned.

Our security team comprises over 500 staff who ensure the safety and security of all passengers and staff at Stansted, and who regularly search up to 35,000 departing passengers in a day. You will appreciate it is not always possible to delight passengers in a security environment, but our passenger scores (see QSM below) for security staff helpfulness are consistently high.

The customer service duty team are enthusiastic, proactive people who are experienced in dealing with almost any situation that may arise – unattended bags, lost children, delay situations, accidents/incidents, distressed passengers, missed flights, VIP movements, in fact any situation you can imagine! No two days are ever the same and they have to be prepared to deal with whatever may impact on the airport and our operation. During inclement weather we have found ourselves looking after 10,000 passengers who were stranded here overnight, ensuring their comfort and welfare as best we could, providing information, reassuring them and trying to make the best of a difficult situation. Strikes, air traffic control problems, surface access problems, or bad weather anywhere in Europe can all bring issues for us to manage, even if we play no part in the original problem.

We encourage customer feedback through an on-line feedback system and a feedback leaflet on site, as well as via letters, e-mail and telephone calls, and each contact is thoroughly investigated and receives a reply. We aim to reduce the number of complaints and track areas of concern and any trends, ensuring that we address these promptly. Should any aspect of our operation attract five or more complaints in a month (not a lot when you consider we handle over 1.5 million passengers a month!) we are obliged to report these in our monthly customer services report to BAA main board and explain our actions to remedy the situation.

We are pleased to receive many compliments about services and facilities, often naming members of staff who have gone out of their way to help passengers and provided excellent service. Stansted is proud to boast an excellent ratio of compliments to complaints, currently 5 to 1.

BAA has a market research team that carries out interviews with passengers at all of our airports as part of our Quality of Service Monitor (QSM) with arriving and departing passengers.

At Stansted some 7,500 passengers are interviewed a year about many of the services and facilities provided, and this helps us to track passenger perceptions about the service we provide and focus our attention where most needed. All managers are given targets in relation to these results, and lower than acceptable scores have to be improved.

I hope this information helps you understand the complexity of customer services provision and some of the issues involved. I wish you all the best in your study of travel and tourism and future career in the industry.

With very best wishes

Paula

Source: BAA Stansted

1  List all the things that BAA Stansted does to ensure a high standard of customer service. What benefits will this have to the organisation?

   This task may provide evidence for P1.

2  Research another travel and tourism organisation. Compare and contrast its customer service provision with that of BAA Stansted.

   This task may provide evidence for P1 and M1.

3  Evaluate the delivery of customer service at BAA Stansted and your second organisation. Can you suggest improvements? If so, you must also justify them.

   This task may provide evidence for D1.

# Issues and implications

We have already established the principles of good customer service and why the provision of excellent service is important to organisations and their staff, as well as to the customers themselves. This section examines some of the issues associated with good service and the benefits of its provision.

## Issues

In order to provide excellent customer service, staff must:

* greet customers warmly and enthusiastically to create a positive first impression

* be aware of their body language – it must be positive

* communicate clearly

* recognise customers' feelings (and treat each one as an individual)

* provide correct information promptly

* deal with complaints effectively

* always be well turned out.

While we are being observed, we can all do this.

However, the key to excellent service is that it is **consistent** and **reliable**.

A consistent service is one which is always the same; for example, the staff always smile, the phone is always answered within three rings, phone calls are returned and staff are always professional.

Reliability means being trustworthy and dependable. Customers need their products and services to be reliable; holidays are usually booked well in advance and looked forward to for months. When thinking about different organisations' reliability, customers may ask themselves:

* is the airline usually on time?

* are the cabin crew friendly?

* has my luggage always arrived safely?

* are the hotel rooms always spotlessly clean?

* is the receptionist efficient?

* does the tour operator provide value for money?

* is the brochure accurate?

Reliability implies consistency – after all, a service is not reliable if sometimes the staff let you down!

If a customer is to consider a product or service to be both consistent and reliable, many aspects of work within the organisation have to be efficient. Organisations must ensure the following.

* Staff are well trained – they know the importance of good service to the customer and how increased sales and repeat business can affect the organisation.

* There are always enough staff present to do the job; if a customer is kept waiting in a travel agency because it is the lunch hour, he or she is unable to book a holiday. A sale is lost and the customer is unlikely to return.

* The right staff are recruited. Some people are naturally good at customer service; they have a positive outlook on life, they are outgoing and are always smiling.

* Staff are motivated. Some motivation comes from ourselves. However, the way we are treated by our manager, pay levels, and the office environment will all affect our levels of

*Customers will notice whether cabin crew are friendly and helpful*

motivation. For staff to feel valued, it is important that organisations provide suitable facilities for them. In small organisations this may simply be a room for coffee breaks. In large organisations staff perks sometimes include gym membership and annual excursions.

* The working environment is clean, healthy and safe. This is important for both staff and customers. A clean and pleasant working atmosphere is good for both internal and external customer service. Staff feel valued and customers are more likely to return. Health and safety measures are also legal requirements.

* The service is available. A travel agency needs to keep regular hours, a resort representative must advise customers when he or she will visit and then do so, and a call centre needs to be operating at evenings and weekends as that is when most people want to book their holidays.

* Resources are available. Travel agencies need computers, resort staff need uniforms, cabin crew need safety equipment. Resources include anything physical (cars for sales staff, filing cabinets, desks, chairs, telephones for offices), and include human resources, such as extra guides for the summer season in Oxford, cleaners in hotels, or reservation staff for a tour operator. Lack of resources can inhibit excellent service.

✳ The product meets customers' needs. Many organisations assess their customers' views through surveys, questionnaires, and suggestion boxes. Some organisations also use focus groups (see Unit 3, Marketing Travel and Tourism Products and Services, page 82).

(see Unit 3, Marketing Travel and Tourism Products and Services, page 82)

## Theory into practice

Obtain a feedback questionnaire from a local travel and tourism organisation. What criteria are being used to assess the level of service they provide? Some will be the same as those above. List additional ones. Do you think any more should be added?

It is clear from the list above that organisations have to spend money on resources, and for staff to be motivated they need to be trained and valued. The provision of excellent customer service is costly.

## Implications

Travel companies have commitments to their customers, not just to satisfy their needs, but also in law. The following Acts of Parliament have relevance to many travel and tourism organisations.

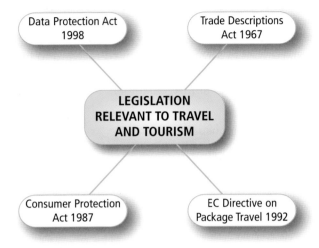

Data Protection Act 1998 — Trade Descriptions Act 1967 — **LEGISLATION RELEVANT TO TRAVEL AND TOURISM** — Consumer Protection Act 1987 — EC Directive on Package Travel 1992

## Assessment activity 5.2

Produce a table like the one below. Select an organisation with which you are familiar and list all the costs associated with providing excellent service. You should consider both internal and external customer service.

Next, consider the implications (costs) of not providing excellent service.

The table has been started for you, taking a travel agency as an example.

| COSTS OF PROVIDING EXCELLENT CUSTOMER SERVICE | COSTS OF PROVIDING INEFFECTIVE CUSTOMER SERVICE |
|---|---|
| Sufficient numbers of staff, all of whom are well trained | If insufficient staff are available, customers may go elsewhere and so sales will be lost. If staff are not trained they will not be able to sell suitable holidays – customer needs will not be met. |
| Clean office – cleaners required | Staff will not feel valued if the office is not clean. Customers will receive a poor first impression. |
| Up-to-date software ... | |
| | |

This activity may provide evidence for P2 and M2.

## Data Protection Act 1998

This act affects all organisations that hold personal details on customers. There are eight general principles to this act. Key points are that organisations are not allowed to pass on information about their customers or sell information in mailing lists. They can keep only relevant information and must destroy it once it has served its purpose.

For example, Tourist Information Centres cannot ask visitors to enter a prize draw and then use their names and addresses for a mailing unless the customers give permission for them to do so.

## Trade Descriptions Act 1968

The key point from this act is that products and services must be correctly described. Hotel descriptions must be accurate, and brochures must contain full and fair information. As brochures are put together a long time before the customers go on holiday, the resort reps have an important role in updating head office staff – who in turn must advise customers of relevant changes, for example that the swimming pool has closed or water sports are no longer available.

## Consumer Protection Act 1987

The EC Directive on Package Travel has now superseded much of this act. The key requirement is that prices for products and services are correctly displayed. For example, a sales promotion might offer a free child place if accompanied by two full-paying adults. Tour operators could not insist that they all share one room unless this had been clearly stated in the promotion.

## EC Directive on Package Travel 1992

The European regulations caused a storm when introduced to the travel industry over a decade ago. They gave customers increased protection, and it became the responsibility of any organisation packaging a holiday (selling transport, accommodation and ancillary services as one product) to provide financial security (a bond) in case its business collapsed. Tour operators became accountable for their suppliers, so that if, for example, a coach company was negligent and caused injury to a client, the tour operator became liable.

There are also requirements to ensure brochures are 'legible, comprehensible and accurate'. Precise details of the package have to be included in the contract, including excursions, itinerary, price and payment schedule. Complaints have to be answered within a specific time frame.

## Health and safety

Other legislation with which travel companies need to be familiar include health and safety legislation. Coach companies and their drivers need to be up to date with the regulations that affect the numbers of hours a coach driver can drive without a break. Airlines need to be aware of the Joint Aviation Requirements (JARs).

### CASE STUDY

Jo is a full-time travel and tourism student. Before starting the course she used to work in a Spanish resort as a transfer rep. She then worked in a travel agency for a few years. She misses her life of travel – and is short of money – so she now works occasional weekends as a tour manager for a company taking weekend tours to Paris.

When doing her training course in Manchester she was surprised by the amount of legislation that now affects tour operators. The trainer made it very clear that Jo's role is really important – and her actions and reports could affect the company if it was ever sued.

On every tour Jo is required to do the following.

- **Check that the hotels used and facilities available are as described in the brochure.** Because the brochure is printed about 18 months before the holidays take place, some things are not accurate. One week the lift was not working (and this is significant as many clients are elderly). Jo rang head office straight away and clients booked on the following week's holiday were told immediately (and many were offered ground floor rooms).
- **Keep accurate records of delays and keep passengers informed.** If there are long delays Jo has to inform the duty officer, who may authorise refreshments.
- **Ensure all the services booked by clients are provided.** For example, one week a special champagne breakfast had been booked by a group – but not provided. Jo spoke to the hotel manager and her own boss. It was provided the following day. Jo was aware that under European directives, the tour operator was liable for any deficiencies of the supplier (the hotel).

Passengers often complain – and for every complaint Jo writes a duty report. She returns this to head office as soon as the tour is over (under the Package Travel Directive, her boss has 28 days in which to respond to the complaint). When completing the report she is careful to be factual and not show any bias – she knows that if the complaint goes to court or arbitration, copies of her report will be seen by many people.

1  **Name four pieces of legislation that affect a tour operator.**
2  **What are the risks associated with a brochure being published up to 18 months before the customer goes on holiday?**
3  **What does 'liable for any deficiencies of the supplier' mean?**
4  **Why must Jo's records be accurate and factual?**

**Theory into practice**

Imagine you work for a hotel. List the ways in which excellent customer service impacts on customers, staff, and the organisation.

Check your answers using the diagrams on pages 147–148.

# Customer service skills

So far this unit has discussed the principles of customer service, why it is important to travel and tourism organisations and the effects (on customers, organisations and their staff) of not providing excellent service.

As mentioned earlier, some people are naturally good at providing excellent service. They have an outgoing personality, appear to be always positive and are not intimidated by difficult situations. Other people have to learn these skills.

When looking at the skills you need, it is important to consider the situations in which they are most likely to be needed, whether when dealing with problems or complaints, giving advice or offering assistance.

## Methods of communication

### Written communication

A vast range of methods of written communication are used within the travel and tourism industry, all of which contribute towards customer service levels and the image a customer will have of the organisation.

Examples of written communication include:

* letters
* e-mails
* memos
* faxes
* brochures/leaflets
* web pages/Internet
* timetables
* menus
* window displays
* notice boards
* welcome packs
* signs.

Written communication contributes towards the overall image the customer will have of a company. The design of the website may attract customers to investigate it further or cause them to look elsewhere for a holiday. If an e-mail has spelling errors, customers will certainly have an impression of poor service levels. Similarly, the language used in letters can indicate whether a company is relaxed and enthusiastic or more formal.

It is important that the correct form of written communication is used. For example, e-mails and faxes are an excellent method of communication if speed is important. However, they are informal and should not be used, for example, to deal with a complaint. Similarly, a memo would be used only for internal customers.

Remember, written communication is more formal than face-to-face communication. It is therefore sometimes used to confirm decisions that have previously been discussed. In some of the choices in the table below, you may decide that face-to-face communication, or a telephone conversation, is needed as well as some form of written confirmation.

## Theory into practice

Write a letter to Mrs D Gill, 22, High Street, Hampton, Shropshire, SG3 9JL. She is a regular customer. She has just visited the travel agency in which you work to complain about her holiday in Greece. The sun didn't shine, the people were rude and the flight home was delayed. Your agency was not open at the Bank Holiday (when she came home) either. You must reassure her and try to win back her custom.

## Face-to-face communication

We are all used to face-to-face communication. When shopping, getting on a bus, greeting friends and working in a team we all communicate

## Theory into practice

Work in small groups. Copy and complete the table below independently, then compare your answers with other members of your group.

| MESSAGE | METHOD OF WRITTEN COMMUNICATION TO BE USED |
|---|---|
| The manager of a travel agency wants to advise a customer of a change of hotel. | |
| A resort rep wants to let head office know that a customer has made a serious complaint about the hotel. She thinks other customers will also complain. | |
| Two hotel receptionists have agreed to swop shifts. They want to tell their manager. | |
| Head office has decided to make 20 airline staff redundant. | |
| A customer has had a great holiday and decides to tell the travel agent and tour operator. | |
| A visitor to a museum has been overcharged. He realises this only when he gets home. | |
| After two weeks of reading about two destinations, Jamal wants to confirm a holiday with the travel agent. | |

*A welcome meeting in a resort is an example of face-to-face communication*

directly with each other face to face. However, it is important to know how to use this form of communication to its full advantage when dealing with a customer. For example, personal presentation is very important – it will give a good or bad first impression. You must also consider your tone of voice and be very aware of your body language – remember it will communicate more to your customer than the words you say (see page 141).

The advantage of face-to-face communication is that you can read your customer's body language, use brochures, leaflets and other materials to help you get information across to your customer, and answer any questions as they arise.

Face-to-face communication is often on a one-to-one basis. However, it can also involve groups of people, for example at a staff meeting or a welcome party in a resort.

## Telephone communication

To be able to communicate well on the telephone you need good listening skills. Remember that you must listen to the tone of voice as well as the words being said! It is particularly important to speak clearly and check understanding when on the phone – as you cannot read the body language or any other non-verbal information (such as gestures and facial expressions).

Other techniques for good telephone communication include:

* be clear – use short sentences and phrases
* avoid jargon
* be concise
* pronounce your words clearly
* speak slowly
* make sure there is minimal background noise
* smile!

> **✳ REMEMBER!**
>
> You should smile when speaking to customers on the phone because it shows in your tone of voice and the customer service you provide.

Many travel and tourism organisations require all their staff to answer the phone in the same way. For example, 'Good afternoon, Travel First. Harry speaking. How may I help you?' This is to ensure consistently good service and to present a corporate image.

## Skills for customer service

### Listening skills

How good are you at listening? Do you interrupt when your friends are talking, look away, or think about something else?

Complete the following questionnaire to assess your listening skills:

| WHEN LISTENING, DO YOU … | ALMOST ALWAYS | SOMETIMES | NEVER |
|---|---|---|---|
| **1** face the speaker? | | | |
| **2** keep focused on the speaker, maintaining eye contact? | | | |
| **3** nod and smile when appropriate? | | | |
| **4** think about other things? | | | |
| **5** look for body language and listen to the tone of voice (to give you more understanding)? | | | |
| **6** think about your answer while the speaker is still talking? | | | |
| **7** interrupt before the speaker has finished? | | | |
| **8** 'tune out' or get bored? | | | |

Consider points 1–8. Which ones indicate that you are listening? Use these (and any others you can think of) to produce some guidelines called 'Improve your listening skills'.

## Key concept

**Active listening** – demonstrating through words and actions (body language) that you understand what is being said to you. For example, you can make appropriate responses ('wow', 'oh dear') or ask questions ('So are you saying that he shouted at you?'). Body language that demonstrates active listening includes nodding, maintaining eye contact, smiling or looking concerned as appropriate.

## Theory into practice

Non-verbal behaviour is an important aspect of listening. Carry out this exercise to assess its impact.

Work in pairs. Each of you should choose a topic to talk about (make sure it is something you know a lot about and can talk on for a few minutes).

Each speaker should talk on his or her topic twice. The first time, the listener will practise active listening (nodding, smiling, maintaining eye contact). The second time the listener will demonstrate (through behaviour) that he or she is not listening. This could include looking away, tapping a pencil, or yawning. Remember the listener is practising non-verbal behaviour, so must not speak.

1 What impact does active listening have on the speaker?

2 What impact does it have on the speaker when it is clear that he or she is not being listened to?

## Identifying behaviour

Identifying a person's behaviour could help you in many customer service situations. You need to be aware when a customer is becoming stressed, anxious or angry. A good resort representative will notice the quiet person who is too shy to join in with things and will offer words of encouragement. A good sales consultant will identify the signals that a customer is interested in buying.

You may already be good at identifying behaviour, but unaware of your skills. How do you do it? Through observing body language! If people are speaking, their tone of voice will also give you a clue if their mood is changing.

## Questioning

Asking the right questions is an important aspect of customer service skills. Whatever your future role in travel you will be asking questions of colleagues and customers. In some situations the type of question you use is as important as the words used. This is especially so when trying to sell or dealing with a difficult situation.

There are four types of questions: closed, open, reflective and leading. These are identified in the table below, together with examples and the limitation of each type of question.

| TYPE OF QUESTION | EXAMPLE | USE | LIMITATION |
|---|---|---|---|
| **Closed**<br>One that can be answered only by 'yes' or 'no'. | Have you sent in your booking form?<br>Will you be staying for dinner?<br>Have you received your tickets? | To clarify facts.<br>Should not be used if trying to gather details. | Closed questions will not provide further information for discussion. |
| **Open**<br>One that cannot be answered by a 'yes' or 'no'.<br>They start with words like what, when, how, who, why, where or which. | What did you enjoy most about your holiday?<br>Why are you upset?<br>How can I help you solve this problem?<br>Where have you been on holiday before? | To start a discussion or conversation, to gather information. | A talkative person may answer at length and take up a lot of your time! |
| **Reflective**<br>One that checks understanding and gives a person the chance to think about what has been said. | So you feel the hotel staff were unfriendly?<br>So you want somewhere sunny, but you are not looking for a beach holiday? | Allows you to check understanding and for the customer to add to what has been said. | Takes time. You may lose the thread of the previous discussion. |
| **Leading**<br>One that suggests what the answer should be, or leads the person into answering in a certain way. | So you feel that if the flight had not been delayed you would have had a nice holiday? | Try to avoid using. | Indicates what you are thinking and is unlikely to obtain a full or true answer. |

In most situations you will need to be asking open questions, for example when establishing a customer's needs. In some cases reflective questions may be useful, for example when dealing with a complaint or making a sale.

| DON'T USE | DO USE |
|---|---|
| Did you enjoy your holiday? | How was your holiday? Or Tell me what you enjoyed about your holiday. |
| Did you learn a lot at the welcome meeting? | What sort of things did the resort rep tell you at the welcome meeting? |
| Do you want to go to Ibiza because of the nightlife? | What is it that makes you want to go to Ibiza? |
| You've been to Spain a lot, haven't you? | What destinations have you been to before? |

### Theory into practice

Change the following closed questions into open questions:

1. Can I help you?
2. Are you OK today?
3. Do you like the view from your balcony?
4. Would you like to go to Greece again this year?

Change the following closed questions into reflective questions:

5. Is your budget £400 per person?
6. You don't want to go to Spain?
7. Was it the airline's fault?

## Establishing and responding to customer needs

You know that in order to provide excellent customer service you must meet customers' needs. But you need to establish what these needs are before you can respond to them.

You may think that simple open questions will establish customers' needs, such as 'When do you want to travel?', 'Where would you like to go?' However, there may be some things that clients don't tell you, either because they don't think it's important, or because they're embarrassed, or because they don't realise it themselves. For example, issues around money or special needs are often unspoken. These are referred to as 'underlying needs'.

It is sometimes very difficult to establish underlying needs until late in a sale. It is therefore important to ask the right questions to try to understand what these might be.

### Theory into practice

Imagine you are working as a sales consultant in a call centre. What questions would you need to ask to uncover the following underlying needs?

- restricted mobility means that a wheelchair is needed at the airport
- one of the four passengers is over 80 and therefore needs additional insurance
- a baby is travelling
- a honeymoon couple don't want other hotel guests to know it is their honeymoon but do want a four-poster bed and champagne on arrival.

## Assertiveness

Assertiveness means standing up for yourself while also considering other people's needs. Broadly speaking, assertive people usually manage to get what they want – but not at the expense of other people. For most people this does not come naturally. Many are passive – they are easy going, often get 'walked over' and will try to avoid a confrontation at all costs. At the other extreme there are aggressive people – those who tend to argue, are confrontational and always get what they want, often at other people's expense. Assertive behaviour is a middle way between aggressive and passive behaviour. It is a useful skill to acquire.

## Recording information

Recording information is an important aspect of providing excellent customer service. You will need to record information in the following situations:

* taking an enquiry for a holiday (establishing customer needs)
* dealing with a complaint
* taking payment
* booking an excursion
* taking a telephone message
* dealing with a problem (with a colleague, customer or your manager).

In many situations pro-formas are provided (a form to fill in). One example is an enquiry form, which prompts the travel consultant to ask specific questions such as dates of travel, number of adults and children, preferred resort, preferred departure airport, and length of stay.

Another example is a customer report form used in resorts. A resort representative will need to use this to write a report if a complaint is received in resort. The rep will need to write a factual report to relay the necessary information to head office. An example of what such a report might look like is given below.

**Customer report form**

Tour operator: _____ Form no. _____

Resort (e.g. Palma Nova) _____ Area (e.g. Majorca) _____

Customer's name _____ Booking ref no. _____

Accommodation _____ UK departure date _____

Customer's UK address _____

Postcode _____ Telephone _____

Details of issues raised:

1 _____

_____

2 _____

_____

3 _____

_____

Actions taken to resolve the issues raised above:

1 _____

2 _____

3 _____

Customer signature _____Date _____

Copy received by _____ (on behalf of hotelier/supplier)

Additional comments _____

_____

Remember when filling in any document that it could potentially be used in a court of law. Therefore take your time over it, be professional and make sure the information is full, accurate and legible. Times and dates must be included. Give facts, not opinions! The guidelines shown below will be helpful.

## Guidelines for resort representatives

When completing documents, forms and reports in resort, please:

* check you are using the correct form before you start – if unsure, ask your manager

* use black ink (this photocopies better than other colours)

* write in block capitals

* write clearly – remember, these documents are of no use if we cannot read them

* make sure you complete all sections – if they are not applicable, write N/A (if you leave it blank we won't know whether you have simply missed it)

* don't use jargon, abbreviations, acronyms or foreign words – we may not understand them

* state facts – your opinions are not to be put on paper; state simply what happened where, when and why

* when you have finished, read the whole form through to check it – remember this may become a legal document

* post all forms to your line manager with your weekly administration reports. If a form is urgent, please use the fax and then telephone to make sure it has been received.

## Conflict management

Conflict is an inevitable part of life. When working in the travel and tourism industry you may have to deal with conflict, both with internal and external customers. This may involve customer complaints, problems with colleagues, disagreements with your manager or problems with suppliers such as flight delays or hotel over-bookings.

All such problems will stretch your skills. You will need to listen, question and be assertive. In addition you will need to know how to deal with the conflict effectively and be aware of your own responsibility limits.

We are all aware that more complaints are received nowadays – customers are more demanding and know their rights. Some people blame the increase in complaints on TV programmes such as *Holidays from Hell*, while others talk of professional complainers and the fact that new legislation is more likely to protect customers than suppliers.

Whatever the reason for the complaint you will need to follow a set process to ensure its resolution. It is important to view a complaint as an opportunity to 'turn a customer around' – that is, an opportunity for you to demonstrate excellent service and produce a satisfied customer. Research shows that if a complaint is dealt with effectively, customers are likely to return.

| DEALING WITH COMPLAINTS | |
|---|---|
| Listen! | Use active listening so that the customer knows you are taking his or her complaint seriously. Ask probing questions, but don't interrupt. Look interested. |
| Apologise | Apologise for the inconvenience – that the customer is upset. Do not accept liability – i.e. do not say 'I'm sorry, our organisation has clearly made a mistake', but do say 'I'm really sorry this has occurred.' |
| Tell the customer that you will investigate the matter | This may be a simple check to see if tickets are in the file, or it may be more complex. You may need to write to an airline, hotelier or other supplier. In this case tell the customer when you will have a response for him or her. |
| Empathise | Try to see the situation from the customer's point of view. |
| Be calm | Remember that even if the customer is angry, you must stay calm. The complaint is not about you, so don't take it personally. |
| Know your responsibility limits – agree a solution or refer to your manager | If you are able to offer a solution, do so. But make sure you know your responsibility limits. If the complaint is outside your area of responsibility, you may need to refer the customer to your manager. Always discuss the solution with the customer. |
| Do what you have agreed to do | Whatever the agreed solution, do it! Make it a priority. This is your chance to turn a bad situation into a good one by being efficient. |
| Record details | Make sure you follow company procedures about dealing with complaints. Fill in appropriate forms and send them to the right people. |

*Customers today are more demanding and may complain about any mishap*

## Consider this ...

Research shows that seven out of ten customers will do business with you again if your resolve their complaint effectively (and in their favour!).

## Theory into practice

Work in pairs. One of you is a customer and the other a resort rep. Role-play the customer making a complaint – you can make up the details. Complete the customer report form for your head office.

## Key concept

**Empowerment** – being given the power, authority or ability to do something. If your manager gives you training to deal with complaints, offers you support and backs up your decisions, he or she has empowered you to take on this role.

## Assessment activity 5.3

1 Imagine you work in a local travel agency. Use the skills you have acquired in this section to demonstrate effective customer service in the following role plays. For a Merit grade you need to be professional at all times. You should appear confident (even if you are not) and demonstrate a high level of service.

   a A very hesitant young couple come into your agency. They seem to want to book a holiday but appear unsure. She is very keen to go to the Caribbean, but he is clearly worried about money. She is wearing an engagement ring.

   b Your manager has asked you to return a call to a client. This client spends a lot of money with the agency, but is very difficult to satisfy. She is never clear about what she wants. You telephone her to establish her needs and offer advice.

   c Mr Gwiner comes into the agency. He is very angry. He called you yesterday and your colleague said you would call him back but you did not (you did not get the message). He is really upset about his holiday. The resort rep did not appear most days, one of the excursions was cancelled as there were not enough people and the pool was closed because of a leak.

   This task may provide evidence for P3 and M3.

2 Evaluate your performance in each of the role plays.

   This task may provide evidence for D2.

# Selling skills

Selling is just one of the many customer service situations that you may be involved in when working in the travel and tourism industry. It may be an important part of your job, or just a small aspect of it. For most travel and tourism organisations, sales are a fundamental activity as the number of sales determines profit levels and the ultimate success of the organisation.

Selling skills can be learnt. Many people are good at selling and earn good commissions through their sales. Examples of sales situations within the travel industry include working in a call centre (whether selling holidays, car hire or insurance), travel agency work and working as an overseas resort representative (selling excursions). In many sales roles your income may largely be determined by the commission you earn from a sale.

In resorts the representatives earn commission for all the excursions they sell. This is an important part of their income.

## Establishing rapport

The first stage of the sales process is to establish a rapport (a positive relationship) with the customer. Customers must feel positive and relaxed and under no pressure to buy. They must trust the salesperson and be confident in his or her ability to find the right product to meet their needs.

Create a pleasant working environment with no interruptions or background noise, and a clear desk

Use positive body language – smile, use open gestures

**HOW TO CREATE RAPPORT WITH YOUR CUSTOMERS**

Greet your clients warmly – offer a seat or drink if appropriate. If regular clients, ask how they are

Use a positive and enthusiastic tone of voice

*The stages of selling*

Establish rapport with the customer

Ask questions to establish needs

Select a product to meet needs → Switch sell

Sell up

Turn features into benefits

Overcome objections

Use persuasion

Customer thinks product does not meet needs

Customer accepts product

Close sale

The environment in which you are working, your tone of voice, body language and what you say to your customer will all contribute towards the rapport.

The environment (office and desk) is important. For example, if purchasing a holiday in a travel agency, customers would expect:

* the office to be clean
* staff to be seated at their desks
* no eating and drinking at desks
* clear, neat desks
* telephones to be answered quickly
* no radios or loud background noise
* staff who are not serving to be working (not gossiping with each other).

As a salesperson you will also establish rapport by:

* first impressions – smiling and greeting your customer warmly
* your appearance – clean, tidy, neat hair and minimal jewellery
* offering customers a seat
* making good eye contact
* positive body language
* not being distracted by other people or the telephone.

## Establishing needs

Once rapport is established, you will need to establish the customers' needs. This is perhaps the most difficult part of the sales process, as customers may not know what they need themselves. Through careful questioning and listening you will have to work out what it is they really want. You have already seen that there is a huge range of customers, all of whom have different needs. Remember that your client may also have underlying needs which he or she does not tell you about.

The first stage is to ask questions to establish factual information, that is the presented needs. For example, if selling a holiday you can ask questions to establish how many people are going, when they want to go and for how long. Clients

may also be able to tell you what type of accommodation they would prefer and their preferred destination. Other clients may need you to guide them. Some clients will know only that they want a holiday and expect you to find the perfect holiday to meet their requirements. Careful questioning will be required!

You will need to ask open questions to make sure you get all the information you need. Open questions begin with what, why, who, how, when, which or where. They will perhaps give you more information than you require, but this may help you discover the underlying needs and guide a customer to a particular type of holiday.

You will also need to practise active listening. This will help to maintain the rapport that you have established and encourage your clients to give you further information. You should take notes, write down key points, nod or say encouraging things ('I know what you mean', 'I see'). If you are working in a travel agency you will be required to complete a customer enquiry form.

> **Key concept**
>
> To establish customer needs you must:
> * ask open questions
> * listen actively
> * use reflective questions to check understanding – 'So you think Greece was too hot for you in August last year?'
> * maintain a positive rapport through good eye contact, positive body language
> * keep asking questions and discussing options until you have established customer needs.

## Selecting the products to meet requirements

Now that you know the customer's needs, you must find a holiday to match them! If the enquiry is straightforward – the customer knows exactly what he or she wants – this can be done through a simple search on the computer reservation system. However, if customer needs are less clear, it is your product knowledge that may determine whether you can meet them. Do you know different resorts, are you familiar with the brochures, do you know which operators offer particular holiday types?

For example, a couple may ask about going to Spain for a romantic beach holiday, but you may be able to recommend a Greek island which you know is very popular with young couples. This is called 'switch selling'. You may also be able to 'sell up', which means selling something more or of higher quality than the customer originally mentioned.

### Key concept

**Switch selling** – the process of selling the client something different from what they thought they needed. For example, a group of young people could come into your travel agency saying they want a clubbing holiday in Ayia Napa (Cyprus). However, you know that Ayia Napa is now much more a family resort than it was three years ago and you 'switch sell' them to Palma, Mallorca.

**Selling up** – selling something of greater value than was asked for. For example, you might sell a client a holiday in the Caribbean when he came into your agency asking for a week in Tenerife, or encourage a client to travel first class. Selling up means the agency (and possibly the travel consultant) earns extra commission.

### Features and benefits

When presenting the product it is important that you identify the three or four things that are most important to the client and describe how this product matches these needs. For example, 'I have just found this holiday in The Gambia. It is available for when you want to travel. I know you want some sun and the temperatures there will be high at that time of year. There is five-star accommodation available and it has a pool, which you particularly wanted.'

It is at this stage that you will introduce the features of the holiday and turn them into the benefits for the customer.

| FEATURE OF HOLIDAY | YOUR BENEFIT STATEMENT |
|---|---|
| The hotel has a large swimming pool and a children's pool | 'This hotel has a really large pool. There will be plenty of room for you to swim and you won't be disturbed by children's games.' |
| The hotel is isolated | 'It is a wonderfully quiet location – no neighbouring hotels to share the beach with. You will also have great views from all rooms.' |
| The hotel is in the middle of a town | 'You will be right in the middle of things. You can stroll out each evening and really get involved in local life.' |

## Overcoming objections

You will also need to overcome objections. Customers may not agree with you that the holiday you have selected for them matches their requirements. This may be because you have misunderstood their needs, or simply have not asked enough questions (and so you don't know the underlying customer needs). If this is the case you must ask probing questions to re-establish their requirements and select a different product.

However, it may be that the customers need more reassurance. They may be hesitating, unsure what to do. You need to establish what it is they are unsure about. For example:

*You:* 'What is it about the holiday you are unsure of?'

*Your customer:* 'The hotel isn't very close to the beach.'

*You:* 'That's true. But it's only five minutes' walk. And you are right in the middle of town, so it will be great for the nightlife you wanted.'

Overcoming objections is really like turning features into benefits. You need to first establish what the objection (feature) is and then turn it into something that the customer can view as a benefit.

You are **persuading** the customer that this holiday really does meet his or her requirements.

In pairs, each write down five objections that a customer might make when buying a holiday. Take it in turns to listen to each other's statements, and reply in a way that attempts to overcome the objection.

## Closing the sale

Once you have overcome objections you must look out for buying signals. These may be things that are said (verbal signals) or simply body language (visual signals). Examples include customers:

* nodding to their partner

* looking in their bag for their chequebook

* asking you to reconfirm the total price

* checking flight details again.

It is important that you never rush a customer. Some people are happy to make quick decisions, while many are indecisive. You must look out for these verbal and visual signals. If they are strong and it is clear the customer wants to book, then you could say 'Would you like me to book this for you, before it goes?' Other customers will clearly ask you to book it, for example saying 'Let's get it booked, then!' In these cases, the sale is closed and you need to reconfirm holiday and payment details with the client, complete the paperwork and take payment.

However, there will always be some customers who remain unsure. You may have overcome half a dozen objections, turned all features into benefits and been extremely persuasive, but they may need time to think or discuss with their family. Offering to 'hold' a holiday or reassuring the customer that there is plenty of availability is all part of excellent service. Make sure customers know your name, how to contact you and when you are available. Hard selling often turns people off – you are more likely to end up with a satisfied customer if you pick up on their signals and don't pressurise them.

## Sales methods

In the travel and tourism industry much selling still takes place in a face-to-face situation, such as in a travel agency. However, there is a growth in telephone sales as a result of the growth in call centres. The Internet is also a key sales tool for many tour operators and airlines. These sales are achieved through written communication, that is web pages and e-mails.

Whichever method is used, the same skills are needed and the same process is followed.

1 Collect three direct-mail letters received in your home. They could be for any product. List the techniques and phrases used to grab your attention. Examples may include free products (such as a pen) or money-off vouchers. Phrases may include 'You're the lucky winner of …'. Note down what is written on the envelope to stop you thinking the letter is 'junk mail'. Do these methods work?

2 Examine three websites of travel organisations. Are they good sales tools? Would you use them? Why?

3 List the advantages and disadvantages of written, telephone and face-to-face sales.

1 Work in groups of three for these role plays. Take it in turns to be the sales consultant while the other two try to book a holiday with you. You will be assessed on you ability to demonstrate effective selling skills.

This task may provide evidence for P4 and M3.

2 Evaluate your performance in these role plays. Were your sales skills effective? What could you do to improve? Why are these improvements needed?

This task may provide evidence for D2.

1  How much does it cost to attract a new customer (compared to retaining an existing one)?

2  What are the benefits of uniforms to organisations?

3  What is meant by body language?

4  How can you demonstrate to someone that you are listening?

5  What is meant by 'rapport'?

6  How does product knowledge help you to provide excellent customer service?

7  Write out the phonetic alphabet.

8  How do you write midnight using the 24-hour clock?

9  What are the benefits of teamwork?

10  What is a customer charter?

11  List the benefits of excellent customer service to the customer.

12  List the benefits of excellent customer service to staff.

13  Describe what is meant by the following terms: competitive advantage, public relations, press relations; customer loyalty.

14  Name four different types of internal customer.

15  Describe a situation when you would use a memo rather than a letter.

16  Give five words which are used to begin open questions.

17  What does being assertive involve?

18  What does 'commission' mean?

19  What is the difference between a feature and a benefit?

20  Give four examples of things you can do to ensure that you give a positive first impression.

# UNIT 5 ASSESSMENT ASSIGNMENT

You have just gained a work experience placement with an independent travel agency in your home town. There are five sales staff, a manager and a part-time administrator who works 20 hours a week.

The manager, Shena Bajart, calls you into her office on the first day of your work experience to discuss what you will be doing. The agency is doing quite well, but Shena is concerned that a competitor is setting up at the other end of the High Street. She wants to improve the customer service her staff give to customers to ensure competitive advantage.

As you have just completed the customer services unit on your travel and tourism course, Shena asks you to complete the following tasks.

1  Research how customer service is provided in two travel and tourism organisations.

   Shena would like you to use this information to write a report in which you do the following:

   • Describe how customer service is provided in the two organisations.

   This task may provide evidence for P1.

   • Compare and contrast how the organisations provide customer service.

   This task may provide evidence for M1.

   • Describe the benefits of quality customer service to the organisations.

   This task may provide evidence for P1.

   • Evaluate the delivery of customer service in the two organisations and make recommendations for improvements (saying why these are necessary).

   This task may provide evidence for D1.

2  Shena wants her staff to know about the issues and implications associated with delivering quality customer service. She asks you to produce some notes for the staff which describe these.

   This task may provide evidence for P2.

3   Some of the staff are not performing well – their customer service is poor. Shena asks you to analyse the implications of providing ineffective customer service for the organisation, the employees and the staff.

This task may provide evidence for M2.

4   All staff need to improve both their customer service and selling skills in order to ensure that they do not lose business to their new competitor. Shena asks you to demonstrate good practice to them. Work with a colleague and write a total of six scenarios. These should include a range of methods and cover both selling and customer service skills. You need to project a professional image and communicate confidently for a Merit grade.

This task may provide evidence for P3, P4 and M3.

5   Evaluate your performance in each of the role plays. Did you provide excellent customer service? Were your selling skills effective? Explain where improvements could be made.

This task may provide evidence for D2.

UNIT
6

# Working in the travel and tourism industry

## Introduction

This unit will provide you with the opportunity to explore all aspects of working in the travel and tourism industry. You will already have had experience of observing some of the career opportunities and job roles in travel and tourism when you have been on holiday or visited tourist attractions. In this unit you will examine those roles, but also be introduced to other 'behind-the-scenes' opportunities. You will find out about the different entry routes, progression and training opportunities.

The process of recruitment and selection will be examined, and you will practise the skills that will prepare you for employment, undertaking a personal review focusing on skills, experiences and attributes. You will learn how to put together your curriculum vitae (CV), a letter of application and personal statement in order to apply for jobs. You will be introduced to business skills and to the skills that are essential for performing well in interviews.

To help you prepare for the workplace, the factors that contribute to an effective workplace will be studied, such as working relationships, performance management teamwork, legal and ethical responsibilities and training and development.

### How you will be assessed

This unit is internally assessed by your tutor. A variety of exercises and activities is included in this unit to help you understand all aspects of working in the travel and tourism industry and prepare for the assessment. You will also have the opportunity to work on some case studies to further your understanding.

After completing this unit you should be able to achieve the following outcomes:

→ Investigate the range of career opportunities in the travel and tourism industry
→ Examine recruitment and selection in travel and tourism
→ Prepare for employment in the travel and tourism industry
→ Explore the factors that contribute to an effective workplace.

# Career opportunities in travel and tourism

Since 1980, tourism-related employment in the UK has increased by over 40%.; it increased by 12% between 1995 and 2000. The biggest increases in employment have been in London and the south east.

There are an estimated 2.1 million jobs in tourism in the UK, which accounts for some 7.4% of all employment. There are more jobs in tourism than in construction or transport. Although the large tourism companies are the best known, there were about 129,500 tourism-related businesses in 2002, of which 77% were small firms with less than £250,000 in turnover.

The chart below shows the numbers employed in tourism in relation to total employment.

|  | TOTAL (MILLIONS) | TOURISM-RELATED (MILLIONS) |
|---|---|---|
| Total employment | 28.5 | 2.13 |
| Employee jobs | 25.1 | 1.96 |
| Self-employment | 3.3 | 0.16 |

Source: Great Britain Labour Statistics, June 2002

Travel and tourism careers vary from sector to sector and even within different sectors, so it is necessary to look at the types of employment in the different sectors. There are some general points to be made about working in travel and tourism, however.

* The work is often seasonal as it varies with demand from tourists.

* Shift work is often required.

* A lot of the work involves direct contact with customers.

* The work is very varied.

* Travel is not always involved.

* Some sectors are low paid.

This unit will examine the following sectors and look at the types of careers, entry requirements and progression opportunities they offer:

* retail and business travel

* tour operations

* airlines and airports

* visitor attractions

* cruising

* conference and events

* hotels and accommodation

* tourist boards.

## Retail and business travel

Many recruits to travel agencies are college leavers. They have acquired a good background knowledge of the travel and tourism industry and are usually enthusiastic and willing to learn the essential travel agency skills.

If you choose to work in a travel agency you can work in retail travel or in business travel. Retail travel agents deal with leisure travel, which usually means holidays, whereas business travel agents organise transport and accommodation for business clients. There are many similarities in the work, but also some important differences. Business clients are usually more concerned about reliability and convenience than cost.

Leisure clients may be booking a long time ahead, whereas business clients may be booking a few days ahead. Business travel agents may hold accounts for large companies and cater for all those companies' travel needs.

There are opportunities for progression in both types of agencies. With chains you can progress to area and then to national management. In independents you can reach management level and then may choose to move to a larger company.

Study the two job advertisements below, one for a business travel agent and one for retail. Comment on the differences and similarities. Decide which one you would prefer, and why.

---

### Sales consultants required

Snow.com is a leading Internet-based retailer specialising in the sale of ski and snowboarding holidays. Due to expansion, we have some exciting new opportunities available in our London office for

#### SKI SALES CONSULTANTS

You will be responsible for booking ski holidays to the European and North American ski resorts.

The ideal candidate will be computer literate, have excellent organisations skills, an eye for detail and preferably telesales experience. You will also be friendly and self-motivated, able to work in a pressurised environment, and have a good knowledge of appropriate destinations.

If you want to join a fast-moving, dynamic company and have a genuine passion to deliver the best, we want to hear from you! In return we offer a competitive salary, a free winter holiday, uncapped commission and excellent career prospects.

Please e-mail your CV with covering letter detailing your experience to recruitment@snow.com

---

### BUSINESS TRAVEL CONSULTANT

Travel Professionals Consultancy is looking for an experienced travel consultant to work in a small, specialised business travel team. We specialise in group travel such as product launches and sales conferences.

A minimum of two years' travel experience working in a business travel environment, together with knowledge of a CRS, preferably Galileo, is essential.

The salary package includes pension, private medical insurance and health club membership.

Apply with your CV to Samuel Okobo at Travel Professionals Consultancy, e-mail sam.okobo@travprof.co.uk

---

## Tour operations

This is one of the most exciting sectors in which to work as it offers a wide range of opportunities.

If you want to work in tour operations in a head office role you will have to move to the head office location. Unlike travel agencies, tour operators are not represented in every town. Tour operator jobs are either at head office or in a resort, often overseas. There is a career structure in each:

* head office roles
* reservations/sales
* marketing
* accounts
* customer relations
* contracting.

Choose one of the types of jobs mentioned above. Find an advertisement for this type of job in the trade press or on a travel jobs website. Give a detailed description of the job including:

- responsibilities
- work pattern, for example seasonal, permanent, full time, shifts
- pay and conditions
- qualifications required
- skills required
- personal attributes required
- entry levels, for example, school leaver; BTEC National; A level; graduate
- progression opportunities.

**Research tip:** The trade press includes *Travel Trade Gazette* and *Travel Weekly*. Websites for travel and tourism jobs include:
www.shgjobs.co.uk
www.travelrecruit.co.uk
www.mytravelcareers.co.uk

### Resort representatives

Many students say being a resort representative is their chosen career, and this is not surprising as it gives an opportunity to meet new people of a similar age and to live in a resort. Some resort representatives are employed all year round, but

MyTravel recruits representatives to work for all of its different brands. The job can vary according to brand. For example, the Escapades brand is aimed at the 18–35 age group and needs reps who want to have a great time with the customers. They need to know all about local nightlife as well as the usual holiday information. They also need lots of stamina to cope with the long hours.

No formal qualifications are needed for this role but applicants need the right skills and personal attributes. These are described as follows by MyTravel:

> Everyone who works in our overseas team has a positive attitude and genuine desire to deliver excellent service to our customers. You'll also need to be friendly, outgoing, self-motivated and above all responsible and resilient. We would love to hear from you if you also have:
>
> • excellent verbal and written communication skills
>
> • a high standard of personal presentation
>
> • the commitment and drive to achieve sales targets (customer service reps and Escapades reps)
>
> • diplomacy and problem-solving skills
>
> • a willingness to take on responsibility
>
> • energy, initiative and enthusiasm
>
> • the ability to work well in a team and make an individual contribution
>
> • effective numeracy skills.

You can find out more about MyTravel at www.mytravelcareers.co.uk.

there are many more positions available in the summer high season. This means there are jobs for students during their holidays. If you do get a permanent job you should expect to move resorts between winter and summer seasons.

The work is often low paid, but accommodation is included and it is possible to earn commission and tips.

Resort representative duties are described by MyTravel as:

✳ holding regular welcome events

✳ carrying out airport duties and coach transfer for arriving and departing passengers

✳ handling complaints and solving problems

✳ ensuring noticeboards are up to date and professionally displayed

✳ selling excursions and additional services in resort

✳ guiding excursions

✳ working with hoteliers to ensure company procedures are followed

✳ monitoring health and safety in the properties you are responsible for

✳ ensuring paperwork and accounts are completed neatly and accurately and to specified deadlines

✳ undertaking hospital and police station visits as required.

## Theory into practice

Choose another tour operator. Find its Internet site and find out about resort representative jobs it offers. Describe the jobs and the qualities and skills needed. Comment on how they are similar to or different from the MyTravel requirements.

## Graduate jobs

Some tour operator positions are open only to graduates. If you are thinking of studying for a degree in the future you might be interested in joining a graduate trainee scheme.

## Thomas Cook graduate training

As part of its strategy to maximise the potential of its people as future business leaders, Thomas Cook's 2004 graduate training programme has now begun. This is the first formal programme of graduate placements at Thomas Cook for a number of years.

Ten recent graduates have now joined Thomas Cook, and will spend the next 12 months working in various business areas to gain a complete experience of the company's operations.

The new members of the team are joining the company after successfully completing a rigorous recruitment process. The business sought high-calibre graduates with an upper-second-class degree or higher. The successful graduates are confident team players who see themselves with a long-term future at Thomas Cook. They have qualified for a fast-track development scheme to become the company's managers of the future.

Three graduates are taking up placements within Thomas Cook's product division to help develop holidays and services for customers. One will be based in yield, the department concerned with holiday pricing. There are two placements in multimedia, two in operations and two for the holiday brand Thomas Cook Signature. Every graduate has a dedicated mentor to support and guide them through their training.

Clive Adkin, director of human resources, said: 'We are very confident that our new people will make a real difference to Thomas Cook's business. Each graduate will gain experience across all our business areas, from working overseas and in our stores to helping develop new brochures and set holiday prices. The future of Thomas Cook depends on the investment in our people now, and we plan to continue to target exceptional graduates in the future.'

Source: Thomas Cook news release, 12 August 2004

Imagine that you want to apply for this graduate scheme or a similar one in a few years' time.

1  Produce a review of the personal skills you have that would be appropriate for this job.
   This task may provide evidence for P3.

2  Compare the entry routes and progression at Thomas Cook with those for another job. Explain why you think you are suitable for one of the jobs. Think about the further education, skills and qualities you would need to develop for the job, and list all your development needs.
   This task may provide evidence for M1.

3  Think about how you will achieve these attributes. Where will you study? What will you study? What work experience will you need? Produce an action plan for the next five years showing how you might work towards a chosen job.
   This task may provide evidence for D1.

**Research tip:** Go to www.thomascookjobs.com to find out more about careers at Thomas Cook. Also useful for graduate opportunities is www.prospects.ac.uk.

## Airlines and airports

Airlines employ a variety of personnel such as air crew/flight crew and maintenance staff. Some airlines contract out the maintenance and engineering to specialist companies. Most airlines also contract out services like baggage handling and check-in – companies based in airports handle these services. Examples are Aviance, Groundstar and Servisair.

*Baggage handlers are among the many types of staff working at an airport*

Many airports in the UK are expanding and that means there are more jobs available at airports. The types of job vary a great deal. There are many unskilled and relatively poorly paid jobs, such as baggage handlers and catering staff who prepare in-flight catering and bar carts. There also highly skilled jobs such as air traffic control (based in air traffic control centres such as Swanwick) and operations management. Some jobs require very few qualifications if any, and others are open only to graduates. At Manchester Airport 19,000 people are employed across 250 companies, so you can see that the type of work is very varied.

Remember that public services such as immigration control, customs, police and fire services are all provided at airports and each of these has its own career structure. Connexions produces a booklet called Working in Airports which includes interviews with staff in airports and gives the entry criteria for their jobs.

### Theory into practice

Visit the website for Manchester Airport, www.manchesterairport.co.uk, and find the education section. Here you can read or download the Connexions booklet.

Travel and tourism students often express a desire to be air cabin crew, but remember that there are many behind-the-scene jobs at an airline. There are opportunities for call centre staff dealing with reservations or customer enquiries. As in any company there are positions in finance, accounts, marketing, human resources and customer relations. In addition there is usually a yield management department which constantly monitors sales and adjusts pricing according to demand. The operations department looks at routes and determines where new routes should be developed.

### CASE STUDY

Visit the Virgin website (www.virginatlantic.com) and find the page on cabin crew recruitment by going to 'All About Us', 'Working for Us', and then 'Job Profiles'.

1 **In the section 'Getting to Know You' on the cabin crew page, you can see that applicants are assessed in a group interview on teamwork, customer relationships and attention to detail. Think of two examples for each of these skills where you can show how you have demonstrated these competencies in your past work or study. Describe these examples to a colleague. Ask for constructive feedback on how convincing your examples are.**
2 **Do you meet the minimum requirements listed for Virgin cabin crew? If not, will you be able to meet them in the future? Write notes on how you meet or could meet the requirements, and share your findings with a colleague.**

### Consider this ...

Think about the nature of cabin crew work – it has a glamorous image, but is it really glamorous? Think about when you have flown. What were the cabin crew's activities on the flight? What is the effect on their bodies of constant flying? What impact would this lifestyle have on their personal lives?

## Visitor attractions

As in every other sector, visitor attractions require marketing, human resources, accounting staff, and so on. These are the people who are needed to run any business.

The other jobs available may vary according to the type of attraction. For example, at theme parks, engineers design and build the rides. At stately homes, guides are needed with a detailed knowledge of the history of the house and grounds. You will also find restorers working on the fabric of the building and on, for example, ancient tapestries and paintings. Historic properties require managers and this is a likely career for you if you are interested in heritage or conservation work and think you can manage a team of people.

### Consider this ...

You have probably been to a visitor attraction near your home. Think about the kinds of jobs you noticed there. There are the obvious ones like the host and retail assistant. What kinds of work might be going on behind the scenes, and which jobs would require special skills?

## Cruising

Cruising is a wonderful way to travel, see the world and get paid for it! Cruise ships offer plenty of positions. Below are some examples:

When a ship comes into port most of the passengers go ashore, so many of the crew are allowed time off to go ashore themselves. If you have a long-term contract on a ship you will visit the same ports several times, so you will have a chance to get to know them well.

To apply for a cruise ship job:

* apply directly to individual cruise lines
* research the products and services offered by the line
* be specific about the jobs you are interested in
* describe your training, experience, talents, and skills.

Be careful when looking for a cruise ship job. There are many companies that will try to sell you books on how to apply, or CV services. It is best for you to apply directly to the cruise ship companies; this won't cost you anything.

## Conferences and events

This is an exciting and growing sector of travel and tourism. There are many jobs in this sector, and even many degree courses specialising in conference and event management.

Jobs may be in the public or private sector. The main function is to plan, develop and promote special events. You need excellent communication skills to do this job, as you will have to liaise with many different people

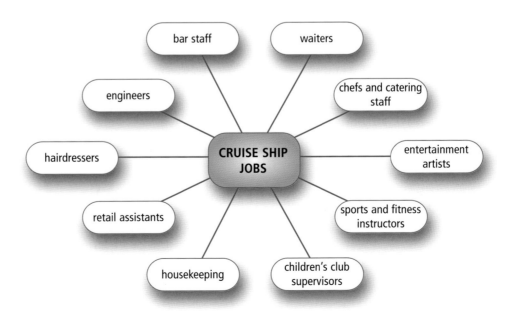

including clients and suppliers. You need to be very motivated, be creative and have plenty of initiative because there is little routine with this kind of work. You will have to be a multi-tasker – that is, able to manage a lot of tasks at once.

### Theory into practice

Are you the kind of person who could work in event management? Try planning an event for a friend or family members, such as an outing or special party. It doesn't have to be a large event – it could be as simple as a visit to the cinema.

Make a list of all the things you have to consider, then work backwards from the date of the event and assign a deadline to each task. What costs are involved? Where will you get the money? What resources do you need? Are there any health and safety considerations? Plan for contingencies, that is things that might go wrong. Evaluate your event afterwards and report on it to your group.

*A career in a hotel may start with working on the reception desk*

## Hotels and accommodation

To work in this sector you need to be able to work in a team, work unsocial hours and use initiative, just like most sectors of travel and tourism! Many students look for work in hotels when they complete their BTEC awards because there are opportunities both at home and away, and a variety of jobs to choose from. Some students are not ready to leave home, and look for employment in local hotels.

Hard workers are soon rewarded. You may start as a receptionist but can quickly move into reservations, managing housekeeping, or managing events or business activities. For those people prepared to travel, the opportunities are even greater as many hotels are part of international chains.

If you want to work in a hotel as soon as you finish your BTEC course, you can combine your career with study for a degree.

### CASE STUDY

**Paramount Management Trainee Programme (incorporating Foundation Degree in Hospitality and Tourism Management)**

If you don't fancy being laden with student debt, but still want to gain a formal qualification, then Paramount can offer you a unique opportunity to combine practical work experience with a Foundation Degree in Hospitality and Tourism Management in just two years! You will be based in one of our hotels, and will attend residential blocks of study with tutors from the University of Gloucestershire throughout the programme.

**What is a Foundation Degree?**
It is a new, modern, higher education qualification, which is designed specifically around workplace needs. As such it is particularly recognised and valued by employers. The qualification gives 240 credits (a Higher National Diploma gives 240 credits). This means you can always extend this if you wish, to a BA Honours degree in Hospitality Management.

## How does the Management Trainee Programme work?

Over two years, you will experience an exciting mix of work-placed learning, as well as block residential study periods, when you will meet up with other Paramount Degree students, at Paramount Hotels throughout the country. You will also spend time at the University of Gloucestershire Campus, and study through distance learning via the Internet. Assignments will be based on work you will be doing within your hotel, applying academic theory to practice!

During your first year you will experience the operational departments of the hotel, including Restaurant, Conference Operations, Housekeeping, Bars and Kitchen.

During your second year you will build on this experience by spending time in the other hotel departments including Events Office, Reception, Personnel and Accounts, then finally Duty Management.

## What is the benefit of a Foundation Degree?

After two years you will have received a national qualification, as well as completing two years' work experience in a top quality hotel. You will have gained working knowledge of every department, enabling you now to further your career, knowing exactly what you want to do, and where you want to go! At Paramount, we will make every effort to find you a position within a department of your choice – it is up to you how quickly you progress!

## What about the cost?

The great thing about this qualification is that Paramount will pay you a salary, and your tuition fees – it couldn't be better!

## What are the entry requirements?

You must be eligible to live and work in the UK, and be of minimum age 18 years. You must have at least one A level grade C or above, a BTEC Certificate or Diploma at the appropriate standard, or GNVQ or NVQ at level 3. We will also consider applications if you do not have the above qualifications, but can demonstrate that you have relevant previous experience in a hotel or similar customer-focused role. Above all you must be smart, outgoing and have a professional approach.

Source: www.paramount-careers.co.uk

1 Do you measure up? Look at the entry criteria and see whether you could apply.
2 Search some other hotel websites and see what their management trainee schemes are like. Try the websites of hotel chains represented in your area.
3 Produce a comparative chart of your findings.

## Tourist boards

You may decide to work in local government – most local councils now have a tourism department. You would expect to enter as an assistant tourism officer and work your way up to more senior positions, such as tourism development officer.

Tourism officers spend most of their time in offices within the local authority. The activities of a tourism officer are described in this extract from www.lgcareers.com:

- promoting existing attractions; working with press and public relations people, designers and photographers to advertise local features. Where there is little history of tourism, the job also involves research into local history and developing potential attractions;
- engineering newsworthy events in order to generate publicity in the local, national and trade media;
- organising exhibition stands at conferences and at exhibitions both nationally and overseas to promote the area;
- assessing the impact that any planned developments may have upon the local environment weighed against of course the potential benefits;
- working very closely with businesses in attracting holiday makers, tour operators, restaurants and guest-houses, to build a picture of how effective existing policies are and what may need addressing in the future. An important part of the work is seeking to attract exhibitions and conferences to the area;
- overseeing the council's tourist information offices;
- operating their marketing and development activities within a set budget. (This financial aspect may also include the need to look for outside assistance – advertising or sponsorship support, for example.)

After your BTEC course you should be eligible for a position with a Tourist Information Centre.

Becca Hammond tells us about working in her local Tourist Information Centre.

After finishing college with an AVCE in Travel and Tourism, I wanted a year out before I went to university, so I decided to stay at my Saturday job, which is at the Cambridge Tourist Office. As I know the job quite well I didn't really need help in settling in and getting some training.

When I started back it was August so it was a busy time for Cambridge and for us at the Tourist Office. Working in a tourist office brings you new things to do each day. No day is the same! Because there are various different things to do in the office we do shifts of one hour in the gift shop and in our call centre. Then we have periods of time on the front desk dealing with enquiries face to face with the public. We also have an accommodation desk at the front which isn't staffed, but if people want to book accommodation we help them.

The past few months I've been asked to do what's called advanced accommodation bookings, which are done over the phone. It is a different perspective on the way in which customers approach you. Personally I have benefited from it a great deal.

At times in the job there is pressure, e.g. visitor numbers, getting them through the door, giving out the correct information. There is another different pressure when working on the advanced booking desk. It's trying your best to get the right accommodation for the customer, and when really busy it's getting all the paperwork right, sent out to the customer and to the establishment as well as getting our own paperwork all correct.

Working full time in the tourist office has given me a great deal of experience for working in the tourism industry and the working world! So I'm off to university to study travel and tourism. I'm going to Buxton in Derbyshire for three years. The course is a Foundation Degree in Travel and Tourism Management. Obviously I hope to work in the tourism side of the industry and maybe work for a big company like the National Trust.

## Training and continuing education in travel and tourism

You are undertaking education at the moment, as you are studying for a BTEC qualification. It is most likely that you will want to continue with education or training in the future, and you need to be aware of the opportunities available to you. There are many different kinds of qualifications and courses, but you will first have to determine where you want to do your studying or training. There are three basic paths:

* full-time education

* full-time work with on-the-job/off-the-job training

* full-time work with college provision.

### Full-time education

Travel and tourism courses are available from foundation level to postgraduate degree level in further and higher education. You may already have completed a GNVQ Intermediate course in Leisure and Tourism before starting your current course. After completion of the BTEC programme you have several options.

| BTEC National Award (6 units) | |
|---|---|
| BTEC National Certificate (12 units) | BTEC National Diploma (18 units) |
| HND, e.g. Travel and Tourism | Degree, e.g. Travel and Tourism |
| Top up to degree | |
| Postgraduate qualification, e.g. MSc in Tourism Management | |

As the table above indicates, you are unlikely to be offered a university place without at least a 12-unit (BTEC National Certificate) qualification unless you also have 'A' levels. A 12-unit qualification at Pass level would allow you to be accepted onto an HND programme, and if you had good grades you might get onto a degree programme. Points are awarded for your grades and each university sets its own entry criteria. If you start with an HND programme (two years) you can convert it to a degree by studying for a third year.

There are other examining boards offering equivalent qualifications to BTEC, such as OCR and AQA, and these programmes are equally acceptable for university entrance.

There are hundreds of travel and tourism courses available at universities. Of course, you do not have to study travel and tourism at all – you may choose to study a different subject. Suitable courses include business studies, marketing and event management. All the details of courses are available on university websites, and it is worth spending time researching courses as each travel and tourism course differs from the others.

You should begin by looking at the UCAS website. This offers you various search options, by subject, university or geographic location. Once you have found courses that interest you, you can go to the relevant university websites for more information.

### Consider this ...

Some students don't like the idea of going on to higher education straight after their BTEC course. This may be for many reasons – the cost, a desire to get straight into work, or having had enough of study. However, you should be aware that many people, after experiencing the realities of working life, decide to go to university a year or two later. You can go to university at any time, but only if you have the entry qualifications – so get them now!

### Theory into practice

Visit www.ucas.co.uk and find six degree or HND programmes that are of interest to you. List them and write down the reasons for your choices.

You will also find details on the UCAS website of how to write your personal statement for your application form. The personal statement is all about you, why you have chosen particular courses and why you are suitable for them.

## Full-time work with on- or off-the-job training

Much of this unit concerns jobs and how to get one, but even when you are employed you will be expected to carry on learning and undergo training. There will be plenty of opportunities open to you. In some sectors training is desirable and in others it is essential – for example, if you work as air crew you must do fire training annually.

**Accredited Travel Professional Qualification** is a new qualification for travel agents. Agents accrue points towards the qualification by completing distance-learning modules and attending conferences. The purpose is to ensure that travel agents have the necessary expertise to cater for complex customer demands and offer an excellent service. There are three proposed levels:

* Bronze – minimum NVQ Level 2 or equivalent plus two years' industry experience

* Silver – minimum NVQ Level 3 or equivalent plus four years' industry experience

* Gold – minimum NVQ Level 3 or equivalent plus seven years' industry experience.

The levels have to be renewed annually with re-accreditation requiring proof of continuous professional development.

One possibility for gaining points for accreditation is attending an educational travel event. These events are provided in resorts by tour operators for agents to learn about the destination and the tour operator's products.

Leisure travel agents who want to learn about business travel can complete a 'Passport to Business Travel' course. These are run by the travel management company, Carlson Wagonlit Travel.

A useful aspect of continuing training for travel agents is destination training. Many tourist boards and companies now offer destination training on-line, and some of it is free. Examples of destinations agents can learn about on-line include Canada, Thailand, Australia and Malta, and more destinations are coming onstream all the time.

The travel agents benefit because they can carry out the training at home if they wish, or at work in quiet periods. The training increases their knowledge and therefore boosts their confidence and helps them sell. There is no pressure – the training is done at your own pace. The tourist board or company promoting the training benefits as they make agents more aware of their products and better equipped to sell them. The programme on Malta has prizes for agents who achieve more than 85% in their on-line exam. If you want to try this training, you will be able to do so if you have work experience or a job at a travel agent. You need the ABTA number to register on-line, but some programmes allow students to sign up.

Cosmos has a similar programme to help agents sell many Cosmos products – not just one destination.

*Agents can learn about destinations such as Toronto, Canada, on-line*

## CASE STUDY

The following is an extract from the website www.specialist.australia.com.

The Aussie Specialist Programme has been designed by the Australian Tourist Commission specifically for the retail travel trade. Who better to provide you with the most up-to-date information on every aspect of tourism to and around Australia?

The on-line format of the Aussie Specialist Programme was created to equip you with the knowledge and skills you need to sell Australia effectively. The on-line learning environment also allows you complete flexibility throughout the course – learn in your own time and at your own pace. But remember – don't take too long. The sooner you qualify, the sooner you will reap the rewards of being a certified Aussie Specialist.

The structure of the programme is simple and straightforward. There are four modules to complete, each with a short exam which needs to be passed with a score of at least 85% before you can move on to the next module. Once you've completed all four modules, the final exam will test your knowledge – successfully complete this, and you qualify.

Each module covers various aspects of Australia:
- Introduction to Australia
- Features and attractions of each State and Territory
- Building effective itineraries

Your membership lasts for 12 months from the date you register, and to remain on the programme, all you need to do is complete our renewal quiz. The renewal quiz is designed to ensure that you are kept up to date with developments in the Australian tourism industry.

1  Go to the site for the Aussie Specialist Programme, www.specialist.australia.com, and find out what the benefits to the travel agency are of putting staff through the training programme.
2  Carry out a search on the Internet and make a list of other destination training that is available.

Travel agents have other qualifications available to them. The Certificate in Travel (Travel Agency) is the standard examination-based qualification for travel agents, accepted by large organisations and independents. The course is available at Levels 2 and 3.

A similar qualification is available for tour operators, the Certificate in Travel (Tour Operators).

A two-level, self-study training course on travel insurance is available from ABTA for travel companies, travel training organisations and any company that sells travel insurance.

For employees of airlines, a 'Passport to Air' qualification is available. Ticketing qualifications are useful for employees in airlines or in travel agents. These are accredited by IATA and are exam-based.

Specialist qualifications are available from BTEC and NCFE for those who choose to be resort representatives.

If you are working in a Tourist Information Centre or for a tourist board you will probably train in the 'Welcome Host' and 'Welcome Host Plus' programme. Welcome Host is the official qualification for the tourism industry and it is designed specifically for the service sector (hospitality, retail, transport, library boards, leisure, etc.). Welcome Host is designed to enhance fundamental standards of service by all staff.

Many of these specialist courses can be added on to full-time college programmes or done in the workplace.

## Full-time work with college provision

### Foundation degrees

There are other ways of doing a degree besides full-time education. They are available through open learning, and a new proposal is the foundation degree. This has been designed for employees at supervisory level who want a qualification in higher education. Once the foundation degree is completed you can progress to a full degree. It can be undertaken at a college of further education on a flexible basis, taking your work commitments into account.

### Modern apprenticeships

These are available only to young people between the ages of 16 and 24. Under this scheme you work full time and study for a National Vocational Qualification (NVQ) at the same time. The most appropriate NVQ is Travel Services.

Modern Apprenticeships are available at foundation or advanced level. This scheme might be of interest to you if you leave college with a GNVQ Intermediate or lesser qualification, but otherwise you should be aware that an Advanced Modern Apprenticeship is a Level 3 qualification and you will already have one if you complete your BTEC National programme.

Lunn Poly is an example of a company with a good Modern Apprenticeship scheme. PGL, a company which offers activity holidays for young people, is another company that offers a Modern Apprenticeship scheme.

## Changing direction

Some students change direction completely after studying travel and tourism, but still find the course useful. Here is Lisa telling us about what she is doing.

I work for a music magazine called *Sound On Sound*. I am an administration assistant so I do reception duties, e.g. answering the phone and sending out the mail. We also have a mail order department where customers can buy magazines and merchandise directly from our shop, and I am in charge of this. I take the payments and send out the goods that have been ordered.

I also help in two other departments. I help the subscription manager by sending out renewal forms and I help in the credit control department by typing up and sending out the invoices. I send out the magazine to our advertisers every month.

Even though I have not gone into the industry, I am glad I did the travel and tourism course. I found it very interesting, especially as when I started the course I wanted to live in Spain! I really benefited from doing the course as I became much more confident and my social skills improved immensely. My favourite part of the course was organising our residential study visit. I loved the fact that we did it ourselves and worked together to organise a trip abroad. It was a very successful trip and great fun to do.

# Recruitment and selection

Human resources departments usually handle the recruitment and selection process for organisations. It is vital to the success of any organisation that the best staff available are employed in the right positions. A system is needed so that recruitment and selection are carried out properly and the employment of staff is not left to chance. The procedure varies from organisation to organisation, depending on the size and nature of the business, but it is possible to identify the essential stages.

In this section we will study how Canvas Holidays, a tour operator specialising in camping holidays, carries out recruitment and selection procedures. You can look at its current vacancies by going to www.canvasholidays.co.uk, going to the 'Contact us' section and finding the recruitment pages. Take a look at the interviews with the operations team – note how many of them started their careers as couriers and enjoyed the company so much they never left.

## Identifying company needs

There should be a staffing plan for any company. This gives ideal numbers of staff in each capacity within the organisation. When a vacancy arises for whatever reason, the impact of the vacancy should be considered against the staffing plan. It may be possible that the post is no longer required, or that the nature of the post should

change. There may be an opportunity to move staff into different positions better suited to company needs.

Sometimes, major restructuring takes place without a vacancy having arisen, due to changes in the business or economic circumstances of the company, for example a takeover of another company or a major economic downturn.

Canvas Holidays looks at courier staffing numbers every year and sets a courier/unit ratio of about 1:8 (a unit is a mobile home or tent). This can vary according to the site and whether it is used as a long stay or overnight stop. Once numbers are established, a staffing budget can be decided for the year. The courier service is deemed to be really important as it directly impacts on the customer's enjoyment of the holiday.

*Adequate numbers of courier staff are important to camping holiday makers*

---

## Job descriptions

A job description is a general statement explaining the purpose, duties and responsibilities of a job. It should include the following information:

* job title and department

* job purpose – the main duties of the role

* responsibilities – to whom the job holder is responsible, and all the responsibilities of the post

* physical conditions – where the work is performed, the hours, any hazards or special conditions

* social conditions – in teams, with clients, or alone

* economic conditions – salary range, commissions, bonuses, pension, sick pay

* prospects for promotion and training.

Here are some edited examples of job descriptions from Canvas Holidays.

---

**JOB DESCRIPTION**

**Job Title:**     **Campsite Courier**

*Reports to:*     Area Manager, Site Manager, Site Supervisor, Senior Courier

*Liaises with*:   Camp Proprietors, Specialist Couriers, Warehouse Personnel, Operations Department

**General Function**

To ensure that every aspect of our customers' holiday is of the highest standard possible by participating in montage, providing excellent Customer Service during the season and by participating in demontage. This will be measured through feedback from Customer Questionnaires and Area Managers.

**Duties and Responsibilities**

* Participate in montage and demontage as and when required.

* Montage clean and prepare units, prior to customer arrival.

* Cultivate and maintain good working relationships with the camp proprietor and campsite staff.

* Clean and maintain all units on site throughout the season, ensuring that they are clean and tidy at all times.

* Reflect appropriate Company Image at all times, as per the Overseas Staff Handbook, ensuring correct uniform is worn at correct times and that guidelines regarding corporate identity, dress and alcohol code are rigorously upheld.

* Where applicable, organise and supervise a programme of events for children, aged 4–11 years, at least twice per week.

* Ensure that local information in Information Book and on notice board is kept up to date and that information is added, where possible, to enhance the level of customer service.

* Provide each customer with a personal welcome on arrival.

* Monitor the quality of campsite facilities, as laid out in Health and Safety Guidelines.

* Ensure that campsite Health and Safety Audits are completed accurately and on time and that they are submitted to your Area Manager by the deadline set by him/her.

* Complete all necessary paperwork promptly and accurately.

* Work in a flexible manner in order to achieve the overall objectives of the Company.

## JOB DESCRIPTION

**Job Title:**     **Area Manager**

*Reports to*:     Recruitment & Training Manager

*Liaises with*:     Operations Department, Campsite Owners and Staff, Warehouse Personnel

### General Function

Be responsible for overseas staff welfare and overall running of a designated geographical area ensuring the best possible standards of customer care at all times, thereby achieving the customer satisfaction levels detailed in the Area Manager Handbook and the Operations Departmental Aim.

### Duties and Responsibilities

Co-ordinate and supervise the complete montage and demontage of all accommodation, storage and specialist units in designated area following procedures laid down at training and in Area Manager Handbook.

Take responsibility for the welfare and performance of all staff ensuring that they are appropriately trained and developed throughout the season and by carrying out regular performance monitoring as outlined at training and detailed in Area Manager Handbook.

Ensure that staff maintain all units (customer and courier) to a high standard throughout the season thereby upholding the correct Company Image in the field, following procedures laid down at training and in Area Manager Handbook.

Cultivate and maintain good working relationships with all Camp Proprietors and campsite staff thus ensuring the smooth running of the Canvas operation on site. Regular communication must be maintained throughout the season with staff, campsite owners and the Operations Department.

Ensure that all administration tasks (e.g. Health and Safety Audits, Emplacement Assessment Forms, Site Visit Forms, Staff Assessments and Appraisals, Demo paperwork) are completed accurately and on time by following the procedures detailed in the Overseas Staff and Area Manager Handbooks.

With the aid of Health & Safety Audits and Defect Forms, monitor the quality of campsite facilities, identifying any problem areas and immediately reporting them to the appropriate personnel.

Ensure appropriate Company Image is being reflected at all times, ensuring correct uniform is worn by all Canvas staff on site at correct times and that, as per the Overseas Staff Handbook, guidelines regarding corporate identity, dress code & alcohol code are rigorously upheld.

Ensure care and upkeep of all company vehicles, reporting any incidents immediately to the Logistics Manager, as per procedures laid down at training and in Area Manager Handbook.

Carry out contracting responsibilities including camp hunting, emplacement selection and contract negotiation as required.

Monitor quality of Canvas product on site, ensuring customers receives the best quality equipment available within budgetary and logistical constraints.

Monitor all expenditure within a certain geographical area, ensuring it is accounted for by means of appropriate receipts, reports and accounts, which are submitted weekly to the Operations Department.

Work in a flexible manner at all times in order to achieve the overall aims of the company.

## Person specifications

A person specification is used to match the right person to the job. It describes the desirable personal attributes of the job holder. It is usually based on a seven-point plan which includes:

* physical make-up – does the job require any special physical characteristics such as strength, good eyesight or height?

* attainments – what type of education is needed? What special occupational experience or training is required?

* intelligence – how much general intelligence should be evident?

* special aptitudes – is a skill in writing or drawing needed? Does the applicant need to be a car driver or speak a second language?

* disposition – what type of personality is desirable? Does the applicant need to be reliable or hard working?

* circumstances – does the applicant need to be mobile? Does he or she have to travel away from home?

* interests.

The job description and person specification are kept on record together and are used to help the recruitment team find the right person for the job.

### CASE STUDY

Study the Canvas job descriptions on pages 190–1 carefully. Using the seven-point plan, draw up a person specification for each of the jobs. Compare your person specification with that of another student.

## Advertising

Advertising is used to find suitable candidates. There are many possible locations for placing advertising. The most important consideration is reaching the right people, but cost must also be taken into account. The following could be used.

* Recruitment agencies – general or specialist. There are specialist travel and tourism agencies. To fill a permanent position, the agency charges a percentage of the annual salary for the post, so they are expensive.

* Job centre – usually used to recruit unskilled or semi-skilled staff. As the Department for Education and Employment provides the service, it is free. Job centres will also pre-interview for the company.

* Press – local press is ideal for local companies.

* Radio – frequently used for recruitment; more suitable for local jobs.

* 'Milk round' – companies visit universities searching for suitable graduate applicants.

* Internet – on their own websites or through specialist recruitment sites.

Canvas Holidays advertises in national newspapers such as the *Daily Mail* and the *Guardian*. An advertising schedule is prepared and shows all the publications that are to be used, along with dates and costs. The extract in our case study shows the publications and websites that Canvas decided to use in 2004.

### CASE STUDY

*Guardian* – **Monday and Saturday**

*Daily Mail* – **Thursday**

*Daily Mirror*

Loot

Countryside Jobs Service

Net Recruit – Internet

Hot Recruit

Summer Jobs Abroad

Job Opportunities

*French Property News*

Anywork Anywhere

Gaptastic

Website Address Book

*Daily* and *Sunday Express*

British Sports Trust

Independent Magazines – *GAT, MS LONDON LAM*

Southampton Uni

*TTG* (Area Manager Advertisement)

*Daily Mirror*

Childworks website (90 days)

Nanny Jobs (website)

Jobs Abroad Bulletin (website)

Travel Weekly – Area Manager Advert

Job Centre Adverts – Children's Courier, Montage Assistant and Warehouse Assistants

*TNT Magazine* (Hoopi Advert)

*The Lady* Magazine (Hoopi Advert)

Vacation Work Publications

Study the list of publications and websites used for advertising by Canvas Holidays and answer the following questions.

1 **Why are particular days specified for the *Daily Mail* and the *Guardian*?**
2 **Why was the *Travel Trade Gazette* (TTG) chosen for the area manager position?**
3 **What kind of people do you think Canvas is trying to attract by advertising in these publications?**
4 **Why do you think Southampton University is included in the schedule?**

## Short-listing applications

The initial methods of selection involve comparing applications to the job specification and person specification. A list of essential criteria may be used, and this will result in many applications being rejected.

At Canvas Holidays an interview checklist is used to help decide who should be short-listed. Essential requirements include availability, a bank account, experience of working with the public, experience of overseas travel or camping. Desirable requirements include a language and experience of working with children.

### Consider this ...

What do you think happens to an application that has spelling mistakes, crossings out or is badly presented?

## Interviewing

An interview is a two-way process and can be described as a problem-solving activity to decide whether the interviewee is right for the job and whether the job is right for the interviewee. The interviewer has to direct and control the discussion in order to make an objective decision.

Successful interviewers prepare well by:

* reading carefully through applications
* deciding on questions
* considering seating and room layout for the interview.

To establish rapport with the interviewee, they:

* smile and maintain good body language
* welcome the candidate
* start by confirming the information in the application.

When questioning, an effective interviewer will:

* start with simple open questions about what the candidate has done
* continue with more difficult, probing questions
* practise active listening
* repeat questions or reword them if necessary
* avoid leading questions
* avoid answering the question for the interviewee
* write notes afterwards, not during the interview
* ask all candidates the same questions to be fair
* encourage each interviewee to talk
* ask if the candidate has any questions
* end on a positive note
* tell candidates what will happen next, for example 'we will write to you next week'.

*An interview is a two-way process*

At Canvas Holidays, one-to-one interviews are the preferred procedure. Interviews are held at head office in Dunfermline as well as in hotels in major cities such as Manchester, London and Bristol. Interviews follow the same format, and interviewers receive both in-house and external training.

## Telephone interviews

When resources are limited or time is short, telephone interviews may be carried out. Canvas will use this method when they are nearing the start of the season and still want to recruit staff. Later in this unit there are some ideas to help you develop your telephone technique.

## Psychometric tests

These are used to test ability or personality. They usually take the form of fairly lengthy questionnaires and the respondent is judged as suitable for a position or not depending on the responses given. The tests are used to support other selection methods rather than as a selection tool that stands alone.

## INTERVIEW ASSESSMENT FORM – Courier

Result: ......

| Name: | Date: | Place: |
|---|---|---|
| Exact dates: | Position: Courier | Interviewers: |

| First impressions/ Reasons for applying | |
|---|---|
| Job awareness CLEANING!! | |
| Relevant work experience | |
| Customer expectations & customer service | |
| Problems (real or theoretical) | |
| Ideas for Hoopi (children's club)? | |
| Language skills | |
| Hobbies | |
| Montage/demontage Driving | |
| Camping/travel | |
| What do they hope to gain from a summer with Canvas? | |
| What would they do 'to make a difference'? | |

| Preferred area & why: | Single or team: | Suggested site: |
|---|---|---|
| | | |

| Any additional comments: |
|---|
| |

1   Arrange to carry out practice interviews within your group. Carry out the following activities to prepare:
   • choose one of the two Canvas Holiday jobs described in this unit
   • complete an application form, which you can download from the Canvas Holiday website
   • the interviewer should prepare questions and the interviewee should prepare to be interviewed.
   You could alternatively download job descriptions and application forms from Internet sites of other companies that interest you.
   Take it in turns to play the role of:
   • the interviewee
   • the interviewer
   • the observer.
   Use an assessment form like the one on the previous page when it is your turn to act as interviewer.
   It is a good idea to videotape the interviews so that you can discuss them in your group.
   This task may provide evidence for P4.

2   Explain how you used information on the job descriptions, the application form and appraisal form to help you promote yourself positively.
   This task may provide evidence for M2.

# Preparation for employment

## Business skills

The business skills you will need include the following:

✱ writing a business letter

✱ writing a memo

✱ using a fax machine

✱ communicating by e-mail

✱ telephone skills

✱ making a presentation.

### Writing a business letter

A business letter is a formal letter. It is often on headed paper, and it is always word-processed. The most common format of a business letter is fully blocked format. This means that everything is aligned to the left.
   You should:

✱ include the name of the recipient if you can, otherwise write to 'Dear Sir/Madam'; never assume a particular gender

✱ use an ordinary font such as Times New Roman, size 12

✱ begin a new paragraph for each new point

✱ if you are responding to a job advertisement, include a reference to the advertisement

✱ end with 'Yours faithfully' if you started with 'Dear Sir/Madam'

✱ end with Yours sincerely' if you started with 'Dear [name]'

✱ print on good white paper

✱ check everything and then ask someone else to check it again.

An example for you to follow can be found on page 197.

### Writing a memo

Memos are not used very often these days as they have been largely replaced by e-mail. However, you should know the format in case you need to write one. Sometimes memos are sent by e-mail.
   A memo is an internal document sent to a group or an individual to give them some information – 'memo' is short for memorandum. It is an informal document and there is no need to sign it.
   An example for you to follow is on page 197. Note that the content is very brief.

15 Somerset Gardens ← *Your address*
Hereford
HG6 4WA

Ms J Atherton ← *Recipient's name and address*
Fanfare Travel
Woodcroft Way
Hemel Hempstead
HP0 1WW

2 May 2005

Dear Ms Atherton

**Vacancy for Travel Assistant** ← *Reference to advertisement*

I am writing with reference to the above vacancy which was advertised in *Travel Weekly* on 27 April 2005.

I am about to complete my BTEC National Diploma in Travel and Tourism at Hereford College and I would like the opportunity of working in a busy travel agency.

I have undertaken work experience in a travel agency in Hereford. They were very pleased with my performance and I was offered a full-time job, but I wish to work in Hemel Hempstead and I know your agency has a good reputation.

I have been working part-time at the local library during my studies. This has given me excellent experience of customer service and improved my administrative skills as I had to use the library database. ← *Note new point in each paragraph*

I am sure I have the necessary skills and experience to succeed in the advertised post. I have pleasure in enclosing my CV and look forward to hearing from you.

↑ *Reference to enclosed CV*

Yours sincerely

Sanjit Atwal

---

**MEMO**

From:     Sanjit

To:        Mary

Date:     29.4.2005

Subject:  Marketing meeting

The meeting scheduled for next Friday (6/5) has been cancelled.

## Using fax

You will be expected to use a fax machine in the workplace. First, complete a fax header form. This has the details of the sender and a space for you to enter the details of the recipient. Each machine differs slightly but the basic operation is simple. If you are using a manual fax machine, insert your papers face down, tap in the recipient's fax number and press Send. If you are using a computer system you will have to attach documents held on file or scan your document to file and then attach. The computer will generate a header form to go with the fax.

## Communicating by e-mail

E-mails are less formal than letters but still important as there is always a record of what you wrote. This means it isn't a good idea to write them on the spur of the moment! If you are writing to an employer be professional, although you do not need to use a formal business layout. Don't apply for a job by e-mail unless expressly invited to do so. Record sent mail into your sent box. Learn how to send an attachment in case you need to attach your CV.

## Telephone skills

You might have to make telephone calls to a prospective employer – you might even be interviewed by telephone. A telephone call can be very important; you create an impression even though you cannot be seen. You should prepare for your telephone call just as you would for a face-to-face meeting.

Before you make a call, think about its purpose. Is a telephone conversation the best means of achieving that purpose?

For example, if you telephone a company and say 'Hello, I'm calling to ask if you have any vacancies', it's very unlikely that the answer will be 'Oh yes, we do, you just called at the right moment. Can you come in tomorrow?' It would be better to send a letter.

Who do you want to speak to? What are you going to say if that person is not in? You could leave your name and number or you could phone back having found out when he or she will be available.

Make a few notes about what you want to say or ask – but don't write a script and read it out, or you will sound very unnatural.

During the call:

* stand up – good body language will affect your voice

* use an appropriate greeting

* introduce yourself – for example, 'Good morning, this is Katy Johnson from Glasgow College. Is Ms Hendry available please?'

What if you don't know who to speak to? Ask the switchboard operator or whoever answers the phone for the name of the relevant person. For example, 'Hello, could you tell me the name of your human resources manager, please?' 'Yes, that's Ms Hendry.' 'Thank you. Is she available, please?' Write down the name so you remember it for next time.

Don't launch into your full speech to the wrong person – the switchboard operator probably won't be interested.

When you are speaking:

* use your voice to make a good impression; vary the pitch, be clear and not too quiet or too loud

* don't ramble, but make your point briefly

* end the call properly – say thank you, make sure your name has been noted and say goodbye.

### Theory into practice

Practise making telephone calls. Ask your tutor for a telephone set. Set up a situation for one of your colleagues and ask him or her to practise it. Listen and give constructive criticism on each other's performance.

Here are some ideas for tasks.

* Leave an answerphone message for Ms Hendry saying you have to change your interview date.

* Telephone and find out the name of the manager at a travel agency.

* Ring and ask for an application form for an advertised post.

## Making a presentation

There are two important aspects to an effective presentation; what you say (the content) and how you say it (presentation).

To ensure the content is correct, make sure you have understood the brief. If you have been asked to talk about Barbados, don't talk about all Caribbean islands. Carry out your research thoroughly so that you know your subject inside out and are able to answer questions.

Select relevant information from your research to fit the length of the talk. What is relevant? Decide what the audience needs to know, the essential facts and the most interesting information. You won't have time to include everything you have found out if you did your research properly.

Prepare the structure of your talk by dividing it into logical sections. Describe these sections to your audience by showing a contents page if you are using an overhead projector or PowerPoint, or tell them clearly what you are going to cover. Once you have introduced your subject in this way, present the information to the audience and, at the end, recap it in a summary.

### ✳ REMEMBER!

The best presentation structure is to:
- tell the audience what you are going to say (outline)
- tell them the information
- tell them what you have told them (summary).

Keep to these basic presentation rules:

✳ speak clearly and more slowly than usual

✳ use your voice effectively – don't speak in a monotone

✳ flag up the different sections by telling the audience or using a PowerPoint slide or overhead transparency

✳ if you have to include figures, give them in written form – on a screen or a handout

✳ don't use slang

✳ use cue cards

✳ never read out information – know your subject and use cue cards as prompts

✳ establish eye contact with the audience – practise scanning the audience, not fixing on one person

✳ practise giving presentations – you will improve!

Think about your body language too. You will probably stand; in fact it is better to stand even if you are allowed to sit – you will immediately feel more confident and in control. Stand up straight and don't shift from one foot to the other. If you have a tendency to play with pens, jewellery, hair or to tap your fingers, put everything down and fold your hands together. This will also stop you waving your arms about in excitement.

You should be smartly dressed, even if you are not in an interview situation.

### Theory into practice

Prepare for a presentation; the subject is you!

Your tutor has asked for volunteers to host an open day on Saturday about your course. Only two people can be hosts. Their task will be to welcome the visitors, charm them and give them interesting information about the course.

As you can imagine, everyone in your group wants to be chosen to attend on Saturday – from 9 am. You have to sell yourself and persuade your tutor that you have the necessary skills, charisma and knowledge to be chosen.

## Other business skills

In the world of work you will also need other business skills such as time management (prioritising, organising and scheduling your tasks), and skills relating to working with other people, including team-working, assertiveness and listening skills. These skills are practised throughout your work for this qualification, and all of them will improve with experience. When at work you can learn a lot by carefully observing how your colleagues go about their tasks, and seeing which approaches seem to be most effective.

## Personal skills and attributes

You must be realistic about your capabilities, and therefore your options – there is no point in applying for a job for which you have no qualifications. If you are lacking in one or two points only, decide how important they are and whether you should try anyway.

It might be useful to carry out a skills audit. This will help you complete an action plan as well.

### Developing an action plan

Here are two examples of planning methods you can use to help set, plan and achieve your targets for the development of your personal skills.

### Theory into practice

Complete the following skills audit. Do this with a partner and discuss how you can each improve on your skills and qualifications.

| SKILL AREA | ASPECT | GOOD? | IMPROVEMENT NEEDED? | QUALIFICATION HELD |
|---|---|---|---|---|
| Communication | Taking notes<br>Spelling<br>Writing letters<br>Writing reports<br>Oral presentation<br>Interviewing | | | |
| Number | Calculating<br>Interpreting statistics<br>Presenting graphs and tables | | | |
| IT | Word<br>Access<br>Excel<br>Internet<br>E-mail | | | |
| Working with others | Contributing to a team<br>Assertiveness<br>Listening | | | |
| Improving own learning and performance | Time management<br>Action planning<br>Organisational skills | | | |
| Vocational skills in travel and tourism | | | | |
| Languages | | | | |

## 1 Setting targets

| TARGET | WHEN? |
|---|---|
| Find an interesting and challenging job | |
| Gain BTEC qualification with good grades | |
| Complete final assessments | |
| Update CV | |
| Contact tutor about possible jobs | |
| Carry out research for assessments, prepare CV and covering letter | |
| Interview practice with tutor, regular reviews of progress with tutor | |

## 2 Action plan

| TARGET | HOW? | WHEN? | RESOURCES NEEDED |
|---|---|---|---|
| Apply to university | Research courses | Summer holidays | UCAS website, prospectuses, friends at university |
| | Prepare personal statement | By beginning of October | UCAS instructions |
| | Complete application on-line | By October | Tutors or careers advisers |
| | Prepare for interviews | By December | |
| Pass course | Keep to deadlines, prepare timetable of work | By June | Tutors, parents, library and Internet |

### Theory into practice

Design a similar target-setting form or action plan and complete it for yourself. You can keep it confidential if you prefer, or you can discuss it with your tutor. If you use the form to show how you will meet your training and development needs, you can use it for your assessment.

## Self-selling

### Preparing a curriculum vitae (CV)

*Curriculum vitae* literally means an account of your life – it is a summary of your work experience, education and skills. The purpose of your CV is to bring you to the attention of an employer and get you to the interview stage.

Your CV should be constantly updated, and although you will keep a basic CV on file you should adapt it to fit the particular requirements of each job you apply for. Of course, this doesn't mean changing the facts – it means altering the emphasis of the CV to make the relevant points stand out.

Your CV should include:

* personal information

* work history

* education

* skills

* references.

## Personal information

Give your name, address, telephone numbers and e-mail address. There is no need to give your gender, marital status or number of children, if any. Age need not be mentioned either, but if you are young it is a good idea to put your date of birth as there may be jobs you are not eligible for because of your age. Some resort representative jobs are available only to over-21s, for example. You do not want to reach interview stage and then be disappointed.

## Work history

This is where you list all your employment, starting with your current or latest job. If you have never had a job, include any periods of work experience or voluntary work you have done. For each job give the job title, the name of the company and what it does, if it is not well known. Add a list of your responsibilities in that position. If you can think of particular achievements in that position, list them too.

## Education

List your qualifications. As with work history, start with your most recent qualification or course. Include schools from secondary onwards. Do not include GCSEs below 'C' grade. Write the name of the college/school and against it the qualifications you achieved there.

## Skills

List any other skills you have. Examples include languages, with an indication of your level, driving licence, first aid certificate or lifeguard qualifications. You can include your key skill and IT qualifications here. For IT, say which software packages you can use.

## References

It is usual to include the names and addresses of two referees. One must be an employer or tutor. Alternatively, you can state that referees are available on request – this gives you time to ask referees for permission to give their contact details.

## Profile

Some people choose to start their CV with a brief personal profile. It sums up your skills and experience and gives the employer an instant idea of whether you are suitable for the post. It can easily be adapted to fit a particular post.

## CV writing tips

* Keep it brief – two sides of A4 is the maximum.

* Don't try to be funny.

* Don't include visuals, special designs, etc.

* Don't add a passport photo unless specifically asked to do so.

* Tailor the CV to the job in question.

* Don't include anything negative.

* Print it on good-quality paper.

* Ask referees for permission before mentioning them.

* Ask someone to check the grammar and spelling.

* Keep a copy of your CV on disk.

An example of a CV is shown on page 202.

---

## Assessment activity 6.3

1 Follow all the guidelines and the example given above and produce your own CV. Make this a basic CV which can then be adapted to fit a particular job application.

2 Read the following job advertisement.

### FRIENDLY TRAVEL

Friendly Travel has been in business successfully for 25 years and has become one of the UK's leading independent travel companies. We pride ourselves on the range of products and the outstanding level of customer service we provide for our clients.

**Customer Relations Executive**

We are looking for a well-organised, customer-focused person to be responsible for logging in-coming correspondence, acknowledging customer complaints and liaising with other departments to ensure customer complaints are resolved. The post is suitable for a new entrant into the travel trade and training will be given. As much of the correspondence is written, applicants will need excellent letter-writing skills and must also be confident in verbal communication. A knowledge of tour operators and their regulatory practices would be beneficial.

Please forward your CV and letter of application to …

a Adapt Charlie's CV (page 202) so that it is suitable for this position.
   • List the Customer Service and Tour Operations units under the BTEC National qualification.
   • In the profile add 'well organised'.
   • Under TIC responsibilities add 'dealing with customer complaints'.
   • Make any other changes that you think are appropriate.

b Now adapt your own CV, drawing on your own experience and skills so that your CV is suitable for this position. If you prefer, you can choose another job advertisement for this task.

These tasks may provide evidence for P4.

## Letters of application

You should never send your CV without a covering letter. Remember your CV is up to two pages long, and the purpose of your letter is to focus on why you are suitable for the job.

If the letter is poorly presented you will not be selected, so make sure you have studied the section in this unit on writing a business letter.

Letters of application may be speculative – this means a letter is sent even if you don't know whether a job vacancy exists. If you are writing in response to a job advertisement, make sure you say which advertisement and give examples of the skills and qualities you have that match the job advertised.

### Theory into practice

Write a letter of application for Charlie for the job advertisement shown in Assessment Activity 6.3 above. Use the letter-writing guidance given earlier in this unit and Charlie's CV (page 202) to help you.

## Interview skills

### Personal presentation

In the travel and tourism industry, staff often have direct contact with the public, so dress code is important. Employers have the right to control their business image, especially when employees are in direct contact with customers, and most travel and tourism companies require their staff to wear a uniform or obey strict dress codes.

Most airlines do not allow visible piercings (except for simple earrings) or tattoos. Thomas Cook does not allow facial studs, body piercings or visible tattoos.

In a resort, employees sometimes wear shorts and T-shirts depending on their role. This would be suitable for campsite couriers, for example. They are still part of a uniform provided by the company.

If you are preparing for an interview you should dress in a conservative way. This means wearing formal business dress, unless you are specifically told otherwise.

*You should wear formal business dress for an interview*

| MEN | WOMEN |
| --- | --- |
| Suit – if you don't have one, wear a plain shirt, tie and smart trousers. No T-shirts | Suit or smart trousers/skirt and top – no mini-skirts. No low-cut tops or thin straps |
| Polished dark shoes – no trainers | Polished dark shoes – no trainers, and heels should not be too high |
| Hair – freshly washed and tied back if long | Hair – freshly washed |
|  | Wear tights with skirts – no bare legs |

Make sure every item you wear is clean and free from creases, and make sure you too are clean and sweet-smelling. If you smoke, do not do so just before you enter an interview – it will not give a good impression. Remember to smile!

Also pay attention to your body language during the interview – try to appear relaxed and open, even if you are feeling nervous. Leaning forward slightly shows you are alert and interested, and maintaining eye contact (without staring) shows you are confident and are engaging with the interviewer.

## Arriving on time

Being late does not give a good impression! Plan to arrive ten minutes before your interview appointment, so that you feel calm and prepared. If possible, do a practice run of the journey to time it – preferably at the same time of day to allow for traffic conditions.

## Demonstrating your skills

Prepare examples of situations where you have demonstrated particular skills. You should be able to guess the skills that would be appropriate from the job description. For example, think of situations where you had to solve a problem, where you demonstrated leadership or where you showed good customer service skills.

## Preparing questions

At all interviews an opportunity is given for the interviewee to ask questions. Make sure you have some ready. Don't ask about the pay and holidays – you can find out about these later if they haven't already told you. Ask about training and promotion prospects. If interviewers want to give you a hard time they will start by asking for your questions. Don't be intimidated, take out your pad of prepared questions and fire away!

## Giving a presentation

At some interviews candidates are required to give an individual presentation on a given subject. You would expect to be informed of this before the interview and given plenty of time for preparation.

It is a great opportunity to show what you are capable of and demonstrate your knowledge and research skills; nevertheless, it can be a nerve-wracking experience. There is no point hoping to give an 'off-the-cuff' performance – the only way to give a good presentation is to prepare thoroughly and practise, and practise again. Use the section earlier in this unit (page 199) to make sure you have prepared the presentation properly.

## Knowing the company

Make sure you have carried out research into the company and its products and services. You might be asked about your opinions of the company; if you don't know anything about it you will look foolish. For example, one unsuccessful interviewee was asked what she thought about the company's new programme to Asia, and she replied that she didn't know it sold holidays to Asia.

# Factors that contribute to an effective workplace

## Teamwork

Teamwork skills are essential in the workplace. You must be able to work with other people in a team even if you don't happen to like them.

A team is a group of people who are working together to achieve common objectives. Even when you are not physically with other members of your team, you can work together by contributing to a sequence of activities with a common aim. If you were working as a resort representative in Spain, you would still be working in a team with colleagues in head office in the UK. In this part of the unit we will consider the factors that contribute to effective teamwork.

## Team roles

Good teams achieve synergy; that is, together they can achieve more than the members could individually. More ideas, energy and resources are generated as a group because:

* the team solves problems and makes decisions together

* the team focuses on priorities, with everyone working towards the same aim

* the team provides a sense of belonging and a sense of status

* the team provides a support network.

Not everyone in a team is the same – each person has his or her own strengths and weaknesses. If each person had the same weaknesses, the team could not work; there needs to be a balance of skills. A method of recognising individuals' strengths and weaknesses is needed in order to build an effective team.

The management expert R. Meredith Belbin has outlined nine team roles necessary for a successful team. One person can represent more than one role, as most people have strengths in more than one area.

Belbin's roles are as follows.

1 **Chairperson/co-ordinator** – the group leader, likely to be relaxed and extrovert, also likely to be a good communicator. He or she will build on the strengths of team members and give them encouragement.

2 **Plant** – the ideas person in the team, a person who is creative in looking for solutions to problems, but not always good at details, and so may make careless mistakes.

3 **Shaper** – the task leader who unites ideas and effort. Needs to be dominant and extrovert in order to make things happen.

4 **Monitor/evaluator** – the team analyst, who is not so good at ideas but pays attention to detail, thus keeping the team directed towards its target.

5 **Implementer** – the organiser of the team, who is able to take the ideas of the plant and shaper and turn them into manageable and realistic tasks. A practical, stable and disciplined person.

6 **Resource investigator** – the person who is outgoing and will explore and report on ideas and developments outside the group; this person always has a solution to problems, is sociable and enthusiastic, and good under pressure.

7 **Team worker** – a very people-oriented person, sensitive to others' needs. The team worker has good communication skills and will be good at motivating others. A natural mediator, who will deal with any conflict within the team, this person is very good to have around in a crisis.

8 **Finisher** – a person who sticks to deadlines and likes to get on with things. Will probably be irritated by the more relaxed members of the team.

9 **Specialist** – this person is single-minded and a self-starter, and provides knowledge and skills in specialist areas.

*People playing different roles blend together to form a successful team*

Each of Belbin's roles acquires a different level of importance according to the objectives of the team and the stage in the team's life.

**Theory into practice**

Which of Belbin's roles do you think you fit? Visit the website www.belbin.com to find out more about Belbin roles. You will find a self-perception questionnaire that is used to analyse roles. You will be able to complete it, but the analysis itself has to be paid for.

## Team development

**Formal teams** are part of the structure of an organisation and are planned in order to meet that organisation's objectives. The formal team will follow rules and regulations and may meet on a pre-arranged schedule and complete administrative procedures. Examples in travel and tourism include sales teams and marketing teams.

**Informal teams** work within or outside formal teams. They are sometimes based on personal relationships between members rather than on work roles. When you complete group work for assignments, you often choose the classmates you wish to work with. You choose to work with people you like and ones you know will be as committed as you are to the work. This is an informal team.

There are several theories of team structure and development, which will help you to understand the effectiveness of teams. Bruce Tuckman (1965) identified four main stages of team development.

1 **Forming** – at this stage, team members form their first impressions of each other and establish identities. They are sounding each other out and finding out what is expected of them.

2 **Storming** – the team members have, by now, become more used to each other. Members are prepared to put forward their ideas forcibly and openly; they are also prepared to disagree and so there may be some conflict and hostility.

3 **Norming** – the team now begins to establish co-operation. Conflict is controlled, views are exchanged and new standards introduced.

4 **Performing** – the team is now working together; it begins to arrive at solutions and achieve objectives.

There can also be a fifth stage, called 'adjourning' or 'mourning', where the team has disbanded and the members miss being part of the team.

## Sources of conflict in a team

Conflict occurs in a team when there is a disagreement among members which affects their interaction. The disagreement may be about leadership, team roles, the aims of the team or the means of achieving those aims. It usually occurs in the storming stage of team development. A high-performing team will air disagreements and make an effort to resolve them. There are two main sources of conflict.

### Personality conflict

This affects the relationships among team members and distracts them from their objectives. It may shows itself as hostility to one or more team members and the breaking of the team into cliques. It can be resolved by allowing individuals to air their grievances openly and engage in free discussion.

### Task conflict

Team members may disagree on how to achieve their objectives, for example on how to increase sales. This may promote a healthy competition among team members as they strive to prove their idea is most workable, or it may unsettle the team and make them insecure. In a situation where individuals are able to get on with their own tasks within the team, the effect will not be so marked.

## Effective communication

Open communication must be encouraged and ideas should be freely expressed in the team. There should be trust and support between team members. An effective leader can encourage good communication and shape the way the team works; different styles of management are discussed in Unit 2 (see pages 54–5).

## Motivation

The motivation and commitment of employees is key to the success of a team and therefore to the company.

> **Consider this ...**
>
> What factors motivate you to go to your job or your course? Think about one of your family who has a good job. What motivates him or her? Is this motivation different from yours?

There are many ways of motivating staff. Here are some examples:

* **Shares** – some companies allow employees to hold shares. If the company is doing well they will be paid a dividend, so the employees have an interest in a successful company. British Airways operates such a scheme.

* **Performance-related pay** – the better you perform or the more sales you make, the more money you are paid.

* **Flexible working** – if employees can work the hours they want, they are better motivated to perform well.

* **Competitions** – staff are invited to enter competitions based on new ideas, high sales or customer satisfaction.

* **Appraisal** – a good appraisal scheme can be a motivating factor for employees if they feel involved in the process and are given

constructive feedback. Canvas Holidays has a typical appraisal system, described below.

---

## Canvas appraisal

### i) Pre-interview preparation

Your Area Manager will provide you with your pre-appraisal interview questionnaire and a date and time for your interview 7–10 days in advance. Using the questionnaire you can then prepare for your interview. You do not have to use this form and you do not need to submit it to your Area Manager before the interview; it is entirely for your own benefit.

### ii) The appraisal interview

This is the time to discuss and agree on your overall performance, taking into account every aspect of the job and to review performance assessments that have been completed during the season.

### iii) The performance appraisal form

The discussion during your interview is recorded on this form and your performance to date is evaluated under the headlines provided. Future job/career aspirations, including future work with Canvas Holidays, should also be discussed at this point.

Once the appraisal has been completed, both parties should sign the appraisal form

- One copy will be returned to Head Office for your personnel file.
- You will retain one copy.
- Your Area Manager will hold one copy.

---

## Consideration of health, safety and security

Safety and security factors must be considered in the workplace, and legislation such as the Health and Safety at Work Act must be adhered to. Specific regulations also apply where food is served or where there are chemical hazards, for example in a swimming pool. All these requirements are important.

For some organisations a lapse in safety procedures can mean the collapse of the business and even a prosecution. Companies that organise activity holidays for children, for example, must make health and safety a priority.

Assessment activity 6.4

PGL Travel provides activity holidays for groups and schools. Established for 48 years, PGL has developed comprehensive, externally verified safety management systems.

This starts with the recruitment procedure. Recruitment officers make an initial selection of applicants based on a detailed four-page application form. Formal written references are obtained from two people who know the applicant in a professional capacity. Qualifications claimed by applicants must be supported by documentary proof in order to be taken into account. Successful candidates are offered contracts of employment subject to vigorous internal vetting and then via the Criminal Records Bureau. They must then successfully complete a probationary period.

All new staff follow a formal induction procedure. Upon successful completion of the induction programme, staff gain a nationally recognised Open College Network qualification. PGL is an approved centre for Edexcel, BTEC and City and Guilds, offering courses such as Modern Apprenticeships at foundation and advanced level. There is a permanent team of qualified staff responsible for delivering in-house training and assessment as well as setting up external courses. Reviews of staff performance take place throughout the period of employment.

Visit www.pgl.co.uk for further information. Look particularly at external accreditations.

*PGL Travel offers activity holidays for groups of young people*

1 Describe the factors at PGL that contribute to an effective workplace. Consider:
   - teamwork
   - recruitment
   - training and development.

   This task may provide evidence for P5.

2 Explain how you could contribute to making an effective workplace at PGL.

   This task may provide evidence for M3.

3 Analyse the effects of all the working practices in the areas mentioned above on the workplace at PGL. Give examples of good practice at PGL.

   This task may provide evidence for D2.

## Legal and ethical responsibilities

Legislation exists to ensure that personnel receive equal opportunities and that there is no discrimination. The Acts of Parliament that you should be aware of are explained below.

### Race Relations Act 1976

This makes discrimination on racial grounds unlawful in employment, training, education and the provision of goods, facilities and services. The act defines two main types of discrimination:

* **direct discrimination**, which occurs when someone is treated less favourably because of his or her colour, nationality, citizenship or national origin

* **indirect discrimination**, which occurs when rules which apply to everyone and appear to be fair, put a particular racial group at a disadvantage in practice.

### Sex Discrimination Act 1975

This act makes it unlawful to discriminate against someone on the grounds of gender, marital status, gender reassignment or sexual orientation.

The act was updated in 1986 to remove restrictions on women's hours of work – it allows women to take jobs with flexible hours. The act not only covers discrimination in the workplace but in job advertisements and interviews.

### Disability Discrimination Act 1995

A person with a disability is 'anyone who has a physical or mental impairment which has a substantial or long-term adverse effect on his/her ability to carry on normal day-to-day activities'.

This act makes discrimination against people with disabilities unlawful in respect of employment, education and access to goods, facilities, services and premises.

Employers are required to make reasonable adjustments to accommodate people with disabilities. Examples include providing specially adapted keyboards for arthritis sufferers, facilitating wheelchair access and relocating people with limited mobility to the ground floor.

### Equal Pay Act 1970

This act was introduced to address the problem of women being paid less than men for the same work. It allows employees to claim equal pay for work of equal value in terms of demands made on them, such as effort, skills and decisions made. There is also an EU Directive that states that for the same work or work of equal value, sex discrimination must be eliminated in all aspects of pay.

## Age discrimination

Legislation prohibiting discrimination on the grounds of age is promised in the UK by October 2006. This is in line with a European Employment Directive. This directive also added sexual orientation and religion to the cases covered by discrimination laws, and these are already in place. The legislation on age discrimination is delayed until 2006 to give the government time to resolve the complex problems associated with its introduction and to allow employers sufficient time to prepare for the changes.

Travel agencies have already increased the number of older staff working in agencies. A Co-op Travel Group manager was quoted as saying 'Mature staff make our customers more comfortable when booking – they are booking with their peers, as most of our customers are 35 plus'. Thomas Cook has been recognised by the government's Age Positive campaign as an 'employer champion' based on its recruitment of older staff for its shops.

### ✴ REMEMBER!

Discrimination is sometimes reasonable and is therefore lawful. For example, at airports female security officers are required to search female passengers.

Discrimination at work is a very serious issue and can result in large amounts of compensation being awarded following successful tribunals, not to mention a lot of bad publicity. Employers need to set up policies to ensure that the workplace is free from discrimination.

Measures to be taken include:

✴ setting up a comprehensive equal opportunities policy covering all aspects of discrimination

✴ training staff in discrimination legislation and on how to implement the equal opportunities policy

✴ setting up complaints procedures for instances of discrimination

✴ ensuring that discriminatory behaviour is never condoned and that action is taken where necessary.

### Theory into practice

Find out about the equal opportunities policy at your place of work or education. Is provision made for all aspects of discrimination? What happens if someone feels he or she is being discriminated against? What training is given to staff or students in equal opportunities? Make notes on your findings and discuss with your group.

### CASE STUDY

#### Equal opportunities awareness quiz

A holiday maker, lying on a sunbed, looks up and shouts 'hey, gorgeous' to a passing lifeguard. The same lifeguard casually mentions this to a senior manager. The manager says 'I'd never do that'. The manager has two grown-up children who are 22 and 30. They get on very well. One is a sergeant in the army, the other is a make-up artist. The manager divorced last year and is currently dating someone.

Complete the table and discuss your results in a group. Are you aware of any stereotyping?

| STATEMENTS | True | False | Don't know |
|---|---|---|---|
| The holiday maker was lying on a sunbed | | | |
| Not every man mentioned would shout 'hey, gorgeous' to a lifeguard | | | |
| The manager is no longer living with his wife | | | |
| The manager has a new girlfriend | | | |
| The manager's son is in the army | | | |
| The younger child is a make-up artist | | | |
| At some point a man spoke to a woman | | | |
| A woman was shouted at | | | |

## Employment Rights Act 1996

When you get a job you can expect to receive a **contract of employment**. This is a legally binding agreement between the employer and the employee. Under the Employment Rights Act, the employer must give the employee a written document including the following information, in writing, within two months of starting work.

* name of employer and employee

* date employment began

* rate of pay and interval of pay

* hours of work

* holiday entitlement and pay

* job title and brief description of duties

* place of work

* notice entitlement and requirements

* sick leave entitlement and sick pay

* pension and pension schemes

* disciplinary procedures and grievance procedures

* date of end of employment if fixed term

* additional details about working abroad if appropriate.

Some terms are 'implied' in a contract of employment, which means they may not be mentioned but they are still legally binding. For example, the employer has a duty to provide safe systems of work, a safe workplace and to employ competent staff who are not a danger to themselves or other staff.

### Notice periods

After one month of continuous employment an employee is entitled to one week of notice if the employment ends. After two years' employment he or she is entitled to two weeks' notice, after three years, three weeks' notice and so on. After 12 years the legal maximum of 12 weeks' notice is reached.

A employee must also give notice of leaving to an employer. After one month of continuous employment, an employee must give a minimum of one week's notice.

Employees are entitled to normal pay during notice periods as long as they are working or available for work.

### Disciplinary and grievance procedures

These must be included in the employee's written statement or contract, or at least there must be a reference to where they can be found.

Disciplinary procedures deal with such matters as warnings to be given before dismissal. Warnings might arise from the following:

* lack of capability or qualifications – although the employer has a responsibility to give training

* misconduct – which includes habitual lateness.

Gross misconduct, for example assault or theft, leads to instant or summary dismissal.

Grievance procedures deal with complaints by employees who are not satisfied with aspects of their employment. Employees must be given the name of a person to whom a complaint can be made and should be informed of rights of appeal.

### Redundancy

Redundancy pay is calculated according to the employee's age, length of service and salary. Employees can claim for unfair dismissal if they suspect

* there is no real redundancy

* they were unfairly selected for redundancy.

Dismissal is treated as redundancy if the whole business is closing or a particular job disappears or requires fewer employees. An employer may offer alternative employment. If the employee unreasonably refuses it, he or she is not entitled to redundancy pay.

## EU directives on hours and pay

The European Working Time Directive was enacted in the UK through the Working Time Regulations, 1998. This lays down the following:

* a maximum 48-hour week, averaged over 17 weeks

* at least four weeks' paid annual leave

* a weekly rest period of at least 24 hours in each seven-day period

* a daily rest period of at least 11 consecutive hours between each working day

* an in-work rest break of 20 minutes for those working six hours or more per day.

Some sectors are excluded from the regulations; one of these is transport.

## National Minimum Wage Act 1998

This act provides workers with a minimum hourly rate below which their wages will not fall. Those who work part time benefit most, because they are often badly paid. The Low Pay Commission advises the Secretary of State on the value of the minimum hourly rate. A special, lower rate applies to 18–21-year-olds.

## Maternity and paternity leave

The Employment Relations Act 1999 provides for basic rights for maternity leave. There are three periods of maternity leave; ordinary maternity leave is for a period of 18 weeks which coincides with the period for statutory maternity pay. This applies to all employees. Compulsory maternity leave extends to a period of two weeks after the birth; the employer must not permit the woman to return to work during this period. Additional maternity leave follows immediately after the original 18-week period and must end within 29 weeks of the birth. Employees with at least one year's service with an employer are eligible for the additional maternity leave.

Under the same act there are provisions to allow parents three months' leave in order to care for a child. This is intended to be taken before the child is five. It is intended to be available to men and to women, in addition to maternity leave. Paternity leave is available to men who:

* have or expect to have responsibility for the child's upbringing

* are the biological father of the child, or the mother's husband or partner

* have worked continuously for their employer for 26 weeks ending with the 15th week before the baby is due.

Eligible employees can choose to take either one week or two consecutive weeks' paternity leave (not odd days).

## Statutory Sickness Pay

An employer must pay Statutory Sick Pay to employees who become sick and who normally earn at least £79 per week. After 28 weeks, Incapacity Benefit or Income Support must be claimed instead.

### Theory into practice

Find out how employment rights are implemented at your place of work. There should be a staff handbook with details of grievance and disciplinary procedures. You should have a contract of employment.

If you do not have a job ask a relative or friend if you can look at the information received from his or her place of work. Remember that issues such as pay are confidential. Make detailed notes on the procedures and systems in place. Comment on how they contribute to a more effective workplace.

## Training and development

### 'Agent training key to 30% sales rise'

AGENT training is one of the key factors behind airport parking operator BCP's rise in bookings this year.

The group claimed to have made 170,000 sales in the first three months of the year, compared with 120,000 for the same quarter last year.

Bookings at regional airports have shown particular growth in the first quarter of 2004 – Newcastle is 50% up; Leeds/Bradford 40% up; and Nottingham East Midlands up 30%.

BCP marketing director Eric Campus said discounted holiday prices were boosting sales of ancillary services as agents sought to make up their income in other ways.

Regular training sessions are held across the country, hosted by regional sales managers Jenny Adamou and Darran Burr.

'When Jenny did training in one shop on the Monday, by the Friday they had made 36 bookings', said Campus.

BCP is investigating opportunities to expand its services to European airports.

*Travel Trade Gazette*, 21 May 2004

*Training brings many benefits to organisations and their staff*

Those employers who wish to ensure an effective workplace will offer ongoing training and development to staff. There are several benefits to organisations and to their workforces. Training can:

* improve individual performance
* improve team performance
* allow staff to be better informed
* equip staff to deal with change and emergencies
* make for a more flexible workforce
* improve morale
* allow managers more time to manage through delegation of other tasks.

## Induction training

Employers have to provide instruction and training to ensure health and safety, and this is usually a part of induction training. The induction is the first stage of training and is given to new employees; it is important as new employees need to be made welcome and to become effective in their work as quickly as possible.

Induction covers:

* the nature of the job
* introduction to the workplace and to staff
* the lines of responsibility

* facilities such as toilets, lockers, canteen
* health and safety basics.

## Mentoring

Mentoring schemes are growing in popularity. They offer employees a one-to-one relationship with a mentor, someone with greater experience and a willingness to listen and advise. The mentor and the mentee meet regularly and discuss aspects of the mentee's job, such as career development.

The mentor does not act as a line manager or superior and is never judgemental, but acts as a sounding board and is able to offer ideas and a different outlook on work issues.

The Hilton hotel chain runs a mentoring scheme for its staff at all levels. Its purpose is to support staff in their career development. Mentors at the Hilton chain are often colleagues of the mentees doing similar jobs, which departs from the traditional model. All of the mentors have had mentoring training.

## In-house training

Large companies offer their own in-house training and may even write their own materials. These training courses are very beneficial as they are tailor-made to meet the needs of the company.

Here is an example from the Saga website to show how the company supports the continual development of its staff.

To help staff make the most of their existing skills, as well as acquire new ones, the Saga Learning Academy makes available a wide range of facilities and resources to all our employees.

Learning Academy sites provide a quiet space for learning, reading or studying and are located in prime locations in each of our buildings.

The scheme offers access to over 250 e-learning courses covering a vast number of topics. These include communication, leadership, human resources, management, customer service, sales, marketing, negotiation, project management, health & safety, team building, typing, languages and first aid. The full range of Microsoft Office courses is also available.

Courses can be taken either at home or on Learning Academy PCs using either CD ROMs or via the Saga intranet. Additional resources include an extensive library of over 150 books, journals and magazines.

1  Go to the Saga website (www.saga.co.uk) and find out what other elements of good practice contribute to an effective workplace at Saga. Make detailed notes.
2  Try to evaluate how the examples benefit staff and the organisation.

## External courses

Thousands of external courses are available. These may be specific to travel and tourism or other professional qualifications in areas such as marketing or human resource management. They may be offered by colleges, by travel associations, or by private companies.

Companies may allow individuals or groups to attend such courses. Some may be long term, leading to advanced qualifications, so a great deal of commitment is required on behalf of the individual. Earlier in this unit you were introduced to some examples of courses and qualifications (see pages 185–8).

### Theory into practice

Consider the advantages and disadvantages of in-house training and external training. Draw up a comparative table showing your analysis. Discuss your findings with your group.

## Investors in People

Investors in People is a UK quality standard developed in 1990. Those companies who gain the award have proved that they invest in the training and development of their staff. This is beneficial to employees and also to customers and suppliers.

The standard for Investors in People is based on four key principles.

1  Commitment from the top to develop all employees.

2  Regular review of training and development needs.

3  Taking relevant action to meet those needs throughout people's careers.

4  Evaluating training and development outcomes for individuals and the organisation in order to continuously improve.

These principles are sub-divided into 24 indicators of effective practice, and the organisation provides evidence for assessment against the indicators.

Once the organisation gets the award it is entitled to display the Investors in People logo on company literature.

### Theory into practice

What do you think are the benefits to an organisation of gaining the Investors in People Award? Make notes on your ideas. Research a travel and tourism organisation which has been given the award and try to analyse what effect this has had on the organisation.

1. What different aspects of travel agency work are available?
2. What does the job role of a resort representative include?
3. Describe the range of jobs in an airport.
4. What kinds of courses can follow a BTEC programme?
5. How would you build up your knowledge of destinations if you worked in a travel agency?
6. What is a Modern Apprenticeship programme?
7. What information would be included in a job description?
8. What is the purpose of a person specification?
9. What are the differences between an e-mail and a letter?
10. What should your CV include?
11. Give five tips for writing a CV.
12. Why is good teamwork important?
13. What are Tuckman's stages of team development?
14. Give some examples of methods of motivating staff in the workplace.
15. What is the principle of the Sex Discrimination Act?
16. What differences will the legislation on age discrimination make to the travel and tourism industry?
17. What legislation covers hours and pay?
18. What is induction training?

# UNIT 6 ASSESSMENT ASSIGNMENT

This assessment is designed to provide you with a portfolio of work which will help you in the future when you are looking for a job or looking for a change of job or promotion.

You will consider a range of different jobs in the travel and tourism industry and select two of interest for comparison. You will analyse your own skills and attributes and prepare to participate in the recruitment and selection process. You will also consider the factors that contribute to an effective workplace and think about how you can use your own skills to make the workplace more effective.

## 1 About the jobs

- Describe a range of career opportunities in the travel and tourism industry. Use the information in this unit and your own independent research to find relevant information.

- Choose two job roles in travel and tourism which are of interest to you. Describe each of these roles in detail. You should include: responsibilities; work pattern (for example, seasonal, permanent, full time, shifts); pay and conditions; qualifications required; skills required; personal attributes required; entry levels, for example, school leaver/BTEC National/A level/graduate; progression. This information could be presented in a table.

  These tasks may provide evidence for P1.

- Compare the entry levels and progression routes for the two jobs and draw conclusions from your comparison.

  This task may provide evidence for M1.

## 2 About the workplace

- Describe the stages of recruitment and selection in travel and tourism.

  This task may provide evidence for P2.

- Describe the factors that contribute to an effective workplace.

  This task may provide evidence for P5.

- Analyse how good or poor working practices impact on a workplace, with examples of good practice from travel and tourism organisations.

  This task may provide evidence for D2.

3 **About you**

- Undertake a review of your personal skills and attributes in preparation for employment.

  This task may provide evidence for P3.

- Select one of the jobs from Part 1. Use your review to evaluate your suitability for the chosen job and describe the development, education and skills you would require to meet the job criteria.

  This task may provide evidence for M1.

- Prepare an action plan which shows how your training and development needs could be met.

  This task may provide evidence for D1.

- Adapt your CV and prepare a letter of application for one of the jobs in Part 1.

- Prepare for an interview for the job. Your interview preparation should cover: company background; prepared responses to questions you could be asked; questions you want to ask about the job.

  These tasks may provide evidence for P4.

- Explain how you have used information from the different stages of the recruitment and selection process to promote yourself positively in the job selection process.

  This task may provide evidence for M2.

- Explain how you can contribute to making an effective workplace.

  This task may provide evidence for M3.

Present all your information in a portfolio for submission.

## Research tips

Use a variety of sources to find information on jobs in travel and tourism. These might include websites, newspapers and trade magazines. If you are interested in a specific area, for example working in an airport, look at the relevant websites.

## UNIT 7

# Retail travel operations

## Introduction

When you finish your studies you may opt to work in the retail travel sector. It offers many advantages as a career; you can choose to work in the leisure or business sector, and there are travel agencies in all localities so it is a flexible option in terms of location. You will have the opportunity to practise your customer service skills at first hand with people who are excited about booking travel or holidays. There are plenty of incentives for staff who work hard, including educational trips to holiday destinations.

The retail travel sector is in a period of dynamic change as new technology is introduced and the nature of the service offered by travel agents is changing.

In this unit you will find out about the retail travel environment, what types of businesses are involved and how they are organised and interrelated. You will examine how they compete with one another.

You will be introduced to the practical aspects of working in a travel agency, including how to select and cost a package holiday and how to tailor-make travel services to suit customers. You will study new developments in the sector and examine how retail travel is changing in the face of moves towards direct bookings by customers.

In addition, we will consider all the add-on services offered by retail travel agents and investigate the importance of working practices and legal considerations.

### How you will be assessed

This unit is internally assessed by your tutor. A variety of exercises and activities is included in this unit to help you develop your knowledge and understanding of the operation of retail travel, and prepare for the assessment. You will also have the opportunity to work on some case studies.

After completing this unit you should be able to achieve the following outcomes:

→ Examine the retail travel environment

→ Investigate how organisations in the retail travel environment seek to gain competitive advantage

→ Examine working practices and legislation in retail travel operations

→ Select and process a range of packaged and tailor-made travel services to meet the needs of customers.

# The retail travel environment

## Types of retailer

A retail travel agent acts as an intermediary (middleman) between the customer and the supplier. The supplier is usually a tour operator but can also be a hotel, transport company or insurance company, among others. The travel agent does not buy the products or services of the supplier and sell them on; rather, they work on a commission basis. The commission is variable between suppliers.

It is possible for travel agents to charge customers for their services and this is becoming more common and more acceptable to customers.

The Association of British Travel Agents defines a retail travel business as follows:

> ❛Retail business is business transacted in the capacity of a travel agent, i.e. a person carrying on business, in whole or in part, as agent for a principal remunerated by commission or otherwise, in respect of the sale or offer for sale of travel arrangements. Retail businesses are not in contract with the client.❜

There are different types of retail travel agents. The main categories are shown below.

## Multiples

Multiples are large chains of more than 100 branches – some have hundreds of branches. The branches are to be found on almost every High Street. They are usually public limited companies who prefer, and can afford, prime locations.

## Miniples

Miniples are chains too, but they are smaller and less powerful than the multiples. They tend to be located in one region where they may be well known and have developed a good reputation. They are often large enough to need a head office as well as retail outlets.

They are often independent companies. An example is Cambridge-based Premier Travel, with 14 retail travel shops throughout East Anglia.

## Independents

An independent travel agent is often owned by a family or partnership. These outlets are more likely to be found in smaller towns as it is difficult for them to afford the high rents of prime locations. Many independents have been bought out by miniple and multiple chains, but those that remain have a reputation for good personal service.

Northenden Travel (www.northendentravel.co.uk) is an example of a family independent. You will see in the following extract that it is a sizeable business employing over 20 people, but is nowhere near the scale of the multiples.

---

### A Family Business

Northenden Travel was established in 1983 and is still family owned and managed. The company incorporates separate business-travel and tour-operating departments alongside a High Street retail holiday shop. As an independent travel specialist and still family-owned business, we are proud to be trusted with the travel arrangements of many leading UK businesses, universities and chambers of commerce.

Directors Nigel and Jeni Schofield are supported by a team of over 20 people. Each member of staff is highly experienced in sourcing the best value from the world's leading operators, airlines, and travel suppliers. They have built the business by trading with integrity and offering a better service where quality, creativity, flexibility and value for money are the watchwords.

### E-agents

Many of the major tour operators have set up travel agents on-line. They recognise that Internet access and use are growing, and that they have to be part of the Internet revolution rather than be overtaken by it. There are also companies that trade as on-line travel agencies without any retail shop presence. They sell packages, flights or accommodation. Examples include Expedia and Lastminute.com

### Holiday hypermarkets

This is a concept introduced by First Choice, the tour operator. They have some very large retail travel agencies and the staff are specialised, with expertise in particular holiday types. They tend to be located in large shopping centres like Bluewater in Kent, where there is a lot of passing trade. They carry a lot of promotions but are expected to hit high sales targets. First Choice's own products are heavily promoted and you will find it difficult to see any other operator's brochure.

### Specialists

There are agents who specialise in selling particular types of holidays or cater for a specific group. An example is STA, which specialises in travel for students and young people. STA has over 80 agents across the UK.

### Homeworkers

Many people enjoy the flexibility of working from home, especially those with family commitments. They can work full time or part time as they choose. There are several companies operating in this market with a network of homeworkers. Examples include Travel Counsellors and Holidays by Phone. Holidays by Phone is a fairly small business with about 40 homeworkers in the UK in addition to its own call-centre staff, whereas Travel Counsellors has about 400 agents.

## Environment

### Vertical integration

The principle of vertical integration was explained in Unit 1. It occurs forwards or backwards in the chain of distribution when an organisation takes over another company or role in the chain. It gives the advantages of control and of economies of scale.

The major multiple travel agents in the UK are owned by vertically integrated companies.

| PARENT COMPANY | RETAIL TRAVEL BRANDS | NO. OF RETAIL OUTLETS | E-BRANDS |
| --- | --- | --- | --- |
| TUI UK | Thomson<br>Travel House | 800<br>100 | Travel House<br>Austravel<br>Callers-Pegasus<br>Sibbald Travel<br>Brittannia Direct<br>Thomsonfly<br>Skydeals<br>Team Lincoln |
| Thomas Cook AG | Thomas Cook | 700+ | Thomascook.co.uk<br>JMC brand website |
| First Choice | First Choice Travelshops<br>First Choice Holiday Hypermarkets | 300+ | First Choice and websites for each tour operating brand |
| MyTravel | Going Places<br>Travelworld | 900+ | goingplaces.co.uk<br>fly cheap<br>late escapes<br>websites for each tour operating brand |

Remember that these companies operate internationally and therefore have retail travel operations in other countries also.

The integration of companies in one group allows the tour operators to control, to an extent, the distribution of their products. Although all agencies sell each other's products, Thomson gives preference to TUI or Thomson brands, First Choice to their own brands and so on. This will be evident in the brochures racking policy, where more of the own-branded products will be on display, and in selling, as agents receive larger commissions on their own products. A policy of promoting own brands is known as 'directional selling', and critics say that it means customers are not given a full choice.

Since a Competition Commission inquiry into this and other practices by the big four tour operators, travel agents are supposed to make their links to tour operators obvious to the general public. They do this by displaying notices with parent group details and by sharing the logo, if not always the name, of their parent. You can read the report from the Competition Inquiry by going to its website at www.competition-commission.org.uk and searching reports from 1997.

However, a survey by United Co-op Travel Group in 2004 claimed that a third of customers do not know multiples are vertically integrated.

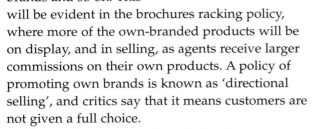

## Key concept

**The Competition Commission** – an independent public body established by the Competition Act 1998. It conducts inquiries into mergers and the regulation of industries in response to requests or complaints from another authority.

## Consider this ...

Before you began this course, did you know which tour operator owned which travel agent? Do you know now?

### Racking policies

Racking refers to the practice of displaying brochures on shelves for customers to browse. Vertically integrated travel agents give prominence to their own products. Independent travel agents select the range of products and services they want to offer based on the quality of the offering and customer demand.

If a brochure is not stocked by an agency its customers will not have access to that product or holiday. However, with the advent of e-brochures, agents will be able to access information about holidays and other products on-line.

### Co-operation with non-travel organisations

Retail travel organisations often have co-operation agreements with other types of organisations. Most examples of such co-operation are found in the media, such as newspapers. They provide exposure for the company and its products and promote sales.

**MASSIVE DISCOUNTS FOR EVERYONE ATTENDING THE SHOW**

Whether you're looking for **inspiration, adventure, fun, relaxation** or the **unusual** there's something for you!

Above is a page from a promotional leaflet for a Holiday Show at Newmarket Racecourse. This was a daytime outside event with exhibitions on destinations and holiday companies, competitions and special offers. The event was promoted in Premier Travel agencies, in the local newspaper and at the racecourse. The event was a collaboration between Premier Travel, the *Cambridge Evening News* and Newmarket Racecourse.

1  Explain why retail travel organisations seek to gain competitive advantage.

   This task may provide evidence for P2.

2  Explain how Premier Travel gains competitive advantage through participation in such an event. Write up your findings as a leaflet explaining the event and its purpose for Premier agency staff.

   This task may provide evidence for M1.

## Trade associations
### Consortia for independent agents

Independent travel agents usually seek to maintain control of their own business, yet they can lose out on the buying power of a large group and find it difficult to compete against the big four.

One means of gaining support for such independent agents is joining a consortium. Consortia allow the travel agents to gain the benefits of being in a group yet retain their independence. Some consortia give the agents the option of using the consortium brand name, which gives the benefit of recognition by the public.

Some of the consortia have grouped together to form the Independent Travel Agents Alliance. This is made up of the consortia Midconsort, Travelsavers, Worldchoice and the Travel Trust Association.

Other consortia in the UK are Freedom Travel and Advantage.

### ABTA

The Association of British Travel Agents (ABTA) is the UK's best-known trade association for tour operators and travel agents. Of holidays sold in the UK, 85% are sold through ABTA agents.

It cost about £1,500–2,000 to join ABTA initially but it is important for agents to join as the public will look for an ABTA travel agent when booking travel and holidays. It gives them a sense of security, knowing that the travel agency follows ABTA's code of conduct and is bonded. However, membership is not compulsory for travel agents.

The main benefit to consumers of booking through an ABTA travel agent is that in the event of the agent or tour operator going bankrupt, ABTA will ensure that people can continue their holiday arrangements with another operator or be repatriated.

Travel agents who wish to join ABTA must comply with four main requirements:

* **Financial:** The requirements are that members should have a minimum paid-up share capital or owner's/partners' capital of £50,000. There must also be net assets of at least £50,000 excluding intangibles. Retail members must have at least £15,000 working capital (net recoverable current assets).

* **Bonding:** ABTA requires that all members protect their clients' money, so providing a bond is a condition of membership. The amount of the bond is calculated by ABTA. It is issued by a bond obliger, which is a bank or insurance company.

### Key concept

**Bond** – a formal undertaking from an approved bank or insurance company to pay a sum of money to ABTA in the event of the member's financial failure, primarily for the purpose of reimbursing customers who would otherwise lose money they have paid.

* **Staffing:** Retailers must have at least one qualified member of staff at each office. There are additional requirements for those selling travel insurance.

  To be considered as qualified, the person concerned must within the five years before any point of time during their employment have had:
  – at least two years' practical experience, or
  – at least 18 months' experience plus ABTA Travel Agency qualifications at Level 1 or primary level, or
  – at least one year's experience plus ABTA Travel Agency qualifications at Level 2 or advanced level.

* **Conduct:** Members must adhere to ABTA's memorandum and articles of association and code of conduct.

All these requirements are explained in detail on the ABTA website.

ABTA provides a range of services to its members, including:

* technology advice
* legal services
* research publications
* financial advice
* seminars
* advice on employment issues
* consumer arbitration.

## CASE STUDY

In summer 2004 a tour operator, Travelscene, went bankrupt. Travelscene had an ATOL bond and was a member of ABTA. However, after the company collapsed it became apparent that there was a loophole in the bonding and some customers were not covered. These customers had booked city breaks but their accommodation was booked through a Travelscene subsidiary, Citibedz. Citybedz was an accommodation-only organisation and a booking agent. Therefore, the customers' contracts on booking were with the hotels, not Travelscene.

This complication caused embarrassment to Travelscene and ABTA. As the ABTA logo was shown on Travelscene brochures, customers thought they were covered. Happily, in this case ABTA agreed to refund payments on the Citibedz bookings. The CAA refunded money on 587 bookings through its ATOL scheme. ATOL is a bonding scheme for tour operators, explained in Unit 11.

1 Why do you think ABTA agreed to pay out?
2 What measures can you take as a customer to ensure your holiday is covered in the event of company failure?
**Write down your answers and compare them with others in your group.**

## Developments in travel retailing

Direct booking with operators or principals is currently the main development impacting on travel retailers. This can be done through call centres, the Internet or other booking channels.

In July 2004 it was reported in *Travel Trade Gazette* that for Thomas Cook, 20% of business comes direct to call centres from its on-line and digital television networks. And this percentage is growing.

Another problem facing travel agents has been a reduction in the commissions paid by principals, particularly by airlines. In 2004 British Airways cut its commission to 1%, and some other airlines followed.

A MORI poll in 2004 showed that young people found it 'uncool' to book with a travel

*Many people are now used to searching the Internet for products, services and information*

agent; 18–24-year-olds prefer to book on-line. The same survey showed that retired people also search on-line.

**Consider this ...**

Do you agree that it's uncool to book with a travel agent? How did you book your last holiday?

The debate continues on the future of the travel agent. There are those who think that they will disappear from our High Streets and that we will all book over the Internet, and others who think that retailers have a future. At a 2004 travel and tourism conference, Thies Rheinsberg, TUI AG's corporate strategy director, gave his company's view (quoted in *Travel Trade Gazette*, 21 May 2004):

> ❛As we create new business it has the potential to cannibalise old business, but we have to manage those changes. Yes, we are closing those agencies which are not profitable any more and concentrating on the ones that are doing a great job. We will continue to employ our hybrid strategy and that will lead to consolidation in the agency arena, but on-line and direct business will grow.❜

One way of responding to the rise in independent travel is to try to cater for a niche market. This means exploiting the demand for independent travel instead of trying to sell packages. Travel agents could specialise in certain area of the world and develop an expert knowledge of that area. Many industry experts think that those retail travel agencies which do survive will have to offer a personal service with expert knowledge of destinations and products.

It is also the case that there will always be some people without Internet access, and people who demand personal service or just can't cope with booking their own holiday arrangements.

Some travel agents are looking for a new source of primary income and are considering charging service fees. Where a fee is charged the service offering has to be excellent or customers will go elsewhere – it cannot be just a booking service.

A typical service charge is £20–25, and if the customer makes the booking then the charge can be credited against it. The system does have the advantage of dissuading time wasters.

Most travel agents will charge for booking flights from low-cost airlines on the Internet for customers, as many of the low-cost airlines do not pay commission to travel agents.

**Consider this ...**

How likely is it that you would pay for service in a travel agency? One agent told of a booking for EasyJet where she booked on-line for four people and charged them £80. They could have booked it themselves and saved the money. Why do you think they didn't?

# Competitive advantage

## Methods of gaining competitive advantage

In order to gain competitive advantage over other retailers, either of the same type or different types, a travel agent has to constantly develop and be innovative. Travel agents often try to gain that competitive advantage by:

✳ vertical integration

✳ horizontal integration

✳ joining a trade association

* offering sales incentives
* promotional activities
* discounting
* staff training
* developing the range of products and services.

## Vertical integration

The vertically integrated companies are so large and powerful that they are able to adapt to a changing market by developing different means of distributing their products and services. Besides having retail outlets, they have developed call centres and websites, and they sell on television, some even having their own television channels. The assessment activity below gives an example of how TUI UK has developed one of its brands.

## Horizontal integration

Horizontal integration occurs when companies are bought out or merged at the same level in the chain of distribution. An example would be one travel agency buying out another. In the table on page 219 you will see that MyTravel has two chains of travel agent, Going Places and Travelworld.

One advantage of buying out the competition is that they no longer compete! Also, the size of the original business increases, with more outlets and economies of scale. Having different brands in retail travel within the same company gives the customer the illusion of choice. Thomson (now TUI UK) bought out the chain Callers-Pegasus for £17 million in 1999, and First Choice bought Holiday Hypermarkets for £45 million from United Norwest and West Midlands Co-ops.

## Joining a trade association

Most UK travel agents are members of ABTA, as described on page 221. There is no doubt that ABTA travel agents have a competitive advantage over non-ABTA agents as the name is well known and holiday makers have been educated to look for evidence of ABTA bonding when booking.

How do the consortia in travel and tourism help the travel agents become more competitive? There are benefits and a few drawbacks to joining one of these associations. The benefits include:

* the consortium negotiates deals with suppliers, such as hotels and airlines
* there is a recognised brand name, e.g. Advantage

---

### Assessment activity 7.2

The Travel House, www.travelhouse.co.uk, part of The Travel House Group, began trading in 1992 when it opened its first branch in Swansea, South Wales. Since then The Travel House has aimed to provide excellent customer service coupled with a policy claiming 'We'll beat any price'. It currently has over 100 retail shops nationwide and a national call centre answering over one million calls per year.

In addition to successful retail outlets, The Travel House is a major advertiser on Teletext, with over 500 pages displayed in the holiday section. Enquiries are answered at a large call centre in Swansea. It also has a website with experienced advisers on hand.

In May 1999, The Travel House became a wholly owned subsidiary of the Thomson Travel Group plc, which is now TUI UK Limited, a part of the World of TUI. The Travel House is an alternative brand name on the High Street for Thomson, offering an independent service on a wide choice of products.

1 Describe the four methods of distribution used by The Travel House.

This task may provide evidence for P1.

2 Explain why all these methods of distribution are used.

3 How does being part of an integrated company help The Travel House gain competitive advantage?

These tasks may provide evidence for M1.

4 Analyse the impact of The Travel House on Thomson travel agencies and on other organisations in the retail travel environment. Write up your findings in a short report.

This task may provide evidence for D1.

* travel agents can retain their own name if they prefer, e.g. those joining Midconsort do not adopt that name

* use of technology systems

* conferences and events

* bonding schemes, e.g. Global has its own scheme as an alternative to ABTA bonding.

The disadvantages include the cost, although it varies a lot between consortia. With Global it costs £25,000 to join and then a percentage of commission, but this includes the technology system and training. However, Global also has another division, Independent Options, and membership of that is free. A consortium like Global operates as a franchise, so the agent is not completely in control of the business.

## Sales incentives

Incentives can be financial, such as a bonus or commission. In the travel and tourism business incentives are often travel-related. Suppliers such as tour operators send agents on 'educationals'. These are trips to destinations to explore what is on offer and increase the agents' knowledge of the destination.

Some companies hold parties as incentives for staff. *Travel Trade Gazette* reports on these; one was held by a north-eastern travel agency owner and staff were plied with champagne and Pimms and entertained by a string quartet.

Call centres often make extensive use of incentives to encourage staff to make more sales. It makes the job more interesting if the staff have something to work towards.

## Promotional activities

Promotional activities include any activity that encourages customers to buy. Agencies may run competitions, for example. Competitions can be held in the agency so that customers want to come in; STA, for example, has offered instant prizes on scratchcards which are given when customers buy foreign currency. Another means of promoting the agency through competitions is by providing a prize – perhaps a voucher towards a holiday – in a competition promoted by another organisation. This can lead to good publicity.

Some travel agencies use professional marketing organisations who will provide promotional materials. At a basic level they provide a central brochure-ordering service so that the agent doesn't have to contact each individual operator for brochures. They will also provide a documentation service providing tickets, invoices, welcome-home letters, confirmations, and so on. The extract below gives an example of a year-long promotional campaign.

### CASE STUDY

Haymarket Travel has announced plans to increase its sales in the UK domestic market, as it seems that many customers are booking directly rather than through agents. The agency will be working with domestic tour operators and the London Tourist Board. The plan is to bombard customers visiting its London flagship store with information on British short breaks.

The campaign began on 1 September 2004 and was planned to last for 12 months.

The store will have agents in traditional costumes serving customers, and Morris dancers on summer weekends outside the shop. Customers will be shown videos of British seaside resorts, posters will be on display and existing customers will receive flyers offering discounts off UK breaks.

1 **Why do you think Haymarket Travel has chosen to focus on short breaks?**

2 **This campaign has to last a year. Perhaps customers will tire of the Morris dancers after a while. Think of at least five other activities which could be used in this promotional campaign at different times of the year.**

Window displays are an important promotional method for travel agents. The window display may have attractive posters showing destinations, but it is certain to have a range of cards advertising special or late offers. These are compiled by staff who search for the offers on Viewdata. They will be informed directly of offers from their own company.

## Discounting

The large chains may run a discount promotion to encourage sales in times of poor trade. Some travel agents ensure competitiveness by constantly checking offers in their competitors' shops and matching the prices if appropriate.

## Staff training

A trained staff is the best means of being competitive. Through training, agents develop their selling skills and their destination knowledge and are thus able to provide personal service to customers.

There are different types of training, ranging from induction for new staff, to on-going training to update skills and knowledge and weekly sessions given by the manager for all staff. Training is discussed in more detail in Unit 6.

## Developing the range of products and services

Travel agents can sell other products. One travel agent now sells a range of luggage. Her theory is that customers are thinking about holidays when they come in the door and they will need luggage.

Thomas Cook is considering selling financial services in its shops:

### Financial services facility put on trial

THOMAS COOK is trialling a scheme to sell financial services to customers as it looks to offer more than just travel in an ever-competitive market.

A proportion of names on Cook's database received a direct mailshot two weeks ago.

Thomas Cook is not running the services itself but, in the same way as Tesco, for example, it will use its name to brand the activities of a mainstream financial services company.

If successful, the facility will be extended to the group's shop network.

Chief executive Manny Fontenla-Novoa said loans and mortgages would be available, as well as overseas currency.

As traditional travel firms face increasing competition for holiday sales from the on-line players, Thomas Cook is looking to generate more profit from its foreign-exchange desks.

While its forex business is 'three to four times bigger' than other agents', Cook's 130 bureaux are threatened by the recent expansion of foreign-exchange services by the Post Office and High Street banks.

Fontenla-Novoa said: 'We have been approached by a financial institution which believes the Thomas Cook brand will work well in that market because of its reputation for trust.'

*Travel Trade Gazette*, 2 July 2004

An important extra service offered by agents is that of tailor-making packages for customers. This means that instead of selling the customer an 'off-the-shelf' package, the agent puts together the different components, tailoring them exactly to what the customer wants. This service is perhaps the most significant in terms of competitive advantage as it offers a very personal service to customers and saves them the time and effort of doing it themselves.

> **Key concept**
>
> **Dynamic packaging** – industry jargon for tailor-making a package for a client.

Selling **add-ons** helps travel agents to gain competitive advantage by giving their customers value-added service. It also helps them make more commission and therefore profit. Top agents persuade 30–40% of customers to buy add-ons – products or services offered for sale on top of the package holiday or tailor-made package. Examples are insurance, car hire, foreign exchange, airport hotels, parking and airport lounge facilities.

An imaginative agent who listens carefully to the needs of his or her customers is able to make many add-on sales. For example, a weekend in London with Superbreak will cost £198 for a couple staying at the four-star Fleming Mayfair hotel. The agent's commission will be up to £35. The agent could discuss customers' needs further and sell first-class rail tickets, along with tickets to the theatre, the London Eye and a Thames cabaret dinner cruise. The package value rises to about £630, and commission to more than £100.

You will be given an opportunity to practise your add-on selling skills later in this unit.

# Working practices and legislation

## Legislation

Most of the legislation covered in this unit is of greater relevance to tour operators than to travel agents. However, when travel agents tailor-make packages for customers, they act as tour operators and therefore must be aware of and abide by all the relevant legislation.

## Agency agreements

Travel agents work on behalf of principals or tour operators. If both travel agent and tour operator are ABTA members they will be bound by the ABTA code of conduct (see pages 228–9). The legal relationship between the tour operator and the travel agent is based on agency law.

An agency agreement will lay out the terms and conditions of the contract, including commissions. If a travel agent stocks a tour operator's brochure and sells from it, there is an implied contract between them, even if there is no written agreement. The travel agent does not have a contract with the customer; the customer has a contract with the principal or tour operator. ABTA provides a model contract for its members to use with their suppliers.

## The Package Travel, Package Holidays and Package Tours Regulations 1992

These regulations impact on retail travel agents as they cover not only the organisation of package holidays but also the selling of them. Travel agents need to understand and adhere to these regulations when they sell, and also when they tailor-make packages for clients. As the regulations are aimed primarily at tour operators, they are discussed in detail in Unit 11.

## Contract law

When a customer books a holiday with a travel agent he or she enters into a legally binding contract with the tour operator offering the holiday. Travel agents ask the customer to read and accept the tour operator's booking conditions before booking, but do not enter into a contract with the customer themselves. They may ask the client to sign a document allowing the travel agent to act on his or her behalf.

## Fair trading charters

These charters usually apply to tour operators, who include them in their brochures. They amount to a plain English interpretation of the Package Travel Regulations.

## Trade Descriptions Act 1968

Descriptions given must be truthful and accurate. This primarily affects tour operators as they have to be careful that brochure descriptions adhere to the act. However, it affects a travel agent too, as any agent making a false verbal statement will be liable under the Trade Descriptions Act.

## Supply of Goods and Services Act 1982

The section of this act which is important is the one relating to a contract being carried out using 'reasonable care and skill'. Travel agents have to ensure that they carry out the booking correctly.

## Unfair Terms in Consumer Contracts Regulations 1999

If customers think that any contractual term is unfair or unreasonable, they have a right to challenge it. The terms of the contract should be written in clear, understandable language.

The Office of Fair Trading (OFT) has written guidelines on the interpretation of this act. The guidelines are aimed primarily at tour operators rather than travel agents as they enter into the contract with the customer, but the travel agent might have to liaise with the tour operator on customers' behalf in a situation where a contract is challenged by the customer.

In 2003 the Office of Fair Trading held an investigation into travel websites. It found that almost half of the websites surveyed were in potential breach of consumer legislation, because they contained claims that the public might find misleading. Most examples were prices advertised that were not really available. The investigators found more than 100 potential breaches under the E-commerce Regulations, Unfair Terms in Consumer Contracts Regulations, Package Travel Regulations and Distance Selling Regulations. Companies that break such rules are pursued by local Trading Standards Officers or by the OFT.

## ABTA Code of Conduct

All members of ABTA, travel agents and tour operators alike, agree to abide by ABTA's code of conduct. The code is available on the ABTA website. Below is an extract, including elements of the code relevant to consumers and travel agents.

### Advertising

- ABTA Members must not mislead you with their advertising and must include all compulsory charges in their prices e.g. UK Air Passenger Duty [Code 1.3].

### Booking procedures

- When you book with an ABTA Member they must give you accurate information to help you choose the travel arrangements that are right for you [Code 1.1].

- ABTA Members must follow all the necessary legal requirements such as the ATOL Regulations and must make you aware of the terms and conditions that apply [Code 1.4].

- ABTA Members must also give you guidance about any health requirements and the passport and visa requirements for your travel arrangements [Code 1.6].

- If you have any special requests concerning a disability or other medical condition ABTA Members must ensure that these are dealt with properly and confidentially [Code 1.4 (iii)]. ABTA Members must also give you information about travel insurance [Code 1.7].

- Before completing a booking, ABTA Members must tell you if the Foreign and Commonwealth Office has issued advice about your destination [Code 1.6 (iii)].

### Once the booking is made

- ABTA Members must notify you as soon as possible if it is necessary to change or cancel your travel arrangements. An ABTA Member cannot cancel your booking after the date for payment of the full price unless it is necessary to do so for reasons outside its control. If this happens, the ABTA Member must offer you the choice of having all your money back or choosing alternative travel arrangements [Code 2.1 & 2.2].

- If an ABTA Member makes a significant change to your travel arrangements they must offer you the choice of accepting the changed travel arrangements or having all your money back [Code 2.2].

- If an ABTA Member does cancel your booking or makes a significant change to the travel arrangements after the date for payment of the full price they must offer you compensation unless the reason for the cancellation or change was outside of their control [Code 2.1 & 2.2].

**Building works**

- An ABTA Member must notify you as soon as possible of any serious building works at your destination. If you wish you can transfer to another holiday or cancel and have your money back [Code 2.5].

**Complaints**

- If you have a complaint about your travel arrangements you should write to the ABTA Member concerned. They must provide you with a full reply within 28 days. If you remain dissatisfied you should write again pointing out the areas of dispute. Again the ABTA Member must respond within 28 days (see 'Complaining') [Code 3.1].

- If you fail to reach a satisfactory position with the ABTA Member you can have the matter resolved through the ABTA Arbitration Scheme (see 'Independent Arbitration') [Code 3.4].

Source: www.abta.com

Any company in breach of the code is reported to a Code of Conduct Committee. If a case is found against the member then disciplinary action may be taken. This could result in a reprimand, a fine or even expulsion.

# Working practices

## A day in the life of a travel agent

Shireen left college in 2003 having completed an AVCE in Travel and Tourism, the same level of course as the BTEC National Diploma. She explains what her job involves.

I start at 9 am – the first thing is to put the kettle on. I am the most junior member of staff but they all take turns to make the tea!

I begin with admin – there's filing to do, checking the post and matching up details on our travel system. If payments arrive I enter them on our system too. This is the time to send out letters –

I don't have to write them, I call them up from our computer depending on what is needed. Sometimes there are tasks to do from the previous day when we have been busy.

From about 11 am it gets busy with customers. We sell a lot of coach tickets as we are the only agent in town to sell them. Whenever customers come in and are looking at the brochures, one of us gets up to greet them and ask if we can help them.

A lot of customers make enquiries and we look up holidays for them on the Viewdata system. They don't always book there and then; I give them information to take away along with my card. You have to listen carefully to find out what they are looking for and you have to know all the different products to be able to find the right thing for them. That was hard at first.

In between customers, I deal with telephone enquiries and sort out brochures – we have cupboards full downstairs. I have to produce tickets and I have to make up files for each client and record when they have booked and when the tickets were sent out, etc.

At about 4.30 pm I do the banking. The computer has details of all payments made and I reconcile that with our takings and put any cash and cheques in the safe.

## Front- and back-office procedures

Most of the tasks described by Shireen are front-office procedures – that is, they are to do with dealing with customers and selling products. Back-office procedures are to do with the suppliers of the products and the running of the office – following up bookings, making payments, banking, ordering brochures, stationery and currency. These procedures do not involve the customer.

All selling procedures used to be done manually with a basic Viewdata system and a great deal of paperwork, but now competitive travel agents use highly sophisticated technology for all procedures. There are several systems on the market and independent agents choose the system they think best meets their needs.

Of course, any system used is only as good as the person operating it, so extensive training is required. Be aware also that computerised systems do not do away with paperwork altogether.

You should be familiar with the terminology used to describe the technology that travel agents use.

The early CRS and Viewdata systems have some drawbacks for travel agents:

* they are not 'real-time' systems, which means the information is not bang up to date and the agent has to telephone reservations departments to confirm

* the agent can search only one tour operator at a time, which means the process of finding a suitable holiday is very slow; the customer's preferences have to be keyed in to each new reservations screen.

These systems are still widely used, but the latest systems are much more advanced and can offer:

* real-time availability
* 24-hour access to the system
* multi-operator searches.

## Key terms

**Viewdata** – the interactive screen system that travel agents use to access the tour operators' reservation systems.

**CRS (Computer Reservation System)** – each tour operator, airline, cruise line, etc. has a computer reservation system accessible by the Viewdata system.

**GDS (Global Distribution Services)** – more sophisticated developments of the computer reservation services. They might combine several computer reservation systems from different suppliers and offer other travel services also. Examples include Amadeus, Galileo, Sabre and Worldspan.

## Assessment activity 7.3

Galileo Leisure is a new Global Distribution Service launched by Galileo in 2004. It is an addition to an extensive range of products from Galileo for the travel industry, and is a sales system for travel agents. It provides access to tour operators' Viewdata systems, gives travel information and processes reservations.

The travel agent can make late-availability searches and view brochures and destination information on-line. The product allows multi-operator searches, a feature which saves a lot of time for the travel agent. Information is also available on coach, rail, air and sea travel and currency conversion.

1 Choose Galileo Leisure or another brand of Global Distribution Services. Find the website and describe the systems offered to travel agents to help them in their daily working practice.

This task may provide evidence for P3.

2 Explain how these systems help travel agents gain competitive advantage. Give specific examples.

This task may provide evidence for M1.

3 Choose one GDS and analyse the impact of the chosen system on the competitiveness of retail travel businesses.

This task may provide evidence for D1.

Some Global Distribution Services include fully integrated back-office systems. This means that all the travel agency's booking and accounting procedures can be automated. Examples are TravelPower and TravelCat. TravelCat is produced by Comtec, a company based in Wales and founded in 1995. The company has received business support from the Welsh Assembly and the Welsh Development Agency. This is important as it reflects the importance given by government to developing the tourism industry.

The company also produces EasySell, a multi-operator holiday search. EasySell is used by MyTravel, TUI, Thomas Cook and First Choice. Like the Galileo Leisure product, this dramatically reduces the searching and booking time for holidays.

TravelPower and TravelCat systems also allow reconciliation of banking as all transactions are entered into the system and the system tells you what the takings should be at the day's end.

Comtec, the company that produces TravelCat, has brought out a new product which gives travel agents their own website. Of course, travel agents often have websites already but this is different as it allows customers to interact and manage their own bookings on-line. The customer is given a booking number to enter on-line, with personal details, which allows access to his or her booking. Customers can make payments on-line and get receipts through e-mail.

There is an initial set-up charge to travel agents and then each transaction carries a small fee. There is no charge to customers. The purpose of the new product is to give a means of Internet interaction to travel agents and help them be competitive. It could save money in administration if successful.

### Consider this ...

Do you think travel agents should encourage their customers to use an on-line facility like the new TravelCat product? Do you think it will encourage even more people to use the Internet and cut out the travel agent?

## Procedures and documentation for selling travel services

We will go through an example of a customer making a booking to show what the travel agent would do at each stage.

The customer approaches the travel agent and is invited to sit down. The travel agent has a computer screen in front of her with the TravelCat system, for example. The customer wants to look for a late-availability cruise.

### Theory into practice

What would the agent need to know? Make a checklist of the details the agent needs in order to search her Viewdata system. Compare your list with that of others in your group to make sure it is correct.

These are the steps the travel agent will follow:

1  Make notes on the customer's requirements.
2  Enter details into the system and check availability.
3  Tell the customer what is available.
4  Give the customer information about the resorts visited, ship, etc.

### ✳ REMEMBER!

The travel agent is not just a booking system. This is the most important part – it's where you lose or make a sale. You have to have this information at your fingertips. This means in your head, in a brochure you can show immediately, in a gazetteer or on-line. A recent survey by *Holiday Which* magazine praised a 'model agent' because he gave perfect answers to the enquiry posed and used the gazetteer and Foreign Office advice. This agent said, 'The secret is not knowing everything, but where to look for it.'

5  The customer chooses a cruise.
6  The agent confirms all the details with the customer and completes the booking form provided by the tour operator. The customer signs it. This form can be downloaded from the computer or may be in a brochure. The agent also enters all the booking details into the CRS. This computer file is unique to that customer and can be updated and altered if necessary.

## Fabulous Cruises

Fabulous House, Ocean Road, Southampton SO38 2XY
Reservation: 0845 111222  Facsimile: 02380 888999
Internet:www.fabulouscruises.com

**Booking confirmation**
Agents Copy

| Date printed<br>11 AUG 05 | Booking ref<br>831XFC | Group name |
|---|---|---|
| Tour | Cruise no<br>E528 | Agency contact/ ABTA<br>CHARLIE   00019543 |
| Departure<br>23 DEC 05 | Grade/Cabin<br>A/402 | Ship name/Registry<br>GOLDEN PRINCESS/BRITISH |
| From port<br>BARBADOS | To port<br>BARBADOS | Number of cruise nights<br>14 |

| Payment schedule | |
|---|---|
| Deposit w/o Ins | Deposit w/Ins |
| 11126 | |
| Due date: | By return |
| Balance amount | Balance due date |
| Total costs:<br>11259.00 | 28 OCT 05 |
| Net bal:<br>9739.04 | 28 OCT 05 |

Mail payments to:
Cruise Payments
Fabulous Cruises, PO Box 6031
Southampton 38 4AZ

### Important notices

With effect from 27 February 2005 the contract for your Fabulous Cruises holiday transferred from Fabulous Cruises International Limited to Fun Cruise Plc, our parent company. This is purely a change of legal entity for our business and will not have any impact on our day to day operations.

### Currency

POUNDS STERLING

| Description | Amount |
|---|---|
| NET FARE | 11259.00 |
| COMM | 1519.96 |
| TOTAL | 9739.04 |
| RECEIVED | 0.00 |

| Dining | Comments |
|---|---|
| Non-smoking | |

| Passengers | Age | City | Air | Ins | Occ Ship | Occ Land | Comment |
|---|---|---|---|---|---|---|---|
| 1 FORTUNE, JANE MRS | 38 | LON | N | OWN | TPL | | |
| 2 FORTUNE, ALISTAIR MR | 45 | LON | N | OWN | TPL | | |
| 3 FORTUNE, SARAH MISS | 12 | LON | N | OWN | TPL | | |

### Itinerary

AIR TRANSPORTATION NOT PROVIDED

| | | | |
|---|---|---|---|
| FRI 23/12 | BARBADOS | | 06:00pm |
| | embark from 02.00pm | | |
| SAT 24/12 | DOMINICA | 08:00am | 06:00pm |
| SUN 25/12 | AT SEA | | |
| MON 26/12 | AT SEA | | |
| TUE 27/12 | NASSAU | 08:00am | 06:00pm |
| | TENDER REQUIRED | | |
| WED 28/12 | PRINCESS CAYS | 08:00am | 04:00pm |
| | TENDER REQUIRED | | |
| THU 29/12 | AT SEA | | |
| FRI 30/12 | TORTOLA | 08:00am | 06:00pm |
| | POSSIBLE TENDER | | |

| | | | |
|---|---|---|---|
| SAT 31/12 | ANTIGUA | 08:00am | 06:00pm |
| SUN 01/01 | ST KITTS | 08:00am | 06:00pm |
| | POSSIBLE TENDER | | |
| MON 02/01 | ST LUCIA | 08:00am | 06:00pm |
| TUE 03/01 | GRENADA | 08:00am | 06:00pm |
| | TENDER REQUIRED | | |
| WED 04/01 | TOBAGO | 08:00am | 06:00pm |
| THU 05/01 | BARBADOS | | 08:00am |
| | OVERNIGHT ON BOARD SHIP | | |
| FRI 06/01 | BARBADOS | | 07.00am |

AIR TRANSPORTATION NOT PROVIDED

IMPORTANCE NOTICE: The terms and conditions which govern this booking are printed in the back of the Fabulous Cruises brochure from which you booked. A copy of these terms and conditions is available from your Travel Agent or from Fabulous Cruises. Please read all conditions carefully as they affect the passengers legal right, particularly with respect to the provision of medical care (conditions 11 and 12), cancellation (conditions 17), matters of security and safety (condition 28), and the Carrier's liability and your right to claim (condition 43 to 46).

*Booking form*

7   The agent will also complete a booking authorisation form and ask the customer to sign it. This is the travel agency's own form and gives it permission to make a booking on behalf of the customer.

8   As the booking is for a late-availability cruise, the customer must pay in full. The agent takes the payment and enters the details of the payment into the system. Payment could be made by cash, cheque or credit card. The customer is given a receipt which has been printed.

9   The agent must ensure that the customer has insurance. This is a sales opportunity and she might sell the company's insurance and earn more commission. However, the cruise customer says she has her own insurance.

10  The agent generates an insurance indemnity form from the computer. This means that the

customer promises not to sue the travel agent if costs arise through lack of insurance.

11 The agent is already thinking about this customer's needs and any add-on sales that can be made. She suggests that the customer buys US dollars for the cruise. These are ordered and the details entered into the system.

12 When the customer leaves, the agent makes a file of copies of all the paperwork completed and files it manually. The agency provides an envelope for this, printed with a checklist so that she doesn't forget any details:

---

## BOOKING CHECKLIST

**1 Passports**
The party leader must ensure that all passengers hold an appropriate British citizen's passport. If not, he/she must advise us of the type of passport held ❏

**2 Visas**
Client advised of visa requirements for British citizens ❏

Client advised that foreign passport holders must check visa requirements with the appropriate embassies immediately, and this information should be rechecked nearer the departure date ❏

**3 Health requirements**
Client advised of any compulsory health requirement and additionally any recommended health requirements. Clients should also check with their GP ❏

**4 Insurance**
a) Taken ❏
b) Operator's compulsory ❏
c) Refused ❏
d) Indemnity form signed ❏

**5 Traveller's cheques and foreign currency** ❏

**6 Contract**
Clients advised that they are entering into a contract with the principal and that they should understand booking conditions in particular cancellation/amendment charges, surcharges and payment schedule ❏

Clients advised of financial security ❏

**7 Itinerary**
Times/stops/connections

**8 Ancillary products**
a) Transport to/from airport, coach/rail ❏
b) Car parking ❏
c) Overnight accommodation ❏
d) Car hire ❏

---

13 In the post five days later, the tickets arrive. The agent generates a standard letter from the computer to inform the customer. Then, as this is a late booking, she also telephones the customer to ask her to collect her confirmation and tickets. The agent updates her computer system noting what she has done.

---

Dear Mrs Fortune

We refer to your holiday reservation and have pleasure in enclosing your confirmation from Fabulous Cruises.

Please check this carefully and advise us immediately if you require clarification of any points.

We would like to take this opportunity to remind you that if you are travelling abroad you must hold a valid passport and be aware of the health requirements for the countries you are visiting. In some cases a visa is necessary. We must also advise that it is your responsibility to check all the above requirements.

We would also like to advise that we can arrange travel insurance, foreign currency, traveller's cheques, airport car parking, overnight airport hotel accommodation and overseas car rental at very competitive rates. If we have not already dealt with this for you please let us know if we can assist in any way.

We thank you for your valued custom and trust that all arrangements are to your satisfaction. If we can be of any further assistance please do not hesitate to contact us.

Yours sincerely

---

14 The customer collects the tickets and the agent notes this on the computer system. When the customer comes back from holiday she will be sent a 'welcome-home' letter to remind her of the expert travel agent who sent her on the holiday.

**Consider this ...**

The computer stores letters to cope with any eventuality – payments due, requests for forms to be signed, complaints being dealt with. Why do you think this is a better system than the agents writing their own letters?

15 At the end of each day a banking print can be generated from the computer. This will state all the transactions that have been carried out and should be reconciled against cash, cheques and card payments. A daily sales summary can also be printed.

## Payment timetable

In the example above, the customer paid immediately as she was leaving on holiday very soon. The usual procedure is for the customer to pay a set deposit on booking and pay the balance eight weeks before departure. The travel agent then makes payment to the supplier, minus their agreed commission. Any customers who fail to pay will lose their deposit as a cancellation charge. If cancellation is for a valid, insured reason, the insurance company will refund the deposit or cancellation charge.

## Client file

Customer files are duplicated – they are kept on computer and in a paper file. The best way to keep the paper files is in order of departure date; that way, it becomes obvious if someone has not collected tickets!

Once clients have returned from holiday the files must still be kept. The client could make a complaint and then the files would be needed. A complaint could be made up to three years after a problem occurred.

## Brochure handling and preferred operators

Day to day, the agent must make sure that there are enough brochures on display and order them (usually from a central supplier) as needed. Preferred operators are those who work closely with the agency, perhaps providing staff training posters and better commissions. Their brochures will be more prominently displayed.

## Merchandising and displays

It is important that the agency looks good and that the window display appeals to passers by. Late deals are a common merchandising tool to attract people and these are often displayed on cards in the window.

Posters are easily obtained and often used to advertise destinations. It is part of the job of the travel agent to arrange attractive window displays.

## Sales targets

An agency has its sales target set by head office or by its owner if it is a small business. The target is subdivided between the staff. It isn't divided equally; more experienced staff are expected to sell more than juniors, and part timers naturally have smaller targets. In many agencies, staff are paid a bonus when they reach their target. This bonus is separate from the commission earned.

## Commissions

Commission is paid monthly and it depends on bookings made. The commission differs with each product or company – higher commissions are paid on own-branded products.

Airline commissions can be as much as 9%, for example Emirates, or zero, for example low-cost airlines. Some travel suppliers operate a tiered system where agents are categorised. Top agents – those who do a lot of business for the supplier – can earn high commissions. For example, Virgin Airlines pays 7% on economy sales, 5% on premium economy and 4% on upper class to top-tiered agents. Other categories of agents earn 3% to 4% on sales.

Some retail travel agents, for example Travelcare, do not pay commissions to staff to sell or promote one supplier rather than another. They say such a practice is not in the customer's interest.

**Theory into practice**

Here are some typical questions overheard in a day's work at a travel agency. Can you answer them? You might have to do some research.

- What do I do if my baggage is overweight at the airline check-in?
- Can I get a visa on entry to Kilimanjaro?
- What is different about going first class on Eurostar?
- I am leaving Heathrow at 10 am. I want to take the airport bus from Stansted. What time should I take the bus?
- Can you take hand luggage and a handbag on a plane?

# Packaged and tailor-made travel services

## Package holidays

We have seen that, traditionally, the role of travel agents has been to sell package holidays on behalf of tour operators. Throughout this unit we have noted that this role is changing, but travel agents must still know how to select and process a package holiday.

The range of package holidays on offer is endless, with a full range offered by the major operators First Choice, MyTravel, Thomas Cook and TUI UK. You can remind yourself of all the brands offered by the big four by visiting their websites, where all their brands are listed.

Cosmos is an alternative to the big four. It is the UK's largest independent tour operator and part of the Globus group of companies, a family-run organisation established in 1928 which includes Cosmos Tourama, Avro, Monarch Airlines and Archers Direct.

Cosmos is a major established operator and carries half a million people per year. The brochures offered under the Cosmos name are:

* Summer Sun
* Eastern Mediterranean
* Villas with Pools
* All Inclusive
* Dream Weddings
* Lapland
* Winter Sun.

You will note that, although they are fewer in number, the brochures cover much the same range of destinations as the other major tour operators, except for Lapland.

As a travel agent you would need to be familiar with the range of brochures offered by every tour operator selling package holidays. This presents quite a challenge. Tour operators help agents (and promote their products) by providing training packs or training sessions for agency

*Cosmos offers Christmas packages to Lapland*

staff. These packs demonstrate how to use the brochures and the booking procedures.

As we saw previously, the booking can take place on-line through the CRS system or by telephone or even post. You need to practise selecting and processing a booking. If your college or school has a travel agency, you should carry out the following exercises there. If not, the exercises are designed to work with Internet access to tour operator websites.

## Tailor-made services

The importance of this service in terms of competitive advantage was discussed earlier. It is more exacting for the travel agent as he or she has to know where to find all the information for the different components of a holiday, whereas when booking a package the tour operator has done the groundwork.

Offering tailor-made services can lead to an increase in sales, especially if low-cost airlines are used as a component. Using them brings the cost down for the customer and gives the possibility of regional departures.

There are a number of booking systems now available to travel agents which bring together databases of accommodation, flights and transfers and help agents to research and book tailor-made packages. The travel retailer adds a margin to the prices charged by the suppliers and invoices the customer. Travel retailers are generally happy with this arrangement as it means they determine the commission. Examples of systems are Holidaysandmore.com (a Lastminute.com trade operation), Holiday Brokers and Cultura Trips, a Thomas Cook subsidiary. These are sometimes called dynamic packaging tools. To use these systems you have to register. Unless your college or school has its own travel agency you will be unable to register, but you will be able to practise with similar booking services such as onlinetravel.com, which is used by agents and consumers.

A customer, Jenny Horrocks, is looking for a very special holiday to celebrate an anniversary. She wants to take her husband back to the place where they first met. Neither has been back since, as with six children and full-time jobs they didn't have enough money or time. In fact they can't remember having a holiday by themselves.

Now the children are grown and the couple are free to please themselves. The two met and fell in love on the slopes of Kilimanjaro while on a climbing expedition. They have no wish to climb any more but want to go on safari in Tanzania for a week, followed by a week in luxury on the island of Zanzibar. They want you to arrange the whole trip including transfers. The holiday will be for two weeks in April or May next year.

Select and process a tailor-made holiday for the couple. Produce an itinerary, along with a full costing. Complete documentation as appropriate. You may want to use a dynamic packaging tool such as Cultura (www.cultura.com) or www.onlinetravel.com.

This task may provide evidence for P5 and M3.

Miss Markham comes into your travel agency wanting to book her honeymoon. You are excited as you think this will be an exotic holiday with a great commission. However, she wants to go to London for a two-night break.

You want to make sure she has a wonderful honeymoon and that you make good commission. Tailor-make a package for her, including rail travel and a good hotel. The wedding is on a Saturday next month and the couple will leave for London on Sunday for two nights. They live in Manchester. Make sure you include add-ons. You can make your own suggestions for the bride, but consider upgrades in the hotel and on the train, theatre tickets, sightseeing tours and flowers.

Produce an itinerary for the couple along with a full costing. Complete documentation as appropriate.

This task may provide evidence for P5 and M3.

## Ancillary products and services

Whenever travel agents are helping customers they should be listening carefully to ensure that they understand their requirements and can add on sales as appropriate. In Assessment Activity 7.4 above, the couple were celebrating an anniversary. They hadn't been able to go away before without children. They are likely to be prepared to spend money to have the holiday of a lifetime. They may want flowers and a dinner for the celebration. They may wish to upgrade from economy flights. There is a lot of potential for add-ons.

Make a list of the ancillary sales or add-ons that would be appropriate for the anniversary couple. Remember that they will be on safari. Start from the moment they leave home and anticipate their needs. Compare your list with that of a colleague.

1   Identify the different categories of retail travel agents.

2   What is meant by racking policy?

3   How does ABTA help travel agents?

4   What are the benefits to a travel agent of joining a consortium?

5   What is an 'educational'?

6   What are add-on or ancillary products and services?

7   Identify three types of promotional activity a travel agent might use.

8   How does the Trade Descriptions Act affect a travel agent?

9   What is the difference between front- and back-office procedures?

10  What is a Global Distribution Service?

11  Describe some resources available to a travel agent.

# UNIT 7 ASSESSMENT ASSIGNMENT

## Part 1

You have recently gained a position as an assistant in the offices of ABTA. Your department deals with travel agency support and is preparing for a conference entitled 'The Future of the British Travel Agent – Strategies for Survival'.

There will be a number of speakers from ABTA and from other organisations in travel and tourism. All ABTA members have been sent invitations to the conference and a good response is anticipated. The purpose of the conference is to help members stay up to date with developments in, or affecting, the retail travel sector and show them how they can remain competitive in a rapidly changing environment.

You are not required to give a presentation but to carry out research. Your findings will form the basis of the presentations from ABTA personnel.

Your findings should be presented as detailed sets of notes with illustrations as appropriate. Make sure the notes are clearly presented with suitable headings and sub-headings.

1   Describe the retail travel environment of today, explaining why it is important for organisations to gain competitive advantage. Explain integration, trade associations and new developments.

    This task may provide evidence for P1 and P2.

2   Explain how organisations gain competitive advantage in today's retail travel environment, giving examples of good practice.

    This task may provide evidence for M1.

3   Analyse the impact of developments in retail travel such as integration, development of consortia, and new technology. Analyse the ways in which such developments help or hinder organisations in their efforts to be competitive. Give specific industry examples.

    This task may provide evidence for D1.

4   Describe the working practices of retail travel organisations including day-to-day tasks and responsibilities. Summarise the key legislation and regulations that affect retail travel operations.

    This task may provide evidence for P3 and P4.

5   Explain how key legislation and regulations affect working practices in retail travel.

    This task may provide evidence for M2.

6   Analyse the impact of key legislation and regulations on working practices in retail travel. Analyse also how legislation and regulations impact on the competitiveness of organisations in the retail travel environment.

    This task may provide evidence for D2.

## Part 2

ABTA has sent you to work in a travel agency on a month's placement. The purpose is for you to experience working practice so that you understand the environment and problems which travel agents face.

In your last week you are allowed to deal with customers and sell products and services. You deal with four different sets of customers. For each one you must select and process an appropriate product, meeting the needs of the customers. Present your findings as itineraries with relevant brochure pages, forms and computer printouts attached.

To complete this part of the assessment you will need access to brochures, relevant forms and the Internet. Ask your tutor if you do not know how to access these resources. If your college or school has a travel agency, you should complete the assessment in the agency. Role plays can be used.

Alternatively, this part of the assessment could be carried out on work placement with appropriate supervision.

1 Mr and Mrs Fremantle are retired and in their sixties. They wish to spend six weeks in Portugal, on the Algarve, for a winter break. They can go in October or November but insist on being home at least a week before Christmas. They want a quiet resort and want to stay in a hotel on a bed-and-breakfast basis so that they can go out for dinner to local restaurants. They want to make sure the hotel has a heated pool and some entertainment. They would prefer a sea view and will pay extra for it. Cost is not an issue. They will fly from the local airport.

Find a suitable package, show how it fits the Fremantles' requirements and complete the necessary documentation.

2 The Jarman family needs a summer holiday. They are exhausted looking after six-year-old twins and their new baby. They want to go somewhere that is warm, has beaches and is not full of young clubbers. However, it has to be in Europe as they don't think they can manage a long flight with the children. They want all facilities to be close at hand as they do not wish to hire a car. They are looking for a hotel with half board and want some kind of children's club for the twins. The budget for the holiday is £2,000. This must cover any supplements (but not spending money). They want to fly from Manchester as it is their nearest airport.

Find a suitable package, show how it fits the Jarmans' requirements and complete the necessary documentation.

3 Sayid wants to arrange a surprise for his fiancée's 30th birthday. He is very concerned that you don't contact her about arrangements or send any documents to their address. He wants to go to Paris on Eurostar from Waterloo and stay in a 'posh' hotel. He lives in Norwich so he wants you to arrange his transport to Waterloo and the transfer from Gare du Nord in Paris to the hotel. He has asked for a bed-and-breakfast arrangement and flowers to be in the room on arrival with a message from him. The break is to take place over the birthday weekend with a two-night stay. The birthday is in six weeks' time. Sayid has told you he can spend up to £1,000.

Research and complete booking documentation for all the elements of this tailor-made holiday and produce Sayid's itinerary. Explain why your choices fit his requirements.

4 Helen is getting married and she is organising a hen party for herself and her friends. There will be 12 of them altogether. She has no idea where she wants to go except that it must be in the UK and within a couple of hours of where she lives – in Oxford. She doesn't fly. She does, however, know what she wants to do. She wants to leave after work on a Friday and spend Friday night in a hotel having a dinner and drinks – no club as they will have lots to talk about. She doesn't want to drive so they will travel by train or coach. On Saturday she wants the girls to have a range of beauty and spa treatments and pamper themselves. They will leave on Sunday morning after breakfast. Each of the friends will pay for herself, but of course, Helen doesn't want to ask them to pay too much so costs must be reasonable.

Research and complete booking documentation for all the elements of this tailor-made holiday and produce Helen's itinerary. Explain why your choices fit her requirements.

These tasks may provide evidence for P5 and M3.

# UNIT 11

# Tour operations

## Introduction

Tour operators have been very important in the development of the travel and tourism industry, from the first Thomas Cook package to today's vast tour-operating industry.

In this unit you will find out about the tour-operating environment, its structure, what types of businesses are involved and how they are organised and interrelate.

You will investigate the range of products and services offered by tour operators and how they carry out their business, including the planning, selling and operating of package-holiday programmes, both in the UK and overseas.

You will examine the factors that affect a tour-operating business including legal, political and environmental factors, and the ways in which tour operators are adapting to their changing environment.

You will undertake some practical activities in designing, planning and costing a package for inclusion in a tour operator's programme. Your package will include a destination, accommodation and transport.

### How you will be assessed

This unit is internally assessed by your tutor. A variety of exercises and activities is included in this unit to help you develop your knowledge and understanding of tour operations and prepare for the assessment. You will also have the opportunity to work on some case studies. *Tutors and students should refer to the BTEC standards for the qualification for the full BTEC Grading criteria for this unit.*

After completing this unit you should be able to achieve the following outcomes:

→ Examine the UK tour operations environment
→ Investigate how tour operators plan, sell and operate a package-holiday programme
→ Examine the external factors that affect the planning, selling and operation of a package-holiday programme
→ Design, plan and cost a package for inclusion in a tour operator's programme.

# UK tour-operating environment

## Structure

A tour operator designs and puts together package holidays and tours for sale to customers. These products and services are sold through travel agencies or directly to the customer through call centres, websites and television channels. To put the package together, the tour operator must contract the services of airlines, hotels and transport organisations.

The importance of the holiday market is demonstrated by information from a KeyNote report in 2004.

> Between 2000 and 2003, the revenues generated by UK travel agents and tour operators rose gradually, by 6.6%, to £41.23bn. The majority of this revenue (91.4%) was derived from outbound travel arrangements and packages. Between 1999 and 2003, the penetration of adults who took a holiday in the last year remained fairly constant and rose by 3.2 percentage points to 65%.
>
> Source: Key Note Travel Agency and Overseas Tour Operators Report, June 2004 and Target Group Index © BMRB 1999/2003

The extract demonstrates two important points:

* most British people take a holiday
* most money is spent on outbound travel and packages.

This is good news for tour operators, who want us to spend our money on their products and services. However, there is a trend for customers to book independent travel and holidays, and tour operators are very aware of this and taking steps to cope with it, as we will discover.

## *Horizontal and vertical integration*

Four integrated travel and tourism companies dominate the market. These are First Choice Holidays plc, MyTravel Group plc, Thomas Cook UK Ltd and TUI UK Ltd. These companies are not only tour operators but retail travel agents and airline operators. According to figures from the Civil Aviation Authority in 2004, the big four operators hold 48% of the package-holiday market.

See the table on page 242 for who owns whom. Distribution on the Internet has not been included in this table. Ownership is correct at the time of writing, but quickly changes as companies buy and sell subsidiaries – you should check for the latest information.

You are already aware of the concepts of vertical and horizontal integration, and the table clearly illustrates the extent of integration in the four largest UK tour-operating groups. You can see how it is possible for the groups to vertically control all of the chain of distribution, from creating the package to selling it via their own travel agents. Horizontal distribution is also apparent, especially in tour operating, where the groups have several subsidiaries.

### Key concepts

**Horizontal integration** – where two companies offering competing products merge or one takes over the other.

**Vertical integration** – where companies merge or one takes over the other at different levels in the chain of distribution. For example, Thomson bought Lunn Poly.

There are benefits to integration:

* economies of scale as the company grows
* control over the supply of accommodation and flights
* control over distribution
* larger market share
* less competition
* established reputations.

A few years ago the big four tour operators were in control of the holiday market and were acquiring everything they could, from hotels to cruise ships. Although these companies are still vast, they are now consolidating their operations, merging similar subsidiaries and concentrating more on specialist operations in the face of a changing market, where customers are no longer seeking mass-market products and are happy to travel independently.

| PARENT COMPANY | UK COMPANY | TOUR OPERATIONS (UK) | RETAIL TRAVEL (UK) | AIRLINES (UK) | OTHERS |
|---|---|---|---|---|---|
| Thomas Cook AG | Thomas Cook | Club 18–30<br>Cultura<br>JMC<br>Neilson<br>Style<br>Sunset<br>Sunworld Ireland<br>Thomas Cook<br>Thomas Cook Signature<br>Time Off | Thomas Cook | Thomas Cook Airlines | Parent company has many other interests including hotels |
| First Choice plc | First Choice | Citalia<br>Eclipse<br>Exclusive Destinations<br>Falcon<br>First Choice<br>Hayes and Jarvis<br>JWT<br>Meon Villas<br>Sovereign<br>Sunquest<br>Sunstart<br>2wentys<br>Unijet | First Choice Travel<br>Holiday Hypermarkets | First Choice Airways | Also has Suncars (hire car) and First4extras |
| MyTravel Group | MyTravel UK and Ireland | Airtours<br>Aspro<br>Bridge<br>Cresta<br>Direct Holidays<br>Escapades<br>Manos<br>Panorama<br>Tradewinds | Going Places<br>Travelworld | MyTravel Airways<br>MyTravel Lite | Global interests including hotels<br>Also White Horse Insurance |
| TUI AG | TUI UK | American Holidays<br>Austravel<br>Club Freestyle<br>Headwater<br>Just<br>Magic Travel Group<br>OSL the Villa People<br>Portland Direct<br>Simply Ski<br>Simply Travel<br>Skytours<br>Something Special<br>Thomson brands<br>Tropical Places | Thomson<br>Travel House<br>Callers-Pegasus<br>Sibbald Travel | Thomsonfly | Parent company has several divisions including large hotel groups |

Both Thomas Cook and TUI UK have German parent companies. First Choice and MyTravel are British companies but have international operations.

You can expect to see major changes in these large groups over the next few years. To remain competitive, they will have to get rid of companies which are outside their core business of holidays, and they will have to change the nature of their products, concentrating on more specialist holidays. In addition, distribution is changing and tour operators have already introduced direct selling and on-line booking, although they have not abandoned the traditional travel agency route.

### Consider this ...

Why do these large tour operating groups have so many brands? Should they make it obvious to the customer that they all belong to a particular group?

### Theory into practice

Choose one of the big four tour operators. Find out how it came to acquire so many tour-operating companies in one group. For example, First Choice has a history page on its website (www.firstchoiceholidaysplc.com). Has the pattern of acquisition changed? Have any subsidiaries been sold? Make notes and compare them with your group.

## Links with airlines, accommodation providers and travel agents

### Airlines

Tour operators use charter flights to provide transport to holiday destinations as part of the package. The big four have their own airlines but still have to charter them within the group as they are run as separate companies.

If the own-brand airline cannot provide enough capacity, the tour operator will charter outside the group. Similarly, if the own-brand airline has excess capacity, planes can be offered for charter to another tour operator.

Charter airlines supply planes and staff to tour operators according to their specified needs. For example, a tour operator may ask for a plane and crew for a once-a-week service from Luton to

*The big tour operators have their own charter airlines*

Ibiza, from May until September. The tour operator orders planes for the routes and the length of time it needs. It has a contract with the charter airline and then sells the holidays itself. Many tour operators sell seat-only flights to fill spare capacity.

### Key concept

**Charter flight** – a flight rented by a tour operator to fly for short seasons to holiday destinations. Small operators can group together to charter a flight.

Tour operators also offer scheduled airline seats on more 'up-market' packages. They may buy a block of seats and then incorporate them into a package, or they may request seats from the airline as customers book the package. Such seats often involve a supplement to the passenger as they are more complicated to arrange and perceived as better service.

### Key concept

**Scheduled flight** – a flight which runs to a set timetable throughout the year, timetables are adjusted for winter and summer seasons.

Tour operator Canadian Affair has contracted a Boeing 757-200 charter flight with Thomas Cook to operate a weekly service from Gatwick to Quebec City. Canadian Affair will also introduce weekly flights to Montreal, Halifax and Ottawa from Manchester. The operator already serves Toronto, Calgary and Vancouver from Manchester.

### Press release

Manchester's long love affair with Canada has been boosted today with the announcement of three new low-cost direct flights to **Montreal** in Quebec, **Halifax** in Nova Scotia and **Ottawa** in Ontario.

Fares will start at just £89 one way including tax to the new destinations.

Canadian Affair, the UK's leading tour operator, will introduce the new weekly direct flights in May next year, bringing the number of Canadian cities it serves direct from Manchester Airport to six.

The flights will be operated by Thomas Cook Airlines on a Boeing 757-200. This is an additional Manchester-based aircraft which will be dedicated to operating the Canadian Affair flights.

Ian Smith, Operations Director, Thomas Cook Airlines, said: 'We know this is going to be an incredibly popular service and we have been able to use all the economies of scale by being part of a worldwide group to provide all the "frills" at no-frills prices to Canadian Affair's passengers.

'Our customers will also have the reassurance of flying with a highly-respected, quality on-time airline and brand, part of the major international Thomas Cook group, which has a 162-year heritage of providing exceptional value and service to travellers.'

Source: Canadian Affair Press Release, 26 August 2004 (www.canadianaffair.com)

1 **Why do you think Canadian Affair chose Thomas Cook for its charter?**
2 **Why do you think the main services are offered from Manchester?**
3 **How is Canadian Affair able to offer such cheap flights?**

## Accommodation providers

Tour operator links with hotels can be very complex. Large tour operators may have global deals organised centrally. There may be multi-property relationships when dealing with a chain of hotels or there may be an individual relationship between a tour operator and one hotel. The tour operator has to contract accommodation – beds, rooms or tents – before the season. The number of units booked is known as the allocation.

Accommodation is central to a package. Both parties must agree what is included and what the terms are. The allocation period must also be agreed. When bookings are taken, they are reserved from the allocation of accommodation units; any further capacity required is 'on request' from the accommodation provider.

## Travel agents

Tour operators traditionally sell their products through travel agents. They pay agents commission – this is variable, but can be in the region of 10%. They also provide travel agents with a range of support services to help them sell. These include training packages, special incentives and educational trips. They provide promotional material including brochures and posters.

The current situation is difficult, as tour operators try to balance their relationship with travel agents alongside offering customers direct booking and Internet services. Even where operations are vertically integrated, tour operators are looking closely at the role of the travel agent and deciding whether to maintain so many branches or switch to other types of distribution.

## Associations and regulatory bodies

There are several associations and regulatory bodies which impact on tour operation. These include:

✳ Association of British Travel Agents (ABTA)
✳ Federation of Tour Operators (FTO)
✳ Association of Independent Tour Operators (AITO)
✳ European Tour Operators Association (ETOA)
✳ UKinbound.

## ABTA

You were introduced to ABTA in Unit 1. Many tour operators join ABTA for the same benefits as travel agents. There are 997 tour operator members, and 85% of the UK's package holidays are sold through ABTA members. The bonding requirements apply to tour operators as well as travel agents, and ABTA holds bonds of about £170 million for tour operators.

## FTO

The role of the Federation of Tour Operators is to act as a point of contact between outbound tour operators and government bodies in the UK, in the EU and in destinations served, on matters relating to tour operation. It represents its members' interests with other trade associations, and co-ordinates members' activities with regard to operational matters, for example on health and safety. It also represents its members at the International Federation of Tour Operators. A full list of its activities can be found on the FTO website (www.fto.co.uk) along with a list of members.

## AITO

The Association of Independent Tour Operators represents about 160 of Britain's specialist tour operators. All the members are independent companies, and often they are owner managed. The companies which join AITO agree to adhere to its Quality Charter, which has three key principles of choice, quality and service. Full details of the charter and a list of members can be found on the AITO website, www.aito.co.uk Like the other associations, AITO insists that its members are bonded and expects to see details of bonding arrangements before membership.

## ETOA

The European Tour Operators Association was founded in 1989 and has 110 tour-operator members. The association was founded to ensure that tour operators were fully aware of the implications of the Package Holiday Directive. ETOA has established a track record of influencing travel and tourism legislation at both national and European levels. It provides individual companies with representation at European level, ensuring that members' needs and concerns are understood by EU institutions.

## UKinbound

UKinbound is the official trade body representing UK inbound tourism. The association represents over 250 major companies and organisations in all sectors of the industry, operating over 5,000 outlets in the UK.

*UKinbound is the association for tour operators working to attract tourists to Britain*

Its objectives are:

* to promote tourism to Britain, and to ensure that overseas operators work with a UKinbound member
* to ensure that UKinbound members adopt ethical 'best practice' procedures with clients and suppliers
* to encourage UKinbound members to adopt eco-friendly practice in their businesses
* to encourage UKinbound members to support educational and training programmes
* to represent the political interests of UKinbound members in Whitehall, Westminster and Brussels.

## CASE STUDY

In 2004, UKinbound worked closely with VisitBritain to represent Britain at the World Travel Market. Representatives from 200 countries visit the World Travel Market, so it was a unique opportunity to raise the profile of Britain and promote the UK as a tourist destination.

Promotions in the future may be linked to the 2012 Olympics bid. The Regional Tourist Boards were also represented on the stand, supporting the Enjoy England campaign.

1 **Why would UKinbound wish to be represented at the World Travel Market?**
2 **Why is VisitBritain interested in supporting incoming tour operators?**
3 **Why might it be difficult for incoming tour operators to get their views represented?**

# Categories of tour operator

## Outgoing

Outgoing tour operators are the ones you will be most familiar with. They package holidays for tourists who are travelling from the UK to European and worldwide destinations. They may be mass-market or independent operators.

## Incoming

Incoming tour operators direct their marketing towards tourists overseas who want to visit the UK. You will not be familiar with these as their advertising and promotional material is targeted at other countries.

## Domestic

Domestic tour operators operate within the UK, persuading us to take holidays in our own country. These are the most difficult packages to sell, as it is relatively easy for us to book and travel independently within the UK.

## Mass market

Mass-market operators carry high volumes of passengers and operate on low margins and low prices. They offer a product that in theory appeals to most people. These operators are usually also outbound operators.

Mass-market packages are typified by beach holidays on Spain's Costa Blanca, with high-rise hotels offering British food, in resorts with pubs. Such mass-market products are becoming less common as the population becomes more sophisticated about travel, and more discerning. Because of their size these operators can order from suppliers in bulk and command cheaper prices.

## Independent

There are hundreds of independent tour operators who offer individual products and services. They are usually small to medium-sized organisations. They carry relatively small volumes of passengers compared with the large tour operators. They may carry 10,000 passengers a year, or up to 100,000. In order to compete with the large integrated companies, independents are more likely to concentrate on niche products and to establish long-term relationships with suppliers. They are more flexible in terms of product offering, allowing greater choice to customers.

## Specialist

Specialists are likely to be independent operators. Specialist operators are growing in numbers as they respond to the public's desire for personal service and a specialist, tailor-made product. However, the integrated companies are also focusing on more specialised products in reaction to market trends.

### Consumers hate making decisions

UPMARKET short-break specialist Kirker Holidays was established in 1986 and now has 33 staff. It features more than 450 hotels, all of which are visited by directors and staff.

About 75% of its sales go via agents and the average spend by clients booking through agents is higher because the agent can add upgrades and other services.

The average spend is about £2,000 per booking and the London-based operator takes 22,000 clients a year.

So what makes Kirker so special?

Sales director Ted Wake says 'You cannot give exceptional service if you give your client or travel agent too much choice.

'Otherwise, what are you offering that they cannot do themselves? They can get choice on the Internet. Consumers hate making decisions and the travel agent needs to ask precisely the right questions and make the correct diagnosis before prescribing the perfect holiday.

'We always try to help the travel agent ask the right questions: a chap asking for a cheap weekend in Paris when it may actually be his wife's 50th birthday. The travel agent is always closer to the client.

'The tour operator knows the hotels and so on, the agent knows the client. It is about trust and the relationship.

'We can book museum tickets, for example to Uffizi in Florence, so they do not have to queue. The client can see that someone has anticipated their needs.

'Our brochure is unique, it has no glossy images [just watercolours] – we have accurate written descriptions and first-hand knowledge.'

*Travel Trade Gazette*, 2 July 2004

1 **What type of tour operator is Kirker?**
2 **How does Kirker compete with large, vertically integrated operators?**
3 **What is the advantage to the travel agent of selling upgrades and other products on behalf of Kirker?**

## Assessment activity 11.1

Carry out some research and find an example of each type of tour operator in the following list.
- incoming
- outgoing
- domestic
- mass market
- integrated
- independent
- specialist.

Note that a tour operator may be in more than one category – for example independent and specialist.

1 Describe each tour operator and say what its products and services are.

2 State which associations each tour operator belongs to and why.

You could present your work as a table, as in the example below. Add explanatory notes as needed.

| CATEGORY | TOUR OPERATOR | PRODUCTS AND SERVICES | ASSOCIATIONS | BENEFITS |
|---|---|---|---|---|
| Incoming | British Tours | Personalised day tours in Britain for overseas customers, particularly from the US | American Society of Travel Agents (ASTA)<br><br>UKinbound<br><br>London Tourist Board | ASTA: To gain representation in the US market<br><br>UKinbound: To get support and representation in the UK<br><br>London Tourist Board: To gain referrals |
| Outgoing | | | | |
| Domestic | | | | |
| Mass market | | | | |
| Integrated | | | | |
| Independent | | | | |
| Specialist | | | | |

These tasks may provide evidence for P1.

3 Consider the integrated example you chose and analyse the impact of integration on the tour-operating environment. Include all the levels of the chain of distribution and horizontal integration in your analysis. Think about effects on competition and on suppliers and distributors. Write a brief report.

This task may provide evidence for M1.

## Products and services

### The package holiday

> **Key concept**
>
> **Package holiday** – a holiday including at least two elements of transport, accommodation and other services, for example, the services of an overseas representative.

This is the definition of a package holiday under the Package Travel Regulations. It must

* be sold or offered for sale
* be sold at an inclusive price
* be pre-arranged
* include a minimum of two of the three elements of transport, accommodation and other tourist services.

Most package holidays are pre-arranged and presented in brochures by the tour operators. Customers visit travel agents and collect brochures on destinations of interest to them, or order brochures directly from the tour operator.

The brochure is an important sales tool for the package holiday. Because of the intense competition in the holiday industry, tour operators constantly review their products and introduce new packages.

*Benidorm is a traditional package holiday destination, and is now to be offered for short winter breaks*

## CASE STUDY

### Operators unveil new programmes

THOMSON is to launch a Beach Breaks brochure next week which will offer short winter-sun getaways for the first time.

Previously a summer-only programme, Beach Breaks will now offer three- or four-night breaks to Mediterranean destinations through the winter.

Prices start at £75 for four nights' self-catering in Benidorm, based on four people sharing, for Gatwick departures on November 23.

Thomson is also launching its summer 2005 Just brochure, featuring the new Just Chill concept.

Geared towards young people looking for an independent holiday in a lively resort, Just Chill is designed as an alternative to Freestyle.

Prices start at £175 for seven nights' self-catering in Corfu, flying from Doncaster in May.

*Travel Trade Gazette*, 3 September 2004

1  **What market trends are these products responding to?**
2  **What would you expect to be included in the Beach Breaks package? Write up your findings as a fact sheet.**

## Ancillary products and services

The marketing activities of tour operators have become very sophisticated in that they offer a vast range of extras that the tourist can add to a holiday – at an extra charge, of course!

The advantage for customers is that all their needs are catered for through one contact. The disadvantage is that all these extras cost money, and in some cases they are services that used to be included in a package, for example a meal on a flight. Here is a list of extras available on a typical First Choice package:

* holiday insurance
* foreign exchange
* airport car parking
* airport hotel
* airport lounge
* taxis
* car hire
* late check-out from the hotel
* upgrades to rooms
* kids' clubs
* tickets for attraction/events.

And on the flight:

* champagne
* chocolates

* meal in flight
* extra leg-room
* seats together
* day-before check-in.

## Tailor-made packages

### Key concept

**Tailor-made package** – a holiday designed for a specific customer. Accommodation, travel and other services are separately researched and put together in a package for the customer.

The holiday market has become very competitive in the past few years. These are some of the conditions which tour operators face:

* profit margins are low and there is a great deal of price competition

* a high load factor is needed on aircraft to achieve margins

* customers are less prepared to book early, hoping for last-minute bargains; this results in poor cash flow and harms revenue

* competition from low-cost airlines

* independent booking, especially on the Internet, has intensified; even though packages are often cheaper than independently booked holidays, there is still a change in customer behaviour in favour of independent booking

* travel agents are tailor-making packages

* there are many new entrants into travel and tourism, such as Expedia, coming in as e-commerce operations and exploiting on-line booking.

Tour operators have had to consider different means of maintaining their market position.

There has been a trend towards the introduction of niche or specialist packages from tour operators (and from travel agents, as we saw in Unit 7). Such packages can be tailor-made or 'dynamically packaged' to meet customers' personal needs. They can be marketed through call centres or through the Internet. Tour operators are less likely to use travel agents for such services as it reduces the personalisation, and travel agents may be in competition with tour operators in these markets.

Some tourists may wonder why they should book a tailor-made package. They may think that they can save money by booking themselves. However, tour operators are often able to command favourable rates with airlines and hotels. Even where there are cost savings to be made by independent booking, there are advantages to using a tour operator:

* good ones have specialist knowledge

* they do all the administration for the customer

* they make all the reservations

* they should be bonded – protecting the booking

* there is only one invoice to pay.

# Planning, selling and operating package-holiday programmes

## Planning

Planning includes the stages of:

* research
* contracting
* pricing.

### Research

Research has to take place on a continuous basis. Tour operators are constantly monitoring their sales, the competition and the market, so that they can make decisions about capacity to be offered in existing destinations, new destinations to adopt and old destinations to drop.

They use many sources of data and trends to inform this process.

* **Sales figures** – when figures go down, perhaps it is time to leave the destination; when figures go up, it may be worth investing in more capacity.

* **Communication** with salespeople in reservations and with travel agents – they can report on customer demand. Internal communication should be efficient – marketing staff should work in conjunction with operations staff.

* **Research findings**, for example, Travel Trends, Mintel reports and Star UK reports.

* **Travel and tourism conferences**.

* **PEST analysis** – analysing political, economic, social and technological factors.

An organisation that is aware of and using all this information will make informed decisions about which destinations to include in a package-holiday programme. In spite of this, there will be occasions when an operator has to pull out of a destination because of factors which could not be foreseen, for example a terrorist attack.

**Consider this ...**

Think of at least three destinations tour operators **cannot** offer at present. Why is this?

## Contracting

Contracts are typically fixed about 12 months ahead of the holiday season. This means that the tour operator needs to make an estimation of capacity in order to agree contracts with hotels and airlines. There will be some adjustments later, but it is difficult to make major changes as prices have been agreed and brochures have gone to print.

It is difficult to contract too far in advance as tour operators have to make decisions, based on sales and other research, about what to include in their programme. Different types of contract that might be organised for accommodation include:

* a fixed contract

* an allocation contract

* a sale-only contract.

The **fixed contract** is more advantageous to the supplier as it means that if the accommodation is

---

## CASE STUDY

### Elegant Resorts Ski 2005
**What's new**

* Southern hemisphere destinations
* More hotels in Val d'Isère

THINK luxury ski resorts – think Whistler, Zermatt and Val d'Isère. But these may be a little too well-trodden for customers wanting to stray off-piste. That's why Elegant Resorts has expanded its brochure to include ski holidays to Argentina and Chile.

Another bonus of these southern hemisphere destinations is that the ski season runs from June to October.

Also included is a collection of luxurious chalets in France, Switzerland and Canada – all with superb mountain views, as well as a host of newly featured hotels.

Prices start at £1,395 for an eight-night ski holiday in Argentina.

*Travel Trade Gazette*, 30 July 2004

1  What research do you think contributed to Elegant Ski Resorts' decision to market holidays in Argentina and Chile?
2  Discuss your ideas with your group, and produce a list of sources that may have been used.

not sold they will still be paid. Obviously this is not so practical for the tour operator.

**Allocation contracts** are also popular with hoteliers. To ensure that all their beds are sold they contract with tour operators for more beds than they have available. The tour operator has to confirm, by an agreed date, how many beds it will actually take. This gives the hotel time to sell remaining beds at a competitive price.

Allocation contracts also apply to flights. A smaller tour operator can't fill a whole charter aircraft, so it buys an allocation of seats on a flight. Once the allocation is sold, it requests seats for any extra bookings or looks for seats on an alternative flight. The customer may have to pay a supplement for these seats as they won't be acquired at the preferential rate of the original allocation. If the allocation is not sold, unsold seats can be returned to the airline, but the deadline for this is six to eight weeks before departure date.

A **sale-only contract** means that the tour operator estimates the amount of accommodation needed and then pays only for what is actually sold. This can leave hotels with unsold rooms which they have to sell at the last minute. They could do this through an agent such as Lastminute.com or Expedia.

Fixed contracts are less common than they used to be as tour operators look for greater flexibility and control over costs. However, the type of contract also depends on who is the more powerful negotiator.

Flights are often contracted more than a season in advance, and again the tour operators have to predict how many people will be prepared to book a particular holiday from a particular airport. If predictions are wrong they will have to make adjustments – but sometimes this is not possible. They may be able to contract extra aircraft if available but it is difficult to cancel one without incurring costs.

Where there is no possibility of achieving the required load factor on a flight, a tour operator may decide to consolidate two flights. This simply means that one will be cancelled and the passengers will be transferred to the other flight. This action causes customer dissatisfaction as departure times and even airports will change. But sometimes it can work in a customer's favour, as they may be given an extra couple of days' holiday to fit in with the new flight.

## Pricing

A number of pricing strategies are commonly used by tour operators. These include the following.

### Fluid pricing

The brochure is issued a long time before the season and is printed with prices. The price at this stage may not be a true reflection of the price that the customer will ultimately pay. Operators may raise prices if costs increase, or if there is a surge in demand.

The Trading Standards Institute has criticised tour operators for such practices and threatened to take legal action against some. This is because the Package Travel Regulations forbid such price rises, or 'fluid pricing'. Also many tour operators may use the same hotel but arrive at different prices for the package.

## Discount pricing

Prices may be discounted if holidays remain unsold. By fixing contracts and therefore prices a long time ahead of the season, tour operators purchase their supplies (flights and rooms) at the cheapest prices. In order to ensure that holidays are not left unsold and that cash flow is good, tour operators must encourage early bookings. When early bookings are high, the tour operator knows whether there will be any excess capacity in holidays – hopefully none – and takes a substantial deposit per person. Tour operators are able to use or invest this money as they do not need to pay their suppliers until the holidays are taken.

When there is excess capacity, tour operators are forced to discount holidays at the last minute. Tour operators aim to sell 95% of holidays available in order to maintain profitability. This means it is important to try to match supply and demand very closely.

Large tour operators achieve very small margins of profit. They may make only 5% of the price of the holiday as profit. The Civil Aviation Authority states that some margins are as low as 3%. If the holiday is discounted, they may not make any profit. In that case the aim is to cover the costs.

You can see why the selling of ancillary products is so vital – this is where the profits are to be made. Tactics employed by tour operators with discounted holidays include charging for the transfer, charging a late booking fee and for a meal on the plane.

Here is an example of a cost breakdown for a holiday costing £499.

| Flight | £214.55 |
|---|---|
| Accommodation and transfer | £149.70 |
| Marketing | £14.97 |
| Distribution | £74.85 |
| Overheads (salaries, offices, administration, etc.) | £19.96 |
| **Total** | **£474.03** |

## Seasonal pricing

Tour operators divide the year into different seasons. First, there is a broad division into winter and summer season. In summer there are more beach holidays, and in winter ski programmes are running. A summer brochure will typically cover the period May to November, and a winter one will run from November to April. Within these periods there are peak seasons, shoulder seasons and off-peak seasons.

Tour operators vary their capacity during the season but must fill the planes they have contracted. This can result in discounted prices at shoulder season. At peak season – the school holiday period of July and August in summer, and the Christmas holidays in winter – demand and therefore prices are at their highest. Tour operators have been heavily criticised for charging their highest prices in school holiday times, but they have to make their profit when they can.

## CASE STUDY

| Week commencing | 12-night base price | +/- per night |
|---|---|---|
| 02 Apr–13 Apr | 430 | 16 |
| 14 Apr–07 May | 360 | 15 |
| 08 May–14 May | 525 | 23 |
| 15 May–21 May | 560 | 26 |
| 22 May–04 June | 675 | 32 |
| 05 June–11 June | 680 | 36 |
| 12 June–18 June | 740 | 43 |
| 19 June–25 June | 850 | 51 |
| 26 June–02 July | 965 | 54 |
| 03 July–09 July | 1,160 | 62 |
| 10 July–16 July | 1,200 | 64 |
| 17 July–23 July | 1,290 | 68 |
| 24 July–13 Aug | 1,340 | 68 |
| 14 Aug–20 Aug | 1,300 | 65 |
| 21 Aug–27 Aug | 995 | 52 |
| 28 Aug–03 Sep | 470 | 20 |
| 04 Sep–10 Sep | 370 | 14 |
| 11 Sep–22 Oct | 370 | 15 |

**Your price includes**
- 12-night accommodation for 2 adults – all children under 18 years FREE of charge
- Return midweek Dover–Calais–Dover ferry crossing for a standard car and up to 5 passengers with P&O Ferries
- FREE Travel Pack
- FREE Representative service
- FREE Children's Pack
- FREE Children's Clubs
- Games to loan (small deposit)
- FREE Barbecues at most parcs
- Local taxes included
- Gas, water and electricity charges included

Source: Haven Europe brochure 2004

1 **The chart shows prices for a holiday in a mobile home in France. Give reasons for the variations in price.**

2 **When are the peak season and the shoulder season?**

3 **What else would a family have to pay for on this holiday?**

**Make notes for discussion with your group.**

## Competitive pricing

Mass-market operators are very keen to remain competitive on price; they will often match prices offered by the competition. Sometimes more up-market operators will do this as well, so it is worth customers asking them.

## Promotional pricing

Tour operators have tried various promotions linked to price over recent years, including a two-for-one offer. This was not very successful as many customers believed that the original prices had been raised to cover the offer. Early booking promotions with price discounts are more credible.

## *Other factors affecting the price*

### Exchange rates

Many of the costs paid by tour operators are in foreign currencies, usually euros or dollars. Such costs include accommodation, airport charges and transport. When the exchange rate varies, tour operators may have to pay more or less than they had originally calculated. This could cause problems if the rate change is not in their favour.

Operators are legally prevented from passing on the first 2% of an increase in costs to customers. Of course, tour operators are aware of this and 'hedge' funds. This means sufficient funds are exchanged in advance of need, or contracted to be exchanged at a fixed rate. The bank charges for this service, but it is invaluable to the tour operator.

### Airport charges

Airlines pay the airport per passenger carried. The airline will pass this charge on to the tour operator. A tour operator that is prepared to offer flights at unsocial times will be able to purchase the flights more cheaply, as the airport charges less for those slots.

Customers wanting regional departures often pay a flight supplement. This is surprising, as airport charges are generally lower at regional airports. However, flights may be slightly longer than from London airports and therefore more fuel may be used. Also, it may be more difficult to fill planes to capacity.

## Accommodation supplements

When tour operators book hotel rooms they agree a price per room, so they need to put two people in a double room to make it cost effective. Single people pay more and a third person gets a reduction.

Single travellers regard this as discrimination, and tour operators have recognised that singles are an important market and have made some changes to policy, as Saga Holidays managing director Chris Simmonds indicates:

> ❛Single travellers make up a significant proportion of our customers and we have always campaigned for single rooms at no extra supplement. We're committed to meeting the needs of single travellers and to providing a wide range of supplement-free holidays in exciting destinations throughout the world.❜

## Selling

### Brochure production

As we saw earlier, holiday brochures are printed a long time in advance of the holiday season. The brochures include prices, and obviously it is difficult to determine prices a long time in advance.

Tour operators produce several versions of a brochure in order to update prices. But this practice is confusing for customers and travel agents, and also wasteful. A solution would be to print brochures without prices and to confirm the price at the time of booking, but this is illegal in the UK – a price must be set for the package.

It has been suggested by Trading Standards officers that a maximum brochure price is set which cannot be exceeded, but which can be discounted. This suggestion has not yet been adopted.

The brochure is an important sales tool and traditionally the main source of information for the customer. Unless the business is new or a new venture for an existing operator, the brochure will be largely based on the previous year's version. This means it is unnecessary to photograph every hotel every year and rewrite all the copy (text). In spite of this, it still takes a lot of time to produce.

Time is needed to:

* design the brochure
* take photos
* write copy
* determine prices.

The brochure must appear in good time to allow sales to take place. A brochure for the summer season will be published in September or October of the previous year.

Brochures are costly to produce, with each costing between 75p and £1.20. This takes up a large part of the marketing budget. First Choice estimates that 25% of its marketing spend goes on brochures.

Many of the brochures never reach a customer; as second and third editions appear, travel agents have to discard the old ones. One agent reported spending £500 on getting rid of them – this amounted to more than three skips of brochures. Travel agents also have to devote a lot of valuable storage space to brochures.

There is a solution to the brochure problem. Technology allows for printed brochures to be abandoned in favour of e-brochures.

**Key concept**

**E-brochure** – an electronic version of tour operator information of the type that traditionally appears in print.

There are advantages to these – e-brochures do not waste paper, ink, space or money. They can also be more precisely targeted, as a travel agent or other intermediary can download information that is of interest to a specific customer.

However, an e-brochures system is not as simple as transferring the brochure to the Internet. It requires investment in a content management system by the tour operator in order to be done properly.

Anite Travel Systems Ltd held a conference at the end of 2003 about an e-brochure system. The following diagram summarises the system.

In this ideal model, tour operators have access to their suppliers' extranet and can access contract rates, images and text. The tour operator selects and inputs relevant data and this then goes through an automatic process which calculates prices according to the operator's margin. The information then goes to brochure production and to e-distribution and reservations.

The main question is whether customers will accept e-brochures in place of brochures they can browse through at home. Also, it is likely that small operators will be deterred by the investment required.

**Theory into practice**

Find a tour operator's e-brochure on-line. You could look at www.kuoni.co.uk. Compare the experience of using the e-brochure with a traditional brochure. Make a comparative table.

### Promotion

Promotion is the work of marketing personnel, as you saw in Unit 3. The nature of promotion depends on the budget available, and ranges from television advertising campaigns to press releases about new products and destinations. You can find examples of the use of press releases in travel trade magazines.

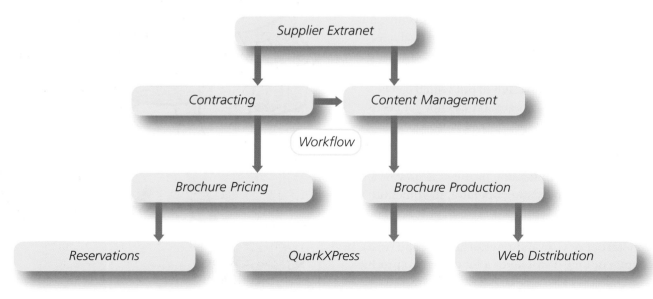

*Integrated Holiday Production*

## Reservations

Most tour operators use computerised reservation systems. Reservations staff are salespeople so they have to be well informed about the products they sell. This is easier in tour operation than in travel agencies, as the salesperson needs to know about only one company's products and will have received intensive training.

Reservations staff may be at a call centre, in which case they have targets to meet in terms of calls answered and sales made. Others take bookings over the computerised reservation system from travel agents, or over the Internet. They will need to contact customers only if there is a query about a booking or availability. Once a booking is made, a reference code is assigned to it alongside the customer details, so that the booking can always be traced through the system.

### Theory into practice

Role-play the part of a reservations clerk in a call centre, with a colleague acting as a customer.
Prepare by choosing some holiday brochures to work with. Make a list of the information you will need from the customer in order to take a booking. Be prepared to answer the customer's questions about the resort, accommodation, etc. If you can, tape the role plays so that you can evaluate them to see whether you missed any important information.

## UK operations

### Administration

Once reservations are made, further administration is dealt with by another team. They issue invoices after booking and send out reminders for payment. They issue any tickets, itineraries and other documentation; this can be quite complex. Camping operators send out guides to the campsite, a guide to the local area, car stickers and maps as well as the booking details.

The administration department has to make sure that suppliers are informed of bookings. Passenger lists and details of forthcoming bookings are sent to airlines and hotels.

The administrative role is important as payments must be received from customers, and customers and suppliers must have all the relevant information.

### Duty office

The role of the duty office is customer liaison. Smaller tour operators may not have a dedicated department, but they always have a designated member of staff on call outside office hours.

The duty office provides an essential link between the UK and the resorts. The office deals with any non-routine occurrences, for example medical problems where an insurance company has to be contacted. If delays occur at airports, they will make sure that passengers receive the information, meals or even accommodation that they require.

### Customer service

In addition to the duty office, tour operators provide routine customer service departments. They may be divided into pre-departure customer service and post-holiday customer service.

Before departure, the customer service agents deal with enquiries and provide information. They may give information about passports, visas and vaccination requirements. They will also deal with any booking amendments and pass on details to reservations.

After the holiday, the customer service department mostly deals with any complaints. The agents answer telephone, e-mail and postal complaints. The large tour operators computerise these systems and scan all correspondence into an individual customer file saved on the system.

Targets are set for responding to complaints and letters are automatically generated as far as possible, although obviously some complaints require a unique response. The aim is always to solve the complaint as quickly and as cheaply as possible. The customer service department's work load is much reduced where overseas representatives are empowered to resolve complaints in the resort as far as possible. The tour operator will try to resolve any further complaint to the customer's satisfaction and to avoid possible legal action. However, many people complain after their holiday because they simply had expectations that were too high, or experienced poor weather, and the tour operator has to respond to such complaints although there is no obligation to provide any form of compensation.

# Overseas operations

## Transfers

Transfers are usually included in the package. The transfer from the airport to the hotel is usually by coach. On many late bookings, tour operators now charge extra for the transfer to compensate for discounting the holiday. Representatives take it in turns to be on airport duty – normally one day a week. These reps meet the plane and accompany the coach loads of passengers to their accommodation. The rep has a list of who should be on each coach and must make sure they are taken to the right place.

The rep has the job of entertaining the passengers on the way, which is not easy if they have been delayed! Most holiday makers probably want to go to sleep at this point. The transfer can be very tedious if the coach visits several hotels. More up-market packages include a taxi transfer, which is much more convenient for holiday makers. It is also offered as an extra on standard packages.

## Representatives

Package holidays include the services of a representative. The representatives are employed directly by the tour operator in areas where the operator has a large programme with many holiday makers. In other circumstances, reps are hired from local companies and will take care of people on holiday with several different tour operators. This latter group is more likely to be made up of local people.

Working as a representative is very popular, although they have a gruelling schedule. The main role is that of customer service; a customer can expect all of the following from a rep:

* a welcome meeting
* choice of excursions (at extra cost) accompanied by a rep

* daily availability of an hour or two at the accommodation
* an information board and file in reception
* help in any situation, from advice on where to eat to an emergency.

The reps are expected to deal with customer complaints and preferably solve problems on the spot so that they do not result in a further complaint when the customer returns to the UK. To this end, the reps have some authority to award compensation in the form of bottles of wine, for example.

In large resorts there will be an office for the tour operator, with administrative and management staff as well as the reps. Someone will be on call 24 hours a day. The staff are in communication with the UK and receive daily information updates, for example passenger manifests and special requests. Sometimes the resort staff have to allocate accommodation where customers have booked late at a discount for 'allocation on arrival'.

The reps will have a degree of responsibility for health and safety. Under the Package Travel Regulations, the tour operator is responsible for the customer's health and safety, not the hotel. If the rep notices any breach of health and safety or is informed of one by a customer, he or she must ensure it is put right.

In addition, the reps must deal with emergency situations. A good tour operator lays down procedures to be followed in such cases. Most emergencies are health-related or involve crimes. The worst scenario involves someone's death; although this is a terrible situation for all concerned, it is not unusual for reps to have to deal with it and there will be procedures to follow.

The most demanding situation for a rep is dealing with a crisis that affects a lot of customers. Examples include mass food poisoning, a bus crash or a hurricane. In such situations there should be a crisis management procedure that can be put into operation, but reps would also expect senior management to oversee these procedures.

# External factors affecting package-holiday programmes

## Environmental factors

Environmental factors can adversely affect a holiday and the whole travel market. Recent examples include a series of hurricanes in 2004, the outbreak of diseases such as severe acute respiratory syndrome (SARS) in 2003, and foot and mouth disease in the UK a few years ago. Other possible problems include floods, avalanches and oil spillages.

*A series of hurricanes swept through the Caribbean in 2004*

Obviously it is difficult to plan for natural disasters, but companies should have contingency plans in place to cover all eventualities.

## Political factors

Sometimes, tour operators have to pull out of destinations completely because of political factors such as war or terrorism. In 2003 Kenya suffered some terrorist attacks which caused devastation to the tourism trade. The British government banned flights to Kenya for several weeks as there were fears that there would be another attack. Holiday sales to Kenya are now improving, but tour operators have to work hard, alongside the national tourist board, to reassure customers that the destination is safe. The Kenyan Tourist Board spent £1.2 million on a tourism recovery marketing programme. The British Foreign Office gives up-to-date information on its website about the safety of destinations.

It is important for tour operators to conduct risk assessments and have contingency plans in place for when things go wrong. Staff should be trained in crisis response. They should also have a plan for dealing with media enquiries if a disaster happens.

---

## CASE STUDY

### Hurricane to hit Bahamas and Florida

Tour operators and airlines are currently working on contingency plans for Florida as Hurricane Frances – a force 4–5 hurricane – is expected to hit the Bahamas imminently and the east coast of Florida and Orlando on Saturday. Orlando airports could be shut during Friday, Saturday and Sunday. As a result it is likely that many flights, including charter flights, leaving the UK for Orlando on Friday will be cancelled.

Tour operators and airlines will be putting the safety of their customers first. They are constantly monitoring the situation and evacuating holiday makers from high-risk areas where necessary.

Source: www.travelmole.com, 2 September 2004

1  What do you think tour operators should do in this situation to ensure the safety of their customers and carry on their business?
2  Present your ideas to your group, and discuss the implications of these measures for the tour operators.

# CASE STUDY

## White Water Rafting Holidays

Enjoy the thrills of white water from an inflatable raft, as you head down one of our featured white water rivers! From gentle rafting on grade 2–3 rivers, to the fast and furious rapids of the higher-grade 4 rivers – we have a range of trips to suit everyone! In all of our resorts you will join experienced local guides for a trip of a lifetime. You will be kitted out with wetsuits, life jackets and a helmet (all you need to bring is swim wear and plenty of enthusiasm). Before you set off you will be given some basic instruction and safety training and then you will join your fellow rafters – normally 6–8 in a raft with the guide. The rivers we feature lead through some beautiful mountain scenery and give you the chance to view the area from a completely different perspective!

Source: www.crystalactive.co.uk

## Airport staff to strike over pay dispute

By Michael Millar

Baggage handlers and check-in staff at airports across the UK have voted to strike in a dispute over pay.

Members of the T&G union working at 17 locations, including Heathrow, Edinburgh, Glasgow and Liverpool, voted by four to one to reject a 2.5% pay offer from ground handling services company Aviance.

The union said it was now up to Aviance management to come up with a new offer, or face a series of strikes.

Brendan Gold, the T&G national secretary for civil aviation, said: 'Everyone is aware that aviation is a tough market, and nobody is better placed to know that than the baggage handlers and check-in staff.

'They also know that the volume of their work is increasing as the industry gets busier, and passenger numbers break record levels,' he said. 'They know a bad deal when they see one, which is why we urge Aviance to listen to their workforce and act to improve the deal on offer, and avoid a damaging dispute.'

The Department of Transport said it was a matter for the two sides to negotiate.

Aviance operations are at the following airports: Aberdeen, Belfast, Birmingham, Cardiff, Coventry, Edinburgh, Gatwick, Glasgow, Heathrow, Jersey, Leeds Bradford, Liverpool, Luton, Manchester, Stansted, Southampton and Teesside.

Source: www.personneltoday.com, 5 July 2004

1 Read the article on Crystal Active white water rafting. Think about all the factors that might affect the operation of this type of package holiday. Prepare a contingency plan to deal with them, and explain how this will make operations more effective.

2 Read the *Personnel Today* article on the airport strike. This is a situation that occurs quite regularly in UK airports. Explain what contingency plans a major tour operator could have to deal with such situations.

Tour operators must also recognise the social and economic situation at the destination and how tourism can impact on issues such as unemployment and poverty.

A group of tour operators from different parts of the world have joined together to create the Tour Operators' Initiative for Sustainable Tourism Development. It is open to all tour operators regardless of their size and geographical location. The aim is to encourage tour operators to accept their ethical responsibilities and adopt practices that promote local economic development and reduce the adverse environmental impacts of tourism. Many tour operators are often criticised for paying lip-service to sustainable tourism, so these initiatives help promote truly sustainable travel policies.

## Legal factors

Tour operators must adhere to relevant consumer legislation. Consumer protection laws affecting tour operators include the following.

### Package Travel Regulations 1992

As a result of a European Directive, since 1993 all UK tour operators offering package holidays have been subject to the Package Travel Regulations. The regulations set out the tour operators' responsibilities to their customers and what customers can do if the regulations are breached. If there is a breach, the customer has a case against the tour operator, not each individual supplier.

The two principal sections of the regulations provide financial protection for prepayments and require tour operators to provide what is promised. The main provisions are:

* tour operators are responsible for the safety of their customers – this means for their safety in the accommodation, on the flight and so on, and must provide assistance in the resort

* tour operators must not give inaccurate brochure descriptions

* last-minute surcharges cannot be imposed

* if the operator becomes bankrupt there must be a guaranteed refund.

There are also regulations about the information that should be provided to the customer, and what happens if the contract is altered in any way.

There are requirements for the customer also. If customers have complaints they should report them in the resort so that the rep has an opportunity to resolve them. If they need to write to the tour operator to complain, this should be done within a reasonable period (usually 28 days).

Compensation and legal redress are available for customers through the UK courts when there is a breach of regulations. Booking conditions are issued by tour operators and explain all the requirements for both parties.

The Department of Trade and Industry provides a free booklet, 'Looking into the Package Travel Regulations', which fully explains the regulations.

### Trade Descriptions Act 1968

Descriptions given must be truthful and accurate. This act primarily affects tour operators, as they have to be careful that brochure descriptions adhere to the rules.

### Supply of Goods and Services Act 1982 (amended 1994)

This act says that the tour operator and the travel agent should ensure that the booking is carried out correctly, and the contract for the holiday should also be carried out using 'reasonable skill and care'. The holiday should comply with any descriptions and be of a satisfactory standard.

### Unfair Terms in Consumer Contracts Regulations 1999

If consumers think that the contract with a tour operator is unfair, they may have a case under these regulations. The Office of Fair Trading gives examples of the kinds of terms which might be unfair. These include contracts where customers are not allowed to change holiday arrangements when they are unable to travel, even when they give reasonable notice, and where tour operators seek to put false limits on compensation for problems.

Responsible companies lay out conditions in a Fair Trading Charter, together with their booking conditions. These form the basis of a legally binding contract between the two parties.

There are many sources of help when customers want to make complaints. They can approach their local Trading Standards Office; ABTA has an arbitration scheme; and there are consumer groups who will help holiday makers register a complaint. Unfortunately, many people complain because they have not enjoyed the holiday and not read the booking conditions. The regulations therefore help both parties.

In 2003 the Office of Fair Trading took action against Virgin Holidays. The OFT was concerned that some of Virgin Holidays' booking conditions were potentially unfair under the Unfair Terms in Consumer Contracts Regulations. Virgin Holidays agreed to change its contract terms to give consumers a fairer deal. A number of points were subject to change but here are two examples, taken from the OFT press release.

- Allowed the imposition of a surcharge if certain costs rose, namely transportation costs including the cost of fuel, dues, taxes or fees chargeable for services such as landing taxes, or for exchange rate fluctuations without entitling the consumer to a reduction if the same costs fell. The term also failed to specify that the Package Tours Regulations 1992 (PTRs) require that no increase should be made within the 30 days before departure. **Change** – the term allowing surcharges has been deleted.

- Excluded payment of compensation for significant changes to a holiday or cancellation of the booking by the company before departure above a set scale, even if a consumer could prove a greater loss. **Change** – the contract now states that the compensation levels payable are the minimum levels payable.

Source: OFT press release March 2003, Fairer Contracts from Virgin Holidays.

## Codes of conduct

In addition to complying with legislation, tour operators voluntarily agree to abide by the codes of conduct of the trade associations to which they belong. The trade associations were discussed in the first part of this unit, but you should also be aware of the role of the Civil Aviation Authority (CAA) and Air Travel Organisers' Licensing (ATOL) in tour operations.

All tour operators selling packages must be bonded or protect the prepayments they hold. That means if they become bankrupt before travel, customers should get a refund, or, if they are already abroad, they will be able to return home without any extra payment.

Package holidays that include flights must be protected by ATOL. ATOL is a statutory scheme managed by the CAA to protect the public from losing money or being stranded abroad because of the failure of air travel firms.

All tour operators selling flights and air holidays are required to hold a licence from the CAA. In order to get the licence the company must provide proof of a bond, that is a financial guarantee provided by a bank or insurance company. If the company fails, the CAA calls in the bond and uses the money to pay for people abroad to continue their holidays, and to make refunds to those who have paid but not travelled.

It is the largest travel protection scheme in the UK, covering 28 million people, and the only one for flights and air holidays sold by tour operators. Unfortunately, companies collapse very often so the scheme is much needed.

The case study below shows different examples of the bonds being used.

### CASE STUDY

Golden Sun Holidays ceased trading in September 2004. About 10,000 people were on holiday with Golden Sun at that time, in Cyprus and Greece. Another 20,000 people had bookings with the company. Those people would have to find an alternative holiday with the refund given to them. People who were expecting to travel the weekend of the company collapse were unlikely to find another holiday, but would get their money back.

The CAA called in Golden Sun's ATOL bonds of £9.8 million and ensured that refunds were paid, and that those people who were abroad were able to complete their holiday. Also in September 2004, Hurricane Ivan caused devastation on the islands of the Caribbean. Thousands of holiday makers were in the area. Tour operators such as Virgin Holidays and Thomson provided people with alternative accommodation and flights home when the airports opened. Those who wished to stay were moved to different hotels.

The treatment of these tourists demonstrates the value of travelling on package holidays with bonded companies. Independent tourists arranging their own flights or accommodation would have had no one to help them. They could have had to pay out more for flights or hotels.

1  **Find out more about the CAA and ATOL by looking at www.caa.co.uk.**
2  **Explain how being bonded helped the tourists in the Caribbean and the tour operators looking after them.**
3  **What other factors about Thomson and Virgin might help in this situation?**

# Designing, planning and costing a package

In this section you will be given the opportunity to work on two case studies so that you can practise designing, planning and costing a package holiday. You must bear in mind that you are unable to access the negotiated rates that large tour operators can achieve. Nor will you be able to find out the costs of chartering an aircraft. These figures are negotiated for each deal and are not in the public domain. However, you will be able to carry out research and go through a process which is similar to that of a small operator.

*You need to research a special spa hotel with luxurious facilities*

## Designing and planning

The first case study is about a specialist tour operator bringing out a new product and brochure called 'Spa Bliss'. The hotels are all over the world and each one is very special, exclusive and offers a full range of spa therapies. Most of them have been sourced and contracted, but the owner wants one more to finish off the programme. Your role is to find an extra special spa hotel in an exotic location and then create a package around that hotel.

How do you do this?

1  Decide on the destination and the spa hotel. The easiest way for you to do this is to search on the Internet for spa hotels. You can't get the information from another package holiday brochure as you need to access the hotel's rates, so you need to visit the hotel's own website. Search for 'spa hotels' and find one that is suitably exclusive and luxurious for the 'Spa Bliss' programme. Make sure that no prohibitive factors apply to the destination – that is, no political or environmental factors would prevent people from travelling there. Select some photos that you could use in your brochure. Check prices, particularly of a twin room per night.

2  Decide how customers will get there. Find out what scheduled flights serve the destination – make sure there is a direct flight. Start by searching British Airways. Check prices and try to find an average price.

3 What type of board will you offer your customers? Check what the hotel offers, from bed and breakfast to all-inclusive. Check rates again.

4 Decide which treatments and activities will be included and which will cost extra. List everything. Check prices.

5 What kind of contract will you arrange with the hotel? This is a new venture and you don't know how many bookings you will get, so perhaps the first season should be on a 'sale-only' contract.

6 Decide how you will transfer your customers from the airport to the hotel. If they are paying a lot of money, they will expect a taxi. How much will that cost? Try www.holidaytaxis.com for quotes.

You are ready to start costing this project – as you are buying rooms, and seats on scheduled aircraft, you don't need to worry about load factors.

## Costing

1 The mark-up on luxury holidays is higher than on mass-market holidays, and you need to get a speedy return on investment, so go for a relatively high mark-up. Start with 20% – this will be in off-peak, and you can price up from that for shoulder and peak times.

2 Note all the costs of everything you want to include in your package in a table. Do this for a seven-night and a 14-night period. Remember you will get commission from the suppliers on everything you book. Assume this is 10% and take this off. Add on your mark-up. The figure you have left is the basic price.

3 At this stage you should look at some other spa packages and see how your basic price compares. Is it realistic?

4 Decide on the season, perhaps November to April. Divide the season into peak, shoulder and off-peak periods and adjust the prices.

5 Collate a list of supplements, activities and excursions with the prices you will charge for them.

Keep all your notes from each stage so that you are able to explain how you arrived at your package. Put your information together as a brochure page.

Present your proposal to your tutor.

Now try another case study on your own in the following Assessment Activity.

In this case study you are setting up business as a French villa tour operator. You will start the season with a handful of properties, but need to describe only one for the purposes of the activity. Tour operators would travel to the region of France in which they were interested, visit properties and contract them. You will have to work through the Internet.

You need to find individuals who are renting villas rather than companies; try www.villadata.com.

1 Choose a villa that you will offer in your brochure for a period of June to September.

2 Decide what type of contract you will arrange.

3 Find suitable transport for your customers by car and ferry.

4 Decide what will be included in the package.

5 Produce a costing for the package, showing your mark-up.

6 Put all the information together as a brochure page with prices.

7 Show your costing separately from the brochure page.

8 Be ready to present your proposal and explain how you arrived at it.
   These tasks may provide evidence for P5.

9 Discuss the external factors that might affect the sale and operation of the villa holiday package. Some ideas to get you started:
   • an oil spillage on French beaches
   • strikes at Channel ports
   • fantastic summer weather in the UK.
   This task may provide evidence for M3.

10 Prepare a contingency plan to deal with unforeseen problems that might affect the villa holiday, and explain how the plan will help you operate effectively. Examples include how you would get your customers home quickly, where you would find alternative accommodation and which staff would deal with emergencies.
   This task may provide evidence for D2.

1 Summarise the different companies in each of the big four holiday groups.

2 What are the benefits of integration?

3 Identify the associations that support tour operators.

4 Explain how tour operators charter aircraft.

5 Define a package holiday.

6 Explain why ancillary sales are important to tour operators.

7 What are the different kinds of contracts between tour operators and suppliers?

8 Describe the different pricing strategies used by tour operators.

9 What is an e-brochure?

10 What can a customer expect from an overseas representative?

11 Give examples of environmental factors which might affect tour operation.

12 Describe the main provisions of the Package Travel Regulations.

## UNIT 11 ASSESSMENT ASSIGNMENT

After finishing your BTEC course you have found a job with a medium-sized, independent tour operator specialising in packaged ski holidays, called Especially Ski. You work in the reservations department. You really enjoy your work but you are keen to learn about other departments and make career progression.

At your appraisal, you discuss this with your line manager and he asks you if you would like to be involved in a project that the press office team has suggested. The press office is constantly receiving requests for information from students who want to know about tour operating and about how the company operates. The press team acknowledges that it is important to help students, but they find they are spending a lot of time answering questions and sending out information.

Their idea is to compile a student pack that can be posted on the Internet. It will be a series of downloadable fact sheets so that students can choose the ones they need. The press team has put together a list of the most frequently asked questions that they receive and they want each sheet to be a response to one of the questions.

Carry out the necessary research to allow you to produce a detailed response to each of the questions, and put together an information page for each question. The pages must be suitable for inclusion on a website.

**Frequently asked question 1**

*What kind of tour operator is Especially Ski, and how does it compete with other kinds of tour-operating businesses?*

1 Describe the different types of tour operators and what they sell.

2 Describe the various trade associations that support tour-operating organisations.

These tasks may provide evidence for P1.

3 Analyse the impact of integration in other tour operators on Especially Ski.

This task may provide evidence for M1.

**Frequently asked question 2**

*How do tour operators plan, sell and operate their package-holiday programmes?*

4 Describe the different aspects of planning, selling and operating the package-holiday programme including:
- research
- contracting
- pricing
- UK operations
- overseas operations.

This task may provide evidence for P2 and P3.

5 Explain how the different operational areas relate to each other, and explain the timescales involved in each area of operation.

This task may provide evidence for M2.

**Frequently asked question 3**

*What external factors affect the planning, selling and operation of a programme?*

6 Describe environmental, political and legal factors affecting the tour-operating business.

This task may provide evidence for P4.

**Frequently asked question 4**

*Can you tell me about problems caused by external factors that tour operators have had to deal with and how well they managed it?*

7 Research newspapers, trade magazines and websites and find two specific examples of external factors affecting tour operators' programmes. They could be examples of natural disasters, political situations or new legislation. Describe the situations and analyse the effectiveness of the tour operator in dealing with the situation.

This task may provide evidence for D1.

**Frequently asked question 5**

*What new packages are coming up for Especially Ski? How did you decide on them?*

8 Design, plan and cost a package for inclusion in Especially Ski's new brochure. Describe each stage of the process.

This task may provide evidence for P5.

**Frequently asked question 6**

*Are there any external factors that might affect your new package?*

9 Explain how external factors could affect the sales and operation of the package you designed.

This task may provide evidence for M3.

**Frequently asked question 7**

*How will you deal with those external factors?*

10 Prepare a contingency plan to deal with external factors that could affect the selling and operation of the package you designed. Explain how having the contingency plan will make the operation of the package-holiday programme more effective.

This task may provide evidence for D2.

**UNIT 21**

# Work-based experience within the travel and tourism industry

## Introduction

**W**ork-based experience is a valuable addition to your programme of study. It helps you to apply your knowledge of travel and tourism in a work context and to develop your practical skills. You will experience the world of work and appreciate the code of behaviour and teamwork essential to the effective running of the workplace.

Your work-based experience may take place in a block of two or more weeks or on a day-release or weekend basis. This unit will help you prepare for your placement, give you guidance on planning and completing a work-based project, and help you review your work experience.

> *How you will be assessed*

This unit is internally assessed by your tutor. A variety of exercises and activities is included in this unit to help you make the most of your work-based experience and prepare for the assessment. You will also have the opportunity to work on some case studies to further your understanding.

At the end of this unit you should be able to:

→ Investigate opportunities for a work-based experience in the travel and tourism industry

→ Prepare to obtain a work-based experience

→ Plan, complete and present an approved project

→ Undertake a personal review of the work-based experience and your own performance.

# Why do work experience?

## Developing your skills

In the work environment you will have an opportunity to develop some or all of the following skills.

* **Customer care** – you will be dealing with members of the public, suppliers and colleagues, and the customer care skills you develop will be of use whatever career you choose in the future.

* **Technical/practical** – you may learn to use specialist equipment and resources, for example, reservation systems, other IT systems or you might be finding your way around directories.

* **Social/personal** – when you go to work you leave your personal problems at home. Develop a professional attitude showing respect and consideration for customers and colleagues alike.

* **Analytical/critical/problem-solving skills** – your work experience will present you with real challenges. Use your initiative to deal with any problems or incidents that occur. Bear in mind your limitations and refer issues to relevant managers if appropriate.

* **Prioritising tasks** – you will be given various tasks to do, sometimes from different members of staff. Learn how to judge which tasks are more important or urgent and do those first. If in doubt, ask.

* **Time-keeping** – punctuality shows your commitment to the placement. Remember to return punctually from breaks as well as arriving on time for the start of work.

* **Self-motivation** – always ensure you have tasks to do. If necessary, ask for something to do or ask staff for an explanation and demonstration of what they are doing.

* **Action planning/research techniques** – you will have a project to complete on your placement. Use the resources available while at work, including people, to develop your planning and research skills.

## Developing your career

Your work-based experience is the first step of your career – whether you eventually go into travel and tourism or not.

* You will gain experience in a sector of the travel and tourism industry – this will help you decide whether your career lies in that sector.

* If you perform well on your work-based experience, your employer should agree to provide a reference for future jobs.

* You will start to build up a network of contacts who might help you in your future career.

* Employers often offer jobs – full- or part-time – to those people who perform well on work experience.

* You will build up experience and skills which can be included on your CV.

## Health, safety and security requirements

These requirements are covered in Unit 6. When you undertake your work experience you will find out how they apply in practice.

When you arrive at work you will be given induction training; this is essential for all new staff and will introduce you to basic policies and procedures relating to your work environment. Basic health, safety and security requirements will be included in induction. Other procedures will be explained to you if they are relevant to the work you are doing.

All health, safety and security requirements will be published in a manual or displayed in the workplace. You should make sure you are familiar with all the procedures.

# Preparing for work-based experience

## How to find a work placement

Many colleges and schools have a work-experience co-ordinator whose role is to help you find a work placement. But the co-ordinator will have to find placements for many students, so you might decide to find your own placement.

## Sources of placements

* **Database** – your college or school should have a database of work placements previously used by travel and tourism students. This may be held by the co-ordinator or the tutor. If a placement on the database appeals to you, notify your tutor and find out what the procedure is for making contact with the organisation. Often, colleges and schools prefer students not to contact organisations on the database directly, as they want to ensure that these organisations are not inundated with requests.

* **Careers advisers** – they may be based in your college or school or in another centre, for example Connexions. They do not find work placements but they will help you decide what type of placement will be suitable for you with your career goals in mind.

* **Newspapers** – look at job advertisements in the local newspaper to get ideas of organisations in your area which are suitable for work experience.

* **Resource centres/websites** – if you are looking for a work placement in a specialist sector such as the airport sector, you will find that there is often a job centre or website for recruitment. Examples include Manchester and Stansted airports. These centres will be advertising jobs, not placements, but will give you ideas on whom to contact.

* **Networking** – perhaps you have a family member or friend who works in travel and tourism. Use any contacts you can to find a work placement.

## Making contact

Make sure any letter you send:

* is addressed to the relevant person, for example the human resources manager or agency manager, by name if possible

* contains details of your course

* contains the dates of your work placement

* has a sentence or two on why you would like to have work experience in that organisation

* is word-processed in a business format

* has been checked by your tutor.

Travel and tourism organisations receive hundreds of requests for work experience. To increase your chances of success, try the following.

* Send out a lot of letters to different companies – some will not reply at all.

* Include a stamped addressed envelope to encourage a reply.

* Instead of a letter, try sending something different that gets you noticed – what about a press release stating you are available for placement, or a tape or CD about yourself?

* Visit the organisation personally, wearing suitable business clothes, and take your CV.

* Send out letters early before the organisation has its full complement of work-experience candidates.

## Consider this ...

How many students from your college/school are looking for work-based experience? How can you stand out from the rest?

## Theory into practice

1 Study the press release shown opposite. Produce a press release for yourself which you can send to prospective work placements.

2 Hold a discussion with your colleagues. What other ways can you think of to get your details noticed by employers?

38, St John's Street, Powertown, Lancs LA4 5DE

1 March 2005

# PRESS RELEASE

## Travel and tourism student seeks work placement!

An ideal opportunity for you to acquire the services of

# Gemma Hudson

## who is conscientious, reliable and enthusiastic

## AND ...
## will cost you nothing!

Gemma is available for work placement from 17 May to 25 June 2005. The work placement is an important part of her Travel and Tourism BTEC course at Trinity and All Saints College, Lancaster.

**Further information about Gemma is attached in her CV.**

**Interested? Please contact Gemma on 0776————, at the above address, or by e-mail at gemma_123@yahoo.co.uk.**

## CV and interview

Unit 6 explains how to produce a CV and prepare for an interview. It is highly likely that employers will ask to see your CV and they may invite you for an interview. You should keep your CV on disk and update it regularly so that it always available. If you are invited for interview, prepare as you would if the interview was for a permanent job. Carry out research into the company, prepare questions for them and answers to their possible questions to you. Wear appropriate business clothes.

## Letter of acceptance

Once you have been offered a work placement, whether by letter or verbally, write a letter of acceptance confirming the dates you will be attending the placement.

---

**Points to consider when choosing a work placement**

- Is the placement going to help you in your career? Don't go to work in a supermarket if you want a career in travel and tourism – find something more relevant.

- Where is the placement? Can you get there? How will you get there if you have to work shifts?

- Do the hours of work fit in with your existing commitments, for example a part-time job? If not, are the hours negotiable?

- Can you afford the transport costs? Can you afford to take time off from your part-time job?

1 Find three opportunities for work-based experience. Describe the three opportunities.

   This task may provide evidence for P1.

2 Explain why each of the placements is suitable for your work experience, considering the following:

   • how each placement relates to your travel and tourism programme

   • how each placement meets your career objectives

   • how each placement is suitable in terms of your personal circumstances.

   You could present this information as a table or as a report.

   This task may provide evidence for M1.

# Getting ready for work

Once you have found a placement, you need to make sure you are fully prepared to start work. Spend some time finding out about the following issues.

## Hours of work

If you had an interview your hours were probably explained to you. If not, telephone and ask. Find out also to whom you are responsible. It is embarrassing to arrive on the first day at the wrong time and not know whom to ask for. Remember you need to know your hours to fit in any other commitments and to arrange your travel.

## Location of placement and travel arrangements

Make sure you have the address of your organisation. Companies with their own websites often provide a location map which you can download. Find out the times of buses or trains before you start the placement. See if you can buy a weekly ticket to save money. Many students do a practice run of their journey so they do not have to worry about the journey on the first day.

## Accommodation

Most students take up work placements in their own locality. If yours is not in your own area, you will have to consider where you will live. Sometimes, although it is unusual, students find placements in resorts and are provided with accommodation. Over-18s finding placements with Butlins are offered accommodation. If you have family or friends to stay with in another area, you can think about taking up a placement in their area.

## Equipment and clothing

Your employer will tell you if you need any special equipment or clothing. If a uniform must be worn, it will be provided. If you are unsure about what to wear, telephone and ask about the dress code. Do this in good time as you might have to buy some suitable clothes.

Always carry a pad and pen to write notes on what you are doing at work. You may have been given a log to complete as well. Consider taking an audio/video recorder to work or a camera. Tapes and photos will add interest to your project. But it is very important to remember to *ask permission* before taking any pictures or recordings.

# Code of behaviour at work

Those students who have a part-time job will already understand that the world of work demands different behaviour from that in a college or school. Think about:

✱ **Time-keeping** – it is unacceptable to be late. Plan to arrive at least ten minutes before your starting time. Your employer will be asked to comment on your punctuality.

* **Attendance** – in a short placement, there is no reason why you should not attain full attendance. If exceptional circumstances occur, for example sickness, telephone your placement and your tutor at the earliest opportunity. Have contact details for work readily available. Make sure you are fit for work by avoiding late nights and drinking before and during the placement.

## Attitudes in the workplace

Of course you are honest and reliable, and these are qualities you will demonstrate in the workplace. Think about how you respond to authority. Are you able to accept that your immediate supervisor will tell you what to do? How do you respond to instructions?

On work-based experience you should not question authority; you should graciously accept instructions and carry them out to the best of your ability. If you are not clear about what to do or need help, ask.

On your course you will study ethics in the workplace. Think about your attitudes to other people. Do you treat everyone with courtesy? Do you act and speak in a non-discriminatory manner? Set yourself high standards and adhere to them.

Consider your reactions to rules and regulations; most workplaces keep rules to a minimum, but there will necessarily be some as they are essential to health and safety, and you must accept them.

## Objectives

What do you hope to achieve from your work-based experience? Look back at the sections on page 268 on skill and career development – do you think you will achieve these in your placement?

*You could do your work placement at a local Tourist Information Centre*

Study this example of Bijan's work placement at the local Tourist Information Centre. The centre puts all new staff through the 'Welcome Host' training programme. Bijan prepared some objectives before he went on his placement – these are shown below.

Bijan's objectives are useful as they remind him of the purpose of his work placement and give him a focus while he is there. They will also help him when he carries out his personal evaluation, as they provide a measure for his achievement.

### Theory into practice

Prepare your objectives for work-based experience under the headings used by Bijan in the example below. Do not complete the comments sections at this stage. If you think you need more information about the placement to do this, discuss the types of activities you will be doing at work with your tutor and carry out some background research into the organisation.

| PERSONAL OBJECTIVES | COMMENTS | CAREER OBJECTIVES | COMMENTS | CURRICULUM OBJECTIVES | COMMENTS |
|---|---|---|---|---|---|
| Develop social skills with new colleagues<br>Learn how to use accommodation reservation system<br>Develop customer care skills<br>Develop action-planning and problem-solving skills | | Gain 'Welcome Host' qualification<br>Gain useful contacts for the future<br>Determine whether this sector is for me | | Collect evidence for completion of Work-based Experience unit<br>Collect evidence for Working in Travel and Tourism, Customer Service, and Visitor Attractions units | |

# The project

## Planning the project

To fully benefit from your work-based experience you should carry out a project related to the placement. The nature of the project should be decided in consultation with your tutor and employer, and it should specifically relate to your work or curriculum. Wherever possible, the project should be negotiated in advance of the placement so that you can plan it before you start work.

Here are some examples of work-based projects that have been carried out.

* Study of the range of career opportunities within the placement organisation.

* Recruitment procedures in the placement organisation.

* Study of the effectiveness of working practices in the placement organisation.

* Study of customer service provision.

* Study of the marketing activities of the organisation and how they meet the needs of its customers.

* Study of marketing research methods used in the organisation.

* Analysis of the range of products and services provided by the placement organisation.

* Analysis of the administrative, financial and communication systems in the organisation with recommendations for improvement.

These are examples only, and your employers may have a particular project they would like you to undertake. The examples given here all provide evidence for units in this qualification.

> ## * REMEMBER!
> The project is a great opportunity for you to provide evidence for two or more assessments. Use it!

Your project must have a defined objective and proposed outcomes. The objective summarises what you hope to achieve in your project, and the outcomes are all the products that arise from the project.

Your objectives should be SMART. Remember that this means:

* Specific

* Measurable

* Achievable

* Realistic

* Timed.

The following case study gives examples of the objectives and outcomes of a project carried out at Middleton Railway, Leeds. These should give you ideas for your own project.

## CASE STUDY

Carl Turner recently graduated from Leeds Metropolitan University with a degree in Tourism Management. In his final year he had to carry out a work-related project, producing a 12,000-word report. This was an assessed project and very important to Carl's final grade.

He worked in a group of five students and they were assigned to Middleton Railway near Leeds. The railway is a non-profit-making organisation and claims to be the oldest working railway in the world. It is a tourist attraction as well as being of interest to train enthusiasts, but did not attract huge numbers of tourists. There are two trains at Middleton Railway and visitors can go for a ride on the trains. It also holds special events such as Santa Claus train journeys. There is a gift shop.

The group was set a brief which had been determined by the tutors at Leeds Metropolitan and agreed with the management of Middleton Railway. The brief was to suggest improvements to the railway and its operation and events, with the aim of increasing visitor numbers. Greater visitor numbers would provide increased revenue which could be re-invested by the railway. Improvements should also lead to a higher and improved company profile.

The students were allocated a budget of £300. This was to enable them to take and print photos, print and bind their reports, etc.

The group began by visiting Middleton Railway and individually carrying out observations and research. Afterwards they reconvened and, using their findings, carried out a SWOT and PEST analysis.

They were able to make many practical recommendations to Middleton Railway following their study. These included improved signage, seating, shelters and improvements to the car park. The students also helped with an application for a lottery grant.

By lateral thinking they provided solutions to problems. For example, it was thought that a 'Thomas the Tank Engine' day would attract family visitors. However, the cost of using this name was too high, because of the permission fees involved. Instead they decided on a 'Thomas' day. There would be no fee attached to using the name 'Thomas', and yet the associations are the same and still attract visitors.

On completion of the project the team made a PowerPoint presentation to an audience of about 150 people including the chairman of Middleton Railway and three tutors. The presentation lasted about half an hour and the team answered questions afterwards.

You will be pleased to know that Carl achieved a first-class grade for this project! For more information on Middleton Railway go to www.middletonrailway.org.uk.

1 **Identify the objectives and possible outcomes from Carl's project.**
2 **Compare your findings with your group.**

### Theory into practice

Decide on the project you would like to carry out. Discuss your ideas with your tutor and employer. Produce a plan for your project – the plan should have:

- key objectives
- proposed outcomes
- timescale
- resources needed.

## Undertaking the project

Your placement may be day-release or an intensive block. Whatever the format, you should start your project immediately and put some time aside each day to work on it. If you leave it until the end of the placement, you will not be able to collect all the relevant information. This is a common problem – don't let it happen to you!

Make sure your employer and the staff at your placement are aware of your project and then they will be prepared to help you. If there is not enough time during the working day to carry out your project, spend a short time each evening working on it, and make a list of information you need to collect the following day.

### Tools to help you

The following tools will help you with your project.

* **Interviews with staff** – most people are glad to talk about themselves. Take notes or make recordings of their responses (with their permission).

* **Resources** – make the most of the resources available at work, especially training manuals and information on policies and procedures.

* **Independent research** – be aware that you will have to carry out your own research, perhaps into competitive activity or head office organisation. You will need to decide what research is necessary for your project. Set time aside for this.

* **Observation** – this is a very useful tool, particularly for looking at customer service. However, if you are observing the way staff operate, be discreet. Write notes later.

* **Keeping records** – you should keep notes on all aspects of your project as you work on it. Note points still to be carried out. Keep copies of relevant documents for inclusion as appendices to your final report.

* **Reviews** – if possible, review the progress of your project as you go along with the employer or your tutor.

## Presentation of the project

Decide on the format of your presentation with your employer and tutor. They may want you to make a formal presentation to them, as Carl did in the case study on pages 273–4. Below are some possible formats for the final presentation.

Whichever format you use, you will need to ensure that you use your communication skills, and the technology available to you, in the best possible way to make your presentation a success. Use graphics to present the data you have found in a clear and user-friendly format.

# Personal review

## Monitoring

Once your work-based experience is at an end you will carry out an evaluation, but you need certain tools to help you carry out your evaluation and these should be used during the placement itself to monitor your activities and performance.

You may have been provided with a log or recording documentation by your college or school. Otherwise, develop your own. You could include:

* a log book
* an interview record sheet
* a witness testimony sheet
* records of an employer review.

Keep all the documentation in a portfolio alongside the materials (letters, CV, objectives chart) that you completed before the placement.

### The log book

The first page of the log book should show your name, your employer's details including contact names and telephone numbers, and your tutor's name and telephone number.

Allocate a page for each day of your placement. It is important that the log is not merely a diary, but records the skills you are developing and any problem-solving you are involved in.

> ## CASE STUDY
>
> Here is an example for Bijan at the Tourist Information Centre.
>
> *Tuesday 26 April 2005*
>
> *Activities*
> First 4 hours of the day spent on the desk with Janine. Had to answer customer queries.
>
> Given time in the afternoon to work on my project – used the intranet and accessed a lot of Regional Tourist Board information on structure and policy.
>
> *Skills developed*
> Customer care – learnt a lot from watching Janine and then dealing with customers myself.
>
> Research – found out a lot about the Regional Tourist Board.
>
> IT – used the intranet.
>
> *Problems and solutions*
> Had to help a German customer and I couldn't communicate at all! Managed to find a staff member who spoke some German.
>
> *Action points*
> Acquaint myself with all the T/C leaflets and literature so I don't have to ask Janine for obvious things.
>
> Learn German?
>
> 1 How do you think the headings help Bijan?
> 2 What could Bijan do if he found he was writing 'made tea' or 'stamped brochures'?
> 3 Design your own log page.
> 4 Discuss your ideas with your group.

## The interview record

You might include some interviews in your project. Remember that interviews can be written, or recorded on audio or videotape. All types of records are valid.

### Consider this ...

Interviews might be useful to collect evidence for other units as well. Can you think of contacts in travel and tourism whom you could interview? Which units would the information be useful for?

## Witness statements

Witness statements could be used to provide evidence of skills you have demonstrated, for example dealing with a customer. The witness must have observed you and will comment on your performance.

## Employer reviews

Your employer will be asked to complete an evaluation sheet on your performance. It is often a series of tick boxes with space for brief comments.

## CASE STUDY

Here is an example of an interview Bijan carried out with Janine to find out more about her job.

### Interview record

| | |
|---|---|
| Interviewee | Janine Nowacki |
| Interviewer | Bijan Roharl |
| Date | 27 April 2005 |

**What is your job role?**
Desk manager at the Tourist Information Centre.

**What qualifications did you need for this role?**
You don't always need formal qualifications, it depends on your experience, but I did an AVCE in Travel and Tourism four years ago. You do have to have excellent communication skills so you need a GCSE in English or Key Skills Communication at a high level. I did Level 3 Communication as part of my course.

**What about the other key skills?**
They are all useful. I did IT and Working with Others at Level 3, and Number at Level 2. I need them all here. I have to use our computer system. You need to be numerate – you do handle money and the customers often ask you what is the equivalent in euros.

**Do you receive training here?**
Yes, all the Welcome Host courses – I'm doing the management one now.

**Is there career progression?**
Yes, I'm already desk manager and I could go on to be in the centre management team. But that's not what I want. We have a conference management department and I want to get involved in that.

**Is that based here?**
Yes, do you want me to arrange for you to interview them?

**Would you be able to give me a copy of your job description?**
It's on file, I'll copy it for you.

1  List at least four useful facts Bijan found out from this interview.
2  How might he use the information found out in the interview? Remember to consider other units of the qualification.
Show your findings to your tutor.

### Key concept

The **Welcome Host programme** is a one-day training programme offered by Regional Tourist Boards which concentrates on improving customer care skills. It is part of a high-profile national initiative. It can help employees acquire new customer-service and communication skills, as well as improving their knowledge of local facilities and services. It has been developed for staff in accommodation and catering, transport, leisure and public sector organisations.
**Welcome Host Plus** is for staff at supervisory level.

Your school or college will provide this and it will either be included in your log book or sent directly to the employer.

## Evaluating your own performance

If you have kept detailed records during the placement, writing your evaluation will be straightforward.

The first stage of your personal evaluation could be a SWOT analysis. Refer to page 69 to remind yourself of what this is. Evaluate the strengths and weaknesses you demonstrated in your work-based experience. Identify any opportunities that arise from the experience. It is unlikely that you will find any threats, unless your experience was completely unsuccessful!

Refer to page 69

**Theory into practice**

1 Copy and complete the following chart. Some examples have been entered for you.

Placement:                              Dates:

| STRENGTHS | WEAKNESSES | OPPORTUNITIES | THREATS |
|-----------|------------|---------------|---------|
| Full attendance | Struggled with the database | I was offered help with future assessments | |
| | | | |
| | | | |

2 The next stage of the evaluation is to measure your achievements on work experience against the objectives you set yourself earlier. Return to the chart you completed before your placement. Consider each of the objectives set and whether you met them. Complete the chart with your comments.

## Benefits of work-based experience

The final stage of your personal review is to summarise the benefits gained from your work experience. You will consider:

* the new skills and knowledge you have gained
* how they can be used in the future
* the personal contacts you have made
* possible career pathways
* other opportunities for progression.

Before you complete your summary, make sure you have the following information to hand:

* log book
* any interviews or witness testimonies
* employer review
* personal SWOT analysis
* objectives chart.

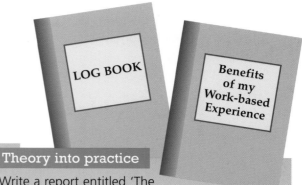

**Theory into practice**

Write a report entitled 'The Benefits of my Work-based Experience'. Use all the information listed above to help you and write the report using the following headings:

* New skills and knowledge gained
* Personal contacts made
* Possible career pathways
* Other opportunities.

Finish the report with a recommendations section which gives suggestions for your future activities and personal and career development.

# UNIT 21 ASSESSMENT ASSIGNMENT

1 Describe three opportunities for work-based experience in the travel and tourism industry.
This task may provide evidence for P1.

2 For each opportunity, explain how the placement will help you meet your personal, career and curriculum objectives.
This task may provide evidence for M1.

3 Set objectives for your work placement (use the chart on page 272 if you wish) and produce a personal code of behaviour for work-based experience.

This task may provide evidence for P2.

4 Negotiate a work-based project and produce a plan for its implementation. This plan must include:
   • key objectives
   • proposed outcomes
   • timescales
   • resources needed.
Carry out the project using a range of research techniques and sources.

This task may provide evidence for P3.

5 Present the project using the following headings:
   • Introduction
   • Methods used to research and undertake the project
   • Findings
   • Analysis of findings
   • Conclusions
   • Recommendations.
Discuss with your tutor the type of presentation you should give.

For a Merit, the project presentation must demonstrate a range of research techniques and sources, and in-depth findings must be coherently and accurately presented.

For a Distinction, the project presentation must show analysis of key issues and make justified recommendations for future action.

These tasks may provide evidence for P4, M2 and D1.

6 Complete a personal review of your work-based experience and performance. Use the documentation and activities in this unit to help you.
This task may provide evidence for P5.

7 Add the following to your personal review:
   • an evaluation of how your objectives were met
   • an evaluation of the effectiveness of your performance.
This task may provide evidence for M3.

8 Add the following to your personal review:
   • critical evaluation of own performance
   • justified recommendations for future personal development.
This task may provide evidence for D2.

**UNIT 22**

# Travel and tourism residential study visit

## Introduction

This section of the book will help you organise a residential study visit. This unit is one of the most exciting and challenging of the programme; students always enjoy it, not only for the visit itself but also the organisation and preparation.

In the unit you have to determine the aims and objectives of your visit, ensuring that you consider how it will benefit you in terms of personal development, the research it will allow you to do and the opportunities it will present for collecting evidence for this and other units. You will produce a detailed proposal for the visit and then participate in it. On your return, you will have the opportunity to evaluate the visit and see whether you met your original aims and objectives.

Throughout this work you will be able to develop your organisational and teamwork skills, show your initiative and solve problems. By working conscientiously, paying attention to detail, considering other team members and evaluating the experience carefully, you can hope to achieve a distinction.

### How you will be assessed

This unit is internally assessed by your tutor. A variety of exercises and activities is included in this unit to help you make the most of your residential study visit and prepare for the assessment. You will also have the opportunity to work on some case studies to further your understanding.

At the end of this unit you should be able to:

→ Establish the aims and objectives for a study visit
→ Deliver a proposal for an effective study visit
→ Positively participate in a study visit
→ Evaluate the study visit.

# Aims and objectives

Remember that your trip is a study visit and, although it should be enjoyable, it is not a holiday! You can determine the aims and objectives before you know exactly where you are going – in fact your objectives will have an impact on the decision about where you go. If you want to do team-building activities, for example, you might choose an outward-bound centre. Once you do know where you are going you can refine your objectives and ensure they are relevant to the destination.

> **Consider this ...**
>
> You have probably already been on some day visits as part of your course. Think about one of those visits. What were its objectives?

## Setting aims and objectives

Start by discussing the aims and objectives as a group, but make sure you record them yourself as you will need them for your portfolio. You should also add some objectives that apply just to the small group you are working in.

Show initiative from the start by setting some personal objectives for yourself. These could relate to collecting evidence for another unit.

The aim summarises the purpose of the trip, and here you have a chance to apply your marketing knowledge and write out the aim as a mission statement for the trip. This example is the mission statement of a study trip to Amsterdam. You'll hear more about this and other trips as you work through this unit.

> *Our mission is to organise a trip abroad that is educational and enjoyable. We want to achieve high standards of teamwork, initiative and assignment work.*

Make sure all your objectives are SMART, that is:

* Specific
* Measurable
* Achievable
* Realistic
* Timed.

See page 85 to remind yourself about SMART objectives.

Here are some ideas to consider when drawing up your objectives.

* Use the study visit to help you collect information for another unit; for example, a visit to an attraction while you are away could be used to complete the assessment for Unit 18, Visitor Attractions.

* The preparation for the visit can also be used to collect evidence for units; for example, finding out about the features of different types of passenger transport.

* Determine the outcome and presentation of your work with your tutor – it could be a portfolio of work, a report or an oral presentation.

> **Key concepts**
>
> The **aim** is a summary of the purpose of the entire exercise.
>
> **Objectives** are more specific and help you achieve your aim.

## CASE STUDY

*The City of Amsterdam*

Here are the objectives determined for a study trip to Amsterdam. Remember that students can add their own group or personal objectives to these.

# Writing the proposal

## Deciding where to go

Your residential study visit may take place in the UK or abroad. It may be located in an activity centre or in a holiday resort; you might visit a city or a beach. Whatever the destination, it needs to be decided quickly so that you can get on with the organisation.

When you are deciding on the destination, bear in mind the following:

* you can't please all of the people all of the time – you will have to compromise

* some students can spend months arguing about where to go – then it's too late to organise the trip!

* you shouldn't book through a package tour company – what would be left for you to do?

* if your tutor has decided on the destination, accept graciously and be positive about the choice – tutors probably know what they are doing!

* be adventurous and look forward to new experiences

* accept that you will probably have to pay to go.

## Considerations for choosing the destination

What do you want to do there? This could include:

* visiting attractions

* investigating local tourist facilities

* looking at hotels and their operation

* taking part in sports and leisure activities

* finding out about the local culture.

Where will you stay? This could be:

* hotel

* hostel

* student residences

* campsite.

Hotels often offer good deals for groups of students, so don't assume you can't afford to stay in a hotel. Student residences will be available only outside term time.

## Finding out about accommodation

You can use the following sources of information about accommodation:

* telephone reservations departments of large chains, e.g. Novotel

* Internet sites of hotel chains
* specialist accommodation websites, e.g. Expedia (which has pictures) or Octopus
* destination guides (books or Internet)
* local universities.

### Theory into practice

Find out about different types of accommodation in Amsterdam. Cost each of them for a group of 15 students arriving on a Monday in April and leaving the following Thursday. Make sure you know what is included in the price and how many boys and girls are in the group.

## How will you travel?

You will need to think about the following.

* What transport will you use – air, train, coach or sea?
* What is the cost of each route?
* How will everyone get to the departure point, and how much will that cost?
* How will you get from the point of arrival to the destination?
* How will you travel within the destination?
* How easy or difficult will it be to book?
* Which route offers the best convenience and comfort?

### *Finding out about travel*

You can use the following sources of information about travel:

* travel websites like Traveljungle or Travelsupermarket
* a travel agent
* enquiries office at the railway station
* coach companies
* airline websites.

### Consider this ...

Booking over the Internet requires a credit card or debit card. Also, there is an extra charge for using a credit card.

### Theory into practice

Find three different routes to Amsterdam from your college or school. Cost each route for a group of 15 students travelling from Monday to Thursday in April.

For each route point out any particular benefits or constraints.

## Features and benefits of the destination

To help you determine the suitability of the destination you should look at its features and benefits. A feature is a fact about the destination, and a benefit is what this means for the visitors. Some examples are shown opposite.

| FEATURE | BENEFIT |
|---|---|
| Wide range of inexpensive accommodation | Affordable for students |
| Mild climate | Suitable for sightseeing in the spring |
| Close to the airport | Easily accessible |
| English widely spoken | Easy to communicate |

## Theory into practice

1 Find out about Berlin and whether it is suitable for a three-day visit for a group of 15 students. Draw up a table describing the features and benefits of the destination.

2 Find out what suitable activities could be included on the trip. At least some of the activities should have an educational benefit. You can add these activities to your table and show how they would benefit students.

3 Prepare a three-day itinerary of the activities showing all departure and arrival points and times.

## Risk assessment

Part of your proposal should include a risk assessment. This will help you determine the suitability of your destination, and it should increase the likelihood of success.

### Key concept

A risk assessment is the process of identifying what could go wrong, deciding which risks are important and planning how to deal with those risks.

These are the steps to follow when carrying out the risk assessment:

* identify the risks surrounding your project
* assess the likelihood of each problem occurring
* decide how to respond to problems
* put in place systems to deal with the problems
* monitor the risks throughout the project.

The possible responses to risks are shown below.

### Key concept

**Contingency plan** – a plan you have ready to deal with anything that might go wrong.

Think of all the risks associated with organising and participating in a residential study visit. Here are some situations that might occur – in fact, they have all occurred on student trips!

* A student joins the trip without a passport.
* A student arrives at Dover with a passport – but it's Australian and a visa is needed.
* A student is taken ill on the first day.
* Two students crash on jet skis.
* A fight breaks out with a security guard.
* Students fail to meet at the check-in desk at the airport.
* A drunken party takes place in the hotel in spite of a no-alcohol rule.
* It rains every day.
* A bag is stolen from a student.
* A bad storm causes diversion of the plane to a different airport.
* A ferry strike means the whole group is stranded in Calais.

Copy and complete the following risk assessment table. You can use the examples given, adding your own, or just use the form to take you through a risk assessment for your own trip.

| RISK | HOW LIKELY? | RESPONSE | ACTION/CONTINGENCY PLAN |
|---|---|---|---|
| Student joins trip without passport | Not very | Reduce risk | Check all passports prior to trip and issue reminders |
| Visas needed | Not very | Eliminate risk | Check passports and apply for visas in good time |
| | | | |
| | | | |

# Administration, information and documentation

## Permissions

You must find out what documentation has to be completed in your school or college to organise a visit. Complete the documentation and ask your tutor to check and sign it. Expect the following as a minimum:

* school/college trip form – details of the trip, participants, staff, dates and costs
* parental consent form – for under-18s
* risk assessment form
* list of participants and next of kin
* list of telephone numbers in case of emergency.

Remember to keep copies of all these documents for the group.

## Passports/visas

If the trip is abroad, each student will require a passport. Make sure they are applied for in good time – it can take a few weeks to process a passport. Some schools prefer to get a group passport. Some destinations, e.g. the Caribbean, require there to be at least six months left to run on a passport from arrival.

Check whether visas are needed, particularly if you have non-UK passport holders in your group. If you are responsible for passports, ask to see each student's passport before the trip and check it.

## Insurance

If you are travelling within Europe, make sure each person has a valid E111 form. This entitles you to medical treatment within the European Union. Ask to see the forms and if some are needed get the forms from the Post Office.

You should also have a group travel insurance policy. Your school or college can arrange this for you through its own insurers – this will be the cheapest option. Otherwise, shop around with insurance companies.

## Telephone numbers

A list of telephone numbers forms part of your contingency planning. If a member of the group is lost or in trouble, he or she must be able to contact someone. The best tactic is to make a list of mobile telephone numbers for all those people who will have mobiles with them, especially staff. The list can be distributed to the whole party. Include the school or college number.

## Code of conduct

Most schools and colleges issue a code of conduct for study visits which students must sign. Why not produce your own code for your visit? Negotiate the terms and conditions with your tutor.

## Medical information

Any student with a medical condition should ensure the group leader is informed. This should also be declared for insurance purposes.

## Itinerary

Each student must be issued with a copy of the itinerary including travel details, accommodation and activities.

## General information

Produce an information sheet reminding participants of essential facts and what they need to bring with them. Include:

* essential clothing items suitable to the climate at the destination

* comfortable walking shoes

* passports and other documents as appropriate

* currency information and suggested amount to allow for spending

* accommodation address and telephone numbers

* safety information.

# Participation in the residential study visit

## Who does what?

Your participation is very important. This means not only going on the trip with a positive attitude, but fully participating in the organisation of and preparation for the visit.

You are likely to be assigned responsibility for a particular aspect of the study trip. This may be an individual responsibility or a small-group responsibility.

Your tutor will make sure that each group or individual has an equal workload. However, be prepared to show initiative and to help out where needed as well as undertaking your own tasks. Once you know your particular responsibilities you can set objectives for yourself or for your group, in addition to those set earlier.

The whole group will have meetings, perhaps weekly, to report on how they are progressing with their objectives and to pass on information to each other. Students may take it in turns to chair and minute those meetings.

Whatever your individual or group responsibility, you should be thinking about how

## CASE STUDY

Study these examples of group responsibilities for a study visit to Barcelona.

Transport group – responsible for:
* transport to and from the airport
* air route research and booking
* transport to all visits in Barcelona.

Administration group – responsible for:
* code of conduct
* letters to parents
* permission documents
* any other internal documents
* insurance
* lists of telephone numbers.

Marketing group – responsible for:
* publicising the arrangements to all participants
* sending out press releases to gain press coverage
* internal newsletter coverage
* photographic record of the study trip.

Finance group – responsible for:
* collection and recording of deposits
* collection and recording of balance
* fundraising – if relevant
* setting budgets
* payments
* keeping accounts.

Health and safety group – responsible for:
* risk assessment
* information on personal safety and security
* E111s
* medical emergencies.

Itinerary group – responsible for:
* researching speakers on the visit
* organising activities and entertainment
* producing itinerary.

Choose one of the groups listed above and produce a list of objectives for that group. Remember these could be added to the original group objectives.

you can participate effectively in the residential study visit.

## Making an impression

Whenever you make contact with an organisation outside your college or school, you are representing your educational establishment, your course and ultimately yourself. Remember to:

* be polite
* greet the contact appropriately
* introduce yourself and your course/school/college.

Sometimes, unfortunately, you might have to deal with someone who does not have your high standards of customer service. Continue to be polite whatever the response. If you are meeting face to face:

* dress in a suitable manner
* speak and act courteously
* introduce yourself
* consider your personal hygiene
* use the host language if at all possible.

If you are contacting someone by e-mail, apply the same rules of politeness and greetings. Say who you are and what you need to know, and sign off with 'regards' – it is less formal than a letter – and your full name. Always keep a copy of your messages and any replies.

If you are contacting someone by letter, use a formal business layout (see pages 196–7) and keep a copy.

(see pages 196–7)

### Theory into practice

You are arriving at your hotel in Paris in a group of 15 students.

Practise greeting the receptionist and introducing your group, saying where you are from. Use French as much as possible – even if just for the greeting and to say thank you.

## Time management

Your residential study visit can be successful only if each person completes the tasks set by agreed deadlines. It is a useful exercise to determine all the deadlines as a group.

The group that organised the Amsterdam visit used a technique called 'critical path analysis' to determine the priority and length of tasks.

The concept behind critical path analysis is that you cannot start some activities until others are finished. These activities are *sequential*, with each one being more or less finished before the next one starts. Some activities are not dependent on completion of others – they can be done at any time during the project. These are called *parallel* tasks.

Critical path analysis:

* helps to lay out all the tasks that must be completed as part of project
* helps to identify the minimum length of time to complete a project.

The group started by brainstorming all the tasks they had to do and listing them. They worked out which tasks were dependent on others and therefore sequential. They also tried to decide how long each task might take.

| | TASK | LENGTH | TYPE | DEPENDENT ON |
|---|---|---|---|---|
| 1 | College permission | 1 week | Sequential | |
| 2 | Consent forms | 3 days | Sequential | |
| 3 | Code of conduct | 3 weeks | Parallel | |
| 4 | Passports | 3 weeks | Parallel | |
| 5 | Set budget | 2 weeks | Sequential | 1, 2 |
| 6 | Book hotel | 8 weeks | Sequential | 1, 2, 5 |
| 7 | Book flights | 1 week | Sequential | 1, 2, 5 |
| 8 | Insurance | 1 day | Sequential | 5, 6, 7 |
| 9 | Business plan | 2 months | Parallel | |
| 10 | Log | 2.5 months | Parallel | |
| 11 | Go to Amsterdam | 4 days | Sequential | 1, 2, 3, 4, 5, 6, 7, 8 |
| 12 | Evaluation | 1 week | Sequential | 9, 10, 11 |

You will note that dates are not used, but the numbers of days or weeks needed to complete the tasks. The completed critical path diagram is shown below.

Although critical path diagrams look fairly complex they are easy to do once you have understood the concept. If you prefer, you can produce a flow chart with dates.

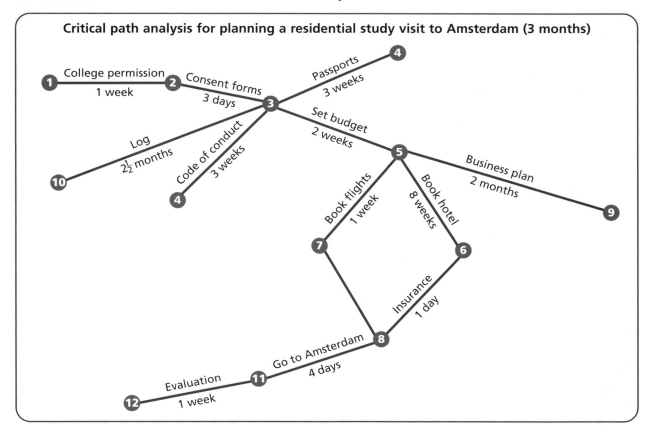

Critical path analysis for planning a residential study visit to Amsterdam (3 months)

**Consider this ...**

In your own study visit, can you differentiate between sequential and parallel tasks?

Regular meetings help with time management. If you have to report back to your group, it is very difficult to confess that you haven't done anything!

## Gathering evidence

While participating in the residential study visit you will gather evidence so that you can succeed in this unit and possibly others. You should keep a log of every task that you carry out, with records of telephone calls and copies of documents.

Below is an example of a log. You could use this format – note how it mentions problems and their solutions, and is not just a diary. The extract is from Rebecca Hammond's personal log, taken from her Residential Study Visit portfolio.

### MY PERSONAL LOG FOR AMSTERDAM

| Date | Task | Problems encountered | How dealt with | Comments |
|------|------|----------------------|----------------|----------|
| 1/10 | Go to Premier Travel agent in Cambridge to pick up Amsterdam brochures | Hotels were too expensive | Now looking at youth hostels | Very helpful travel agent |
| 4/10 | I was chairperson for the first meeting. Natalie booked flights on the Internet with Buzz | Didn't know Claire's surname | Rang Charlie to see if she knew and she did | Poulter |
| 10/10 | Research hotels on Buzz website | Youth hostels were too cheap! | Now looking for 3-star hotels | Found Hotel Barbacan. Accommodation budget limit £1,200 |
| 11/10 | Check Buzz website for Hotel Barbacan | | | Price has gone down to £948 |
| 11/10 | Decide who is sharing with whom | | | 3 singles, 4 twins, 2 triples |
| 17/10 | Telephone the hotel | Could not find telephone number | Looked again on Buzz. Had to contact international enquiries | The group decided to book directly |

**Key concept**

A **log** should record not only what you do, but all the problems you encounter and how you deal with them.

In addition, you should prepare a checklist of evidence which you hope to collect for other units. Here is an example for Unit 18, Visitor Attractions.

Celine is participating in a residential study visit to Paris. While in Paris she hopes to collect evidence for her Visitor Attractions assessment. She has made a list of the basics she will collect in Paris. Further research before and after the trip will ensure she provides detailed evidence.

She has chosen three attractions from the itinerary.

**Disneyland Paris**
✓ collect leaflets on products and services
✓ make notes on interpretation techniques
✓ impact – make notes on transport routes, surrounding retail/industrial activity
✓ visitor types – research on Internet, observe while there.

**Palace of Versailles**
✓ collect leaflets on products and services
✓ make notes on interpretation techniques
✓ make notes on impact and transport routes
✓ visitor types – ask at the information desk if any stats are available – observe visitors.

**Musée d'Orsay**
✓ collect leaflets on products and services
✓ make notes on interpretation techniques
✓ buy postcards
✓ research history on Internet.

# Communication skills

During the course of this study visit project you will have the opportunity to develop your communication skills, both within your group and with other parties.

## Effective questions

Remember to use open and closed questions effectively when you are enquiring about something. Closed questions are those which require only a limited answer, such as yes or no. They do not gain much information. Open questions are more useful – they encourage a full answer. Practise using them with your group.

**Theory into practice**

1 Decide whether these questions are open or closed.
 • Can you tell me how we could reach your hotel from the railway station?
 • Do you have accommodation for 15 students – 10 girls and 5 boys?
 • What sort of information can you give me on the types of visitors who come to this attraction?
 • Do you have statistics on visitors to your attraction?

2 Turn them into the opposite type of question – closed or open.

3 Write down five open questions to be used for collecting evidence for another unit while you are on your study visit. Practise these questions on your colleagues.

## Active listening

Active listening means listening with a purpose to what someone is staying. The purpose might be to discover whether accommodation is available, or to benefit from a talk given on your visit. One technique you can try is to mentally repeat the speaker's words as they are said – it can help you concentrate.

**Consider this ...**

People speak at 100 to 175 words per minute, but they can listen and understand at 600 to 800 words per minute.

Use body language to show you are listening – smile, nod and make eye contact. Another technique of active listening is to give feedback, summarising what you have heard and making sure that you have understood correctly. This is more difficult to do in a group.

## Barriers to communication

Good communication is essential to the success of the project. However, there may be barriers to good communication. Here are some examples:

* the group may be too large, so not everyone gets a chance to have a say

* absence of group members from meetings may mean no one knows what they are doing

* meetings may not take place on time and messages and reports may not be passed on

* some group members may feel intimidated by others and not comfortable reporting back

* people may not listen or concentrate on reports.

**Consider this ...**

What do you think can be done about these problems? Are you aware of any of these barriers in your own group?

## Consequences of ineffective communication

If communication problems are not dealt with, the project will fall apart. Group members will not understand what is expected of them and will be unable to perform efficiently. There will be a breakdown in teamwork and a lack of respect between team members. Resentment will build up against those who do not communicate with the group.

For all these reasons, regular group meetings, held properly, are essential to enable good communication to be established and maintained.

# Evaluating the residential study visit

## Criteria for evaluation

You have produced the criteria for evaluation as you have gone through the organisation of and participation in the study visit. You have set aims and objectives, both for your group and for yourself. You have made checklists of materials to research and collect for your assessments. You should also have made a log showing how you came up against problems and dealt with them. All of this information can be used in your evaluation.

The following ideas for evaluation take you through the full process of group and individual evaluation and will ensure you do the work thoroughly.

## Group evaluation

Consider carrying out a group evaluation half-way through the project. This is called a formative evaluation and it will help you tackle any problems which are apparent.

The easiest way to do this is to carry out a SWOT analysis as a whole group. Remember that this means identifying the strengths, weaknesses, opportunities and threats for the group so far.

Repeat the SWOT analysis at the end of the project and keep records of both.

The next stage of group evaluation is to meet as a group and decide whether you have met your objectives. List all the objectives and go through each one commenting on how successfully it was met.

Make notes and make sure you include recommendations for improvements in the future.

You can add extra questions if you think they are appropriate. Here are some examples.

* Were you within budget?

* Was the accommodation suitable?

* Were there any travel problems?

* What would you do differently next time?

Here is Rebecca's summary of what should be done differently next time. It followed a full SWOT analysis.

> If we were to do the trip again or a similar project, I think we should keep having a weekly meeting because it showed that everyone knew what he or she was doing and everyone had to communicate with each other. Working in small groups within the whole group works well as every group has allocated tasks. We need to concentrate more on keeping to deadlines to avoid stress and I think we should interact more between groups. Having a strong chairperson in the meetings is vital. Rotating the chair is fair and democratic.

### Key concept

When you **rotate the chair** you take it in turns to chair a meeting. The chairperson has to produce the agenda and run the meeting properly. Someone else will take minutes.

## Small-group evaluation

If you have worked in small groups their performance also needs to be evaluated. This time the evaluation can be done in a different way; each group evaluates the other groups.

They can do this by deciding whether they met their objectives, or they can design a form to use. Each group then presents their evaluation to the evaluated group, explaining what they think could be improved next time.

### Theory into practice

Design an evaluation form for each small group. Include the following features:
- objectives and whether they were met
- comments on teamwork
- comments on time management
- comments on communication skills
- recommendations for improvement.

## Self-evaluation

You don't have to share your self-evaluation with the group, so be very honest with yourself.

Again, you or the group can design a form if you wish, but make sure you ask yourself the following questions.

✳ Did you achieve your personal objectives? List them and comment.

✳ How much did you contribute to the group objectives?

✳ Did you attend all the planning sessions?

✳ Did you meet deadlines?

✳ Have you improved your communication skills, and how?

✳ Did you work well in a team?

✳ Did you work well independently?

✳ Did you show initiative?

✳ What would you do differently in the future?

Give examples of all your skills and successes.

## UNIT 22 ASSESSMENT ASSIGNMENT

Produce a report on a residential study visit you have participated in. If a written report format is chosen, ensure that the correct layout, appropriate headings and sub-headings are used. The itinerary and log may be attached as an appendix if your report is a written one.

Your report should contain the following sections.

1 The aims and objectives of the study visit.
This section may provide evidence for P1.

2 Explanation of how the destination and itinerary allow the objectives to be met.

3 Explanation of how constraints and considerations are taken into account.
These sections may provide evidence for M1.

4 Features and benefits of the chosen destination.

5 Full itinerary for the visit including transport, accommodation, day visits, entertainment.
These sections may provide evidence for P2.

6 Risk assessment with contingency plan.
This section may provide evidence for M2.

7 Log of participation.
This section may provide evidence for P3.

8 Evaluation against objectives.
This section may provide evidence for P4.

9 Evidence that your evaluation stems from a range of sources of feedback and evaluation techniques.
This section may provide evidence for M3.

10 Evaluation of the group's performance, with justified recommendations for future trips and planning.
This section may provide evidence for D1.

11 Evaluation of your own performance, with recommendations for improvement.
This section may provide evidence for D2.

# Index

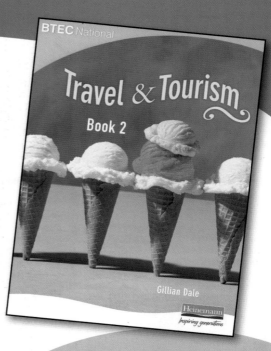